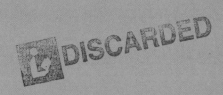

Writing
GEOGRAPHICAL
EXPLORATION

THE

STRANGE
AND DANGE-
ROVS VOYAGE OF

Captaine THOMAS JAMES, in

his intended Discovery of the Northwest

Passage into the South Sea

WHEREIN

THE MISERIES INDVRED, BOTH
Going, Wintering, Returning; & the Rarities
observed, both *Philosophicall* and *Mathematicall*
are related in this Journall of it.

Published by HIS MAJESTIES
command.

To which are added, a Plac or Card for the
Sayling in those Seas.

Divers little Tables of the Author's, of the Va-
ration of the Compasse, &c.

WITH

An Appendix concerning *Longitude*, by Master
Henry Gallibrand, Astronomy Reader,
of *Gresham* Colledge in *London*.

AND

An Adreise concering the Philosophy of these late
Discoveryes, By W. W.

LONDON:
Printed by *John Legatt*, for *John Partridge*.
1633.

Writing
GEOGRAPHICAL
EXPLORATION

James and the Northwest Passage
1631–33

Wayne K. D. Davies

UNIVERSITY OF
CALGARY
PRESS

We acknowledge the financial support of the
Government of Canada through the Book
Publishing Industry Development Program
(BPIDP) for our publishing activities. We
acknowledge the support of the Alberta
Foundation for the Arts for this published
work.

Canada

 Canada Council   Conseil des Arts
for the Arts   du Canada

Printed and bound in Canada by
Transcontinental Printing

∞ This book is printed on 50% recycled,
acid-free paper

Cover design, page design and typesetting by
Mieka West.

National Library of Canada Cataloguing in Publication

Davies, Wayne K. D.
  Writing geographical exploration: James and the North West Passage,
1631-33 / Wayne K.D. Davies.

(Northern lights series ; 4)
Co-published by the Arctic Institute of North America.
Includes bibliographical references and index.
ISBN 1-55238-062-9

  1. James, Thomas, 1593?-1635. 2. Northwest Passage—Discovery and
exploration—British. 3. Arctic regions—Discovery and exploration—
British. 4. Discoveries in geography. 5. Narration (Rhetoric) I. Arctic
Institute of North America. II. Title. III. Series.

FC3961.2.D39 2004   910'.9163'27   C2004-900162-0 *for Bronwen*

NORTHERNLIGHTS SERIES

William Barr, general editor

University of Calgary Press and the Arctic Institute of North America are pleased to be the publishers of the Northern Lights series. This series takes up the geographical region of the North (circumpolar regions within the zone of discontinuous permafrost) and publishes works from all areas of northern scholarship, including natural sciences, social sciences, earth sciences, and the humanities.

Other books in Northern Lights series:

Nunavik: Inuit-Controlled Education in Arctic Quebec Ann Vick-Westgate · Copublished with The Katutjiniq Regional Development Council · No. 1

Many Faces of Gender: Roles and Relationships Through Time in Northern Indigenous Communities Edited by Lisa Frink, Rita S. Shepard, and Gregory A. Reinhardt · Copublished with University Press of Colorado · No. 2

New Owners in their Own Land: Minerals and Inuit Land Claims Robert McPherson · No. 3

War North of 80: The Last German Arctic Weather Station of World War II Wilhelm Dege · Translated and edited by William Barr · No. 4

As Long As This Land Shall Last: A History of Treaty 8 and Treaty 11, 1870-1939 · René Fumoleau · No. 6

CONTENTS

LIST OF TABLES AND FIGURES

Geography has had a long and intimate relationship with the study of exploration, because a great deal of the information used by the earliest geographers to map and describe the world came from narratives of discovery. From the end of the nineteenth century, the association between the two fields began to wither. The world had been largely explored; the interests of most geographers moved to regional studies and the analysis of the processes that create spatial differentiation; and cartography and map-making developed into specialist fields. Nevertheless, even in the 1930s, geographers were still writing important books about exploration; for example, in studies by Taylor (1930, 1934) and Baker (1931). Even in mid-century, Griffith Taylor's (1951) influential set of edited essays describing the main themes of contemporary geography contained two essays dealing with the exploration and character of the Arctic and Antarctica, whilst Wood (1951) summarized the results of world discovery. In the last quarter of a century, geographers such as Allen (1975), Barr (1995), Davies (1984), Lewis (1979), and Wallis (1999), have continued the geographical research tradition in exploration, frequently providing new insights into the journeys of exploration. In addition, students of the development of cartography obviously still spend a great deal of time on the maps of explorers (Warkentin and Ruggles 1970, Harley and Woodward 1987), which has produced many new insights into the meaning of maps and the cultural influences and forces lying behind their development. But these are exceptions. In general, relatively few academic geographers have been actively researching exploration topics in the last fifty years, so most of the academic research literature on exploration has come from historians or retired military personnel who have brought their own expertise and methods of enquiry to the field. But the last two decades have seen another change in the academic background of individuals contributing to the study of exploration. Literature specialists have used hermeneutic perspectives to provide radically new interpretations of the writings of explorers. This type of research is very different to the older studies of exploration by geographers and historians. Most of these emphasized the *products of journeys* – the *why*, *where*, and *when* of exploration, as well as *what* they saw, described, and measured. There can be no doubt that the often painstaking scholarship of what can be called the *exploration result* approach has produced major insights into the context, progress, and consequences of the various voyages and expeditions of discovery. Certainly, there were many examples in which more subjective factors were dealt with, such as the influence of myths, political intrigue and rivalry, or justifications for conquest and settlement. But the tone of much of the literature – especially the contributions by geographers up to two decades ago – was usually very empirical and positivistic. The new, literary-inspired approaches of individuals such as Campbell (1988) and Greenblatt (1991) have focused on the *writings* of explorations – upon the exploration *narratives* – rather than primarily on the *results of the journeys*. They concentrate on two key questions: the first relates to interpretation and meaning; the second, to the influences that affect the construction of the narratives. In the former case, a key question is how explorers *represented* the sights they saw and what ideologies lay behind these interpretations; in the latter, the emphasis is upon how the exploration narratives were *written* – recognizing that a multitude of influences affect the writing process and that ideas and experiences can be written in very different ways. Relatively few geographers have adopted these ideas, but the recognition of the way that geography can be considered to be a cultural field in the last decade (Davies and Gilmartin 2002) has led to increasing interest in these ideas and to what amounts to a new cultural geography that underpins the field. In the context of travel writing, these ideas can be seen in a recent book edited by Gregory and Duncan (1999, 2) in which it was succinctly observed that the essays in the collection dealt as much with the "production of a space of knowledge," as the "production of a space of power," in the sense that the new discoveries led to European political or economic domination in the newly discovered areas.

A key difference between the traditional approach to the study of exploration and these new, literary-inspired perspectives is that the new researchers reject the implicit assumption of realism; essentially this is the idea that explorers simply wrote down what they saw, as some type of mirror-like process. Certainly, there were disputes about where an explorer had been, and what he saw, for many explorers made speculations that were presented as facts. But in most cases, the *cultural setting* and the *process of construction of the narrative* were taken for granted, and were rarely considered to be topics of great importance. In contrast, exponents of the new perspectives argue that the narratives of exploration are cultural productions whose meanings can only be properly understood in relation to the context of their construction. In other words, the writings of explorers, whether in the initial daily logs or journals, as well as the final published narratives, tell the readers as much about the previous ideas, motives, culture, and representative practices of the explorer as about the new worlds that were discovered and described. Particularly important in these new perspectives is the way that the writings of western explorers can be shown to encode European agendas, interests, and dominance, demonstrating how particular ideologies infuse the writing. One of the pioneering workers in this field incisively summed up the approach in the title of her book, *Imperial Eyes* (Pratt 1992). This went to the heart of the idea that explorer-authors wrote about the worlds they discovered from a particular perspective – a perspective that unconsciously legitimized European attitudes and beliefs as well as marginalizing those of the indigenous peoples; conquest, trade, and imperialism were often the dominant objectives and assumptions.

Interest in these hermeneutic approaches to textual study has rapidly spread to other disciplines. In the past decade, an increasing number of human geographers have been applying these ideas – although rarely in the study of exploration. In their introduction to a groundbreaking set of essays written by geographers, Barnes and Duncan (1992) identified some of the major tasks involved in the study of textual construction and meaning in the general field of geography, arguing that these issues – the underdeveloped *writing* or *graphy* part of the subject – need far more attention than just the *geo*. This book attempts to contribute to this relatively neglected part of geography, using exploration literature as the raw material the literature that provided much of the raw material for the geography of recently explored lands in the past.

The book has two objectives, one general, and one specific. The specific function is to reassess the exploratory work of Captain Thomas James who searched for the Northwest passage in 1631–32 and who wrote a book about his experiences in the following year. It is the contention of this study that James has not always been treated fairly by people who have commentated on his book over the centuries, and his work needs to be reappraised. However, to appreciate the basis for this reappraisal necessitates an understanding of the way that James chose to write his book, which means that his narrative needs to be regarded as an exercise in *construction or writing*, the type of issue identified by Barnes and Duncan (1992), as well as one of *interpretation, by readers of the book*. Recognition of the literary value of James's narrative gave rise to the general objective of this study: a survey of the way that exploration is written and received. Exploration narratives cannot be looked at simply in terms of the description of discovery of new lands since many variables – other than the stimulus of the exploration experience – affect the way the books are written. Although this may seem obvious, the focus upon one type of reading, such as the 'exploration result' approach described above, can easily lead to misunderstandings of the value of the descriptions, because it deals with the *product* not how this product was created; what Turnbull (2000) has called the "*creation of knowledge spaces*" in his stimulating book. This objective meant that it was necessary to provide a review of the factors that affect the creation of an exploration narrative, the effect of writing, the relationships between exploration, or travel writing in general, and literature and the problems posed by textual representation. These issues are complex and problematic, for they go to the heart of the construction and communication of meaning in written texts. It is obvious that the digression into such issues does take the reader away from the objective of re-evaluating the work of James, but the survey does provide a context for his work and for the evaluation of his contributions. The discussion shows that the translation of the experiences of the explorer into the apparently static and timeless written words of the book that records the exploration cannot be seen as a series of mimetic statements about the areas explored – statements of authority because they were the first words written about the new lands. The older, implicit assumption that exploration narratives are 'realist' or copyist accounts of some external reality is rejected, and replaced with evidence from many exploration narratives, and also critics of these books, that these texts are *constructed representations*, subject to a large number of influences. Of course, most of these ideas will be familiar to those working in literary criticism, and could be taken for granted. But the application of these ideas to exploration narratives by geographers, is still in its infancy. Hence, it seemed appropriate to provide a review of these concepts, and, in the process, to try to create a more systematic introductory approach to the issues of *writing* and interpreting *exploration* narratives.

The dual objectives of this book led to the decision to separate the work into two main sections: Part A, dealing with the broader issues of exploration writing, and Part B with the rest of the chapters that review the specific case of James. But since the purpose is to apply the new approaches to James's work, it seemed necessary to begin this study by introducing his contribution to exploration and providing a rationale for the need to re-evaluate his contributions in Chapter 1. However, the basis of the argument that James's work needs a new assessment necessitated a review of the issues of textual construction and the relationships between exploration writing and the field of literature. This discussion forms Part A of the book, composed of Chapters 2 and 3. The new approaches to the interpretation of the narratives of exploration, reviewed in Part A, contrast with the older geographical and historical approaches, which normally focused on the *results* of explorations, and tended to view the texts as empirical statements of what was seen. These views were only modified as new information was produced from new discoveries, or the explorer was shown to be falsifying or misinterpreting his discoveries. Yet, recognition of the utility of the new interpretations does not mean a rejection of all of the older, traditional methods in the study of exploration. In the birth of these new perspectives, it is almost inevitable that advocates of the new approaches downplay older, traditional ways; to draw attention to their case it is often necessary for those using the new approaches to ignore, or even to denigrate the old. Indeed, some of the new hermeneutic studies seem to be so concerned about meaning and cultural interpretation that key issues such as the process of discovery, or the identification of specific locations and the characteristics of the new lands, are almost ignored. This makes their approach as *partial* as the older focus upon *exploration results*.

In this study, it is argued that many the older contributions to the study of exploration are still an important part of the record, but their findings need to be integrated with, or at least related to, these new perspectives. Hence this study attempts to combine the new and old approaches, in an attempt to provide a more balanced approach to an understanding of the process of writing exploration narratives in general, and the significance of James's work in particular. One important by-product of the new perspectives is that exploration narratives, such as the one considered here, should not be seen as finished empirical accounts, valorized because they are the first descriptions of an unknown area. Rather, they are part of the new discourse of understanding about exploration. This is a discourse that relates as much to the cultural meanings and preferences of the world of the explorer, to the encoding of positions of dominance and subservience in the writings, as to the lands discovered and the effect of the discoveries upon these areas, as well as the fact that explorers may be trying to entertain, perhaps even to astonish the reader with their experiences. Part B applies many of these ideas, as well as the older approaches, to the work of James, in Chapters 3 to 7, showing that he was a more significant figure than critics have previously allowed. But his work – not so much his *discoveries*, as his *writing* about the exploration – needs to be read from several different perspectives if its value is to be fully appreciated. This emphasis provided the title for the book.

The development of this book has involved a circuitous path; it was itself a process of discovery, rather than one that started with a planned purpose. In origin, the interest in James came from the chance finding of Kitchen's 1776 map of North America in a second-hand shop in my hometown in Wales during a visit in the early 1980s. I confess I had forgotten my history and was surprised to see the label New South Wales emblazoned across the lands bordering the south west of Hudson Bay. This led me to review the work of early explorers and promoters of Canada and to search for Welsh connections. These admittedly aimless readings were focused when I was asked by Professor Muriel Chamberlain to provide an introductory survey of the role of the Welsh in Canada at a conference on this topic in the University of Wales, Swansea, in March 1985; a college where I had held a lectureship before going to Canada (Chamberlain 1985, 1999). Although I was able to include a small part of the information on James in my survey, it was largely from secondary sources. I was still far too interested in my main academic interests in urban geography to seriously pursue what seemed to be esoteric interests in seventeenth century exploration, despite the fact that my paternal grandmother, a Shelvocke, may well have been connected to the famous eighteenth century explorer of that unusual name. However, a few years later I received an invitation to lecture on James at a one-day conference on Canada held in Swansea in 1996 when it was the 'city of literature'. This was organized by Peter Stead, then senior lecturer in history at Swansea, and now visiting professor at the University of Glamorgan in Treforest (Pontypridd), located in my hometown. This invitation gave me the opportunity to spend more time looking into James's contribution and the new approaches to exploration in general. After the original sources were consulted, I gradually came to the conclusion that many of his reviewers had been unfair, and James's exploits and contributions needed to be reassessed. But the real impetus to writing a book on James, rather than an article or two, came from increasing awareness of the hermeneutic turn in human geography, which meant that I incorporated this material into my senior and graduate courses on the philosophy and methods of geography at the University of Calgary. I began to realize that the narrative of Thomas James needed to be read on several planes and that his work could be seen as contributing to science and exploration as well as literature. However, it was soon apparent that any comprehensive reassessment of his work needed a book-length manuscript if his work was to be given a new valuation. I was fortunate to obtain a Killam Fellowship at the University of Calgary in 1998–99, which provided me with partial release time from a heavy teaching schedule to work on research projects, especially that of James, which was unrelated to my main research and teaching interests in urban geography. Part of the book was written during this period and it was completed during my subsequent tenure as Craig Dobbin Visiting Professor of Canadian Studies in University College Dublin, where the Department of Geography, under Anne Buttimer and Angret Sims, provided important assistance and interest. This position in Dublin also provided time for reading more widely in literary and cultural fields and was a convenient location from which to visit archives and libraries in Wales, London, and Bristol that contained material pertinent to this project. Hence, I must thank the trustees of the Killam and Dobbin awards for their generosity, which gave me time to complete this project.

During the lengthy gestation of this research, I have been extremely grateful for the help of friends in many parts of South Wales and surroundings who have listened far too often to my tales of James when I returned from various libraries and archives. I must thank, in particular the two Peters, Eleanor, Elaine, Graham, as well as Arwel, Jan, Gill, Gwynne, Guy, Muriel, Roy, and Andrea: The Bristol Society of Merchant Venturers helped by allowing me to view their records on James. In University College Dublin, the final writing was made easier because of the friendship of several people – and the assistance of their relaxing Guinness breaks – especially the Visiting Professor of Australian Studies, Judith Brett, Graeme Smith, Gerald Mills and Mary Gilmartin; the latter was kind enough to read the almost complete manuscript and provided some useful criticisms because of her extensive background in contemporary cultural geography. In addition, I must also acknowledge, with thanks, the assistance of the staff of the University of Calgary Press, the Arctic Institute, the cartographic skills of Robin Poitras in Calgary and Stephen Harmon in Dublin, the proofreading help of Amanda, Allison and especially Jean Llewellyn, and the encouragement of my daughter Rhiannon and her invaluable assistance with ideas from literary theory. Finally, the support provided by my department head, Diane Draper, and my former doctoral student, colleague, and friend, Ivan Townshend, now in the University of Lethbridge, was appreciated, although he still thinks I should spend my time on quantitative urban geography. He may be right. But what I have discovered in the writing and publication of this work is the utility of my old school motto: Ymdrech a lwydda.

The engraving contains the following text: Ætatis suæ 40 — THE TRVE PORTRAICT OF CAP: THOMAS IAMES IAMES — Some has a time.

FIGURE 1.1. A PORTRAIT OF CAPTAIN THOMAS JAMES C. 1633

Chapter 1

Captain Thomas James:
The Case for Reassessment

2 *Captain Thomas
James*

On 22 October 1632, the *Henrietta Maria*, a small seventy-ton ship, battered, leaking, and crewed by eighteen exhausted men, limped back into the port of Bristol, a year and a half after it had set off to find the Northwest Passage to the Orient around the north of America. The voyage was sponsored by the Society of Merchant Venturers in Bristol; a city associated with the search for such a passage since the 1497 exploration of Cabot that rediscovered part of the American continent. In common with so many of its predecessors, and subsequent successors, the expedition failed to find the elusive passage. But unlike many similar voyages, the harrowing experiences of James's journey were not forgotten. They were brilliantly described in the book written by the ship's captain, Thomas James, published early in 1633. Little is known of James's life before he undertook the voyage. Yet it is clear that he was brought up in the Welsh border parish of Llanvetherine, near Abergavenny in the county of Monmouthshire, and had qualified as a lawyer before turning to the sea and becoming a privateer captain based in Bristol. James must have attained a considerable reputation to be entrusted with the leadership of such an expensive and significant expedition by the Bristol commercial elite.

We are fortunate to have James's portrait (fig. 1.1), which was included as an addition to the map showing his voyage included in his book (James 1633). The portrait is accompanied by a rather pessimistic motto: Some Has A Time. Was this proud-looking, sharp-featured man, dressed in the finery of the period, implying that fame is ephemeral? Did he mean that his *time* was the harrowing voyage of exploration that made his name and led to the privilege of audiences with King Charles? We shall never know. But in a personal context, James's succinct comment proved accurate. He only lived a few years after his horrendous and challenging experiences in the ice-encrusted conditions of Hudson Bay and its shores. It was an environment that was unfamiliar and often terrifying in its cold. The area was only marginally habitable for sailors restricted to the western European technology of their day. But in terms of the history of scientific exploration, exploration writing, and literary genres, James's terse four word comment may have underestimated his real achievements — especially now that exploration narratives are being seen as more than the descriptions of the events of discovery. These writings can no longer be interpreted as mimetic copies of environments that were seen – produced by simply writing down the sights that were seen. They need to be interpreted through the new intellectual perspectives of the last two decades provided by contemporary literary criticism, cognitive science, the new historicism, and by the hermeneutic trends in historical and cultural geography. These conceptual changes mean it is worth adopting one of the words in James's motto and suggest it is *time* to review and to reassess his work. The rest of this chapter makes the case for such a new evaluation, setting James's contributions to knowledge within a summary of the traditional approaches to the study of exploration narratives, the opinions of James's principal commentators, as well as a review of the relationship of his work to two literary genres.

✛ 2. TRADITIONAL STUDIES OF EXPLORATION

James's voyage was one small part of the explosion of European exploration undertaken from the mid-fifteenth century onwards. Although the period has often been described as an *age of exploration*, voyages of discovery by Europeans were not unique to this period. Phillips (1988) has shown that Europeans made many new discoveries in the medieval period, whilst it is well-known that the work of Chinese and Arab navigators in the same period surpassed these achievements. The discoveries of the Europeans in the Renaissance proved to be vastly more extensive in geographical scope. In addition, they took place at a time of increasing technological advancements, which gave Europeans the ability to colonize new lands and to explore and establish transoceanic trade routes – of which the search for the Northwest Passage was the most spectacular failure. The general success of these initiatives meant that, for the first time, a group of people on the earth were able to think globally and initiate the process of regular and direct commercial connections between its distant parts, rather than through trade by intermediaries (Davies 2004). Together with the social, intellectual, and economic developments within Europe, the continent was transformed from a backwater, to the centre of world development within a few centuries.

These expeditions coincided with the invention and diffusion of the printing press, a growth in literacy and wealth, and expanding state power. All contributed to enhance the effect of these new discoveries upon the imagination of the peoples of Europe. The published reports of explorers attained a wide readership, helped by the fact that most were written in the languages of the emerging nations of Europe. The public was no longer dependent upon oral reports filtered down from presentations made at court, or to sponsors and friends, and whose detail rarely survived beyond the life of the explorer. However, not all the results of explorations were accessible to the general public. One must remember that the accounts of some expeditions and the resulting maps were deliberately repressed because of national rivalry or commercial secrecy. Moreover, it was often decades and even centuries after some explorations that many unpublished notes and letters were found by scholars in various archives and in sets of long-forgotten family papers.

This voluminous literature – books, pamphlets, letters, and charts – has been assiduously mined by students of discovery in the search for the motivations of the explorers, and the results and consequences of the expeditions. However, the very scale and scope of the explorations, and the conflicting claims, often made the discoveries difficult to comprehend, especially in the years immediately after the new lands were seen. The first of the traditional strategies to cope with this volume of data was to collect and codify the information brought back by journeys of exploration, in order to compare different sources and evaluate the claims. During the medieval period, this was a difficult task. Much of this information was only available in a few manuscripts or charts, scattered in private libraries or in personal files in different countries. The Renaissance brought a new interest in compilation. Henry the Navigator's decision to collect as much information as possible about Atlantic exploration at his palace on Cape Sagres in the mid-fifteenth century, was one of his major achievements. It helped the Portuguese in their exploration of Africa, South America, and Asia (Russell 2000). Over a century later, Richard Hakluyt (1600; Quinn and Skelton 1965) adopted a similar comprehensive approach, but went beyond the collection of maps, to edit and publish a summary of the major voyages of exploration. There is little doubt the act of publication was as much designed as an enterprise to establish English claims to parts of the New World, as one that provided a dispassionate, compendium of knowledge. Hakluyt's pioneering path was followed a generation later by the clergyman, Samuel Purchas (1626) in his multi-volume description of world exploration, using extracts from many exploration narratives as well as summaries and comments.

The collation and compendia approaches continued to be used in subsequent centuries as shown by the two-volume work of Harris

(1705), which was revised and extended in 1744 to 48 and reprinted in 1764. This approach became more and more difficult as the volume of information increased. They were gradually replaced by attempts to summarize the main contributions of a group of explorers in particular regions or times. A good early example of the former approach was provided by Barrow's (1818) survey of Arctic exploration, a theme which subsequently led to scores of books: from Rundall's (1849) survey of the voyages to 1631, to the most comprehensive recent works by Savours (1999) and Delgado (1999). Pioneering work on Tudor and Stuart explorers by Eva Taylor (1930; 1934) shows the focus upon a particular period rather than an area, whilst an area, period, and country focus is shown by Glyndwyr Williams's (1962) work on the British search for the Northwest Passage in the eighteenth century. These and other surveys were complemented by innumerable articles on the work of individual explorers in the pages of publications such as the Geographical Journal, whilst increasing interest in individual explorers has led to a voluminous body of literature on their significance and work. The work of the Hakluyt Society in the last century and a half provides the major resource in the study of exploration. Almost three hundred volumes on the history of explorers and exploration have been published in two series. This sequence of publications includes the reprinting and editing of the journals of many expeditions throughout the world, such as Thomas's (1998) recent work on the Russian explorer Semenov in central Asia, or those of Middleton, More, and Smith (Barr and Williams 1994; 1995) in the Canadian Arctic. The Hakluyt Society's publications are complemented by national series of explorations, such as the Champlain Society in Canada, as seen by Davis's (1995; 1998) comprehensive reviews of Franklin's early expeditions in the arctic mainland of west central Canada, or Cooke and Holland's (1978) catalogue of all Arctic journeys, which even includes lists of seamen known to have travelled to the area. In addition, the journals of discovery written by many individual explorers in particular areas have been generalized to show how knowledge of remote areas was painstakingly built-up from many sources over the centuries, as shown in John Warkentin's (1964) selection of extracts from exploration journals in the western interior of Canada. The result was a book of what can be described as *first voice descriptions* of the area; although it is worth observing that James's work was not used, presumably because most of his narrative is set in Hudson Bay itself. However, James's 1633 map of the bay was included in a comprehensive collection of historical maps of Manitoba (Warkentin and Ruggles 1970).

The main emphasis of these studies of exploration has been to provide accurate and comprehensive editions of the narratives left by explorers, together with evaluations of the significance of these works. But the information has also enabled subsequent investigators to summarize the general trends in world or continental exploration, culminating in such important late-twentieth-century surveys as those of Parry (1964), Morison (1978), or Quinn (1977). In general, the traditional approach to the study of exploration has been on the *results* of the exploration. Certainly, this has led to a comprehensive understanding of the way that the world has been explored, the motives involved, and the effects of the discoveries. However, most of these studies unconsciously adopt a realist approach to interpretation: they assume that the explorers simply described what they saw. Since these were the first persons from Europe to see and write about the new lands, the descriptions were considered to be mimetic; in other words, the words of the explorer simply reflect the underlying reality that was found. Of course, this does not mean that students of exploration were unaware of the fact that explorers often lied, added imaginative passages, or reached erroneous conclusions. Rather, it was assumed that such views could be corrected by evaluating the claims of the explorer in the light of subsequent findings. These essentially positivist approaches have been complemented by new ways of investigating exploration narratives from the 1970s. The work of literary analysts in particular has shown that a difference can be drawn between the actual explorations and the narratives that describe them. The latter involves a writing that takes place at a later date than the progress of discovery, is affected by many more influences than the journey itself, and always involves interpretation and bias because the author is writing within the context of his or her own culture and beliefs. Hence, the new approach to the study of exploration literature has been hermeneutic or interpretive in approach, searching for the forms of representation and the meanings that lie behind the words, as seen in the pioneering studies of Campbell (1988), Greenblatt (1991) and Pratt (1992) among literary scholars, and Gregory and Duncan (1999) in geography. But the search for representations within an explorer's writing can be complemented by the same type of search in the works of writers who have written about the explorers; after all, most of our knowledge of exploration comes from these secondary sources, whose authors have tried to interpret the work of explorers in the context of other discoveries and with the benefit of hindsight. So, the first question to be addressed is how James's work has been evaluated in the past.

Most reviews of James's work still focus on his voyage as a journey of geographical exploration, whether in Britain (MacInnes 1967; Jones, Emyr W., 1996), or in Canada (Bodilly 1928; Helfrich 1972; Kenyon 1975). As such, James's achievements are bound to be of limited significance compared to major trailblazers, such as Magellan or Cook, for his exploration only took place in the area in and around Hudson Bay – incidentally, this is the form usually used today, rather than its original designation as *Hudson's Bay*. Moreover, James was not the first to explore in the area of Hudson Bay, as is obvious from its name; this was a label that had been given to the area to immortalize Henry Hudson's voyage and wintering in 1610–11. His expedition ended in a mutiny and the abandonment and subsequent death of Hudson and his loyal associates. Yet it is possible that Hudson was not the first to venture into the bay. Sebastian Cabot may have journeyed to the bay in 1508, mistaking the large sea for the Pacific, although there are real doubts about whether such a journey did take place (Cooke and Holland 1978, 18). Thomas Button's expedition of 1612–13 was also sent in search of the Northwest Passage, and his two ships ventured into the same bay. He was the first to find and explore much of the western shore, and wintered in the vicinity of the Nelson River, although not without losing a ship and a large number of men from his complement of 160 original adventurers. The Danes, under Jens Munk in 1619–20, also sailed into the same area searching for the same passage. But only two men, in addition to the leader, out of the original sixty-four members of the expedition, survived the wintering (Hansen 1970). After these three major voyages there were a few additional but failed expeditions in search of the elusive passage (Rundall 1849; Cooke and Holland 1978). But it was not until the early 1630s that two new successful journeys into Hudson Bay were again made, in the hope of finding a shorter route to the Orient in order to participate in the rich returns from trade with this area.

James's 1631 voyage from Bristol was complemented by Foxe's expedition from London, each sailing within a few days of one another (James 1633; Foxe 1635; Christy 1894). Both failed in their quest, spending most of their time fruitlessly in Hudson Bay. But since Foxe managed to get further north than James, well into Foxe Channel (south of Baffin Island), he is often seen as the more successful explorer, although James had the courage to winter in Hudson Bay and try again the following summer. James's original achievements in discovery were limited to the south coast of Hudson Bay and to the west coast of James Bay. Compared to the discoveries of many of his contemporaries, these were relatively minor additions to the new geographical knowledge, although it will be shown that his narratives contained a great deal of useful information that was used by subsequent explorers.

For almost two hundred years after James's book was published, the account of his experiences and explorations continued to be held in high regard. The original book proved popular enough to be republished – a century after it first appeared – by Payne in 1740 and in abridged form by Lemoine and Roe in 1807. Long extracts appeared in the authoritative English-language survey of world travels written by Harris (1705) that was revised in 1744–48 and republished in 1763. An influential Hakluyt Society series edition (Christy 1894) of two volumes contained both James's book and its appendices, along with Foxe's journal, which also included extracts from fifteen previous voyages to the Canadian northwest. These books still provide the most accessible source of the first published narratives of both James and Foxe, and provide a detailed commentary on both the preparations for the voyages and a series of informative footnoted comments on their discoveries. Christy's editorial introduction (1894, 183) also showed that James's narrative appeared in abstract or abridged form in eighteen different sources from 1705 to 1870, proving that his work was well-known. Bodilly's book (1928) also reprinted most of James's original text and provided informed commentary directly after the long quoted passages from James's book. Increasing access to the Arctic in the 1960s and 1970s led to new interest in the early geographical explorations of the area, leading to two new Canadian publications on James. Payne's 1740 edition was republished in the early 1970s (Coles 1973), bringing James's words to a new audience, although the appendices were not part of this edition. Kenyon (1975) tried to make James's work more suitable to a contemporary audience by rewriting the text of James's narrative in contemporary language. Again, the appendices were excluded, which means that the justification for James's calculations on locations, for example, is not apparent to readers of this version. Fortunately, a complete reprinting of James's entire work, based on the edition held in the Bodleian library in Oxford (Theatrus Orbis Terrarum 1968), had previously provided an accessible source of the original text.

The fact that James's book, or a summary of it, was reprinted so many times, shows that many publishers saw value in his work. But as time passed, it is clear that not all commentators have viewed James's expedition in the same way. The first published commentary on James's work came from his rival Luke Foxe (1635). He suggested, without any real evidence, that James had limited navigational skills, although it will be shown that this and other opinions about James's ability can be seen as the carping comments of a less successful explorer, whose work was only published two years after that of James. For almost two centuries, the comments made about James were generally favourable. Harris's (1705) survey of travels in the world contained a sixteen-page summary of James's text, and chose not to include anything from Foxe. This indicates that Harris viewed James's work as superior to that of his rival, in the same way that he ignored Button's expedition, in favour of including descriptions of Hudson's voyages. The 1748 revision and extension of the 1705 survey of Arctic expeditions, probably completed by Dr. J. Campbell, contained much more commentary and a different selection of explorers. It is worth noting that this edition only contained small extracts on the major previous expeditions to the area: nine lines on Frobisher, twelve on Hudson and twenty-nine on Button. Foxe was again largely ignored, whereas James was accorded twenty-five pages in this new edition (Harris 1748, vol. 2, 406–30). The new editor justified his selection in several ways, commenting that James's book is

> *very justly looked upon as the very best work of its kind that ever was published ... (so) ... it will free us from the Necessity of inserting any more voyages into the Northern sea. (Harris 1748, vol. 2, 406)*

But in the early nineteenth century, opinion about James's achievements changed dramatically. The influential Second Secretary of the British Admiralty penned a series of scathing comments on James in his book that reviewed Arctic expeditions (Barrow 1818). Barrow claimed that James's book was either an exercise in exaggeration, or the mark of an incompetent. He accused James of being overwhelmed with conditions that should have been anticipated and dealt with, because of knowledge of the conditions gained from previous expeditions to the area. He also made the following sweeping condemnation:

> *Captain James's history ... may be called a book of Lamentation and weeping and great mourning; it is one of continued strain, of difficulties, dangers*

and complaining ... the observations it contains are at this time of no use whatever. (Barrow 1818, 250)

These criticisms seem to have had a major impact upon subsequent views of James. For example, the influential Hakluyt series edition of Foxe and James (Christy 1894, 177) concluded that Foxe's work "is of greater geographical value" although he did acknowledge that James's book was respected for its prose. Neatby's survey (1958, 40) of the exploration of the Northwest Passage is typical of the early- and mid-twentieth-century references; it only contained thirteen lines on James and Foxe, repeating the latter's view that James was "no seaman," although he goes on to describe him as a "brave and amiable gentleman ... who over-dramatized the voyage." Thomson's (1975) vigorously written survey of the search for the Northwest Passage was less critical, and took pains to praise James's survival during the winter. The entry on James in the Dictionary of Canadian Biography carefully summarized James's achievements, noted his knowledge of mathematics, and praised the "fluid grace of his exposition, learning and scientific accuracy," but still described the voyage as full of "amateurish misadventures" (Cooke 1966, 384). The thumbnail summary of James's expedition in Cooke and Holland's (1978, 29) review of all Canadian Arctic voyages also noted that "James was not a trained seaman." James's work was even debated under the sub-title of "fool or hero" by Helfrich (1972); the first of these words indicates the critical manner in which James has been regarded by many readers, although the article did more than most in this century to rehabilitate his work. Finally, most books on the search for the Northwest Passage in the past quarter century contain only a few lines, if that, on James, or Foxe for that matter (Keating 1970; Pharand 1984; Berton 1988; Savours 1999), and often repeat the accusations about James's lack of seamanship. Fortunately, Delgado's (1999, 45–49) recent survey of expeditions to the Arctic Northwest redresses the balance somewhat, by devoting several pages to James and Foxe, but pays more attention to the work of the former and even includes his portrait.

It will be argued in subsequent chapters that these largely negative opinions are biased, and are often unfair when evidence from James's own narrative is reviewed. Technically, of course, James's decision to turn south into Hudson Bay and winter in James Bay, and his inability to go further north than Foxe, meant that his contribution to the attempts to find the Northwest Passage *was* limited, especially as nineteenth-century expeditions sailed further north and deeper into the Arctic archipelago. However, it is important to remember the context of the voyage: James was *instructed* by his sponsors to try and find the passage *through* Hudson Bay. We now know that James was too far south to be able to penetrate far into the Canadian arctic islands that rim the direct, although normally ice-blocked passage, running from Lancaster Sound to the Beaufort Sea and Bering Strait. Hence, James's exploration could never have found the passage, given his instructions to traverse the sub-arctic area of Hudson Bay. But even here, James's exploration and contribution to knowledge of the area were only briefly acknowledged in the historical surveys of the development of the Hudson's Bay Company (Rich 1966; Newman 1986), which controlled all the lands west of Hudson Bay until 1870. In Newman's book, the macabre events associated with the disastrous journeys of Hudson and Munk — mutiny and large numbers of deaths respectively — are given more attention than the successful survival of James and his crew. Indeed, it is worth noting that even the normally stoical Barrow (1818, 234) described Munk's "unparalleled sufferings" as having "an air of romance," whereas he attributed the dangers faced by James's crew as due to the captain's incompetence. Surely, this is hardly fair?

The critical comments on James, and the fact that he has been often ignored in discussions of Arctic exploration, mean that from the early nineteenth century onwards James's work is usually seen as being of limited value, a contrast to the first hundred years of positive opinion. Perhaps the main exception lies in the praise he has received for the quality of the writing in his narrative. The 1748 revision of Harris's Travels noted:

> It is justly looked upon as the very best work of its kind that was ever published.... The Author being a knowing, careful and experienced Seaman, one who wrote every thing [sic] as it occurred and framed the History of his Voyage while it was making and not after his return Home from loose papers, or a bare journal. (Harris 1748, vol. 2, 406)

Even Barrow (1818) had some praise, at least for James's prose, whilst Christy (1894), who was generally critical of James's achievements noted:

> In his narrative he expresses himself so clearly, his diction is so good, and what he has to say is so interesting, that it is a pleasure to read his book,

while to peruse that of Foxe (which took a much longer time to prepare) is a tedious and difficult occupation. (Christy 1894, 177)

Nevertheless, the general tone of James's critics indicate that such *literary* merits are of far less importance than the discovery of new lands – the so-called *geographical* results – to which James seemed to contribute little. Moreover, the comments about James's literary skills are usually assertions about his book's readability, with no supporting evidence justifying the opinion.

If the opinions of these reviewers were justified there seems little purpose in pursuing an interest in James. But when James's book is read on its own terms, the skill of its construction soon becomes apparent. James's narratives contained vivid descriptive passages, identifying the perils the crew faced and the emotional responses that resulted – in prose and verse. This means that James's narrative was not only a mimetic account of the new-found geography of the Hudson Bay area; it was also a melodramatic account of his experiences. The book is a tale of tribulation and terror, as well as being educational and entertaining. There is little doubt that on one level James's book was typical of the more thorough maritime expeditions of the day. Its frequent descriptions of position, of the character of the land and sea, of tides, depths of sea, magnetic variation, and the provision of a chart for sailing in the area, represented the typical content of nautical narratives of exploration. Certainly, James can be regarded as producing one of the earliest journals of exploration that adopted the emerging scientific practises of precise measurement. On another level, James's fast-paced descriptions of the constant perils that were faced in the frequently stormy, icy seas – with crisis succeeding crisis – represented a breakthrough in exciting exploration writing. The book conveyed a real sense of the dangers experienced during the eighteen months of the expedition. To consider James's narrative as a dispassionate, mimetic journal of exploration seems misplaced. Rather, it seems to have been deliberately constructed to entertain – perhaps even to excite – his readers with accounts of the omnipresent problems and the horrific environmental conditions that so frequently threatened to overwhelm James and his small crew. Indeed, the reputation James gained in his lifetime was based on the heroism of the journey, rather than by his achievements in discovery. So to judge James's book only from the traditional single context – as a journey of discovery – seriously diminishes its value and probable objective. James's *book*, viewed as a literary construction and achievement, may be more important than the *voyage of discovery* that stimulated it. But since the process of *writing* was not really important to those students of exploration who were interested primarily in the results of expeditions, this interpretation of its utility has been overlooked. Perhaps it is ironic, given the subsequent separation of what became viewed as literature, as opposed to science writing, that just before James's work was being dismissed by Barrow (1818), the explorer had attracted the attention of two of Britain's most famous romantic poets. Southey and Coleridge (1812) published, with approving comments, one of the poems that James wrote in Hudson Bay and included in his narrative. Indeed, the former registrar of the University of Wales (James, I., 1890) argued that James's work may have been the source for some of the images that Coleridge used in one of the most famous poems of the English language: *The Rime of the Ancient Mariner*. Despite these two nineteenth century exceptions, the literary significance of James's work seems to have met the same fate as his explorations; it has been underestimated, or virtually ignored in the last two centuries, especially in the context of the two national genre most relevant to his work, namely Canadian and Anglo-Welsh literature.

⊹ 4. JAMES AND CANADIAN LITERATURE

There is no doubt that James is usually recognized as one of the first explorers to write about part of the Canadian north – in this case, the lands around Hudson Bay. But it is rare to find reviews that argue James made an important contribution to Canadian literature by being one of the first writers to construct an exciting and readable account of the difficulty of surviving in the perilous environment of northern Canada. Part of the limited recognition of James's work is a consequence of the limited attention paid to the value of exploration journals in the development of national self-knowledge, or of literary styles and conventions in Canada – at least until about twenty years ago. One eminent literary critic in a well-known conclusion to the first Literary History of Canada (Frye 1965, 822) castigated the writings of explorers in the following words:

The literary, in Canada, is often only an incidental quality of writings which, like those of many of the early explorers, are as innocent of literary attention as a mating loon.

14 Captain Thomas James

However, it must be noted that Frye did not consider that the field of *literature* included works whose major aim was descriptions about the world. Nevertheless, Galloway's essay (1965) on "The Voyagers" in the same Literary History collection briefly acknowledged that explorers did influence literature. He specifically mentioned James as:

> *that stubborn and pious old British seaman ... [who] provided ... with a certain grim satisfaction in his hardships, the raw material for a new Inferno, all ice. (Galloway 1965, 16)*

By the 1980s, a change in attitude had taken place. It was increasingly recognized that the journals of explorers – however limited in literary phrasing and in interpretations of the human condition – represented a significant genre in literature. In Canada, MacLulich's (1979) pioneering paper has been particularly influential in putting forward the case for treating explorer narratives in literary terms. He emphasized that the final texts or written works of explorers *imposed order* upon the places and events that were visited and experienced. Although these places were *given*, not *imagined*, as in most works of fiction, the fact that these books were subject to deliberate construction and organization meant that they needed to be considered as literary works. Moreover, since they represent some of the first, or certainly surviving, commentaries on the world that the Europeans saw in their overseas expansion, they provide evidence of some of the first interpretations of the land. In the specific context of the genre now called *exploration literature*, Germaine Warkentin (1993) has edited a collection of extracts from the journals of major explorers in Canada. In her incisive introduction, she made the case that they represent not only some of the first discourses about the land, but also contribute to the emergence of Canadian culture and identity.

Attempts to summarize the seminal Canadian experience have frequently identified the "terror of nature," (Frye 1965) and "survival" as basic themes in literature (Atwood 1972; 1995). Historians such as W. L. Morton (1963), who focused on the settling of the land and its economic and political development, almost inevitably see the wilderness as areas inimical to progress and civilization – something to be conquered if a settler is to survive and make a living off the land. But MacLaren (1985b) has argued that such interpretations only capture one set of views expressed by writers in Canada; there are other *readings* of the land, as shown in the very different aesthetic views of various parts of the Prairies by members of Palliser's expedition, 1857–59. Also, it is worth emphasizing that historians, such as Innes (1930), maintained that the history of the fur trade could not be appreciated without fully understanding the life cycle of the animals on which it was based. In addition, the twentieth century has seen the development of interest in the observation of animals and vegetation for their own sake. So MacLaren argued that there is a strand in Canadian history and literature that looked at the significance of the land in *nature's* terms, not those of *humans*. The difference is that the former deals with the *intrinsic* value of the environment and all it contains, rather than its *incremental* value, which is linked to some use. This approach incorporated regret for the destruction of the forests and other resources, as well as the aboriginal way of life which was intimately linked to the land and subsistence. These writings also recognized the accommodation that was made by Europeans to enable them to survive in the early period of exploration and settlement; an alteration in lifestyle that was often linked to the borrowing of native ways — as the examples of the fur traders show. When added to more recent ideas of viewing the wilderness as a place in which to renew one's spirit, it seems clear that these views contribute to what Draper (1998) described as the developing ecological world view; one to set alongside the expansionist, exploitive attitudes upon which so much of the settlement of Canada was based — essentially the intrinsic, as opposed to the incremental, attitude to the environment.

In a more literary context, Glickman (1998) has recently argued that the themes of survival, or the presence of garrison cultures, are far too simplistic to summarize the responses made by writers and poets to the Canadian environment. She showed how the European Romantic Movement influenced interpretations of the Canadian environment. By the mid-eighteenth century, many poets, painters, and novelists were rejecting interpretations of the natural world based only on the emerging rational and scientific views (Barrell 1972). English exponents of these views had developed ideas of sublimity (Burke 1756) and the picturesque (Gilpin 1792) as schemata with which to view the world, describing new experiences and feelings. These feelings could be obtained by visits to areas such as the Lake District or the mountains of North Wales. These wet and mountainous areas had previously been disregarded for their harsh environment and poor agricultural land. Now they became destinations for travellers seeking to achieve new experiences. Several authors, from MacLaren (1984; 1985a; 1985b) to Glickman (1998), have used this well-known background to show that the western European ideas of the picturesque and sublimity were applied to Canadian landscapes, which were then *seen* and *represented* in terms of these aesthetic principles. These works illustrate that one must be wary of accepting a single literary response to nature, an issue that will be explored further in chapter 3. Such a perspective can be further illustrated by the literature of the Canadian Prairies. Kreisel (1968) has shown that its environment has produced a series of impressions on the human mind, including feelings of confinement, because of being possessed by the land, or where man is seen as the conqueror. In both cases, the immensity of the grasslands and forests, as well as the hazards of settling the area, provides a constant backdrop to fictional and historical accounts of the land.

These new interpretations demonstrate that the Canadian environment has been viewed in a number of different ways through literary history. Whether perceived as a land to be conquered, to reach accommodation with, to fear, find solace in, or to see beauty within its varied landscapes, it is clear that environmental themes permeate the development of Canadian literature. James does get a brief mention in some of the discussions of the development of literature in Canada. But relatively few literary sources, or critics other than MacLulich (1979), have given James much credit for more than the timing and content of his work. Long before the various environmental themes that have been identified above were used in novels, poetry, or the letters of settlers, the explorers – who were the first Europeans in the land – had to learn how to battle against the previously unknown, and often unimagined elemental forces of nature. This strife was reflected in their writing. Yet James's work is barely mentioned in Atwood's studies (1972; 1995) of the importance of the theme of *survival* in Canadian literature. Although not expressed in terms of the aesthetic concepts of the Romantic period, there seems little doubt that James's frequent near-death experiences – or rather his description of his voyage and wintering in such terms – had all the elements of the feelings of fear and terror that underlie the sublime. This is why it is curious that most of the exponents of environmental themes in Canadian literature ignore James's work or mention it very briefly. The reason may lie in the date of James's writing; in the seventeenth century there were only a few thousand white people in the land that became

Canada. Also, he was an explorer, a visitor from Britain, not a settler. In any case, James described an area that was unsuitable for agriculture, one that did not attract subsequent settlers, or experience continuous occupancy – apart from the small numbers of people engaged in the fur trade. Nevertheless, it will be shown that James's book may be one of the first descriptions of part of Canada to use the seminal Canadian concept of fear of the environment, and of man's battle with it – what is normally described today as the *man against nature* theme. The fact that James created two of the first poems ever to be produced in the area also seems to have been forgotten by Canadians, for they do not appear in surveys of early Canadian poetry (Davies and Gerson, 1994) – probably because James was not a permanent resident of the country. Yet, curiously, one of James's poems was well enough regarded in Britain for it to be reprinted in a recent collection of seventeenth-century poems (Fowler 1991, 335).

The limited attention paid to James makes it appropriate to look again at James's work. Even the most superficial reading seems to indicate that it has the potential to represent an important stage in the development of literature, in and about Canada. Although James's book was written in England and Wales, the experiences and notes on which it was based, were made in Canada, so there seems little point in dismissing James because he was a temporary visitor. Perhaps the most obvious utility of the narrative lies in James's descriptive ability, which created one of the first and enduring images in English of the raw and savage lands around Hudson Bay. In many ways, James's accounts of the environment he experienced are more vivid than the descriptions that Cartier (Trudel 1966) and other French sailors made about their expeditions. However, their comments were written in French, so it is dubious that they were familiar to English readers at the time. James wrote in English; it was a book that had the king's approval and seems to have sold well. So, not surprisingly, James's descriptions had considerable impact in Britain. They must have created an enduring and negative image in Britain of the land around Hudson Bay – an environment that was unsuitable for agriculture and which possessed a vicious freezing winter climate that was almost inconceivable to those used to the benign climes of the British Isles. But one must not forget that James had explored a bay that seemed to lead nowhere and was regarded as possessing few resources to attract subsequent expeditions. These findings certainly eradicated interest from James's sponsors, the powerful Bristol Society of Merchant Venturers. Their old rivals, the London merchants, were probably affected in the same way by the negative images that James created. It was over thirty years before another English ship sailed into Hudson Bay; a voyage that led a few years later to the formation of The Hudson's Bay Company in 1670 to exploit the fur-bearing animals of the region.

✛ 5. JAMES AND THE ANGLO-WELSH TRADITION

The argument that James's book should be seen as an important contribution to the literature of Canada is not the only literary issue that needs to be revisited. James was brought up in South Wales and named the south shore of Hudson Bay after his homeland. This means that another important question has to be addressed. Should James's work be considered as part of the Anglo-Welsh literary tradition? There is little evidence that this has been seriously considered. Since James was born in South Wales and wrote in English, his writings could – and perhaps should – be considered as part of the development of Anglo-Welsh literature. James's work, however, merits only eight lines in the most recent authoritative reviews of Welsh literature (Stephens 1986; 1997) and has been largely ignored by those (Garlick 1970; Mathias 1986) who have searched for the origin of the Anglo-Welsh tradition of writing. There were many examples of literary works written in English by Welsh people from the sixteenth century onwards, but the term Anglo-Welsh was not coined by Evan Evans until the late eighteenth century. Previously, Welsh scholars working in England had written in Latin, the language of the educated classes, or in Welsh, their own language. Once Welsh scholars began to write in English, an Anglo-Welsh tradition was created. Garlick and Mathias both suggested that this genre is older than other hyphenated Anglo literatures, such as Anglo-American, which is usually dated back to Bradstreet's work in 1650. Despite this long history, there has always been confusion about the nature of the field of Anglo-Welsh literature.

Writers from Wales who wrote in English were considered by many *English* literary critics to represent *Welsh* literature – which does ignore the fact that there is a thousand or more years of tradition of literature in the Welsh language (Mathias 1986). *Anglo-Welsh*, therefore, has become a convenient way of distinguishing the body of literature from people born or brought up in Wales – and not necessarily resident in Wales – who write in English. Such debate about the nature of Anglo-Welsh literature is further complicated when the geographical setting of the literature is considered. Glyn Jones (1968) observed in his work *The Dragon has Two Tongues*, that it was not appropriate to restrict the genre to topics based in Wales; this would ignore the fact that a lot of important literature written in English by Welsh writers dealt with other locales. For example, Jones argued that since Richard Hughes's best work *High Wind in Jamaica* was set in the Caribbean, it did not make sense to restrict the genre to those who only deal with Welsh topics. The situation is further complicated by the fact that those who have reviewed Anglo-Welsh writing were unable, when this was the vogue, to find a single style, content or set of associations that are common to all people who have been classed as Anglo-Welsh writers (Garlick 1970; Mathias 1986). It led one reviewer to define the term Anglo-Welsh in the following way:

> *Writers who by birth or strong family derivation and residence in Wales were Welsh but whether from necessity or choice wrote in English. (Mathias 1986, 16)*

This interpretation allows writers with Welsh heritage to be considered as part of the Anglo-Welsh tradition. Captain Thomas James clearly qualifies as a member of the group, although it is rare to find much reference to his work in reviews of the development of the genre – if such a word can be used for such a disparate group of writings and prose. But since it has been contended that James has been regarded for far too long as an explorer – a discoverer of new lands, rather than a writer – his contributions to the Anglo-Welsh field may have been underestimated. James, by living in Bristol and writing about an area outside Wales, may not be the only casualty of the preoccupation of Anglo-Welsh literature with Welsh topics – although the emphasis is perfectly understandable.

To construct a series of categories as to what is – or is not – Anglo-Welsh literature may be a useful intellectual exercise, but does not really provide much in the way of insights into the quality or significance of such writing. What does seem almost inevitable, however, is that literature dealing with descriptions of places outside Wales that are written in English, even by Welsh-born writers, may be downplayed, or even ignored by those searching for the origin or even the character of the field. This seems to have happened to James. After all, the very basis of the Anglo-Welsh tradition may be to provide insights on Wales and its people, and to address them in a distinctive voice – the insider, the fellow countryman or woman, rather than the outsider. James's work is rarely discussed in discussions of the Anglo-Welsh tradition, presumably because he was dealing with a distant land and, incidentally, with conditions that had not been seen in Wales since the end of the Ice Age – twelve thousand years previously. Also, James's work was usually seen as an account of exploration, which as we have seen was often dismissed as having any *literary* value by those who provided reviews, or critiques of literature. All these factors have combined to disguise James's contribution to the Anglo-Welsh tradition.

✠ 6. SUBSEQUENT ORGANIZATION

This chapter has argued that James's contributions are in need of a new evaluation, for his work has often been ignored or criticized on dubious grounds by many students of exploration and literature. But a more detailed review of James's expedition and his book is needed before the standard critical views can be challenged to determine whether James should occupy a more substantial place in history and literature. Before the details of this evidence are presented, it is worth remembering that this type of work is one that is difficult to produce definitive conclusions. Campbell (1988, 2), in her illuminating essays on exotic European travel writing before 1600, claimed that the translation of actual travel into a written record is always a "fraught project," for it is based on unverifiable private experiences of the past. Of course, the text of an explorer can be read literally – a description of the places seen and the events that occurred. Moreover, a great deal of important knowledge can often be derived from such a reading – especially in view of the previously blank database about the newly discovered lands. Yet it is increasingly recognized that the knowledge that we have of the new worlds seen by explorers, and the apparent facts they recorded, is not direct or mimetic; many factors influence how the experiences of exploration are written down as narrative. The texts that provide information on the journeys of exploration should also be viewed as literary constructions, influenced by factors other than the need to describe the new worlds that were discovered. These books often have functions other than the one of describing the facts of exploration. The pioneering works of individuals such as Campbell (1988), Greenblatt (1991), Pratt (1992) and Warkentin (1993), have shown that exploration narratives can provide cultural insights into the world into which they were written, for at base these writings are representations, not realist descriptions.

The new interpretations of exploration narratives have demonstrated the inadequacy of realist assumptions in interpreting these descriptions. As such, the realist ideas used to interpret the narratives in the past could just be dismissed out of hand. But many of these new ideas are less familiar to geographers and to historians of exploration who have been primarily concerned with what might be called the *products of exploration* – the way that explorers helped fill in the map of the world. Hence it seemed important, at least for this group of readers, to try to summarize the basics of the new ideas as a background to the specific interpretation of James's work, especially as an important part of James's contribution is seen as his narrative, not his new discoveries. This discussion is found in Section A of the book, which consists of chapters 2 and 3. Obviously, it does take the argument away from the particular contribution of James. But it does have the advantage of providing, in one source, a conceptual overview of the main tenets of the new approaches to the study of exploration literature for the benefit of those students of exploration who are less familiar with the new literary and cognitive ideas of the past twenty years. Chapter 2 sets the scene for this review by discussing the relationships between exploration and travel writing and what is considered literature, as well as some of the implications of the fact of writing and the nature of representation. All travel writing, whether based on the known world, or the unknown worlds of the explorer, selects and also represents information in ways that are culturally dependent. Frequently the writings have objectives other than the empirical description of the new worlds. Appreciation of this issue makes it difficult to sustain a belief in realist description, whilst recognition of the fact that readers bring their own valuations and judgments to the books of exploration provides another source of instability in the meanings derived from these narratives.

This argument is taken further in chapter 3, which summarizes the variety of influences that affect the construction of a narrative of exploration. It will be shown that these writings are conditioned not only by the cognitive filters through which the explorers see, or rather construct, the world – which depend on the influence of their prior views, based on their imagination, previous experiences, and reading, as well as their cultural mores. In other words, the new worlds that are *seen*, are interpreted and represented by the cultural conditioning of the Old World that nurtured them. But the way that the written text is constructed depends upon a large number of influences that affect its form and content, whilst it can be interpreted by readers in many ways. Hence, analysis of the construction of exploration texts can provide a multitude of alternative insights into the process of exploration, especially upon contemporary representative practises and the effects of the journey. The narratives are the result of a very complex evolution and are not as simple and direct as was believed in the past. All too often in exploration studies, the narrative of discovery was taken literally – as some mirror-like representation that simply involved the choice of suitable words to describe the new environments – criticized only by the factual inaccuracies revealed by subsequent explorations. The chapter concludes by identifying the principal functions performed by exploration narratives, in order to provide a template to assess the utility of the texts of particular explorers.

The second part of the book, Section B, returns to the specific case of Captain Thomas James. It consists of four chapters in which the template is used to provide a detailed review of his work. Much of this review comes from a textual analysis of James's book, which was published in 1633, and also incorporates a great deal of additional material by reviewing previous readings and interpretations of James's work. Chapter 4 deals with the background to the voyage and uses information from manuscript sources held in the archives of the sponsors of his journey, the Society of Merchant Venturers who still have a presence in Bristol. Chapter 5 describes the more traditional geographical utility of James's work in terms of locational identification, his achievements in finding previously unknown places, measurements of location and mapping, as well as his understanding of environmental conditions. Chapter 6 deals with the interpretative significance of his book, detailing the ways he portrayed such issues as the power relationships, the environmental processes, as well as describing the organizational structure and style that was adopted. Chapter 7 summarizes the book's instrumental value, the way that James's work had significance beyond itself; that is, in the way that it affected others, not only in terms of exploration, but also in literary imagination. The conclusion, chapter 8, reviews previous criticisms of his work in the light of the evidence of the previous chapters. James, the Renaissance man that he was – trained lawyer, privateer captain, explorer, and author – was a multi-faceted and multi-talented individual who achieved a great deal in his life. It is the contention of this chapter that his achievements have been downplayed and underestimated in the last two centuries, and that James should be regarded as a more substantial figure in the development of exploration literature, not for his geographical discovery, but for his contribution to the early literature of Wales and Canada.

Part A

INTERPRETING EXPLORATION NARRATIVES

Chapter 2

Exploration Writing
and Literary Concepts

Literature is not something given once and for all, but something constructed and reconstructed, the product of shifting conceptual entitlements and limits.... There are no transcendent or absolute rules about what belongs in the zone of literature and the zone of the non literary.... On the contrary the lines can be drastically redrawn.... Continual refashioning is at the center of the profession of literary study; it is both a characteristic of the texts we study and a crucial means to keep those texts and our own critical practice from exhaustion and sterility. (Greenblatt and Gunn, Redrawing the Boundaries, 1992, 5)

Surveys of literary criticism have shown that a real revolution has taken place in the field within the past twenty-five years (Belsey 1980; Eagleton 1983; Greenblatt and Gunn 1992; Selden 1995). This chapter's introductory quotation deals with one of these changes, and emphasizes that what is considered to be *literature* is no longer confined to a high canonical tradition. Many formerly disregarded forms of prose, such as exploration journals, are being re-examined and interpreted using the new literary methods. In the past, the narratives of explorers have been valued primarily for their utilitarian value in indexing the progress of geographical exploration, although it has been recognized that these texts have an instrumental value in stimulating the development of other literary forms such as the novel (Adams 1983). In recent years the new perspectives of literary criticism have been applied to books on exploration in the search for meanings encoded in the texts – meanings which reveal the cultural and power relationships within the society in which they were written. The result is that exploration narratives, and travel writing in general, are no longer seen as being outside literature. In the past, literary critics such as Frye (1965, 822) argued that studies attempting to obtain descriptive accuracy of the world were not part of literature. In the last decade these writings have become one of the discourses of the past that are being scrutinized by literary criticism methods, as shown by individuals such as Campbell (1988), Greenblatt (1991) and Pratt (1992).

The basis, at least, of these new perspectives, needs to be understood before any effective evaluation of the work of Thomas James can be made, so that his work can be situated within the context of these interpretations. The next two sections of this chapter set the scene for this appraisal. They show that the contemporary view of literature and travel writing having little in common is of relatively recent origin; historically, there has always been intimate relationships between exploration and some of the major forms of literature. The third section shows that from the late Renaissance onwards, a divergence took place between the two – a separation that played a key role in the marginalization of exploration writing in literary terms. In addition, it must be recognized that the process of writing the experiences of travel is not a neutral act. The construction and publication of these accounts endowed them with prestige and power far beyond anything that accrued from the verbal discussion of these expeditions. Following Purchas's (1626) commentary on the value of travel literature, this can be described as the *literal advantage* of writing, the discussion of which forms the fourth section of this chapter. Yet exploration narratives can be written for a variety of reasons; they are not simply dispassionate accounts of the process of discovery, written simply as contributions to the accumulation of knowledge. The fifth section highlights the fact that narratives often had other functions, especially that of a commodified value – linked to their role in providing entertainment to readers, as well as profits to authors and publishers. These and other objectives frequently condition the way that the sights seen in the new worlds were selected for inclusion, and how they are described and interpreted. Recognition of this issue begins the process of casting doubt upon the so-called *factual* basis of exploration literature, the idea that these accounts simply reflect what is seen – in other words that they are mimetic or direct representations of some objective real world. This question is explored further in the sixth part of this chapter, using specific travel and exploration studies to show that this type of writing is never about simple description. All travel writing is interpretive and it is the skills of interpretation that give value to the texts – value to the *general* reader, rather than to specialists interested in the results of exploration. This point inevitably leads to a more formal questioning of the realist approach, which is dealt with in the seventh section. The discussion begins by showing how geographical studies of the importance of perception and images in exploration provided empirical evidence that began to undermine the realist approach. More conclusive evidence comes from the way that contemporary literary critics have destroyed what Belsey (1999) described as the empirical-realist or common sense approach to understanding. The theoretical ideas of post-structuralist writers such as Derrida and Barthes maintained that the production of meaning from any text is always problematic since our words and our language do not reflect the world, but condition how we understand and represent it. Hence, the meanings derived from exploration texts must be as unstable, and as contested, as those from any other genre. These interpretations lead to the conclusion that our understanding of the world is not *reflected* by our language, but is *constructed* by it. Explorers, and the native peoples in the lands they explored, may have experienced the same physical phenomena, but they processed these sights, in words and other signs, through culturally dependent sensory screens. The interpretations produced were inevitably different, since they are embedded in diverse cultures. In the context of exploration literature, these ideas indicate that the words on a page cannot be interpreted simply as literal descriptions of some real world. They are *representations* that reflect the culture that produced them and may provide insights into the social formation of these societies: they are cultural constructions. The objective, therefore, of the new literary approaches is to search for the representations and meanings that lie behind the words on a page. The new critical approaches also show that the meanings derived from individual texts may also be the product of a reader's interpretation and valuation, providing another source of instability between words and what they represent. Yet the construction of knowledge cannot be simply seen as a product of the author's writing or the reader's interpretation. Recent work in cognitive psychology has shown that the mind itself actively creates or constructs knowledge of the sights and sounds that are experienced. In other words, a process of construction, linked as much to prior knowledge and beliefs as to the experiences of exploration, affects how we *see* and *know*. Obviously, the review of these features takes the discussion away from the specific case of James, but was required to provide evidence of the inadequacy of the realist perspective and the division between literature and exploration writing that has so affected previous evaluations of his work. It is the association between these different kinds of writing that must be looked at first.

✦ 2. EXPLORATION, TRAVEL AND LITERATURE

Studies of actual exploration or travel rarely rank among the exemplars of literature. But it is worth noting that there has been a long and intimate association between literature and exploration or travel in general. Many of the earliest and most highly regarded works of prose in the western literary tradition use journeys as a theme to hold the narrative together. Some, such as Homer's *Odyssey*, were based on real travels (Steiner 1996). Originally seen as myth, as invented stories that describe heroic behaviour and illustrating moral precepts, most contemporary classicists believe the stories have a factual basis. However, before they were transcribed into a written and standardized form, the original experiences were distorted and exaggerated – a result of being modified in oral presentations over the centuries. Elsewhere, the *Icelandic Sagas* were regarded for a long time as a series of stories that were a mythic history of a people. But it is now accepted that their accounts of journeys of exploration to Greenland and North America have a strong factual basis and have stimulated attempts to find out more about the peoples and settlements that were described. Yet, it must be admitted that these epics of travel have been hard to interpret, especially from the perspective of the present period. Most are written in an imaginative style and are often so laden with symbolism that it is difficult to separate the *real* from the *invented*.

Other exemplars of western literature using exploration or travel themes are mainly fictive in origin. From *The Canterbury Tales* to *The Pilgrim's Progress* the journeys provide a medium for introducing new people and places, providing moral messages, and displaying the weaknesses or strengths of human character – frequently enlivened with passages of humour, despair, and hope. In addition, influential literary works have used journeys as the way of connecting together satirical comments on the accepted mores and idiosyncrasies of society, as seen in such literary classics as *Don Quixote*. It was probably the exaggerated claims made by some seventeenth and early-eighteenth-century explorers that led Swift (1726) to use an exploration theme in *Gulliver's Travels* upon which to base his cutting satires of the social practises and contemporary figures of his day. Indeed, Adams (1983) suggested that the development of parody was closely associated with actual travel stories. However, one of the strongest associations between literature and exploration writing, or travel descriptions in general, can be seen in the novel. Adams's (1983) comprehensive account of the relations between travel writing and the novel argued that accounts of sixteenth- and seventeenth-century voyages of exploration were important stimuli to the evolution of the novel. They provided tales of adventure, greed, success, and disaster, as well as descriptions of exotic places and races – many of whose practises were beyond the experience and imagination of the readers of Europe. Although parts of the exploration narratives were certainly invented, most explorers from the Renaissance onwards tried to produce factual statements that provided new information to the readers. Nevertheless, the unique and unusual nature of these experiences meant that it was but a short step for authors to use these ideas to create imagined events in the new literary form of the novel. Indeed, some of the first and most powerful of these early novels relate to journeys or sojourns in unknown lands, where the hero has to cope with the unfamiliar in conditions of isolation – the theme of one of the most famous early examples, the story of the castaway, *Robinson Crusoe*.

Of course, most of the examples in which travel or exploration is used as a major theme, fall into the fictional category. Their stories are essentially inventions, books of imagination that were meant primarily to entertain, or to explore the human condition. As such, they seem to have little in common with that body of writing about exploration and travel to real places, which purported to deal with actual events and locations. But the field of exploration literature has always been plagued by descriptions that were presented as fact but were actually inventions. The most famous example of a travel hoax is the well-known medieval text, *Mandeville's Travels* (Seymour 1963). Apparently describing journeys made in the mid-fourteenth century, and almost certainly originally written in French, the book was one of the most popular of medieval prose works. Indeed, it was one of the first texts to be printed in 1470, which shows its popularity, and was subsequently translated into many languages and reproduced in many editions. Mandeville – or rather whoever the author was – is sometimes regarded as the father of English prose, although Campbell's (1988) insightful review of his contribution argued that the author may equally be regarded as the father of modern travel writing.

Mandeville's book was a mixture of different types of information. Some incidents were drawn from existing sources, which made the text plausible to readers; other passages were pure invention. Much of the fascination of the book lay in its tales of the mysterious East – occupied by monsters and people with strange cultural practises – as well as its comments about the location of Paradise. But amongst the mixture of fact and fancy was the frequent reference to the world being round, at a time when the church authorities that controlled so much of learning taught that the world was flat. This assertion provided encouragement to those European explorers of the Renaissance who sought a new way to Asia by travelling west around the globe, instead of the long and dangerous eastern route. However, the book's popularity may also have come from its opposition to contemporary doctrine, in a medieval age in which opposition to church doctrine and ideas was considered blasphemous. Since Mandeville's book described the different customs and peoples of lands outside Europe, it postulated the *other* to Europeans – frequently describing behaviour that would be considered scandalous or unacceptable in Christian Europe. Such ideas could not be openly expressed in other written forms without running the risk of religious sanction. By implying these were *real* people in *real* lands the aberrant characteristics could be safely described – perhaps even pleasurably read – by those whose moral standards were far from the accepted Christian norms. Even guardians of the accepted moral codes could read them, obviously with repugnance, as they provided examples of what was considered to be abominations in the lands that did not possess the Christian message. In other words, Mandeville's narrative seemed to provide actual evidence of *heathen behaviour* that could be deplored. Modern scholarship has shown that much of the text is pure invention, although Greenblatt (1991) has reminded us that most readers in the fifteenth and sixteenth centuries – including important explorers such as Columbus, Raleigh, and Frobisher – regarded the work as factual. So Mandeville's work was literalized. It was used to justify, perhaps even to guide, the voyages of some of the principal explorers of the Renaissance. Mandeville's work was not the only one that led actual explorations to be based on fictive sources. Many expeditions searched for what we now know as the mythical lands of *Prester John* or *El Dorado*, or even the Northwest Passage. To the hopeful explorers searching for the wealth that could be found in such places, or because of passages to them, these lands and routes were considered to be real, and worthy of pursuit.

The origins of so-called factual writing about unknown and known lands is usually traced back to Herodotus's *The Histories*, although this work is not travel writing per se (Gould 1989; Lateiner 1989; Blanco and Roberts 1992). It certainly contains reports of the places that the author had seen, the characteristics of the land, its people, animals, and a potted history of the areas. But the author also includes accounts of places he had not visited, information derived from other contemporary accounts, or from people who claimed knowledge of such places, most of which are almost mythic in their form. Hence Herodotus is writing a history and geography of the known world, a third person summary of real content – not an actual travel account – a form that was followed in subsequent geographies of the world, from the work of Strabo onwards. Perhaps the first type of travel writing to have widespread appeal was the form now known as the gazetteer, designed to provide factual data on different places and represented in Roman times by the *Antonine Itinerary*. This is essentially a verbal chart, with lists of roads, places, and distances apart, with occasional comments on places of interest. Although they make sterile reading, they are eminently useful for travellers needing to plan their journey. Through the centuries, the gazetteer has become more and more complex. The list of places and distances is complemented by more and more detailed information about places – from sights to see, through the cost and quality of accommodation, restaurants and entertainment, to problems to be faced, as well as potted histories of the areas. In such forms, they developed into the modern guidebook. In addition, innumerable accounts of the commercial opportunities present in various places were published from the seventeenth century onwards; such compendia were essentially gazetteers of trade. One of the best known of these early-seventeenth-century accounts was *The Merchant's Map of Commerce*, published by Lewis Roberts, originally from Beaumaris in Anglesey (Roberts 1638), another demonstration of the way that James and Button were not the only members of their land actively participating in early British exploration and commerce. Yet all of these guides and reviews involve *selection* in the material about places that they *choose to include*, a choice based on the purpose of the book as well as the values of the editor.

These examples show that the fact-fictive division in writing about journeys of discovery is not such a simple dichotomy as it may initially seem. In any case, there are often close parallels between books of exploration based on real journeys and the wider body of fictional literature. Indeed, MacLulich (1979) argued that exploration narratives fell into three major categories: quest, odyssey, and ordeal. Each of these had strong associations with the three major forms of fictional narrative: romance, novel, and tragedy. Yet, he was careful to note that his classification represented points on a continuum, not rigid categories, and that the features were often combined in individual studies of exploration. It is notable that MacLulich used quotations from James's book to illustrate some of his points. For example, he observed that James's voyage started as a *quest*, a search for something new; in this case the Northwest Passage. But it ended up describing an *ordeal*, because survival in the ice-ridden and difficult winter environment of Hudson Bay − not discovery − became the major function of the expedition. Many other examples exist among these accounts of real exploration and such books could have as much power on the imagination of any reader as any fictive account. Nevertheless, from the early seventeenth century onwards, exploration narratives have rarely been considered as being of value in literary terms, a paradox that needs to be explained.

From the seventeenth century onwards, new styles in exploration writing developed. In addition, a separation developed between these writings and the work that came to be considered as literature; the latter was fictional in nature, whereas studies of exploration were assumed to be factual, unless there was evidence of fabrication. Given the often wildly inaccurate medieval speculations about the location of places and the character of the land, it is almost inevitable that the role of the exploration writer in the Renaissance was to provide *factual* statements about the newly discovered worlds. Such information was authenticated by the author's own experience – although it will be shown that insights from literary theory in the last twenty years indicate that what constitutes a *fact* is itself problematic. One result was that the imaginative passages, or displays of emotion linked to the adventure of the journey of discovery, were considered peripheral and perhaps unnecessary to the main theme of the narrative. But a more general explanation lay in the way that exploration narratives began to be written from the seventeenth century onwards.

Many of the earliest Renaissance expeditions were led by men of education and status, especially those expeditions that led to books about their experiences. In later years, most expeditions were led by individuals from lower classes, who had lesser educational attainments. Most were individuals with a practical nature – a quality necessary for survival in life-threatening environments. Their limited education meant they wrote in unadorned, direct prose. The majority had little flair for description; even if they did, imaginative insights were often repressed. This sparse style became more and more apparent as scientific and rationalist approaches were developed. As Kittay (1987) has noted, metaphors and the use of figurative language was deplored from the seventeenth century onwards by those advocating rationalist ideas, especially by individuals such as Locke, who harked back to the opinions of philosophers such as Plato who warned against eloquence as the use of emotions to replace reason. This led to an emphasis upon what were considered factual statements, especially about where places were located, the depths of seas and conditions of the harbours, and the general character of the areas explored. The concern for so-called objective, rational facts, adoption of the detached view of the empiricist, as well as concern for greater precision in measurement, marginalized the parts of the written exploration record that dealt with other features or emotions. By the mid-eighteenth century, narratives of exploration were being written in an even more precise scientific style, emphasizing particular types of information and using specific forms of interpretation. There is no doubt that the narratives frequently contained heroic, and often dramatic stories of survival in unfamiliar and often threatening environments. But such descriptions were increasingly viewed as being side issues – especially by the investigators who mined the narratives for evidence of the locational results of explorations. For such readers, these imaginative, emotional passages seemed to be unworthy of serious attention by many students of exploration, perhaps because they were part of the weakness of human beings, or represented the mistakes of explorers and their lack of preparation. In an increasingly rational and mechanical world, the emphasis was upon the practical – that is, upon what was discovered – not upon the story of survival or of the dangers that were faced. It was left to the Romantic Movement to re-emphasize the use of figurative language. Such approaches were not welcomed by the more practical men who controlled, or carried out explorations in the name of science, empire or trade (Wright, L.B., 1970).

Yet, it is vital not to over-emphasize the degree to which a detached rationality was brought to bear on the new lands and the peoples that the Europeans found in the Americas. Even when one discounts travel writings that are known to be invented works of fiction, or those whose claims to veracity have been rejected, it is clear that the accounts of actual journeys also contain fictionalized or imaginative additions. In some cases the writer may be simply speculating; in others there is the deliberate invention of places and experiences, or the use of stories that had been told to the explorer about the nature of lands beyond the horizon, or the next bend in the river. Many reasons account for such additions. Some may have been genuine misunderstandings; the information provided was accepted, or interpreted as *fact* by the author and was simply passed on and accepted by subsequent readers. Others were deliberate additions, speculations that were either added to provide excitement or mystery for readers, or were included to hold out the hope of future unusual findings and easily obtained riches – riches that might encourage readers to sponsor and finance some future explorations. Together with examples of exaggeration, or even the addition of downright lies, it is easy to understand how the phrase *travel liars* became popular to describe the authors of some exploration books (Adams 1983). However, we might be judicious and call these *speculative additions*. It can be argued that they are only part of the text, not the main substance of the narrative, at least when the text is reviewed from its value as an account of discovery, not as a book of adventure that was designed to entertain.

The most significant intellectual trend leading to the divergence between what was regarded as literature and exploration writing came from the development of a *high culture* approach that valued certain writings over others. From the mid-eighteenth century onwards, this approach began to dominate attitudes to literary works, both in prose and poetry. Graff and Robbins's (1991, 417–36) review of cultural criticism argued that until the 1970s there was almost a consensus that the literature to be cultivated was "the best that has been thought and known in the world" – a line from Matthew Arnold's famous poem *Sweetness and Light*. This type of literature, produced and identified by the major intellectuals, came to occupy a primary role as the new interpreter of life. Exemplars of the approach provided prose, paintings, music, and poetry that appealed to, and fed human emotions, consoled their souls, and sought to interpret and sustain their humanity in an increasingly material and mechanical age. In this context, it is easy to see that most of the plainly written descriptions of voyages at sea, or expeditions on land, were unlikely to reach such heights of achievement. Apart from the problems posed by the limited vocabulary and style of explorers, one must remember that the notes on which they were based were often scratched out on the banks of freezing or humid and fetid rivers, or on ships tossing endlessly on stormy seas. Frequently exhausted, half-starved, and concerned primarily with survival, few explorers would have had the time or energy to produce the cultured, and imaginative prose of the newly valued type – even if they had the skills to do so. The result is that the prose of explorers rarely ranked among the canons of western literature, especially given the intellectual cultivation brought to literature from the Romantic Movement onwards. Few of the explorers or those engaged on scientific expeditions have passages in their journals that stir the higher emotions through the thrill of words, or provide insights into the rivalries, passions, and despair of the human condition. Most were content with brief, prosaic descriptions of the lands and peoples they discovered and provide markedly Eurocentric views of the culture of the indigenous peoples. Of course, exceptions do exist. For example, when Darwin dropped his emphasis upon scientific observations, he revealed his emotions at experiencing the beauty and mystery of the world during his voyage on the Beagle (Keynes 1987;

Stoddart 1986). David Thompson's main journal of his discoveries in the late eighteenth and early nineteenth century in the Great Plains and the Pacific has a number of entertaining, even exciting passages (Tyrrell 1916; Glover 1962), although it is worth remembering that he was unable to get his journal published during his lifetime.

Just as the scientific method was a particular way of organizing thoughts and observations, so it can be argued that the high culture approach to literature was also an invention – a constructed approach dependent upon particular values. Graff and Robbins (1992) emphasized that the valuation of this type of literature was designed to be a bulwark against the rationalism and routinization of a new and often brutal industrial age, which had dissolved the older organic orders of society. This attitude to literature was aided by the growth of nationalism. Nations priorized the writings of their own citizens as evidence of their cultural distinctiveness. By the nineteenth century, this literary approach was promoted through the emerging educational system as a way of acculturating the newly literate classes and immigrants, giving them identity and pride in their nation's achievements. Although it fulfilled such objectives, there is no doubt the approach was elitist. It marginalized or dismissed the writings of others, especially those outside the mainstream by reason of their location, colour, gender, sexual preference – or in the case of the theme of this study, by their content, as descriptions of new lands. In the last twenty years this canonical approach to western culture has been challenged, if not largely overthrown, by a new cultural criticism, which stresses the value of very different types of literary expression. One of its key tenets is that all types of written material, other than what was called *literature,* should be investigated to provide more detailed insights into the nature of the society in which they were composed and to ensure that the expressions of other cultures are not lost. It is possible to use the flexibility of the new cultural criticism to argue the case for paying more attention to writings of explorers. Once these narratives are reviewed in literary terms, rather than only in terms of their utilitarian value as evidence for completed discoveries, it is clear that they perform several crucial functions. These are described in the next two sections.

Explorers who discovered new lands, or rather lands unknown to the peoples who sent out the expedition, have always had high status in European history. But what is often underestimated about narratives of exploration is the way that the mere fact of writing down the experiences of the journeys has provided the descriptions with power – with an aura of authority that may be difficult to breach. This is not simply a product of the fact that the accounts of exploration became fixed in words and were more reliable because they are expressed in writing. In preliterate periods, the temporal transmission of accounts of expeditions did occur, but were dependent upon unreliable memories, and were often distorted because of successive oral recitations; after all, the storyteller is always prone to embellish the original information as part of his personal performance. When recorded in a writing culture, the completed exploration text is frozen in time and seemed largely immutable; an authority is implicitly imparted by the text, one that outlives the verbal interpretations. One reason for this authority comes from knowledge of the previous achievements or rank of the author, which provide subsequent books with a reflected status. For example, the works of individuals such as Francis Drake, who carried out daring and successful raids against Spanish shipping and travelled around the globe, or those with well-regarded books to their name, would have an advantage over unknown authors. Most explorers gain status through the singularity of their access to the new lands – in the sense that the author was the only, or first person to have seen the sights. Marco Polo's famous account of his travels in China provides a good example (*The Travels of Marco Polo*, Latham 1958; Critchley 1992). Yet we must remember that Polo's fame rested not on his travels alone – for Phillips (1988, 109–18) has shown that there were certainly many other Italian contacts with China. Rather, Marco Polo's fame rests on the *publication* of his experiences, even though Polo was not actually the author of the book. The honour of authorship goes to his ghostwriter, Rustichello of Pisa, who was able to write down Polo's recollections when they shared a jail cell (Phillips 1988, 113). Frances Wood (1995), in a recent review of the evidence, inclines to the view that Marco Polo never went further than the Black Sea. She argues that Polo probably repeated information about China that was derived from historic and existing trading contacts along the ancient Asian Silk Road. Since this oral history was gradually forgotten, or just unknown in western Europe, Marco Polo's thoughts – whether fabricated or not – provided the most accessible surviving source of the *old* knowledge because it was preserved in written form. Later it was made available to generations of readers through the printing press. Hence, it was the presence of a written text, not necessarily an original exploration, which gave him immortality. Recently, Selbourne (1997) translated and published the previously unknown account of how Jacob of Ancona left his Adriatic city for China in 1270, returning three years later. The narrative provides a fascinating account of Jacob's experiences, but since the source material has not been authenticated by other scholars, there is some doubt as to its credibility.

The biggest advantage of written texts came from the fact that they were normally authored by representatives of the culture that first saw, and usually prevailed over, previously unknown peoples or environments. This priorized, and made permanent, the viewpoints that were expressed in writing. Hence, the real effect of the exploration on the *other*, the indigenous peoples, became largely unknown after a generation or two. After all, their views depended largely upon oral transfer among these peoples and through time was usually debased and forgotten as the culture of the native peoples was destroyed. Ronald Wright (1992) has provided an eloquent testimony on the devastation that Europeans wreaked on the native peoples of America, based largely on European accounts, with additions from the limited and often incoherent fragments of what the non-literate peoples in the Americas really thought about European exploration. Even the peoples who had a writing culture, such as the Maya, had many of their records destroyed by the Spanish invaders. Some writings survived and were preserved, but despite years of study they are still not entirely understood, although considerable progress has been made in recent years. Yet knowledge in preliterate peoples was not based on a lifetime; it was passed through the generations by word of mouth. There are many examples of important stories and genealogies being recorded through time by oral transmission with surprisingly little variation. After all, the ability to memorize and recall tribal histories was a prized skill. When invaders killed the small number of people with such skills, or demeaned and destroyed the living culture, the memory of the conquered people's past was destroyed. Their cultural past was eradicated along with their loss of possession of a land. Even the most painstaking archaeological study can only guess at the richness or poverty of a dead culture. It is also worth noting that Spanish colonial habits, such as writing things down to establish possession, or to proselytize by reading from a bible, led to a deep fear of the written word and books in many Andean areas. It is a fear that Wright (1992, 188) claims to be still present – because the written word and books symbolized foreign domination, and the loss of the land and its indigenous cultures. Since only the written records of the conquerors still exist, the historic descriptions of the new lands, or the effect of contacts on non-literate peoples depend upon these interpretations: opinions of the dominant culture. Alternative communication systems in other societies, such as the Incan quipu – which may be a form of information other than just a tally system – have yet to be translated and understood, so few alternative views exist. So the written accounts we possess represent western views, the interpretations of the *outsider* over the *insider* or *other*, whether environments or peoples. So the first writers, often the explorers, were able to control and promote a particular view – at least until other information became available from new explorations. Since many journeys to remote places in the world were not repeated for years, new and perhaps rival opinions often took a long time to emerge. Moreover, we must also remember that practically all the known written literature on exploration comes from European sources. The extent of Muslim exploration in Africa is still imperfectly known, as written records were not always kept. More generally, Menzies (2002) has argued that the Chinese, under Zheng He, circumnavigated the world in a two-year expedition that sailed in 1421, but rivalries in the Chinese imperial court, in Zhu Di's reign, soon after their return, led to the abandonment of long distance junks and the self-imposed isolation of the Chinese. Convincing evidence for such journeys has still to be provided. Even if true, the absence of continuing linkages means that these are singular explorations, not stimulative discoveries, and parallel the Viking discovery of America. It was the Portuguese and Spaniards who provided the initial contact that began the *continuing* process of commercial and political globalization (Davies 2004).

All this means that it was the first written reports that give the findings of European Renaissance explorers an authority much greater than the act of a mere exploration alone. Certainly, verbal accounts, through personal presentations to court and later to lecture halls, have always provided temporary fame for explorers, but usually only in their own lifetime. But books bestowed a status upon their author, an authority beyond the mere fact of exploration alone. Traditionally, publication had high barriers to entry, due to the cost of production, and the need for a publisher to underwrite the commercial risk in the hope of future returns. This meant there were limited numbers of bound books. Moreover, each book has its own mystique, such as its size, the order and organization employed, the references to other sources, and general knowledge that displayed erudition. Such factors combine to give a published work an authority that the handwritten page cannot match, assigning superiority and prestige to authors. In the last few decades, the relative ease of self-publication through computing systems, the presence of vanity presses, and the increased volume of books, reduced the impact that a single publication would have had in the past. Moreover, the appearance of other forms of communication – by radio, T.V., and internet – has meant that the five-hundred-year-old primacy of the published word has been rivalled in the discourse of representation. But for a Renaissance explorer, there were few alternatives. If the exploration narrative was well regarded, it could provide additional and lasting status, as well as making the author an authority in the eyes of contemporaries. In his famous twenty-volume survey of world exploration, Purchas had no doubt about the significance of the text. But he followed the practise of his culture in denigrating non-literate peoples:

> … amongst *Men*, some are accounted *Civill*, and more both *Sociable* and *Religious*, by the *Use* of letters and *Writing*, which other wanting are esteemed *Brutish*, *Savage*, *Barbarous*. And indeed much is the literall advantage; by speech we utter our minds once, at the present … but by writing *Man* seemes immortall … by his owne writings surviveth himselfe, remaines (litera scripta manet) thorow all ages a Teacher and Counseller to the last of men. (Purchas 1626, vol. 1, 486)

There were also disadvantages to what Purchas called *the literall* [*sic*] *advantage*. One of the most important problems facing students of exploration literature is simply the voluminous nature of the material available. The European discovery and settlement of lands beyond their continent led to a veritable avalanche of writing and other textual representations about the new environments and their inhabitants, such as explorer's journals and maps, promotional pamphlets, letters, official and commercial reports, royal proclamations, speculative essays, and epic poems. Nobody could find or read all this information. This made the pioneering work of men such as Hakluyt and Purchas, who tried to collate the material in a single publication source, of real and lasting value. Also, not all the material was available to the public at large – some was repressed because of state or commercial secrecy. For example, Bawlf (2003) has recently maintained that Francis Drake probably went much farther north than California in his late sixteenth century voyage along the Pacific coast of North America, exploring much of the coast of British Columbia in a search for the Pacific entrance to the Northwest Passage. He argued that the subsequent accounts and maps of Drake's voyage deliberately obscured the evidence, to prevent the information being known to England's rivals. In addition to this type of disinformation, there seems little doubt that other barriers to general knowledge existed. For example, some narratives were written in minority languages; other explorers did not publish their experiences. Their reports mouldered, unknown, in state or commercial archives.

✤ 5. ALTERNATIVE FUNCTIONS OF EXPLORATION NARRATIVES

During the past two hundred years, the primary utility of *narratives* of exploration, as opposed to the *journeys*, lay in the provision of new and original information about the location and character of the newly discovered lands and peoples. Although the rationale for many voyages lies in the search for new lands, personal glory, or commercial and national advantage (Wright, L.B., 1970), the exploration itself was not the only way that individuals could achieve rewards. Additional status and wealth may be obtained by writing a book about the events of the journey. But such books rarely sell on the basis of the descriptions of discovery alone. Readers were attracted to particular books on exploration because of the excitement provided by the descriptions of events and new lands. In skilled hands, narratives of exploration can become spellbinding descriptions of exotic locations and peoples, as well as thrilling adventures — books that had as much power on the imagination of any reader as any fictive account. In our contemporary world, flooded with tens of thousands of novels and with so many different fictive forms, it is difficult to appreciate the role played by these early books of exploration within an increasingly literate Europe. From the sixteenth to the eighteenth centuries, descriptions about the newly discovered lands and their peoples represented the primary literary sources of the *novel* — in both senses of the term. The exotic findings and the emotional appeal of the books were often more important to the general public than the provision of new locational knowledge, the religious goal of converting native peoples, or the discovery of resources – such as the gold, good agricultural land or trade goods that interested state authorities or merchants (Wright, L.B., 1970). This means that these books of exploration are not only texts of discovery; they also performed a variety of other different functions.

The most obvious function may be a personal self-serving role – casting the explorer-author in a heroic light, or justifying his actions. It is probable that many explorers embarked on their voyage in search of adventure, in a gallant attempt to gain fame, or perhaps even to challenge themselves. Schöene-Harwood's (2000) recent survey of how men are portrayed in literature revealed that the conquest of wilderness was one of the traditional ways in which males could prove their masculinity. But exploration narratives often had an ideological role, relating to an expansionist state policy, or as a crusade to spread the word of a god, or, after the Reformation, the ideas of a particular church. A more immediate goal came from the realization that narratives could be a useful source of profit, for publisher as well as author. Narratives written for the public domain were rarely the dispassionate, pseudo-scientific texts that readers searching for evidence of the results of journeys – the so-called facts of discovery – seem to imply. Instead they can be regarded as commodities to the writer; once published, the book becomes a product with commercial value. Indeed, the commodified value produced by book sales may be considered of primary importance to the author, especially those with limited wealth – a tangible reward for the tribulations faced on the journeys of exploration. From a reader's perspective many exploration narratives were bought and read because they provided an escape from the world the readers lived in – and many an explorer deliberately wrote their books in styles and with particular content to attract such attention. But the written accounts of the explorations fulfilled different functions. For a puritan seventeenth-century mind such as Purchas, travel may have been seen as some kind of self-improvement for the elite, but he was perfectly aware that his volumes summarizing world exploration catered for a different purpose:

> *I speake not against Travell, so useful to usefull men … at no great charge I offer a World of Travellers to their domestike entertainment. (Purchas 1626, 44)*

These words show that Purchas had pinpointed one of the key issues of exploration, or indeed travel writing. Readers may gain vicarious pleasure from reading about the tribulations of others — whether long dead explorers or contemporary travellers — and in the comfort of their own home. They could be titillated, as well as informed, by the descriptions of the new environments and previously unknown cultures, without leaving their own chairs. There is little doubt that explorers who wrote accounts of their journeys were aware of the potential rewards from their books if they were written in a style that entertained the public. This purpose remains important today. Some of the results of establishing trade routes to Asia and searching for resources in distant parts of the world still delight and horrify contemporary readers. One recent example is Milton's (1999) fascinating study of the intrigue and enormous loss of life among the crew of ships engaged in the nutmegs and spices trade from several small islands in the East Indies. Another is Philbrick's (2000) recent revival of the story of how a huge bull whale sank a Nantucket whaler in the Pacific during the mid-nineteenth century. The few survivors subsequently experienced a hair-raising journey, in which they resorted to cannibalism before being rescued. It was a story that was almost too improbable to be true and was used by Melville to create his own fictional version in the classic novel, *Moby Dick*.

However, the link between any exploration and the commodification of the subsequent narratives is not simply a one-way connection. The search for profit in the descriptions of exploration, as opposed to a journey seeking new trade routes, resources, or precious metals, is not simply a consequence of the journey. Sometimes it has generated expeditions. This point may be best illustrated by the mid- and late-nineteenth-century race among Europeans to explore the parts of the world that were still unknown, especially central Africa and the two Poles. Their expeditions captured a new audience of fascinated readers. Despite the rapidly developing industrial technology that made the journeys less difficult than for those of their predecessors, the explorers still faced great privations. Knowledge of these privations and findings of the explorers was spread through the medium of newspapers — the new form of communication — and newspapers vied with one another to be first with the news. Riffenburg (1993) has shown that they created the news by actually sponsoring rival expeditions. The expeditions were often linked to nationalist rivalries and to individual desires for fame and glory. There was an obvious desire to be the sponsor of the first explorer to reach unknown lands. But newspaper editors deliberately created tension among readers, by the promotion and manipulation of news, to ensure that readers would buy the newspapers. The sale of extra copies would add to the profits of the newspapers. Hence, it was profit maximization that was the primary motivation of the sponsors, not the knowledge of new lands. Perhaps the explorer still saw the exploration as an expedition of discovery, or as a vehicle for personal glory, adulation, and possible wealth. But the newspaper owners who sponsored the journeys *created* news of the discoveries, rather than waiting for others to produce it, in the hope of generating extra profits from increased newspaper sales. So much for the dispassionate nature of exploration!

✣ 6. INTERPRETATION IN EXPLORATION AND TRAVEL WRITING

If narratives of exploration are written for reasons other than simply describing the progress of discovery – so as to add to the corpus of knowledge about the world – then doubt has to be placed upon the apparent objectivity of the work, despite the initial assumption of authenticity. Such doubts are magnified when it is appreciated that all writings about places, or travel to places, involve interpretation, rather than so-called factual reporting. What may be considered as *fact* in travel writing is not simply a matter of an explorer writing things down that he saw. The written record of travel or exploration is always about representation and interpretation and is often based on prior views or personal insight. Hence, it difficult to sustain the idea that the exploration narratives or travel descriptions are simple realist accounts. The argument can be illustrated by examples from various types of travel writing, beginning with some of the earliest accounts; those based on pilgrimage.

Egeria's *Peregrination to the Holy Land* written between the fourth to sixth century, has long been regarded as one of the first examples of travel writing (Campbell 1988). Written as a letter to her fellow nuns, the descriptions are not really about the places she saw on her visits to the sites described in the Bible. The places are not significant in themselves; rather, the sites are valued because they are the locale of the religious events that were the foci of her spiritual life. What she *sees* – or more correctly what she *records* about the sites visited on the basis of the opinions of the people who lived there – are viewed from within her belief system. Egeria's descriptions are acts of reverence, not of real personal discovery, for she makes very few additional comments about the nature of the places. Similar accounts of pilgrimage can be found throughout history (Turner and Turner 1978), where the written record is largely a result of the whole spiritual experience, although by the early modern period additional secular experiences may be added to the texts. These accounts of pilgrimages parallel the descriptions of the European men of leisure who were able to undertake the *grand tour* to classical sites in Italy and Greece from the sixteenth century onwards (Tower 1985). Some of these travel accounts provide more personal commentaries about what was personally seen, but the emphasis is still upon what was *expected*. The sites (and sights) experienced are described; however, their significance lies in the fact that certain historic events occurred in such locations and left relics of their presence. So, the visits are designed to interpret or understand the past. Certainly, those travellers who took the time to immerse themselves in such places derived a great deal of knowledge of the society that created such forms – especially the artistic or architectural methods of construction. Others did more than just observe the expected. The Romantic poets, in particular, had their imaginations stimulated by personal experiences in these lands, or by reading accounts of these environments. This led to the creation of new prose and poetry forms, which became part of the high canonical tradition in literature. These writings, of course, had their principal appeal in stirring the passions and emotions, or to evoke a particular ethos of place; these were not the objectives of most scientific approaches to travel.

By the nineteenth century, a new version of the *tour* became popular. Men of wealth and leisure were able to use the new transportation facilities to travel to the still largely unknown interiors of continents to get their own experiences: such as in North America, to see and shoot the buffalo herds; in Africa, to slaughter a variety of big game and observe its very different cultures and environments. In MacLaren's (1985a, 32) succinct words, such travellers sought "the frisson of seeing exotic peoples and strange scenery"; a tradition that is fulfilled today by safari trips and ecological tourism. Many of these contemporary journeys are often carried out by formula: so many days here and so many there. They were essentially brief visits to *expected* places, with the sights, sounds, smells, and tastes skilfully arranged by the operator. Although less formal perhaps, and more involved with the exotic landscapes, it has been argued that a great deal of modern travel takes the same form of journeys to expected places. Moore (1985) described how Japanese visitors to California have a hierarchy of places that must be visited, from

Disneyland to Universal Studios. Indeed, contemporary tourists are exhorted to visit X, Y and Z, to make and record their own visit, following in the footsteps of a million or more of their predecessors. Perhaps some may have their own personal experiences in such places, discovering the enhanced feelings or consciousness sought by the Romantics. But it must be remembered that tourism is about the *creation* of local atmosphere, and vacation centres are *manufactured* to create such illusions. The consequence is that the authenticity of the original place and its culture is lost (Cohen 1988). Most travellers simply *see* what others have seen; their visit is often without imagination or personal experience. It is aptly summarized by a cynical modern aphorism: *Been there. Seen it. Bought the T shirt.* Indeed, travel has never been without its affectations. Purchas pinpointed the issue as far back as 1626 in the introduction to his compendium of key explorations of the world.

> As for Gentlemen, Travell is accounted an excellent Ornament to them; and many of them comming to their Lands sooner then to their Wits, adventure themselves to see the Fashions of other Countries, where their soules and bodies find temptations. ... & bring home a few smattering terms, flattering garbs, Apish things, foppish fancies, foolish guises. ... without furthering of their knowledge of God, the World, or themselves. (Purchas 1626, 1, XLIV)

Purchas identified a common problem, as relevant today as in the past. But the quotation also makes it clear that a puritan such as Purchas regarded travel as a type of self-improvement.

Adams (1983) has queried whether travel literature is really needed today. After all, the ease of modern travel and ability to fly in and out of areas makes personal experience of many of the remote parts of the world increasingly possible. But descriptions of contemporary explorations, by the people who make land or sea journeys to the remote and largely uninhabited parts of the globe, still command a popular audience. Travel writing still provides a convenient, if armchair approach to experiencing distant lands – certainly second-hand, but often stimulating and entertaining to many readers. New technologies, such as satellite communication and the use of the internet to link explorers and viewers, allow daily views of the experiences of the contemporary explorer. Yet the new communication devices mean that contemporary explorers are never completely alone with their companions in the wilderness or at sea: the situation that characterized the journeys of historic discoveries. Despite the attempts to recreate voyages or travels using reproductions of the vehicles of the day, there is always the possibility of rescue – at least in earth space – if things go wrong, and of moral support, by radio or laptop computer, from the home base. Obviously, such technological trends do not diminish the dangers that are faced, or the bravery of the explorers. Rather they simply confirm that the loneliness and isolation of the original explorers can rarely be repeated. Moreover, the hand-held global positioning system device, linked to satellites in space, ensures that the eternal problem of the old explorers is solved. A precise location can always be obtained. It may be symbolic to note that the position is still fixed from space, this time by a man-made extraterrestrial object, not by any understanding of the eternal orbits of stars or planets – the guides of past explorers!

However, the best travel books are never simply about providing descriptions that the readers would have seen and experienced for themselves in foreign lands, if they had the means or motivation to travel to such places. The authors of popular travel narratives of the past, and the well-known travel writers of our day, such as Bruce Chetwin and Jan Morris, use their insight, wit, and imagination to write about places and regions in particular and usually idiosyncratic ways – ways designed to expose issues that the reader would not have seen for themselves. So travel writing need not only be a description of the *expected*, as in the pilgrimage and its secular offshoots. Neither is it designed primarily to inform; it is to *interpret* as well as to *entertain* – a key feature already discussed by Morris (1976). This raises the question about how travel writers are able to create these interpretations. Morris (1988) has made the point that it is often important to visit new places as uncluttered by previous views as possible – whether from books or images. In this way, writers can obtain their own unique experiences of the place visited. But this is almost impossible to achieve in the modern world. Most of us have a lot of information of many distant places, some obtained through films and television, or through past educational experiences in geography and history. Nevertheless, Morris's argument is an important one. A personal odyssey or engagement with a place may be the only way to get one's own *sense of place*, to find one's own view of the distinctive character of a town or region. Subsequent reading in the voluminous writings about any area can provide additional insights, or even add significance to the places visited. But the original insights represent primary material for the travel writer, providing the unique interpretation of the places visited, although the final text of most contemporary travel books is subsequently enlivened with a potpourri of local history and geogra-

68

phy derived from other sources. This is not to deny that an important by-product of such travel writing may be to inform; the travel writer certainly adds to the reader's knowledge of places. However, its primary role is to provide a unique and entertaining interpretation – in effect, it is a *personal invention or construction* of what the place meant to the author. Unfortunately, such writings have encouraged many readers to follow in the footsteps of the author, to try to recreate the feelings that the author experienced. Since we now have relatively easy and inexpensive transportation to many places, people can travel in large numbers. The result is that the place described in the travel book or exploration narrative is irrevocably damaged; its authentic ethos is usually lost. To cater for the tourist, new versions of traditional culture forms, especially in song or dance, are simply invented, or copied from some other location, if the promoters find little of local interest. Stripped of their original meanings, that were often fundamentally linked to the social formation or relationships of peoples, they become entertainments – hollow and meaningless representations of the original.

The result of this review of the role of interpretation in travel writing shows that accounts of actual journeys can rarely be considered as simple, empirical descriptions of the lands that were experienced. Rather, travel writers and explorers are affected by their belief systems, or their imaginations, to *interpret* or translate the character of places for the reader. But these interpretations are inevitably influenced by the culture of the writer, who is an *outsider* in a strange land, interpreting it for readers from his own culture. Most writers view these worlds through their own cultural biases and regard the *other worlds* as strange or exotic. They forget that for the people of the *other* it is the explorer or travel writer who represents the curiosity. It has already been noted that the opinions of native peoples are rarely found, since their views and forms of representation have disappeared, or have been deliberately destroyed. But there are a few writers who recognized the inevitable Eurocentric bias and tried to interpret European customs through the eyes of others. Montesquieu's (1743) famous *Persian Letters* is a classic of this approach. Reputedly written by the Persian ambassador to Paris, the letters describe his amusement at the strange customs he 'sees' in France. They are even made amusing because many objects and practises in the Paris of his day represented the cultural reversal of features to those found in his homeland: for example, men in Paris wore trousers, whereas women wore flowing robes or gowns – a gender reversal from Persian practises. To poke fun at the mores of this society, and especially religious beliefs, was at least disrespectful, at worst blasphemous, which often provided the authorities with justification for imprisonment or worse. The French hierarchy was not impressed by Montesquieu's book, although his social position meant he escaped serious retribution from the authorities.

In general, European power meant that the social practises of this continent were assumed by explorers to be the *natural* form. They were imposed, often in modified form, upon other cultures, rarely completely, for fragments of other cultures still remain. On occasion, the process was the other way around, which often provoked controversy. For example, Raleigh's adoption of tobacco smoking did not endear him to his king, who was already critical of his expeditions. James I was so opposed to smoking that he took the trouble to write a critique of the practise in 1604, equating the habit with the behaviour of savages: "shall we … abase ourselves so farre, as to imitate these beastly Indians" (quoted in Whitehead 1997, 55). The cultural superiority implied in King James's choice of words illustrates how the *natives* and their ways-of-life were often viewed. Despite James's strictures, this was one Native American social practise adopted by people in other cultures, and only recently is it being restricted because of its effect upon the health of people. In general, it is salutary to recognize that the indigenous peoples of the New World were just as mystified by many of the behaviours of the invaders, although few of their opinions have survived. The descriptions in the exploration narratives usually reinforced the moral or cultural mores of the Europeans: the practises of the invader were considered to be normal or natural; those of the others were unacceptable or even abhorrent. Most European explorers made little attempt to understand the behaviours of other peoples or their reasons; the new worlds were interpreted and valued through the cultural mindsets of the old.

✛ 7. NEW PERSPECTIVES FOR EXPLORATION WRITING

The critique of the copyist or realist argument to date has been based on evidence that exploration and travel writing – even if based on the real – is affected by the way that the writers interpret, not simply describe objectively, the things they see in the newly discovered lands. Recognition of the role of interpretation in description began the process of shattering the old implicit assumption that there was a one-to-one link between the so-called reality of the world, and how explorers saw it; an approach which valorized eyewitness accounts of the first explorations of a new land. During the past few decades, very different approaches to the study of exploration narratives have been developed which have seriously damaged, if not destroyed, any lingering belief in the utility of the realist approach. The next four sections deal with the relevance of these new intellectual perspectives to the study of exploration, namely: how images and values affect the cognition of the new environments; the way that literary criticism has questioned the nature and construction of our understanding about the world, first in terms of our allocation of words to objects and ideas, second to the way that meanings are derived from texts; and finally, to the way that psychologists have discovered that knowledge is constructed through our cognitive facilities. The findings also help us understand how explorers constructed their images of the new worlds that they saw.

A. THE ROLE OF IMAGES AND VALUES

During the 1960s, many humanistic and behavioural geographers moved away from descriptions of the everyday and empirical, towards an examination of the role of images, imagination, and values in interpreting the landscape (Tuan 1974; Watson 1969; Allen, J. L. 1975 b; Simpson-Housley and Mallory 1986). Such approaches contrasted with several hundred years of geographical tradition where rationalist approaches tended to dominate. This, of course, does not deny that early-twentieth-century French possibilist geographers (Buttimer 1971) touched upon the role of images and acknowledged perceptual factors in their studies of the differentiation of areal variation. And even earlier, Ratzel used the spirit of the people as an explanatory factor in accounting for differences in the human relationships with the land. However, there were few systematic explorations of these themes in geography, either theoretically or empirically. Not until thirty years ago were new conceptual interpretations of place and space made by geographers; interpretations that stressed the need to understand the images and mindsets used by the observers to interpret the land and to account for spatial differences in human occupancy. Geographers, such as Lowenthal (1961; 1967; 1975), Tuan (1974), Watson (1969) and John Allen (1975a,b), building on previous work by individuals such as John Wright (1947), applied some of these new ideas to the study of exploration and landscape description. They showed how prior beliefs and images influenced the initiation and the progress of exploration, as well as the persistence of ideas about the location and characteristics of unknown lands. Some empiricists were able to downplay the importance of the imagination by showing how many of the beliefs, such as older ideas about the location of places, were revised as more and more accurate knowledge of the areas being explored became available. Imaginative ideas were regarded as simply representing inaccuracies – problems that were corrected when explorers actually found and carefully measured the location of places they found. But not all the images could be dealt with in this way; many were persistent and reflected particular feelings that influenced exploration behaviour. However, it was soon recognized that the role of images and perception was not simply a matter of introducing these ideas as new mediating factors in the interpretations of the world by explorers. Rather, it began the process of what amounted to a self-reflection on the nature of geographical knowledge, as seen in James Wreford Watson's succinct phrase in an article dealing with the role of illusion in geography: "the geography of any place results from *how* we see it, as much as *what* may be seen" (Watson 1969, 10; italics added).

Once this question of *how we see* was raised, students of geography and exploration narratives started to appreciate the relevance of the work of scholars in literary studies who began to get interested in the field of exploration literature. It may be worth noting, as an aside, that Watson was also a man of literature. Apart from being a distinguished geographer who held professorial appointments in many Canadian universities before returning to Scotland to the University of Edinburgh, where he also established the Canadian Studies Centre, he was a poet who won the Canadian Governor General's award for poetry under the pseudonym James Wreford. This other side of his work enabled him to appreciate the role of literature in geography, which he summarized in his presidential address to the Institute of British Geographers (Watson 1983). But it was MacLulich (1979) who provided one of the first comprehensive examples of the relevance of literary interpretation to exploration narratives. Not only did he show how explorers favoured particular landscapes in their descriptions, but demonstrated the way they interpreted the new worlds through western European concepts of landscape aesthetics, such as sublimity or the picturesque – a theme further illustrated in studies by MacLaren (1985a, 1985b) and extensively developed in a recent book by Glickman (1998). These examples demonstrate, once again, how much of the early exploration literature on the Americas was based on Eurocentric aesthetic views, and on values that priorized scenes or objects thought worthy of description. They illustrate the argument that exploration narratives should be seen as *cultural representations*, linked to the conceptual ideas of the Old World, rather than being interpreted as unbiased interpretations of what was experienced in the new worlds. Other forms of communication about the new lands, such as paintings, have also been shown to convey particular meanings, hidden behind the apparently natural representations of everyday life on the frontier. For example, the nineteenth-century canoe paintings of Frances Hopkins in the Canadian wilderness have long been regarded as classic realist descriptions of a lost Canadian past; paintings based on her own experience of travel in the wilderness. However, Feltes (1993) has shown that the content and the arrangement of people in the paintings were carefully constructed to reflect imperial and commercial power, ethnic and gender inequalities, as well as sexual tension and the aesthetics of a wilderness. In other words, the paintings are more than a simplistic study of a group of people in a canoe. The choice and organization of features to incorporate in the painting communicate a set of fundamental meanings related to the very nature of the fur trade and the social and political relationships that sustained it.

These examples show that representations of landscapes – whether known from exploration writing or from paintings and sketches – cannot be interpreted empirically; evidence drawn from the experience of travel that produces mimetic reproductions of a distinctive reality. Rather they are interpreted through the conceptual apparatus we use to process this raw material and the ideology or system of beliefs that condition our interpretations. Lowenthal's (1961, 87) classic essay on experience and imagination in geography observed that each different social system or culture, "organizes the world in accordance with its particular structure and requirements." Lowenthal illustrated his thesis by providing examples of how various peoples have developed very different ways of describing location, orientation, shape, territoriality, colour, or even categories of experience. He argued that although humans share the same sensory apparatus, the world is not seen or described in the same way; essentially our knowledge of the world, what we think we know, is affected by the culture of the observers. It is important to emphasize that the word *culture* is being used in the sense of the *ways of life* of peoples, not the refined artistic achievements of the Romantic tradition that produced particular aesthetic views. Although culture is brought in as an explanatory variable to account for the variations, it is really being viewed as an end in itself. This means that it is a way of describing the differences in perception, and does not produce explanations about how any particular culture affects the creation of representations about the world. Fortunately for the sophistication of our explanations, two other groups of scholars – critical theorists and cognitive psychologists – have been studying the questions of how we *see* and *understand* the world, as well as how knowledge is *created*. The next two sections describe the utility of the work of critical analysts to our understanding of first, the writing, and then the reading, of exploration narratives.

B. REFLECTING OR CONSTRUCTING REALITY?

Recognition of the role of perception and culture in affecting our views of the world was initially seen to illustrate the principle of epistemological dualism. This assumes that there is a gap between our knowledge, as expressed in thoughts and words, and some objective external world. However, this concept still posits the existence of some objective reality from which words are derived to describe particular features, and this assumption can be criticized. When we grow up in any culture, we learn the words and categories of experience used by members of the group to distinguish and describe varied objects and events. Without comparative knowledge of other languages, or when one comes from a culture of technological superiority, it is easy to assume that these definitions are the *natural* ones, that words and texts simply reflect the real world, the argument that underlies the realist perspective. In the 1930s, some cultural anthropologists attempted to explain why traditional societies had such very different views of the world and expressed things in varied ways. They showed that people in different cultural groups do not see, or rather interpret, their milieu in the same way, even though all humans share the same basic sensory apparatus. This is not simply a matter of differences in the allocation of words or concepts to specific phenomena. If it was, we could simply translate the symbols used in different language groups directly and have immediate comprehension. The situation was far more complex and seemed to defy interpretation. The cultural anthropologist Benjamin Whorf (1956) suggested a solution to the problem through his linguistic relativity hypothesis. He believed that language was not just a communication medium, namely, a set of symbols for expressing thoughts about objects or concepts. Rather, he argued that language must have primacy in the way we think and express ideas about the world. This means that language is not seen as some *derivative* of experience, but is a major element in the *formation* of thought.

The basic thesis is that without the words to express thoughts, we would be unable to think about the objects we see, or to share ideas with others about particular objects or ideas.

Similar ideas about the primacy of language in our thought processes also emerged from the work of theoretical linguists and literary theorists, but they were able to provide more convincing arguments about the basis of the relationships. In the early twentieth century, theorists such as Saussure in linguistics, and Levi-Strauss in anthropology, had shown that language systems are really sign systems, in the sense that any word is a sign or *signifier* and its meaning is what is *signified*. They went on to argue that distinctive objects and activities in particular cultures could be interpreted as systems of signs that are connected to each other for particular purposes. Behind these sign systems, whether the myths and stories, or the rituals carried out, were rules by which they were connected together, and which could be related to some universal meanings. Therefore myths or rituals were not just stories or objects, but particular sign systems that were expressions of networks of implicit communication about how their reality, the world they lived in and the history of their peoples, was organized and understood. This means that signs, as seen in words or in rituals, were only a type of surface reality. What were more important were the underlying structures of meaning that underlay these surface forms. Although some fascinating advances in understanding have been made by these so-called structuralist views, many literary critics from the 1950s were uncomfortable about such interpretations. They saw the search to uncover these *deep structures* as another attempt to impose some central meaning on objects or literary texts, similar to the materialist ideas of Marx in the socio-economic context. They cautioned against the assignment of unequivocal meanings to what were, in fact, particular signs, since it implied the loss of individual interpretation and experience.

After World War II, literary critics such as Derrida, Foucault, and Barthes, returned to the question of the relationships between signs and meanings. Their ideas have become accessible to a wider audience through reviews and extensions by theorists such as Belsey (1980; 1999), Eagleton (1983) and Bonnycastle (1991). It is not an exaggeration to state that these literary critics have completely transformed our understanding of the way that our knowledge is derived. The work of these critics may seem a long way from the field of exploration – after all, exploration was carried out in large part by very practical men, whose major concern was to get from one place to another. But the insights of contemporary literary criticism has shown us how we actively *construct* the world we *see* through our words and language. This reverses the older view that what we see is some *reflection* of the world, however much affected by intervening processes. Language, as in the ideas of Whorf (1956), is assumed to come first; and the work of the critical analysts has provided a more complete explanation of how the process of understanding works. To appreciate the basis on which these new ideas rest, it is worth returning to the essence of realism, as described in one of the major surveys of new literary criticism.

> *In the ideology of realism or representation, words are felt to link up with their thoughts or objects in essentially right and incontrovertible ways: the word becomes the only proper way of viewing this object or experiencing this thought. (Eagleton 1983, 136)*

But the new literary critics argued that if language systems are really sign systems, these signs, or words, are differentiated from each other, not by their relationship to entities in the real world. But meaning – or what is signified by the word – is not immediately present in any sign, for the sign or word used to label any object or meaning is an arbitrary one and varies between cultures or languages. Meaning is only assigned to the word, and understood by the people who use the label. Eagleton (1983) maintained that part of the huge impact that the French literary critic Derrida had on the construction of meaning, was his observation that many words are partially defined by what they exclude. Hence, part of the identity of any word is what it excludes, a type of binary opposition; its identity is really the result of its difference from other signs, created by the marks or sets of symbols that we accept in any written language as representing that word. Part of the problem here is that the meanings of all words are expressed in other words, or signifiers, so one cannot arrive at a final meaning, or what is signified by the words – without using some other word or signifier. Since the meaning of a word can only be expressed in terms of other words, there can be no fixed point of origin, which means that all words must be ambiguous in the last resort. Also, words frequently have many meanings, even within one language system. It is also apparent that the meanings of many words change through time, as they are used in different contexts or circumstances, producing another source of instability. The result is that the meaning of any words or sentences should always be understood as being elusive or at least not concrete. When these are combined, and used in particular language systems, or in particular rhetorical structures, the meanings become even more problematic and open to dispute or negotiation over meaning.

The allocation of particular symbols as a sign for any word that describes an object, feeling, or concept, is always a matter of cultural and historical convention. Somewhere in the history of communication within a social group, a decision was made to allocate some word to an object, idea, or feeling. This decision was accepted by others, and is consciously or unconsciously accepted by members of any language group, through either the socialization process of growing up in a society, or by education, or simply by participation in group activities. However, it is well-known that a word that may express a particular meaning in one language group may differ in another. Moreover, there are always objects, or events, which are difficult to express – a particular problem for explorers coming across previously unknown features. Their first descriptions usually involve attempts to use words from objects they know; those from their own culture. By assigning them to the previously unknown objects, the objects are understood through the conceptions of another world. Later, contact with indigenous peoples may lead to the adoption of native words for the previously unknown features, such as the case of the canoe, kayak or chinook in Canada.

These essentially post-structuralist arguments have led to the conclusion that the meanings expressed in our words and language are only represented in shifting and unstable ways, so there cannot be any final, determinate truth or concrete meaning at all. It leads to a condition of relativism in terms of the multiple meanings that can be derived from any written text. At first, this seems to lead the reader into a chaotic world of multiple meanings, where individual readers have their own interpretations. Fortunately, in practise these alternatives may not be as infinite as one can theoretically postulate. Raymond Williams (1973, 122) argued in his classic book *The City and The Country* that: "we all learn to interpret by local conventions of thought and language." This means that groups of people with shared mindsets and cultures express things in the same way and share meanings in the words they employ. Without the shared communication, there can be no group understanding. Certainly we can accept that these expressions or representations are culturally relative; other cultural groups may have different interpretations. But acceptance of meanings within a culture or subculture is sufficient to provide shared communication, which creates basic understanding within the group. So the words used to express certain objects and activities are a product of certain shared systems of signification; in other words, people create meaning by the use of their own sign systems. Again, Eagleton has effectively summarized the point.

> *Meaning was not something which all men and women intuitively shared, and then articulated in their various tongues and scripts; what meaning you were able to articulate depended on what script or speech you shared in the first place.... Reality was not reflected by language but produced by it. (Eagleton 1983, 107–8)*

This perspective provides another example of the way the critical analyst school reverses the nature of the relationship between the so-called *reality* and the observer; language is understood as the major element in the formation of thought about the world. In the words of another literary critic:

> *There is no unmediated experience of the world; knowledge is possible only through the categories and laws of the symbolic order. Far from expressing a unique perception of the world, authors produce meaning out of the available system of differences, and texts are intelligible in so far as they participate in it. (Belsey 1999, 45)*

If these two interpretations are accepted, they comprehensively destroy the older realist views, and provide a very different approach to explaining how we understand and communicate. In addition, since words are defined by what they exclude, it means that language needs to be regarded as more than some kind of labelling process. As Belsey observed:

> *Language is experienced as a nomenclature because its existence precedes our 'understanding' of the world ... thought is in essence symbolic, dependent on the differences brought about by the symbolic order. (Belsey 1999, 46)*

Of course, this does not deny the *presence* of objects, such as trees or rivers; rather, it informs us that our ability to identify, think, and communicate about these objects is a function of the presence of language. Other animals may perceive and use these objects, because they are socialized to do so, or learn from experience, but humans can think about the objects and communicate their ideas to others through the presence of a shared language or other sign systems. Once language or the sign system is given primacy in explaining how we understand the world, the copyist or realist approach is shown as flawed, however natural it seems. Belsey is able to succinctly summarize the reason for this situation:

> *Realism is plausible not because it reflects the world, but because it is constructed out of what is (discursively) familiar. (Belsey 1999, 47)*

C. TOWARDS TEXTS AS DISCOURSE

The third new trend that needs to be applied to our understanding of exploration narratives also comes from post-structuralist views; this time it is not about what we see, understand or represent the world, but about how we *read*. Since the work of critical theorists have shown that our words — and hence interpretations and meanings — are essentially unstable, it is but a short step to appreciate that people may read texts or hear speeches in quite different ways, deriving understandings that are affected by individual viewpoints as well as their cultural background. Hence the meanings derived from the words and phrases found in the types of books under investigation here — apparently straightforward observations on a previously unknown land — can vary greatly, as the following observation makes clear.

> *The reader or critic shifts from the role of consumer to that of producer ... it is a shift from seeing the poem or novel as a closed entity, equipped with definite meanings which it is the critic's task to decipher, to seeing it as irreducibly plural. (Eagleton 1983, 138)*

In other words, the meanings obtained from the texts do not simply depend upon the explicit intentions of the author and the ideological context within which it is written. The meanings derived from any text rely as much upon the attitudes and concepts brought to bear on the narrative *by* the readers. So books cannot be regarded as completed works, in which only the authors create meaning. In the phrase of another literary critic, a *reader's plural* must also be seen to apply. (Bonnycastle 1991). Readers participate in the creation of meaning since they may derive different interpretations or even feelings from the text, so that

> *meanings circulate between text, ideology, and reader, and the work of criticism is to release possible meanings. (Belsey 1999, 144)*

The idea that words and actions can be interpreted quite differently, is, of course, quite obvious to patrons of the theatre, where different productions of a play create different meanings, although the same words may be used. This concept of the reader's plural is similar. So far, relatively few geographers have begun to explore the implications of these issues in their work. For example, in a recent defence of one of his articles, Cresswell (1996, 420) identified the key issue in the following words: "acts of interpretation involve linking texts to contexts." He argued that the derivation of meanings relates to the historical conditions of the production, as well as the consumption, of the text – in other words the way that the book is written, the cultural conditions present, as well as how it is read. Applied to exploration narratives, it opens the door to the possibility of additional interpretations of the new worlds being described, their representation, and how the text is received. The problem for all interpretations of texts, as Cresswell (1996) noted, is that of determining *which context is privileged* amongst the multitude of alternatives, for no interpretation can be informed by every possible context. He suggested that the identification of the *purpose* of the reading may be one of the ways of solving this dilemma. In the context of exploration narratives this need not be the traditional empirical approach of most geographical work, of trying to relate the written description to what is considered to be *reality*, which is itself constructed from our language. The purpose may, for example, be to search for the ideological biases of the author that are encoded in the work, or simply to read the book for pleasure.

All these ideas mean that there has been a major shift in emphasis in the way that books are viewed. It has been succinctly summarized as showing "a critical shift of focus from forms of the signified to the processes of signification" (Greenblatt and Gunn 1992, 5). So, interest is now upon the construction of meaning – what is *signified* in the jargon of semiotics – namely that which lies behind the empirical form, or character of the object. These new perspectives mean that it is no longer enough to simply review the findings the explorer reported as empirical observations of what was *there*, or *seen* in the new lands. The text must be seen as a *constructed representation*, not a mimetic copy of some assumed objective reality, and this construction may have quite different purposes to those of the exploration of new lands, as was shown in the previous discussion dealing with the many functions of exploration narratives. The result is that any written text can now be regarded as the site of interactive relationships, rather than a static, one-way, author-to-reader connection. As such, it becomes part of the whole system of communication and meaning between people, so it is appropriate to apply the word *discourse* to these ideas. Mills (1997) has shown that *discourse* is not an easy word to define, because of the different ways in which it has been used. Originally used in the sense of a verbal communication, initially between speaker and listener (or sets of them), it can be extended to apply to the communication of any social activity, recognizing that this is underlain by sets of beliefs, values, or ways of looking at the world. But the communication does not have to be verbal; it can apply to other interactive acts or devices. In the context of a book, such as an exploration narrative, the written text becomes the site of discourse, one where readers can extract their own meanings from the text, at least once the authoritative author-dominant approach is set aside. Literary critics have argued that what is important is the search for the way that one term, one interpretation, or one text, is privileged over others, which may identify oppression, or some hidden authority – the basis of the concept of deconstruction. But as Bonnycastle's (1991, 97) review of new literary theories observed: "deconstructionism is a tool rather than a desirable philosophy in itself." He argued that the approach is useful in uncovering the alternative meanings in any text and may liberate one from oppressive authority, but it cannot create the conditions in which we want to understand the meanings behind any text. To this argument may be added the view that it may well ignore important interpretations derived from what might be called realist approaches. An incisive essay by Godlewska (1995) can be used to illustrate the point. She accepted recent deconstructionist opinions that western maps reflected power structures and have been tools of colonialism in many countries. However, she maintained that they are still descriptive of the world they seek to portray, as well as the system from which they have been derived. In addition, they have been a powerful vehicle for spatial understanding and interpretation about the lands depicted. The purpose of western maps may well have driven their particular construction and use, but they are still important vehicles of spatial understanding – even if they only communicate *some* of the available information about the places they describe, and their construction depends on some shared decisions about representation.

Application of the concept of reader's plural to the field of exploration literature does provide an opportunity for new insights into the traditional valuation of texts. From the Renaissance onwards, exploration narratives were regarded as a new form of truth; the fact that the explorers saw the new lands with their own eyes gave their written descriptions an authority that replaced the prior speculations of the philosophers or geographical theorists. It created a different authority structure for interpretation. The author-explorer described something about which he knows a great deal, and which the reader accepted because of a lack of previous or personal knowledge. This altered the way authority was assigned to books in this area. Of course, we must again exercise caution, for this is not simply about errors of fact, or interpretation in books. These new arguments go much further. It can no longer be assumed that the intention of the writer necessarily has priority in the interpretations made even in non-fiction works; readers may derive their own views, based on the values and the context within which they interpret the text. Nevertheless, a note of prudence may be in order, for not all interpretations are likely to receive the same value. Readers, if they seek to convince others — and some may not — still have to justify their own interpretations of a text, based on the context, purpose, and words of the written work; the court of justification still mediates between alternative interpretations based on evidence.

The result of this new emphasis upon the alternative meanings of the text means our interpretations of exploration texts go far beyond Watson's ideas that were quoted earlier; namely about the importance of *how we see* the world. Equally important is *how we write and read* — how the words convey meaning. We need to know how the text is constructed, what is encoded in the words of the text, and how alternative meanings and interpretations are derived by the readers. These trends provide a stark contrast to the totalizing agendas of previous approaches to texts, which tended to allocate canonical authority to certain key works based on the opinions of some erudite scholar or literary critic. In the context of the *high culture* tradition created by the Romantic Period, the descriptions were assumed to represent the *right* interpretation — the apex of insight, or the creation of intensified feeling. Applied to the literature of discovery, it will be obvious that the written words of the first explorer in an area were often priorized because they represented the initial, and presumably unique descriptions of the unknown land. Little thought was given to the possibility of contamination by the explorer's culture. Such bias, we now realize, is inevitable. Most of the words used to describe the new lands and the interpretative insights made, are borrowed from the culture of the observer. The *new lands* are only *seen, described and read* in terms of the old, whilst the context of subsequent reading can produce additional alternative meanings. These arguments, once more, lead to the rejection of realist interpretations, of the empirical or common sense interpretations.

Although the new insights have expanded our understandings, these new, critical analysis approaches are not without their problems. It can be argued that some of the research tends to overintellectualize the straightforward tasks that explorers set themselves in writing their books, although the derivation of new meanings through critical reading often reveals issues that the author may not have been aware of. In addition, some of this new literature has its own jargon and obtuse style, which often makes it difficult for the general reader to understand the arguments. Moreover, the search for cultural meanings may result in the key objective of the narrative – the discovery of a new land and the charting of routes for others to follow – being ignored, or at least downplayed. The routes taken, the locations identified, the additions to the known map of the world that were made by the explorer, are often taken for granted in these studies. This danger means there may be a need to incorporate the new ideas of critical analysis without losing all of the old interpretations. Finally, the tendency to stress the uniqueness of each explorer's descriptions usually leads to singular interpretations, producing a literature composed of what can be called *fragmented discourses* – a phrase used by Greenblatt (1991) to describe a field of individual studies with few attempts at generalization. Despite these problems, there seems little doubt that the new interpretations and insights from literary theory have ensured that there can never be a return to the old realist views of any exploration narrative, as some single, authoritative standard of descriptive authenticity – one that simply involved the translation of the so-called *reality of the new environment* into words. But insights from literary theory are not the only ways in which knowledge of how people perceived the new environments can be derived. The work of cognitive psychologists also needs to be taken into account.

D. COGNITIVE PROCESSES

Philosophers have long speculated about the relationships between sensing, perceiving, and thinking for centuries. With the development of psychology as a research science, an experimental basis was added to the derivation of knowledge about how the mind works. During the early twentieth century, research was dominated by investigations of the role of the unconscious, and what could be called a direct perception view, which questioned people about what they saw when ideas, words, or images were presented to them. This was followed by the so-called *behavioural* tradition, which focused upon the physical outcomes or responses that people made to various stimuli. The approach was based on the belief that the mind was primarily a passive organism that simply responds through innate processes and conditioning. From the 1950s, the cognitive approach has become more and more important. This has been described as "an empirical research science that has its principal goal understanding the processes that underlie the work of the human mind" (Payne and Wenger 1998, 3). Unlike the behaviourists, cognitive psychologists accept the principle that the mind plays an *active* role in the creation of meaning. In other words the mind is involved in the selection, processing, and reinterpretation of information received via the senses; it is not just a receptor. Hence, cognitive psychologists have focused on understanding the processes and products of the mind by which sensory input is transformed, stored, and understood. These produce our faculties of perceiving, knowing, and conceiving, what is usually called cognitive development, as opposed to the outcomes produced by other features, such as involuntary actions and emotional feelings. The former are the higher order abilities that are normally associated with what is considered to be human intelligence. A key difference with previous studies of the mind is that cognitive scientists use controlled experiments to obtain insights into the way the mind works, and have access to a whole range of new techniques that enable them to explore how stimuli in the form of electrical and chemical messages are transmitted through the brain. The result is that an *information processing* approach is favoured, rather than the direct perception approach described earlier, in which features such as prior images and aesthetics simply modify our knowledge and understanding of places.

At first sight, the application of ideas from cognitive psychology to the field of exploration literature appears rather far-fetched. After all, we obviously cannot go back and apply experimental techniques to how long-dead explorers experienced the new worlds of their discoveries. But cognitive psychology research provides an outline of the way that the brain receives and processes stimuli from the outside world which enables us to better understand the way knowledge is created. To take one example, it shows the way that the so-called *experience error* is so often made; namely that because human perception works so well, it convinces people that perceptual understanding is a direct result of the stimulus. However, cognitive psychologists have shown that this is not the way the brain works. The cognitive system *selects* and *interprets* the stimuli presented by the environment to create the understanding we have of our world. This is not the simple process of *object and reflection*, by which individual objects are perceived in the brain as mirror images of the real world objects. Rather the cognitive system *constructs* knowledge in a series of stages, to produce our understandable images of the world by selecting and reinterpreting the physical stimuli we obtain from the environment, with comparisons to existing knowledge and expectations.

The precise nature of these relationships is still the matter of debate, but the general structure of the stimulus-knowledge connection and at least parts of the processes involved do seem to have been identified (Posner 1989; Osherson, Kosslyn, and Hollerbach 1990; Posner and Raichle 1994). The cognitive system can be summarized in terms of three broad categories. The first, the *sensory processes*, pick up signals from the environment, such as light or sound, and convert it into information that can be used by subsequent processes. The second set of processes, known as *perception processes*, convert this information into what we understand as knowledge, via series of different mechanisms. The third cognitive stage is usually summarized as the *thought processes*, which also contains a series of different types of processes. It is tempting to view these processes as some kind of linear sequence, but research in the last few decades has shown that it is not possible to draw lines between these processes, whilst there is little doubt that the context of the stimuli also plays crucial roles at various stages. However, much the idea of stimuli passing through a series of stages is intuitively satisfying; experimental psychologists are at pains to stress that many of the cognitive processes are not simply the separate bundles of activities that analytical research seem to identify. So even though there may be specialized areas associated with particular functions, there are also complex and simultaneous interactions between the fifty billion neurons that seem active in creating cognitive responses among the 180 billion or more neurons found in the typical brain.

There is little doubt that psychological research has enormously increased our understanding of the processes of cognition through reasoning and experimental research, but it must be admitted that research is still in its infancy. This means it is not always possible to determine whether particular outcomes are the direct result of one process or another. A related group of problems is linked to the fact that most of cognitive research is carried out in laboratories, or under very controlled experiments, and often depends on studies of people with brain damage, making it possible to study what functions are impaired. It is not always easy to apply the research results to the rich and complex real world environment experienced by historic explorers. Also, most research still tries to identify single, or perhaps joint effects, using the analytical processes of science, whereas in practise the cognitive processes operate together in complex, mutually affecting ways. Despite these problems, cognitive psychologists are gradually providing a basic outline of the factors and processes involved, and the way the system seems to operate, which are useful in throwing light on the way that explorers viewed their new worlds. What is clear is that the creation of knowledge from the stimuli of the senses does involve a process of *construction* that is not simply a direct and passive conversion of physical stimuli into what we understand as images and knowledge of the world. The conversion involves a great deal of personal and cultural input. Hence the cognitive processes construct or create images of the real world and these are, in large part, socially constructed. This, of course, does not deny the physical presence of objects and processes that create the stimuli recorded by our sensory apparatus, merely that the identification and interpretation of the new worlds made by explorers through the cognitive functions of the brain is linked to a series of cultural and personal factors, as much as to the environmental stimuli themselves. Cognitive psychology provides a very different approach to critical theory in showing how our images of the world are created and communicated. But research in this field does help us go beyond speculation and reasoning, since it is based on experimental methods and shows that our cognitive processes *construct* rather than simply *reflect* the world we see.

✛   8. CONCLUSIONS

This chapter has tried to make the case against a realist view of exploration narratives by reviewing the way that they are constructed and the linkages with the field of literature and literary criticism. The discussion began by showing that there has been a close connection between exploration and literature since the invention of writing. But for most of the last two hundred years exploration narratives were not regarded as *literature* because of the closed, canonical way that *literature* was viewed from the Romantic Period onward, and the way that descriptions of exploration were written. In the last two decades, the old restrictions have been broken down as the scope of literary studies has expanded; the old dichotomy of exploration narrative and literature has been dissolved. One result is that exploration narratives are themselves being *explored* using hermeneutic methods. These have shown that all such narratives involve some interpretation, and the written texts of all new discoveries were affected by a number of factors, such as ideologies, aesthetics, or even the desire to make profits from the written text, not simply the process of geographical discovery. So, the narratives of exploration cannot be considered to be the dispassionate scientific accumulation of knowledge that our past focus upon the results of geographical discoveries sometimes pretend. The narratives involve a great deal of interpretation at various stages and cannot be viewed as literal representations of some new world seen for the first time by Europeans. But the empirical demonstration of the way that explorers and travel writers interpreted, rather than reflected, the new landscapes in their words and texts, is only one way of illustrating the flaws in the realist assumption which underlay most reading of exploration narratives. A second and perhaps more fundamental change relevant to how we view exploration narratives has come from insights provided by the new literary criticism. Literary theorists have used critical analysis to show that how we *write or construct* is essentially problematic, creating the possibility of different representations of what was seen or experienced during the exploration. But the problematic also applies to the reading of the narratives, for readers derive their own interpretations, using their own beliefs and values to construct their own understanding from the words on the page. But a third new insight also needs to be added to the way that we understand exploration texts. Cognitive psychologists have begun to show that the process of construction of meaning by author and reader is not simply a matter of writing and reading. Our perception of the world around us and, by extension, the world *seen* by explorers, can also be viewed as an act of *construction*, this time in a cognitive context, for our cognitive processes depend on factors such as prior knowledge, expectations, beliefs and values, and do not only reflect the stimuli provided by the new environments.

This inevitably simplistic review of some of the key issues relevant to the critique of realism illustrates one important point. The relationships between the words that explorers use, and the meanings they try to express through these words, are much more complex than the common sense or realist view would have us believe. The world we describe is represented through words and concepts of our own construction, not

FIGURE 2.1. STAGES OF INTERPRETATION

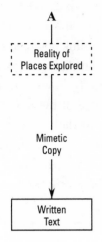

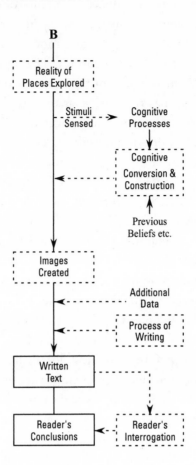

through the intrinsic structure of objects; whilst readers also construct meanings from the text – meanings that are also influenced by their values, ideologies, and motives. Figure 2.1 portrays the relationships that have been uncovered. The copyist idea of a direct link between some assumed reality of the new worlds discovered and our knowledge of it, shown as route A, is far too simplistic a view. Route B shows that there are three sets of influences that affect our knowledge of the new lands that were discovered: the cognitive understanding of the new environments seen; the creation of a written text; as well as its interpretation by readers. At each stage different representations of what passes as knowledge can result, providing a great deal of indeterminacy in our understanding.

Geography's practical and largely empirical past ensures that many practitioners in the field have traditionally been uncomfortable about understandings that stress the elusiveness of meaning. But since language is infinitely variable and varies by culture, it seems inevitable that people with different languages see, or rather communicate about the world in different ways. Even groups within languages with different practises and lifestyles divide the world in different ways and select different features to emphasize as the feminist approach shows. So our knowledge of the world cannot be a simple reflection of some material reality. Rather, what we understand about the world is a product of the way that our cognitive processes and languages work to differentially divide up the world into different categories. Communication between people can only occur if there are some shared meanings. These are frequently imperfect, but without them there is only the relativist chaos of multiple meanings and misunderstanding. The analogy may not be exact, but in the new world of electronics, computer scientists have to agree on the protocols they use to allow machines to communicate with one another and with humans. Decisions are made to facilitate this purpose. Perhaps it is easier in the physical world to make equivalences – unlike the constantly evolving interpretations of the human world, in which the words that represent meaning involve a subjective act of allocation, constantly change, can apply to alternative ideas, and are loaded with symbolic or emotional meanings. Individuals within human groups have developed their own protocols to communicate effectively, but the types of protocol used frequently depends on the purpose of the exercise. Scientists have been particularly effective in developing methods that allow others to accept or reject certain conclusions. Even though the scientific approach has produced such enormous gains in understanding, most adherents to these views recognize these are only partial representations of the real world. Yet this does not lead them to accept the relativist attitudes of many of their humanistic colleagues. Since exploration narratives inevitably attract interpretations from those with scientific, as well as humanistic preferences, it seems important not to privilege one over the other; both approaches may provide useful, but partial interpretations – although the varied values of readers may weight them differently, whilst those with power may be able to impose their views on others. What is shared, however, is a recognition that the realist assumption of most interpretations of exploration narratives cannot be upheld, since all travel descriptions are bound to be representations, as shown in the various sections of this chapter. All exploration texts are based on several separate, yet interconnected stages – from the initial thoughts, to the sights seen, through the stage of writing or constructing an account of the exploration, as well as its reception by readers. This chapter has shown that it is difficult to assume that the explorer operates objectively. In the words of a perceptive contemporary novelist: "the eye is never innocent, it is always committed" (Ironside 1998, 72). The sights seen and interpreted by the explorer, the words created by the author, and those read by the reader, are never absorbed only in a literal way; they are created by prior knowledge, values, language, and processed through the lenses of individual perception and choice, which are themselves biased by the culture of the interpreter and previous beliefs or ideologies. Similarly, readers usually interpret the narrative through the concerns and beliefs of their own period, not through the contexts of the historic time in which they were written. All these issues mean that any exploration narrative, and the impact it makes, cannot be seen as some mirror-like description of the progress of discovery, that the emphasis upon what has been called the *products of exploration* imply. Although initiated by the journey of exploration, the written text – the words on the page, whether initial drafts, or the final book – is subject to a large number of influences, of which the journey itself, and the way the environment and peoples are seen and described, are only a part. It is now necessary to take the thesis one stage further – to identify the details of the various ways that exploration texts, whether the perception and construction of writers, or their use by readers, are always affected by influences beyond the experiences of the journey. This is the objective of the next chapter. It provides a more systematic framework for the study of the influences that affect the production of meanings from of an exploration narrative: a framework which may also, perhaps, be called a poetics of exploration.

Chapter 3

Interpreting Exploration:
The *Three Stages* of *Construction*

The previous chapter has shown that the realist approach to exploration writing conflates the journey of discovery and the subsequent narrative of the expedition. Instead of the textual description being seen as some kind of direct copy of what was perceived in the newly discovered lands, it should be conceptualized as a separate entity; one that is affected by a large number of additional influences – of which the interpretations of the sense experiences of the journey are only part. Any study of these influences may reveal as much about the culture of the explorer and the meaning of the various forms of representation, as about the newly discovered lands. Once the exploration narrative is seen as a culturally produced representation, the relevance of Barnes and Duncan's (1992) call for students of geography to become more interested in the issue of textual construction in their writing, the *graphy* of geo-graphy, becomes apparent. But our understanding should not only involve textual construction. The previous chapter has also shown that narratives can be differentially *read*, which is clearly another type of construction, whilst it is equally important to understand the influences that affect our understanding of the *geo*, for our cognitive system *constructs* our initial perception and knowledge of the world, rather than simply reflecting the stimulus it receives. Since Turnbull (2000) has shown that different groups of people construct knowledge in different ways, we should be wary of privileging one tradition, as we have done so frequently in the past. This argument means that we cannot continue to believe in the exploration narrative as a mimetic reflection of the new worlds discovered; the type of model shown on the left-hand side of figure 2.1a. Instead, the narratives involve complex processes of what Turnbull (2000) called the "creation of knowledge spaces" or Gregory and Duncan (1999) termed "the production of a space of knowledge." In the context of exploration and understanding about the new lands, this knowledge construction can be summarized in terms of three broad categories that encompass a variety of influences: the *cognitive processes, the writing of the text, and the derivation of meaning by the readers*. These deal successively with: the construction of the images or knowledge held about the new world, derived from the exploration itself and prior knowledge or values, which creates the apparent reality that is seen; the factors that modify these views in the writing or construction of the book; and the factors that affect the way the text is interpreted by readers.

FIGURE 3.1. INFLUENCES ON THE CONSTRUCTION OF AN EXPLORATION TEXT

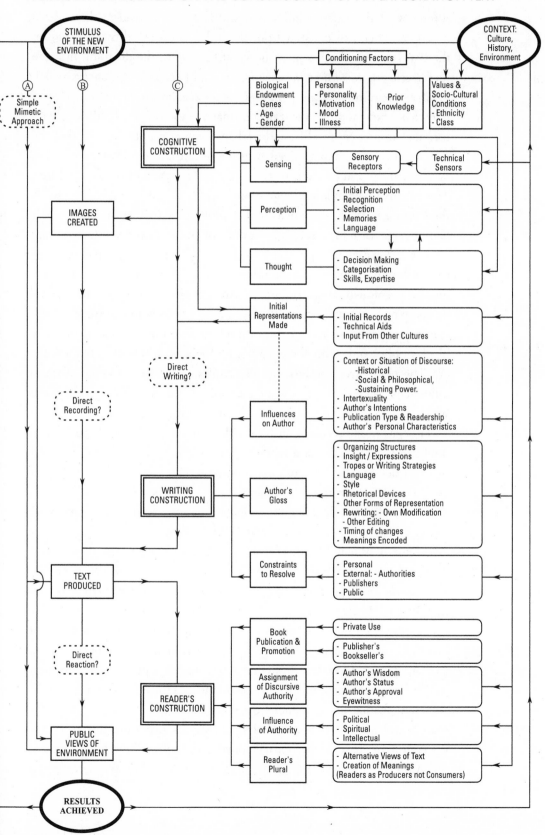

Figure 3.1 extends the ideas of figure 2.1 to provide a more detailed summary of the various influences and factors involved in these three broad categories of construction. It can be interpreted by focusing on the two key sets of influences shown at the top of the diagram: first the *various stimuli provided by the environments*, and second, *the context*, which involves the *cultural system of the explorer and the historical context in which it is written*. The rest of the diagram summarizes the range of additional factors that influence, modify, and perhaps even corrupt, the way that the new worlds were experienced, written about and read. Many of these factors can be linked back to the cultural background of the explorer. This means that the knowledge of any reader about the new worlds, or the *results achieved* in the words of the summary shown at the bottom left hand corner of figure 3.1, is a product of the multitude of factors that affect the construction of meaning. Just as the sights seen by the explorer cannot be interpreted as some mimetic copy of the environment entering the previously empty memory banks of the explorer, so the words on the page cannot be thought of as a direct translation of the exploration experiences; also, the exploration text does not fill some previously blank public void, with some single, uniform interpretation from readers. The next three sections of this chapter describe the range of these influences, as far as possible using examples from the field of exploration writing. Before dealing with these features a few caveats are needed.

First, as more research in the field becomes available, there is little doubt that the number and variety of factors identified in figure 3.1 will be extended and the organization modified. So figure 3.1 should be seen as an *introductory* framework designed to clarify the range of influences, rather than being a final definitive one; a framework that tries to provide some guidance to what Greenblatt (1991) described as the fragmented discourse of the field of exploration literature. This structure is not designed to study the *results* of explorations but *how this knowledge is created and the factors that affect the construction*. Second, there is little doubt that the analytical separation of the various factors is artificial, since many of these interact with one another, whilst some have more influence than others in various narratives. Lines of connection are drawn between the various stages and factors in figure 3.1 in an attempt to draw attention to the most important of these inter-relations. However, this may not do sufficient justice to one crucial question, namely whether the author's words, and use of prior knowledge and values, are a product of either the cognitive phase or the textual construction phase. To take one example, did early-nineteenth-century British explorers in Canada really see the landscapes as expressions of particular aesthetics or did this interpretation come later, when they put pen to paper? Since our information source lies primarily with the writings of explorers, it is assumed that the construction is at the textual stage; of course, it could be at the perception stage, or both could apply in the context of different times or in relation to various influences.

A third issue that must be noted about figure 3.1 is the need to recognize that all the various factors are influenced by the context of the expedition. An important part of the context involves the cultural background of the times and historical moment involved, as shown by the quotation that began this chapter; ideas derived from the work of one of the first Canadians to apply literary ideas to exploration narratives (MacLaren 1984; 1985a; 1985b). This view lies at the heart of what is normally called the new historicism or cultural poetics today (Hamilton 1996). Veeser (1989) has shown that this term has been interpreted in many different ways, although its common purpose is to critique the typical myopia of the present period, namely applying the ideas of the present to interpret past societies and events within them, and searching for common themes, of interest to the present, to elucidate the period or problem under review. Hence interpretations should take into account the *temporal context of the discovery*. The societal conditions of the time and the particular sets of political and social circumstances that are involved represent important aspects of this context. The emphasis is to *look at the past on its own terms*, which can provide very different interpretations to the views of the present. For example, Mayhew (2000) has shown that the geography that was well regarded and popular in the seventeenth and eighteenth centuries was very different to the ideas usually identified in twentieth-century surveys of the development of the field, which stress issues of interest to the present. In addition, the objective of the new historicism is to understand the cultural relationships of the discoveries, the meanings and representations current in the period that are encoded in the documentary record of the past. An important theme is to uncover the sources of power that underlie the creation of works of literature or art; a theme that can also be applied to the texts of exploration. It is argued that power is often intimately involved in the social formation of societies, which are created by particular ideologies, and specific economic and political practises. But any historical past can only be properly interpreted through the mindsets of the people at that time. One can never reconstruct the past completely, for it is impossible to go back. However, the fragments of historical evidence that survive, in this case in the form of exploration narratives, can be interrogated in the search for the meanings which lie behind the particular representations, whether in words, in art, in landscapes, or in any form of communication. In the examples dealt with here, the emphasis is upon western representations; the texts of western explorers, whose words frequently displayed an insensitivity to the peoples they encountered, although there are exceptions. Most, but not all, viewed the new worlds as places to conquer, to master, and to derive wealth from. As Pratt (1992) has shown, these represent an imperial and commercial agenda that is reflected in the expressions used to describe their experiences, expressions that are based on particular ideologies, and specific economic and political practises. These issues will be dealt with in more detail in subsequent sections.

Cultural and historical circumstances are not the only contextual features involved. The possibility of changing environmental conditions must also be taken into account. There seems little doubt that some explorers were unlucky, in the sense that their expeditions failed because they were exploring particular areas at times when the climate had deteriorated, either from some short-term change, or part of some long-term deterioration. For example, Solomon (2001) has recently argued that the death of Scott and his companions on the way back from the South Pole was not only due to their preparation, but was also linked to the exceptionally severe cold conditions in March, which hindered their travel. When people are operating at the extreme of their endurance, such unexpected changes can cause catastrophe. Yet the death of Scott's two companions was, in part, a cultural issue, for they chose to remain with Scott, rather than trying to reach their base camp without him. Their values led them to choose companionship and probable death over possible survival. In the context of longer-term change, the medieval climate deterioration led to the demise of the Scandinavian settlements in western Greenland, which had been served by an annual ship from Bergen. Had this climate recession not occurred, the settlements might have provided the first real bridgehead into the continent of America, rather than being rediscovered by Columbus and later by Cabot. Later, the colder conditions of the Little Ice Age undoubtedly hindered the late eighteenth and early-nineteenth-century attempts to prove the Northwest Passage. These examples could be complemented by situations in which explorers may have been favoured by the fortuitous trends of climatic amelioration.

Last, but perhaps not least, it must be noted that figure 3.1 is not particularly useful as a framework to investigate any *particular* exploration narrative, since it deals with the *construction* of knowledge and images, texts, and interpretations by readers, rather than with the *results and consequences* of the exploration, which involve additional factors. Hence, the last section of the chapter is designed to have a more integrative role for the comparative study of exploration narratives. It identifies a series of themes that can be proposed as a template of ideas; this is essentially a pedagogical device for assessing the utility of any book describing a journey of exploration. In other words, it can be seen as a guide to the reading of exploration narratives that will be used in subsequent chapters to interpret the work of Captain Thomas James.

✢ 2. COGNITIVE CONSTRUCTION

The previous chapter has already outlined the way in which research from cognitive psychology can help us understand the factors that affect the construction of what is seen as reality by any observer, in this case explorers confronted by some new worlds. It has been shown that the brain is not a passive receptor of information derived from external stimuli; rather it plays an *active* role in the creation of meaning, since it is involved in the selection, processing, and reinterpretation of information received via the senses. Although the details and precise functioning of the cognitive system is far from understood, psychologists have outlined the general structure of this system (Osherson, Kosslyn, and Hollerbach 1990; Payne and Wenger 1998). These ideas were summarized to create the framework shown in the top part of figure 3.1, which provides a brief outlineof the most important stages of cognitive activity, and the influences upon these activities, that seem relevant to help interpret the representations and decisions made by explorers in new lands. The diagram shows that the range of processes and influences can be conveniently summarized for the purposes of this discussion in terms of three main broad categories; *the sensory receptors, perception, and thinking*, together with a set of *conditioning factors* that affect the operation of the system for particular individuals.

The first part of the cognitive system involves the *sensory receptors* that convert the physical stimuli such as pressure changes or light reflection into responses in the brain's neural cells; responses that code or represent the stimulus received by the sensory receptor and also store the information. The coded information is then passed on and transformed by a second set of processes, which may also lead to particular actions by the body's motor mechanisms. This *perceptual stage* consists of five different processing and reception mechanisms. In the case of vision, there is an *initial perception* stage that produces an internal representation from the coded messages of the stimulus. This is followed by the *recognition* stage, which involves the identification of objects or patterns, either by comparing it with some prior knowledge of similar objects stored in the memory, or by a feature-matching approach, such as the *interaction activation model*, which involves comparing parts of objects, one at a time. The fact that the receptors are confronted with a barrage of sensory information at any time means that the perception process must also involve an *attention or selection* phase, in which the cognitive system seems to withdraw from consideration of the whole, so as to focus and deal more effectively with the part of immediate interest. It is still not clear whether this vital stage operates before or after the recognition stage. Various types of *memory*, short-term and long-term, play their part in the process, not only by storing information at various stages but also by releasing prior knowledge with which to interpret the stimulus. Finally, the human cognitive system has a highly developed *communication system*, the most important part of which is language, by which we can describe the sources of the stimuli, although gestures and other forms of action may serve a similar, yet less expressive purpose. The third category shown in figure 3.1 contains the higher-level cognitive processes, often summarized as *the thought or thinking stage*. This involves the manipulation of the representations and beliefs to yield new knowledge or understanding, as seen by such processes as decision-making and judgment, categorization and conceptualization, and skills or expertise. In the last few decades cognitive researchers have shown that it is not possible to draw lines between these distinctive processes, whilst there is little doubt that the *context* of the stimuli also plays crucial roles at various stages, which influences the interpretations that are made. These are not simply the proximal relationships, namely who we are with and how they affect our views – obviously a very important feature in the early stages of human development – but also the way that recognition is affected by prior knowledge. What is also vital is the society-culture-historical moment, each with its own valuation of particular skills, behaviours, and thoughts. These common functions in human cognition are also affected by what can be summarized as a fourth group of influences: a series of *conditioning factors*. These affect the cognition of any particular individual, factors ranging from biological endowment, through personal or operational issues, such as personality and motivation, to the effect of prior knowledge and values, and the socio-cultural conditions involved.

It must be emphasized that this framework is *not* designed to show how the perceptual process of any explorer actually worked, but to provide examples of the range of factors that affect perception of the apparent reality of the new worlds. These examples cannot be true experimental tests, since they do not depend upon direct observations of explorers and how they viewed the new worlds. Rather, the source material is the comments expressed, in words on a page, by the explorers some time after the event of exploration occurred. Nevertheless, they do provide at least circumstantial evidence to illustrate the key point of this discussion, namely that cognitive processes are not simply reflective of the environment. Rather the *constructions of reality* that lead to knowledge of the new worlds are affected, or conditioned, by information and attitudes already in the mind of the explorer, and which operate at various stages in the cognitive system, and the cultural background (Lave 1988; Berry and Irvine 1988; Posner 1989). Moreover, this construction is often problematic in the sense that the cognitive processes are always subject to a series of errors at every stage, from the way that we collect information and interpret it (Gilovitch 1993). This, of course, does not deny the physical presence of objects and processes that create the stimuli recorded by our sensory apparatus, merely that identification and interpretation, through the cognitive functions of the brain, is also linked to a series of cultural and personal factors. What is of particular relevance here is the way that prior knowledge and attitudes are used by the cognitive system to convert the stimuli received from the environment into the knowledge that explorers believed they had about the new lands they discovered. As such, the ideas are useful in throwing light on the way that explorers viewed their new worlds. What is clear is that the creation of knowledge from the stimuli of the senses does involve a process of *construction*, that is not simply a direct and passive conversion of physical stimuli into what we understand as images and knowledge of the world. Rather the conversion involves a great deal of additional input that relates to prior knowledge and attitudes. It is this part of the cognitive process that is of particular interest here. Comments about the relevance of the other stages and factors are also provided, although these are very brief, since there are few examples of exploration narratives being interpreted through the concepts of cognitive psychology.

Figure 3.1 has shown that the cognitive system does not operate in isolation. It is affected by a set of what can be called *conditioning factors* that can vary between individuals. Although the basic structure of the cognitive system may be the same for all humans, there seems little doubt that the way it operates in particular circumstances may be affected by a range of factors that vary from individual to individual. These include at least the following features: *innate biological endowment*, such as genetic makeup, age, gender, and physical capabilities; *personal or operational attributes*, such as personality and motivation (the conscious ones linked to determination, courage etc., as well as moods and illnesses, especially mental ones, which may affect cognition; *prior knowledge and values* possessed by individuals; *and cultural attributes*, such as ethnicity, class, education etc. In addition, one could also add the need to incorporate the link to contextual factors, the societal or cultural setting shown in figure 3.1, which should also include the proximal influences on the explorer's development, such as parents in early childhood, or the influence of family, school, or social connections. Given the type of source material being used, only brief insights into the relevance of these various features can be given here; the emphasis is upon the way that the prior knowledge and values of the explorers affect the way the new worlds are seen or understood by the first explorers. Moreover, no attempt is made to deal with the automatic responses that the body may make to particular stimuli. But before dealing with these examples, it must be noted that the application of ideas about the cognitive system focuses upon the example of sight and perhaps sound, because these are the things recorded in the exploration narratives. Figure 3.1 does not deal with all the other senses and motor functions because it is designed to apply to a database that comes only from textual data. Obviously, this restricts the content of the discussion, especially of influences based on actual exploration, such as those that could be investigated today through experiments on explorers travelling across new lands. In this context it is worth remembering Belyea's (1990, 13) observation that the overwhelming sensory experiences of explorers in the Canadian Arctic were of pain, cold, silence, fatigue, and hunger. Certainly these sensations are often mentioned in exploration narratives, but the military tradition of many explorers meant that such deprivations were often downplayed in their books, since to complain was a sign of weakness. The result is that one can only glimpse at the effect of the journey upon the complete set of sensations, for the textual emphasis is usually on the visual. Hence this study focuses upon the sense of *seeing*, on features that find most resonance in the narrative since they deal with the new environment, not the effect of the land upon the explorer.

I. PRIOR KNOWLEDGE

Exploration provides a personal experience of a new land, in which the new or transmitted knowledge is based on first-hand observations. But explorers do not set out on their journeys without ideas and beliefs. Their view of the unknown regions of the world was often based on the myths – perhaps based on long forgotten journeys – held by the society, or views created by the abstract reasoning of philosophers, from speculations based on current belief systems, or even information obtained from people who claimed to have travelled in the unknown regions. Pioneering work by John Wright (1947) and Lowenthal (1961), for example, has described the importance of the imagination in geographical enquiry, whilst reviews by geographers, such as John Allen (1975b), or historians, such as Phillips (1988, chapter 10) have shown the relevance of these ideas in the context of exploration. The importance of prior knowledge to the discovery process is not something that can be dismissed as some corruption of the reality of the new land, a reality only created by exposure to the new lands. Cognitive psychologists have shown that an important part of the *recognition* of objects consists of prior expectations; these help construct our knowledge of the discoveries. Piaget (1954), in his theory of cognitive development, called the first stage "assimilation," followed by a process of "accommodation." By assimilation he meant the way we use our existing knowledge to interpret new objects that are seen, whereas accommodation is the adjustment of existing knowledge to take the new information into account, perhaps by modifying the previous knowledge or creating a new category of understanding. Piaget emphasized that these two features operate almost simultaneously by what is known as a feedback process. The result of these processes is that it is possible to separate what can be called *sensory perception* from *cognitive perception*, the former involving the identification of an object or event produced by some stimuli, the latter involves interpretation, and hence meaning. For example, we can accept that a member of some isolated hunting and gathering tribe, or a contemporary western man, may both *see* an eclipse, a sensory perception. But to the former it may be understood as a 'god' eating up the moon, because of his beliefs, whereas a modern man will *see* the unusual event as an example of the earth's shadow passing over the moon. These different cognitive perceptions are usually regarded as a product of prior knowledge or beliefs and demonstrate that whilst cognitive perception is certainly relative, sensory perception is unlikely to be relative. However, Payne and Wenger (1998, 70) caution that the distinction between a sensation and a perception should be regarded as one of convenience than of scientific fact and many authors demonstrate the complexity of the relationships between what seemed, initially, to be a simple dualism (Dretske 1995, 98–122; Griffin, 1998, 125–51).

Appreciation of the workings of these cognitive processes now makes some of the initial interpretations of explorers, or by people in the new lands, easier to understand. Three examples can be used to illustrate the point. Frobisher's contact with the people we now call Inuit, rather than Eskimos, during his three searches for the Northwest Passage in 1576–78, revealed they had high cheekbones and narrow eyes, the so-called *tartar features* of Asian peoples (Stefansson 1938; Morison 1978, 287). This probably reinforced opinions that the expedition was close to Asia, or at least the passage to it. In the context of gestures and sign systems, Columbus's voyage to the island now known as Trinidad led to frustration when canoe-loads of local natives kept their distance from the exploration ships, although Columbus wanted contact to enable him to trade (Greenblatt 1991). Columbus gave orders for some of his crew to dance and cavort in time to music, to give the impression of a jovial party that the aboriginals might be tempted to join. Instead, the display was met with a shower of arrows! It is very likely that the natives interpreted the dancing as threatening behaviour, as some type of ritual posturing before an attack – a typical situation found in their culture, as well as among South Sea Islanders. A third example can be taken from one of the rare examples that survive about the way that aboriginal peoples viewed the first appearance of European explorers. Usually, the size of the ships and the way they could be manoeuvred, was regarded with awe. But the Tlinget people of the northwest coast of America in 1786 interpreted the black ships of Perouse's French expedition to the Pacific as large ravens, for they had no other category of experience to understand the new object they saw floating on the water. In the mythology of the Tlinget world ravens were considered to be tricksters, and were able to turn a man to stone. So once the ships were 'seen,' or rather 'represented,' as ravens, they were regarded with fear.

The values and ideologies held by the explorer-author are also of significance in the way that sense information is processed, for these condition how objects or areas may be represented to others. Given the vast variety of information in the environment, the choice of data to describe is itself a matter of values – of what sights and events are considered by the observer to be significant enough to comment on. But the process of communication is vitally linked to the linguistic label given to objects, something that provides a form of recognition, or identification for others. Perhaps the most basic form of representation in exploration are the names given to places, which often provide the first signs of European imprints on the land. To a logical positivist, the assignment of a unique name is simply an act of identification, empty of meaning. But the label provided may have a great deal of meaning for particular groups of people who share the sign system. In semiotic terms, this means that the signifier (any sign) is a marker for what is signified (what is meant). Indeed, the whole process of naming may perform several functions. A name is often used to create familiarity with a place. By applying European names, the New World is made to conform to the Old, to the previously known universe. Unknown places are made familiar, such as by calling places after the explorer's home region, town, family, or sponsors. Symbolically, therefore, the places on the new and often threatening periphery of the world may be tamed, or at least made less threatening, and easier to interpret. But the naming is more than a simple link to the homeland; the specific names allocated often honour the sponsors of expeditions or important figures at court, a process of flattery, but also an immortalization, if they stick. The choice of labels frequently provides important clues to the power relationships among the influential persons of the day. Spiritual associations were also important. Roman Catholics, in particular, tended to use the names of saints for new settlements, honouring religious leaders as well as providing the expectation of spiritual protection. Yet the act of naming is also one that signifies possession, a means of extinguishing aboriginal title. It explains why European names usually replaced aboriginal designations, although many of these older designations were simply unknown, or were only known in their Europeanized form. Some of the pseudo-aboriginal names may be easy to unravel. Others are quite distorted from the original form, or simply provide almost comical examples of European misrepresentations, if the results were not so tragic. For example,

Greenblatt (1991, 104) suggested the word Yucatan is probably derived from the Mayan, *uic a than*, which roughly means *what did you say* – surely the probable Mayan response to Spaniards who asked for the name of the land. Contemporary opinion attributes the origin of the word Canada to the Iroquois word for village or settlement, *ka-na-ta*, again the generic response given when early French explorers asked for the name of the area and gestured to the population concentration. On hearing the response, the European explorers simply transcribed the sounds into their own language, assuming the sounds represented the name of the land. It is also possible that the Portuguese, in their early-sixteenth-century expeditions along the Labrador coast, used the slang phrase *aca nada* (nothing here) to describe the new land, because they were disappointed not to find a land of easily exploitable resources. But in thousands of other cases, Europeans applied their own labels to the land. Although corruptions of some aboriginal words were used, most labels had nothing to do with native descriptions; they were replacements that signified the new power. Finally, it must be noted that naming was an important act of possession. So conflicts between European powers often led to the substitution of the victor's title over the older version, except in those cases where a large population of the defeated group remained, or where the name had been used by several powers for generations.

The values of the explorers also led them to engage in particular rituals that had meaning for themselves, but created little understanding in the minds of aboriginal peoples who did not understand the significance of the events. A particularly good example is provided by the events that took place when explorers landed on a new shore. Europeans took great care to ensure that they marked the new land with some formal ceremony, through some rituals of possession. This usually involved the planting of their king's standard, or some flag of a commercial company or group, followed by a precise declaration of possession, declaring the authority of their king, and perhaps their religion. The ceremony alone, however, was rarely enough. The words were usually carefully written down and later communicated to the royal court. A flag, or some token of the new possession, was frequently left at the site as a marker. Both text and marker became tangible representations of the act of possession. Aboriginal peoples who witnessed such ceremonies must have been mystified at the events. How could they understand the significance of the ceremonies to Europeans? The ceremonies were symbolizing the fact that the invaders were taking over their land, and would later incorporate it into a tenure system of which they had no comprehension

– one based on the ideology of private ownership. Even if aboriginals did observe the ceremony, the European explorers often took the absence of any response as a sign of acquiescence. The assumption was an egotistical mark of the self-confidence of the intruders to assert their claims above all others, buttressed by their faith as servants of what they considered to be the only true God. The rituals of possession may seem a simple *act of theatre* to people who did not understand the meaning. To European explorers it was an accepted, and carefully constructed, part of the process that legitimized possession, one that was subsequently recorded in the written record. This approach did not stop after the act of discovery. Settlers often negotiated contracts with native peoples, to signify and justify their possession of the land. In the Americas, there were few contracts between Europeans and aboriginal peoples for the first few centuries. In western Ontario and the Canadian Prairies in the nineteenth century, the major settlement of the area was preceded by a series of land treaties, but these were based on very unequal power bases. The Europeans gave the natives a small portion of the original land, cash, or annual payments and the promise of medicine and other welfare rights – possessions that only provided for bare survival. Many of these rights were often lost through the subsequent venality of the neighbouring settlers or the administrators (Carter 1990). Negotiations as virtual equals only took place in Asia during the early explorations, where the wealth, strength, and population size of the local kingdoms outweighed the initially puny ranks of the European traders. But as European mastery of the increasingly powerful technologies applied to war, based on the new industrial processes, progressed during the nineteenth century, trade negotiations with Asian peoples became almost as one-sided as their American predecessors.

III. PERSONAL CHARACTERISTICS

The cognitive system is also influenced by a number of personal attributes of the explorer. The insight that an explorer possessed, the ability to see new things, to adjust goals, or anticipate dangers, could be vital elements in the success or failure of an expedition, as were their spatial, especially way-finding skills. In contrast, illnesses, a frequent companion of explorers travelling in new lands full of unfamiliar diseases, or exhaustion, frequently impaired judgment, whilst the onset of depression, due to the circumstances faced, often had the same effect. In reviewing the influence of the range of personal attributes of explorers, the presence of courage and determination were frequently vital in pushing an expedition on to its goals, sometimes in the face of contrary evidence. Mackenzie's account of his expedition to the Arctic down the river named after him in 1798 (Lamb 1970, 182), describes how he consulted a group of natives who warned him – or rather his Chipewayn translator and guide – that it would take several winters to journey to the sea and there were monsters in the way. This is a good example of a situation in which native knowledge was either false or obstructionist, for native peoples on the exploration route did not always have a clear idea of the lands over the horizon. Mackenzie dismissed these views and continued on his way, which proved to be a 1,075-mile round trip journey from 3 June to 12 September 1798. Some idea of the strength and endurance needed to undertake the task can be gauged from the fact that the explorers usually started at 3:00 A.M., and travelled for fifteen or sixteen hours each day. Of course, determination can also lead to disaster, if linked to errors of judgment, and inability to take advice, as in the case of Scott's Antarctic expedition, or Franklin's disappearance in search of the Northwest Passage. But the flawed leaders of these disasters were often glorified as heroes in subsequent jingoistic accounts written by their supporters, because they had became symbols of their nation, examples of courage conquering adversity, with a discreet veil drawn over their mistakes or flaws. But to be regarded as a hero, to have everlasting fame, is not the preserve of the dead. There seems little doubt that many explorers were driven by an inner compulsion to be successful, for exploration was a method whereby men of limited means could achieve fame and fortune, similar to that produced by war. Moreover, many of the well-known explorers and conquerors of peoples in the newly explored lands came from relatively poor parts of their countries, such as Pizarro and Cortes in the sixteenth century, to Cook and Stanley in the eighteenth and nineteenth centuries. The determination to succeed may have been borne from their hardships during their early years; failure would have condemned these men to a similar future, giving them a great determination to succeed at all costs, for they had little to fall back on. Obviously, these examples only identify a few of the characteristics of individuals that affect perception, especially the ability to persevere with a journey, despite the apparent reality of insurmountable environmental hazards. What does seem clear is that the personality of the explorer can be influential in several aspects of an expedition. The ability to convince the sponsors of the expedition to give the applicant the leadership of the expedition is the most obvious feature. More important, in terms of the success of the venture, may be the type of personality that inspires others, that of welding the disparate members of a crew into a harmonious team, which can overcome the hazards of the journey. Of course this did not always occur. For example, despite his previous experience, Henry Hudson and a few companions were cast adrift and left to their deaths in the bay named after him, after the crew mutinied against his leadership and his plans to continue the search for a Northwest Passage. In another context Davis (1995) has argued that part of Franklin's failure of leadership in his first expedition to the Canadian arctic was linked to an authoritarian style in which he was unable to appreciate the individual characters of his native and voyageur assistants and companions, or to listen to their advice about how to live on the unfamiliar terrain in which he travelled.

IV. BIOLOGICAL ENDOWMENT

Cognitive psychologists have spent a lot of time illustrating how age affects the way the world is perceived, especially in early childhood when the system is still developing and motor skills are not yet coordinated (Piaget 1954). In the context of our interest in the application of these ideas to explorers, is less clear whether age affects their cognition since most undertake their expeditions at the physical prime of their life. Nevertheless, there seems little doubt that the decline in physical and even mental abilities may well have affected the ability of some older explorers to achieve their goals. Another important factor of the biological endowment that can affect cognitive ability comes from gender. Since there were relatively few female explorers until quite late in exploration history, the differences in gender perceptions and constructions are more difficult to identify. Historically few societies allowed women to undertake explorations, even if they wanted to; a situation that has changed radically in the last thirty years. However, Brown (1993), Blunt (1994), Blunt and Rose (1994) have begin the work of showing how female explorers and travel writers have differentially constructed the worlds they experienced, demonstrating that it is another category that should be taken into account. Whether the differences are a result of biology, or values chosen by females, or roles they are conditioned to play, is difficult to determine. After all, differences in perception and skills that seem to vary by gender, such as spatial ability, could be a product of social conditioning not biological differences, since boys in most cultures are allowed more freedom to wander further, which would give them more knowledge of other places. Although the work of feminist writers have started to show gender differences in interpretation within exploration texts, it is also worth noting that there are a few examples of women playing other roles in exploration, for some historic explorers had female companions. For example, David Thompson's pioneering journeys in the Interior Plains of Canada were helped by the presence of his native wife, who played an important supporting role, whilst the Lewis and Clark expedition was helped by the addition of Sacagawea. She was a Shoshone teenager who had been captured by other Indians and was living in a Mandan village when the expedition camped in the vicinity. Clark, in particular, did not want this young and pregnant woman to join the expedition, mainly it seems because he believed that an unattached woman would be a source of jealousy and dissention. This, of course, was a powerful reason why women were not welcome on most expeditions until recently. However Sacagawea soon demonstrated her ability to find edible plants, which showed an important environmental perception and skill not shared by the white explorers. In addition, she later proved invaluable as a translator when different Indian tribes were encountered, whilst her mere presence helped prove the peaceful intentions of the explorers in the face of frequent native suspicion (Ambrose 1996).

There seems little doubt that some individuals have exceptional talent in specific areas of intelligence, for example in music or mathematics. So at first sight the influence of genetic makeup could account for a range of particular cognitive skills that might help exploration, such as spatial, mathematical, or language ability. However, it is still not clear if such skills are really the product of inherited genes that provide some specific ability, or the presence of a more efficient cognitive system – through increased density or interactions of neurons – or the motivation to use and develop some latent ability that is found in the population at large. For example, in the development of athletic skills, Payne and Wenger (1998, 452) summarized several research publications that showed the variations between athletes was a result of dedicated training, not genetic endowment, in other words a development or acquisition not an innate capacity, although this does not deny there may be people with exceptional innate abilities. The link between genetics, skills, or even motivation in explorers, has not been the subject of any comprehensive research. But some people associated with exploration did have certain types of skills that seem to run in families and imply a genetic base. For example, William FitzWilliam Owen (1827) is regarded as one the most eminent naval surveyors of the early nineteenth century. He rose to the rank of admiral in the navy, just like his brother, a remarkable achievement in class-bound Britain, for two orphans whose parents never married. The father, Captain William Owen, came from a family of upwardly mobile landowners that hailed from Berriew in mid-Wales. He had pioneered the settlement of Campobello Island in what is now New Brunswick and had a distinguished, if minor naval career (Davies, W.K.D. 1999; 2000). But Owen's prowess in the mathematics needed for surveying was not an isolated family trait; two of his cousins won the prestigious Senior Wrangler mathematics prize as undergraduates at Cambridge University, an ability that seemed to continue in subsequent generations in the family. Obviously this is only circumstantial evidence, and can never be proved in a scientific sense since the individuals are long dead. But as more and more knowledge about genes become available, there is increasing evidence that genetic variations can have important effects on cognitive abilities. For example, there has been a recent breakthrough in the association of genes with language development. From the 1950s, the work of Chomsky (1959) and others postulated a link between genes and language, because children of whatever language group seemed able to learn language so effortlessly. However, evidence proved elusive. But in November 2001, a group of scientists (Lai et al. 2001) reported the discovery of a gene linked to speech dysfunction, the first time such a link has been confirmed. Many members of a three generational family were unable to learn certain rules of grammar and break words into sounds. These problems could not be explained by other explanations, such as low intelligence or social opportunity. The researchers found a deficiency in a specific gene in all those who had the difficulty, which indicated the problem was inherited. If replicated and extended these results will confirm that problems of the *hard wiring* in the brain, as expressed in genetic capabilities, can inhibit or alter the functioning of the cognitive system. However, one must be cautious to assign causal explanations to genetic composition in all cases. Not only are there a number of other explanations for variations in particular cognitive abilities, but it is known that when parts of the brain associated with particular functions are damaged, other areas can take over some of these functions.

This part of the cognitive system deals with the processes that convert physical stimuli from the environment into information that can be used and understood by the perception and thought processes. These can be illustrated by examples of sound and sight, although there are obviously other senses that respond to different stimuli. The physical energy we know as pressure changes in the air, or reflected light from objects, is picked up by the sensory mechanisms of the ear and the eye and converted, by the process known as transduction, into responses in the brain's neural cells; responses that code or representation the stimulus received by the sensory receptor and store the information. The precise nature of the form of the representation is far from being understood, but it is known that there are millions of neuron receptors in the various sensors and these pass on messages to different levels of what amount to higher-order neuron receptors. Although most discussion of the relationships between the cognitive system and the role of prior knowledge is concerned with vision, it is worth making a comment on another of our senses. Our ability to describe some sense experiences, such as smell, by means of words, may be less rich than those derived from other senses. For example, it is known that experienced wine tasters, are able, through odour, texture, and taste, to distinguish between a very large number of different tastes that are based on chemical compounds. Recent scientific advances have meant that these differences can be distinguished by their chemical composition through new technical apparatus, whilst the operation of the neurons in the olfactory areas of the nose are also being explored using MRI and PET devices. Although the functioning of the processes, their sites of activity and interaction paths in the brain are being unravelled, the end product, namely explanations for the nature of the communications, are still weak. What does seem clear from the stock of everyday words we have to describe such smells, is that our verbal ability to discriminate between them is pathetically limited. The limitations of human ability in this area may be compared with the much more powerful ability of many animals to discriminate between different smells and to sense them over considerable differences. More significant in the context of exploration is the recognition of the superior navigational properties of many animals and birds. Many birds, animals, and reptiles are able to travel thousands of miles each year to particular feeding or breeding grounds. The navigational processes involved are far from understood, but seem to relate to the ability of fish to identify the particular taste of rivers, for birds and animals to use the earth's magnetic fields or positions of the sun and to encode memories of migration routes. However, such migrations seem to be related to some innate urges – urges outside the consciousness that humans have been able to bring to the process of migration. Nevertheless, it is salutary to remember that other living beings, with different perceptual abilities, see, hear, and even taste things in different ways, and over greater distances; so their experience of the world is very different. In the context of spatial ability, many fish, animal, and bird species regularly navigate over vast distances, presumably using sensory devices more sophisticated than our own. However, these migrations seem to depend on innate urges, rather than the conscious decision-making that underlie human migrations and explorations.

The physical processes by which external stimuli are received and the ways that the cognitive processes convert this information into understandable knowledge is not the end of the process of cognition. Humans have been able to build machines or devices that not only enable a more precise understanding of physical phenomena, but to extend the range of their senses through what might be called *technological sensing*. Much of the increased knowledge we have of the environment is due to the ability to see more and more detail, and to understand more of the more detailed physical processes in operation. In part, this is a matter of training the eye to see the phenomena under investigation, as well as the use of experimental techniques, helped initially by the standardization of approaches to measurement, such as temperature gauges or latitude-longitude systems of representation. The strict categories used in these systems enabled comparative study, and the accumulation of more and more data and knowledge about the phenomena under investigation. But during the last hundred years, we have seen the application of more powerful measuring devices, from microscopes to radar and remote sensing from satellites. These are based on the ability of humans to create machines that record light spectra and sound waves that lie outside the range of human senses. In the same way, sound and light waves have been harnessed by the development of radio and television, which enable communication across greater and greater distances. All the new machines sense or communicate these stimuli and convert the information into data that we can understand. Most of these new technical devices are a product of the last hundred years, with a huge increase in their scope within the last twenty years because of the increasing use of electronic techniques. The result is an accelerating knowledge base of the environment, based on new sensory devices that have immensely increased the scope and quality of human perceptions, far beyond the constraints of our biological heritage.

C. PERCEPTION OR COGNITIVE CONVERSION

The importance of the role of perception in understanding how explorers viewed the new lands has already been discussed in the previous chapter. But cognitive psychologists have shown that the conversion of information from the senses into the initial images of the places is not the result of a single stage or process. What we know of *reality* seems to be conditioned by a large number of distinct, yet interacting processes. Hence what we see, or hear, or taste, is as much a product of our cognitive and interpretative processes as the initial environmental stimuli. They are not some abstract reality. Our cognitive processes *condition* what we see, or consider important enough to describe, so there cannot be an unequivocal one-to-one relationship with some assumed reality.

I. INITIAL REPRESENTATION, RECOGNITION, AND SELECTION

Cognitive research has shown that the first stage of what we know as visual perception involves the conversion of the physical stimuli into an internal representation from the coded messages of the stimulus. Little is known about the nature of this representation because it is subsequently modified. The perceptual process also involves the *selection* of information from among the barrage of sensory information available to the senses. Our sophisticated perceptual processes automatically seem to focus on parts of the information of interest. However, the selection of information from the variety of potential stimuli in the environment can vary from individual to individual, and what is chosen, frequently involves prior knowledge. For example, successful maritime explorers were aware of particular cues that they selected from the environment. Some may have been encouraged or depressed during the journey when comets or meteors were seen, because these were interpreted by their beliefs in cosmic or heavenly intervention. But at a more mundane level many maritime explorers used previous experience to interpret the appearance of seagulls or drifting vegetation as indicators of nearby land. Leaders of expeditions often used such signs to convince their doubting crew to sail on. Other environmental features, such as the set of the tides, were often used to support ideas about the presence of sea passages through what was first seen as an inlet – a feature that crops up time and time again in early-seventeenth-century discussions about a route from Hudson Bay to the Indies. In another context, the way that the perceptual process of individual explorers focused upon, or favoured, particular land assemblages, involved selection through aesthetic preference, as shown by previous discussions on how nineteenth-century explorers of Canada adopted the English principles of the picturesque and sublime to describe the new country they explored (MacLaren 1985, 51).

The examples show that the processes of selection of information from the various stimuli and the ability to recognize it as something distinct or useful for the purpose in hand depends in part on previous knowledge. But the discussion of the recent work of literary critics in chapter 2 has shown that there is no guarantee that the interpretations that we make are the same from person to person, or from group to group. Yet it has been observed there is often a broad consensus between individuals in a society conditioned by a similar culture, otherwise there can be no communication or agreement on what is seen and accepted (Lowenthal 1961). Of course, there is no reason why different groups of people would see the world in the same way. So, the sights that are seen, or more precisely the sights that are interpreted, do not have a simple one-to-one relationship with the reality. Behavioural psychologists have spent a great deal of effort in trying to understand how we represent and understand information. For example, in the specific context of our perception and representation of space, a major review paper by Deregowksi (1989) showed the effect of cross-cultural influences in understanding pictures of objects. She argued that contrary to the work of some philosophers, pictorial space is not simply a representation based on conventions, but is a derivative of real space. However, the way this space is *seen* varies among cultural groups. This gives rise to major cultural differences in understanding what is represented. In the context of exploration, Europeans were intruding upon peoples with quite varied cultures, who looked different, and had alternative systems of representation. So the interpretations Europeans placed on the appearance and character of the indigenous peoples, as well as their words, gestures, and actions, could be very different from those intended by these peoples.

II. MEMORY

An essential part of the process of cognition is played by memory, which essentially involves the three fold functions of acquisition, retention, and retrieval of information received by the senses and other sources. Again understanding of the detailed structure and functioning of memory is only gradually emerging and there is still disagreement over whether all the information originally stored in the mind is always there and can be recalled under certain conditions, rather than being lost. Obviously the ability to retrieve information about the exploration accurately is an essential input for subsequent stages of knowledge construction, but there seems little doubt that memory is subject to selectivity, distortion, and all-out failure. It is well-known that memory in elderly people, or people suffering from severe trauma, is prone to failure, but a recent book by Schacter (2001) argues that such errors are inherent within the processes of memory, so all can be affected by these problems. Among the seven major sources of memory error that he identified, the follow-ing three seem likely to be very important in the context of exploration: Misattribution, in which a thought or dream is substituted for the real event; Suggestibility, in which distortions are produced subsequently by biased leading questions or conflicting evidence; Misremembering, that of making the past seem more like the present. These seem to be par-ticularly influential in leading to distortions in the way that the *memory* of explorers operate, in addition to the other main factors he identified: forgetfulness, absentmindedness, temporary blocking, and persist-ence, such as when the effect of severe emotions persist and distort the memory, when they would be best forgotten.

III. LANGUAGE

The brief discussion on the role of language in chapter 2 has shown that critical analysts and cognitive scientists both regard language as a key component in the process of understanding. However the precise role is a matter of debate, with the former convinced that language comes first, whilst many psychologists believe that language and thought may be inextricably mixed or may be a reflection of the world. The basis of former perspective was found in the linguistic relativity hypothesis of the 1950s (Whorf 1956; Saunders and Van Brakel 1997). This argued against the standard scientific view that there were universal categories behind sense experiences, such as a basic set of colours derived from the physical colour spectrum. Instead, the hypothesis maintained that people do not see the world simply with their eyes, but with the language they use to express the things they see. This means that the act of identifica-tion, and the ability to share this information with others, depends on the presence of categories of language, words, and terms that are used to describe the features seen. But it has already been noted that literary theorists have argued that words are only arbitrary codes for the objects, events, or ideas. Since there can never be a complete one-to-one relationship between any word and with the feature it represents, there is always room for inaccuracy in representation. In addition, the world has been described and recorded in many different languages, each with their own structures and subtleties, producing even more basis for variations in the relationships between the real world and how we perceive it. Also, languages are more or less rich in the range of words that are available or have been invented. The English language is particularly complex, in part because it has adopted a large number of words from other languages to describe previously unknown features; the Indian word *chinook*, or *snow eater*, for a føhn-like wind from the Rockies, is one of the best-known Canadian examples. But beyond the stock of new words may be the recognition that some cultures have far more words for objects that other cultures may see as being of a single type. The classic example may be the recognition that the Inuit of Northern Canada have words for six different seasons and have over twenty different words for snow, and a similar number for ice (Whorf 1956; P. Pressman 1995). Each of these relates to a different condition, crucial for a people who live in an environment that is snowbound for most of the year. So, the simple word *snow* or *ice*, or rather their Inuit equivalents, fail to communicate the nuances of an environment of different types of snow. Only people who live in an environment with many different snow conditions, who need an intimate knowledge of the differences to be able to survive, are likely to possess a language so rich in snow or ice categories. Similar situations exist in languages of people who live in other unique environments. The problem of translating the experiences of people of one language into another, is made more difficult, or even impossible, when one also recognizes that words have symbolic associations and alliterative values that may not work in another language and may be designed for quite different audiences (Venuti 1992).

Although the linguistic relativity hypothesis is still controversial, a recent study seems to have provided new support (Davidoff, I. Davies, and Roberson 1999). The Berino, an isolated Stone Age people in Papua New Guinea, were shown to have the same colour vision as people from economically advanced societies, but had different word categories to identify colours. The Berino had fewer colour categories, did not recognize the blue-green division, and separated colours called *nol* and *wor*, categories that did not exist in English. This evidence means that the Berino tribe's description of the world, and their ability to communicate these variations with others, is bound to be different. Hence, the identification of the character or quality of any new object is not a simple matter of choice of what to record, but the linguistic categorization of the features. Our understanding, in other words, is crucially dependent upon how we conceptualize and label objects and their variety; this is culturally conditioned. Davidoff, I. Davies, and Roberson (1999) argued that their results showed that colour categories could not be considered to be universal, a product of some formation around natural breaks in perceptual colour space; instead words from different societies use different divisions in what may appear as a continuum to categorize phenomena. However, it might be noted that the study was based on a Stone Age tribe. It is possible that the spread of modernization in the world may impose a set of general categories upon those affected by contemporary life, but again, this is a cultural effect, not a perceptual one. Gage's (1999) comprehensive overview of the perception of colour also supported the cultural conditioning view. But linguistic relativity ideas are heavily criticized by those who believe that all languages depend on some basic generative grammar linked to the genetic human ability to acquire language in whatever form (Chomsky 1988; Devitt and Sterelny 1986). Cromer (1988, 245), a leading cognitive psychologist, started research with the premise that language comes first, but changed his mind on the basis of his experimental results and the work of others, although noting that evidence supported both views. Yet many still argue that the concept may be *one* of the features affecting our interpretation of the environment (Lave 1988; Berry and Dasen 1974). Applying the complex and interactive system approach favoured by cognitive psychologists led Cromer to the conclusion that there is a two way process of interaction and modification between language and thought within the mind. So it can be suggested that the *language first* and *language reflection* views may both be partially right.

D. THOUGHT PROCESSES

Figure 3.2 shows that cognitive psychologists have identified at least three important sets of processes in the ability to create thought: decision-making and judgement, conceptualization and categorization, and expertise or skills. Although these issues refer to the internal mind processes that affect cognition, the ideas are still useful for conceptualising some of the key issues that can affect the process of cognition in any explorer confronting the new worlds and affecting his or her understanding of these areas.

I. DECISION-MAKING AND MODIFICATION

John Allen's work on various explorers (1975a,b) has argued that the role of prior ideas was not simply a factor influencing the initial exploratory goal. As significant was the way the subsequent behaviour was modified as discrepancies between a preconceived image and the new information of personal observation emerged. In John Allen's words:

> *Imagination becomes a behavioural factor in geographical discovery as courses of action are laid out according to pre-conceived images; later decisions based on field observation may be distorted by these images. (Allen, J. L. 1975b, 43)*

Allen's essay went on to suggest that it is possible to view the behavioural changes experienced by explorers in terms of transitional zones, or areas where the initial images begin to be recognized as being inconsistent with the emerging reality. The successful explorers, at least in terms of the expedition's survival, were those who made the modification quickly. They used the personal experience of the new lands to modify the route being travelled, or to recognize and use locally available foods. Allen emphasized that explorers in new lands could not depend upon prior personal experience. They usually had to use information derived from abstract reasoning or previous belief systems, with the result that "when efforts are made to describe *terrae incognitae*, extrapolations from the known become confused with the believed, conjectured, or desired" (Allen, J. L., 1975b, 42). The result is that the actual path of the journey of exploration often showed a discrepancy between the pre-conceived image, and the emerging reality of the distribution of land and sea or the destination that was sought. Allen argued that unless explorers were able to modify their behaviour in the light of the new information, the expedition often ended in disaster. This argument means that a new criterion for judging the success of expeditions can be postulated. It would be based on whether explorers modified their behaviour and survived, with minimum loss of life among their crew, enabling them to produce an account of the lands that were traversed. This type of evaluation could replace the older standard of evaluation, based on whether explorers found what they were looking for – in retrospect, often an impossible task, since often the expected place or route did not exist.

In the case of many explorations, the emerging empirical reality uncovered by the journey was often very different to the image held by the explorer. There is little doubt that many explorers only reluctantly altered their initial images. Some of the greatest myths continued to exert their power even after many negative findings – as can be seen by the frequent attempts to search for the land of *Six Golden Cities*, *El Dorado*, the *Land of Prester John*, or even the Northwest Passage. John Allen (1975b) noted that negative results in search of these objectives did not lead to the abandonment of the belief or the myth. If explorers did not find the sought-after place or route in one location, they often felt it must exist somewhere else. The result was a transposition in space, a new image or expectation of where a place was supposed to be, new locations that attracted their own expeditions. Moreover, even when new lands were found, they were often interpreted on the basis of the old ideas. For example, up to the time of his death, Columbus still seemed to believe that he had found the edge of Asia, not a new continent. So it is ironic that we celebrate Columbus for discovering America, which was a continent he was reluctant to believe in. Perhaps the greatest of these beliefs was the search for the Northwest Passage, the persisting idea that there was a water route around the north of America, despite centuries of contrary findings, at least about a commercially viable route. Hence, the strength of these pre-conceived views, what we can now see as erroneous images, cannot be underestimated. They often drove explorers on, well beyond any rational evidence that was accumulated during the journey. In some cases they represented a futile attempt to accomplish goals that we can now see were impossible to achieve. For other explorers it was only this persistence based on false images that allowed new discoveries to be made – often of places never conceived of. Of course, determination can also lead to disaster, if linked to errors of judgment, and inability to take advice, as in the case of Scott's Antarctic expedition or Franklin's disappearance in search of the Northwest Passage. But the flawed leaders of these disasters were often glorified as heroes in subsequent jingoistic accounts written by their supporters, because they had became symbols of their nation, examples of courage conquering adversity, with a discrete veil drawn over their mistakes or flaws. To be regarded as a hero, to have everlasting fame in an explorer's life-time, is not only the reward of the dead.

An important stage in our understanding is the way that the variety of the world is reduced to manageable proportions by putting objects, events or ideas into different groups. But an important stage in our cognitive understanding of the new worlds lay in the ability to reduce the complexity of the individual experiences to more manageable proportions by categorizing and conceptualising, putting objects into summary categories, of form or experience, or in the case of concepts, into categories of ideas. A simple example of this process can be seen by the way that the native peoples of North America are still often known as Indians, since this was the term given to them by explorers who thought they were on the edge of the Indies. More derogatory was their categorisation as 'savages,' a term with all sorts of negative implications. Olive Dickason's (1997) comprehensive survey of the early contacts between the Europeans and aboriginal peoples in Canada has shown the way the latter were represented as savages, a category based on the mistaken idea that they were people without any real culture or social order; as such, the natives were considered to be little different from animals. So mistaken prior knowledge was used to interpret and categorize a continent of people. Given this misconception, Europeans thought it was their duty to introduce order, as well as Christianity; all part of what they saw as bringing civilisation to replace the 'barbaric' practises of the native peoples of the New World. It has taken centuries for researchers of European origin to acknowledge that aboriginal peoples had highly stratified societies with complex rules and intimate links with the local environment. Most native societies were virtually destroyed by European contact and the survivors are still struggling in many areas to gain recognition of their historic land rights, especially in those areas where there was a great deal of seasonal migration. In general, therefore, the pre-conceptions of the explorers often led to dangerously inaccurate misinterpretations of the empirical evidence. Campbell expressed the point clearly in her essay on Columbus:

> The narration of Columbus is occluded by a dense veil of preconceptions: he has a word for everything, and an imaginary map to whose features everything he finds can be made to correspond. (Campbell 1988, 233)

In some ways this problem is reminiscent of the way that the medieval world maps were based on religious beliefs, rather than a representation attempting locational accuracy. But this medieval approach was not to last. The new worlds that Columbus's voyages heralded, began to be described in empirical terms – at least in their locational content – rather than in allegorical terms. Nevertheless, the underlying European beliefs in moral superiority, and the right to exploit and settle, still conditioned much of the rest of the writings of explorers and settlers, which often became justifications for particular ways of thinking and writing about the new worlds and their peoples. In the context of the natural world more dispassionate approaches were developed as part of the Enlightenment passion for ordering and cataloguing. By the late eighteenth century, scientists interested in botany, geography and geology were added to the complement of many naval expeditions, whilst scientists such as Von Humboldt organized their own expeditions. These specialists produced their own systems of classification that provided greater understanding of the variety of species and landforms in the world, leading to new explanations of the processes of differentiation in the physical world and the development of the separate sciences. But it was the writing and dissemination of these scientific reports that was crucial, since they provided a storehouse of knowledge and ideas that subsequent investigators could use and expand or modify. Exploration was not simply about finding out about unknown places; it was increasingly dominated by attempts to understand the variety and origin of natural features.

III. COGNITIVE SKILLS AND ABILITIES

The range of different cognitive skills that affect the conversion of physical stimuli into what we might call understandable information is far from clearly understood. In the context of exploration, however, certain types of skills and abilities, such as way-finding, memorizing ability, or problem-solving abilities seem to be especially helpful. Most researchers in human biology argue that humans have similar innate cognitive abilities. But, there is little doubt that some individuals or groups in particular environments have developed much greater cognitive skills – perhaps through trial and error, intensive training and their methodological approach – rather than from new innate mechanisms particular to the group. But the skills of the European explorer now seems quite limited when compared with those of many so-called 'primitive' people who were able to travel over large distances using attributes that are almost forgotten and were often denigrated by Europeans. By the sixteenth century most European explorers operated deductively, working out a specific plan and applying these principles to the details and events of their journey. However, the deliberate plan approach, based on a map using latitude-longitude conventions, was only generally adopted from the Renaissance onwards, although older systematic systems had been used, such as the use of portolian charts in medieval times. The deliberate plan approach using the systems of latitude and longitude led to major transformation in how journeys were conducted, making the provision of accurate maps a major requirement if others were subsequently able to replicate the voyages. Moreover it was not until efficient time pieces were developed at the end of the eighteenth century that the problem of longitude was really solved. In contrast, the ancient Polynesians were able to travel vast distances across what seemed to be trackless oceans to the first Europeans without using maps. In a study dealing with the effect of culture on cognitive ability, Gladwin (1974) argued that Trukense navigators operated in a completely different way to their European counterparts. These seamen had a unique set of spatial skills, based on what Turnbull (1999) has called performance, rather than representational, navigation ability. The Polynesians based their navigation upon an intimate knowledge of star systems and what stars could be seen from different locations, as well as the ability to know how far they had travelled each day under a variety of different weather conditions. In addition, their navigators constantly modified their voyage, by reacting to the environmental conditions that were found, such as the set of tides, winds and the stars and their perception of minute changes in environmental conditions, such as waves bouncing off some unseen land. These modifications were done non-verbally, adjusting their journey almost by instinct; although the behaviour must have been learned they seemed to operate in an almost inductive fashion, without a detailed plan. This was probably the type of method adopted by pre-literate humans, who purposely travelled over large distances throughout history. Hence, the progress of the Polynesians was constantly adjusted, as much by instinct, as a prepared plan. Some of the knowledge was taught, or came from experience; but as much may be from perception of environmental clues that would be unappreciated by Europeans who did not live so close to the environment and came from different climes. Few modern Polynesians now have such skills; this is a geographical ability that has almost been lost, linked to skills that were developed and valued in another culture. Yet there is little doubt that many European explorers, especially the land-based explorers, recognized that they needed local peoples to help them in their work. Their knowledge of the location of places was complemented by the ability of their guides to question at least some of the people that they met, and to make them feel more able to trust the strange white men. Although the information obtained was not always accurate or believable, in many cases the native guides *were* literally 'guides,' taking the explorers to the destinations sought after. Hence it could be argued that the white explorers only 'discovered' new lands and routes because of the pre-existing knowledge of the indigenous peoples, although this was certainly not true in all explorations. Where there was a great deal of indigenous knowledge, the achievement of the white explorers was to cobble together the local or regional understanding, and made it available to a world audience in their books and maps; their discoveries, after all, were discoveries for outsiders, not those who lived in the lands explored.

The different approach to way-finding used by Polynesians and other Pre-Renaissance voyagers was not an innate condition. Rather it seems to be a honing of the perceptual abilities latent in humans. These are a consequence of other influences, such as previous knowledge and the extent of training, although there may also be differences in the locational ability of individuals, as well as cultural differences in the ability to achieve such skills (Berry and Irvine 1988), since some societies would value and encourage these abilities over others. Nevertheless, however much we may admire the skills of the ancient navigators, there seems little doubt that humans have relatively limited innate ability to navigate large distances compared to other living species, such as salmon, birds and turtles, which are able to travel vast distances to their breeding grounds or food sources. How this behaviour evolved is still a mystery. Humans, by developing more sophisticated rational processing and technological skills, are able to duplicate long distance movements through learned and plan-led methodologies, rather than from innate ability.

✛ 3. THE CONSTRUCTION OF THE NARRATIVE

It has been shown that the various components of our perceptual processes condition and filter the raw sense experiences of the journey of exploration. The process of writing a narrative about the exploration is also affected by a large number of factors that involve a further transformation of the initial cognition of the new lands, which can be more easily understood by using the term 'construction' not simply 'writing,' to stress the way that the text is actually built up. There is little doubt that similar modifications took place when the explorer gave speeches describing the journey. But the production of a written text usually takes more time, is more considered, and if diffused via the printing press, reached a wider audience. The result is a new form of discourse, that is far from the direct relationship between the perceptions and the final written text – the type of relationship posited as route B on figure 2.1.

Before discussing the various elements within the construction of a written text it is worth re-emphasizing a point made earlier, namely the advantage of a written culture in priorizing interpretations. Since most of the peoples of Africa and the Americas who came into contact with Europeans had no means of permanently recording *their* views of the environment, or *their* views of contact with other cultures, it is primarily the European views that have survived. These have been regarded as the 'facts' that described the new worlds. In addition, it must be remembered that any written text describing an exploration is not simply reflexive of what was seen; it is 'constructed' by authors who are affected by a large number of factors. Of course, these features are intertwined in complex ways in practise, whilst individual authors are affected by many different influences. Nevertheless, the analytical separation of these influences helps us to understand the factors that condition the construction of narratives of discovery. There are some parallels here with studies that involve field work in community settings, where researchers always have to try and define the character of a distinctive group or people, and identify the factors that affect how the community is represented. For example, Arensburg and Kimbal (1965) identified the types of data and methods needed for studies of communities and the influences on these groups, whilst the dimensions of community variation are being conceptualised and measured (Davies and Herbert 1994; Davies and Townshend 1999). More generally, Clifford (1986, 6) provided a checklist of the factors that influenced how anthropological accounts are written. He proposed five major sets of influences: the institutional setting of the text (audience, school of thought, etc.); the genre (such as scholarly or newspaper article); the power that sustains the authority of the author (colonial administrator, major journalist, famed explorer etc.); the social milieu in which the work was written; and the historical context that makes all the factors contingent upon a time and place. It seemed appropriate to extend and re-organize this list to provide a longer summary of the influences that have more relevance to the specific field of exploration literature. These factors are shown on the right hand side of figure 3.1, but for the sake of comprehension they have been grouped into four broad categories: *the initial representations, the influences on the author, the author's gloss, and the constraints that are faced.* The first category of influences describes the initial representations that are made, especially the notes and records made in the field during the process of exploration. The second category deals with the factors that affect the explorer, once the task of rendering his experiences into a written form is undertaken. The third refers to the organizational and stylistic practises that are employed in the actual writing. The fourth relates to the various constraints or difficulties that the author has to resolve if the text is to be completed and published. Each of these categories contains a number of more detailed influences that demonstrate the complexity of the forces affecting the content, organization and style of the exploration narrative; in addition, figure 3.1 shows that all are subject to the contingencies of the context, in time and space.

A. INITIAL REPRESENTATIONS

A vital source of material for any person constructing an account of an expedition is, of course, the specific records that were usually made during the journey, such as occasional notes, journals or regular daily logs. The practise of keeping a daily log was a common procedure on board ships, indeed the British Admiralty made it mandatory for naval captains. The log recorded daily location, environmental conditions, especially tides and harbour conditions, as well as the major events of the day. It had the advantage of providing a formal substantial record that could be consulted at a later date when the final book was constructed. Many land explorers adopted the same practise. The accuracy of David Thompson's maps of the interior of the Canadian Plains and Western Canada in the early nineteenth century (Tyrrell 1916; Glover 1986; Belyea 1994), were a product of his meticulous observations. Each twist and turn in his journeys, often by river, was carefully described. These records provided a mine of locational information and were used to construct detailed maps of the west, maps that were prized as being the best of their kind for over a half a century – quite an achievement at a time of increasing technical sophistication in map construction. Many of the daily measurements made by explorers, as well as additional ideas and observations, were jotted down under difficult circumstances, often in wet or freezing conditions. In many cases these original records have been lost, so the primary sources are no longer available to scholars. But for most late-eighteenth and nineteenth-century explorers the original journals, daily logs and field observations still exist, but are often in poor condition because of the passage of time and the conditions under which they were made and kept. Interest in the primary material of the explorations has led to the publication of books reproducing this material in the last twenty years.

The emphasis of most written daily records of explorers was upon location. But by the mid-eighteenth century there was increasing interest in the relief of the land, its minerals, climate, flora and fauna, as well as the character of the people and their customs. Verbal descriptions in notebooks were supplemented by detailed charts, sketches, or even paintings. Much of this work involved the cataloguing of locations and the character of places, often supplemented by the collection of minerals and plants, or even the capture of native peoples to exhibit to the curious in the homeland. In part, this interest in exotic plants can be seen as the overseas version of a new eighteenth-century passion in Britain, as exemplified in the mid- to late-eighteenth-century work of Gilbert White in Dorset. Raymond Williams (1972, 119) argued that White's work was a new way of looking at the facts of an area. It provided the beginnings of the study of a nature separated from man. The approach was complemented by the new and very different perspectives of the romantic poets, who described the way that certain landscapes provided emotional reactions, although the primitive compilers of environmental information were not averse to making their own aesthetic comments about landscapes. But White was far from the only pioneer of the new study of nature and the environment. In the early eighteenth century, Hutton and other early geologists studied other aspects of nature through the developing scientific eye. Their emphasis was upon process, upon the origin of landforms and the geological conditions that made them, not on the aesthetic qualities of the land. It was gradually realized that landforms had taken millennia to create, a new understanding that eventually displaced the older Christian belief that the earth had been created by God in only a few days. Initially, this unravelling of the processes of geological and landscape evolution was seen by many as enhancing man's understanding of the mechanisms of the world. The new knowledge simply provided proof of the variety and complexity of a God-given ordered nature, providing many investigators with a re-assertion of their faith.

In the cultural sphere, the journals of discovery provided accounts of the number and racial character of the peoples encountered, aspects of their character, customs and artefacts. There is often an important interpretive component in such descriptions, which provides an overlap with the next major domain of functions. Given the eurocentric views of the observers, the native peoples encountered were often described in derogatory tones. David Thompson may have had a better regard for native Indians than many of his fellow fur traders, for his aboriginal wife was a constant companion throughout his adult life and was able to do her share of moving goods and setting up tents. But he still judged many aboriginal practises by his Christian values. For example, in December 1797 he described one of the Mandan ceremonies as "detestable" and went on to state that "the curse of the Mandanes is an almost total want of chastity." (Thompson, in Glover 1962, 177–78). Mackenzie (Lamb 1970, 183) on his voyage down the river named after him, described the native peoples he encountered near the Great Bear river in the following pejorative language: "they are all ugly, meagre, ill made people, particularly about the legs ... many are sickly, owing, I imagine, to their Dirty ways of living." Mackenzie (Lamb, 1970, 184) even attributed the absence of any sense of shame about nakedness among the males, whose genitals were often exposed, as a product of their creation at the Arctic Circle. This meant their consciousness was not affected by the ideas associated with the Christian view of creation and the roles played by the serpent, Eve, or the tree of wisdom – presumably occupants of semi-tropical areas! But the cultural characteristics described were not an inventory of what was seen, rather they were the characteristics that impressed the writers enough to be recorded. Moreover, their descriptions of human character, settlement, or culture, were rarely systematic, whilst they were not as amenable to precise recording as the physical features were, such as the height of the land, or the temperature – although these records were primitive until the late eighteenth century, when more accurate measuring instruments became widely available. Yet there are a few examples of almost systematic recording, especially by artists, such as Catlin's (1845) pioneering series of the portraits of mid-western American Indians and their manners, customs and conditions. However, this survey was carried out at a much later date than the first exploration of the land and the portrayals were affected by the artist's beliefs and values.

The ability of explorers to describe and understand the land in which they travelled was not simply a matter of their own personal cognitive ability; it was also linked to the technology of measurement. Eva Taylor (1930) demonstrated how more and more sophisticated measuring devices were used to estimate latitude and longitude in the Tudor and Stuart periods in England, whilst Waters (1958) has described the whole history of navigation in detail. Latitude proved relatively easy to estimate. The problem of longitude was not really solved until Harrison's work in the mid-eighteenth century led to the development of accurate mechanical clocks which would keep Greenwich time, enabling the explorer to estimate his longitude by comparing this information with the time of the local sunrise. Sobel (1996) has provided a fascinating account of the difficulties that Harrison experienced, not simply in creating accurate mechanical devices, but getting others to believe in his project, given the opposition from so many scientists, navigators, and members of the Admiralty who believed that the compilation of accurate lunar tables would provide a better method – one far cheaper than the expensive timepieces that were made by people regarded as mere artisans! But despite the opposition, Harrison's H4 clock proved its worth, although it was his colleague Kendall's K-1 clock that was selected for Cook's second and third Pacific voyages beginning in 1772 and 1776. By the late eighteenth century reasonably accurate, and more to the point standardizestandardized, means of measuring temperature were used. Similar examples of more sophisticated measurements applied to other aspects of the physical environment, provided the ability to gain much more knowledge of the physical environment and its spatial variations, especially after the mechanical and scientific inventions of the Industrial Revolution. These, in turn, led to greater understanding of the processes involved. The consequence of these changes was that the knowledge of where places were becomes technologically determined and dependent. Unfortunately, similar progress in measurement within the cultural sphere was not possible, given the huge number of variations in the cultural attributes of various peoples. However, there was an important advantage in this context. The explorer frequently came into contact with aboriginal peoples who had their own knowledge of the local environment. Most major expeditions used native peoples to guide them; help either based on the guide's own experience and knowledge, or by their ability to get the required information from other indigenous peoples they met along their line of travel. The information was vital in the success of many European explorations, but the names of the native guides, with a few exceptions, are forgotten and rarely honoured.

Figure 3.1 shows that four major types of influences can be identified as having significant effects upon the author of an exploration narrative: the historical and social context; the sources that were available and used; the intentions of the author, especially the audience to which the book was aimed; and the personal characteristics of the author.

The first set of influences upon any author are those usually taken for granted, namely the *context of the work*, the cultural and historical circumstances in which the work was written. Three of the influences identified by Clifford (1986) fall into this category, namely: the historical context, social setting and sustaining power. The new historicism (Veseer 1989, Hamilton 1996) has shown that any text can only be understood in the terms of the broad cultural conditions in which it is written. This is not to deny the fact that people from different cultures or time periods can provide their own interpretations of some historical event or text. But without an appreciation of the particular contingencies of time and place – such as the technology or knowledge base of society, and the political and social conditions – any text is likely to be drastically misinterpreted if the mores and interpretations of a different period are used. In most cases explorers almost unconsciously adopt the standard philosophies and attitudes of the day; if they adopt very different approaches their work runs the risk of not being understood by their contemporaries. Moreover, the authority that is provided by the sponsors of the journey, the wealth of the author or family, or the publication source, provide the author with the means to carry out the exploration, and frequently the time and resources to write their work. Yet this authority may also create many constraints. Although these will be discussed in a subsequent section, it is necessary to note here that the sponsors may not wish all the facts about a journey to be made public, and often requested that their own contribution was reported in a flattering light. All these factors ensure that the writings of explorers can only be fully appreciated within their own, and frequently self-absorbed cultures, based on the specific political or commercial circumstances that generated the journey. In large part, therefore, explorers not only *see*, but *write or construct* the new world through the mirror of their own. Yet we must be careful not to denigrate the importance of hindsight, and the way that the exploration fits into the wider context of knowledge. The significance of many explorations was not always understood at the time of the initial discovery. It is only with subsequent use, either of the land or new products, that the utility of the discoveries was subsequently appreciated and understood.

The second main set of influences upon the writer relate to the *additional sources used* to construct the text. Some have already been discussed, such as: the role of prior beliefs, the personal experiences obtained, the initial records made during the expedition, and information obtained from indigenous peoples. What became increasingly important in the Renaissance was the availability of other written sources. In literary theory terms these are usually described as the intertextual influences, where observations and meanings are derived from other published sources and are often reproduced related publications (Eagleton 1983, 138). During the early Renaissance, classical sources were often a treasured source of information. These sources were endowed with an historical authority because of the reverence given to Greek or Roman authors and philosophers, although the new explorations often showed that many of these valued sources were incorrect.

Another problem in interpretation comes from the fact that not all the sources used are identified or acknowledged in the final narratives of explorers. Whitehead's (1997) appraisal of Raleigh's classic 'Discoverie ... of Guiana' published in 1596 demonstrates how Raleigh used previous Spanish narratives as the basis for much of his book and also how he benefited from the capture of Antonio de Barrio, who had detailed knowledge of the area. Whitehead (1997, 40–44) maintains that Spanish and Latin American scholars do not hold Raleigh's work in high esteem because they consider that much of the book is not original. The so-called 'discoverie' may have been new in England, but it described areas well-known to the Spanish, for they had been trading with, and exploiting the area for over eighty years. Nevertheless, Raleigh did add important original information to his narrative which could only have been derived from the results of his own expedition, and his book did have a significant impact on public opinion given its wide readership, helped by its translation into many languages. This example also reminds us of the importance of non-written information as source material. Explorers frequently interrogated native peoples at length about their knowledge of neighbouring lands. Sea-borne explorers did the next best thing; they sought information from sailors who had been near the areas into which they were venturing. Although there are few sources that enable investigators to pinpoint the influence of this acquired knowledge, the practical advice from experienced seamen must have been a crucial asset. Most contemporary authorities (Quinn 1961; 1977; Wilson, I. 1991) believe that Bristol seamen had knowledge of the fishing grounds off the Newfoundland Grand Banks for at least a decade before Cabot reached the northern shores of America. This may account for the reason why John Cabot deliberately moved to Bristol, the small, but still premier port of western Britain, rather than basing himself in London, near the royal court whose permission was also needed for his expedition to be legal.

A third major set of influences relate to the *intentions* of the explorer, to the way that author tries to address or respond to the audience that is expected to read the book, or review the problem that was faced. Perhaps most explorers were trying to describe the new lands in their journals, primarily to inform their readers. But those that are writing about newly discovered peoples were also writing what amounted to a social commentary – given the inevitable comparison made by the author or the reader, either implicitly or explicitly, to their own practises. Many of the indigenous aboriginal behaviours were viewed with horror, as the examples of Thompson and Mackenzie have already shown. Unfortunately, we do not have written records to remind us that natives viewed many European practises with the same repugnance. But it must not be forgotten that explorers may also be emphasizing particular emotions and feelings about the new worlds, as much for their target audience as an expression of their own feelings, whether it be expressions of 'wonder', or the 'pleasure' to be found in a new environment, or 'fear' or 'apprehension.' Also, the author may be trying to convince some sponsor, or his countrymen, of some deeply held opinion, that could act as a future catalyst of change. Much of the promotional literature associated with plantation or colonisation schemes falls into this category. Vaughan's (1626) classic work The Golden Fleece represents such an example; it was a book designed to encourage emigration to the new colony of Newfoundland. In the context of exploration, many leaders of expeditions who failed to achieve their main objective were not averse to adding recommendations for another expedition to complete their task. Other European explorers often recommended that missionaries should be sent to the new lands to convert the native peoples into Christian ways.

But however much individual values affected the decision of what to include in a book, one question faced all authors; who is the work written for? Hence, the construction of the text, its content and phrasing usually took the anticipated audience into account. But we must be careful and recognize that not all exploration writings were destined for a mass audience. Greenblatt (1991) has reminded us that much of the literature was initially written as a private account for a monarch or commercial company and may only recently have been made public. Davis's (1998) work has shown that Franklin was very much aware of the considerable financial rewards that would accrue from publication of a narrative of his expeditions – if the book was able to attain a popular readership. Davis provides examples of the way that Franklin altered his initial version of events, to broaden the appeal of the text. For example, in his initial log, the reason provided for climbing hills was largely of a utilitarian nature: it was a typical aid to subsequent navigation across unfamiliar terrain, one that achieved more near sunset when one could normally see much further. But Franklin's subsequent narratives often rephrased the initial descriptions, such as the explanation that: "the softened light at this time is more conducive to an appreciation of a delicately textured landscape" (Davis 1998, 74). This illustrates an artistic rather than a utilitarian purpose for hill-climbing, although it can be argued that both functions can apply. The example demonstrates the way that the initial impressions were changed during the writing process. Davis's introduction to his edited version of Franklin's daily records encapsulated the key issue.

> *Franklin, like all of us, was a product of the culture in which he lived, his writing, like all writing, not only reflected his culture's values but was shaped to win the favour of that culture. (Davis 1998, 75)*

Yet recognition of the need to write for a particular readership, especially the choice between alternative writing styles, may be more of an issue in the specialized literate worlds after the mid-eighteenth century, simply because there are so many different types of readers. Moreover, in the early Renaissance it was almost mandatory for the explorer-author to demonstrate erudition by referring to classical sources and often interpreting what was seen through this knowledge – even if we can now see that they distorted the world that was seen. In the contemporary period it is obvious that writing for the audience of a scholarly journal or society requires a very different approach to that required for an article in a mass circulation newspaper. Given popular interest in the discovery of new lands, or the need to reach some difficult objective such as the North and South Pole at the end of the nineteenth century, newspapers deliberately sponsored expeditions, often rivalling those set up by their competitors. The journey of discovery was turned into a race. Sensationalism characterized the writing style. Readers bought the paper which described the latest exploits of *their* explorer (Riffenburg 1993). So some accounts of explorations were not only deliberately *shaped* (Davis 1998), but were a record of events that were *created* by the perceived demands of the readership.

Another set of important influences on the construction of any exploration narrative come from the *personal characteristics* of the author. It has already been suggested that these influence how the author perceives the world, features that complement the general cultural background that conditions so much of the description. But they also affect how the text is written, since people of different interests, gender, ethnicity, religion, personality and stage in life cycle may choose different features and issues to describe, or stress different features out of all the new environments encountered. Gregory (1999) describes the 'specificity of vision' seen in Flaubert's accounts of nineteenth-century Egypt which emphasized the sensuality he found, whereas his photographer concentrated upon tombs and temples. Burton's travel accounts of West Africa were initially banned because of their sexual descriptions. Most emphases of explorers are either permanent or stable over a few years. But some other characteristics, such as moods, or the effect of particular experiences, may show more rapid changes that may be reflected in the type of writing that an author produces at particular times. In the context of fiction writing or poetry it is known that some authors have deliberately taken mood-enhancing drugs to alter their perceptions and subsequently 'see' the world in a different way. But there seems little doubt that the very experience of a hard and difficult journey, as well as contact with other peoples, can change the attitudes of explorers, and influence how a narrative was constructed and phrased. Moreover, it must also be remembered that there may be more than one account of an expedition. On some of the bigger expeditions from the mid-eighteenth century onwards several books from different authors were produced, offering fascinating glimpses into the alternative views of various participants about the new lands. The existence of multiple accounts became more and more common once explorations were based on scientific objectives. Journeys were transformed into expeditions, to discover and to exhaustively record the new plants, animals, minerals, or even the social structures of aboriginal groups. The written record of various specialists usually focused upon particular features. Yet there are also cases where individuals left more than one record. Cook's surgeon, David Samwell from North Wales, wrote several accounts focusing on different features of the journey; medical comments were in Latin, descriptions of the new lands in English, whereas his comments on the customs of the South Sea Islanders, considered scandalous to Puritan eyes, were concealed in Welsh (Bowen 1974).

C. THE AUTHOR'S GLOSS

All explorer-authors adopt particular writing strategies and employ personal skills in the construction of the narratives that describe their experiences and findings. However, the decisions made, and the alternatives considered, are rarely the subject of any comment. The most important of these features consist of: *the general organization of the narrative; the insights and expressions used, especially the aesthetic preferences adopted; the specific writing strategies employed, which includes features such as style, language, rhetorical devices; the addition of other forms of representation or portrayal, from maps to sketches; the extent of rewriting; as well as the meanings encoded.* But since the last category deals with insights that are usually a feature of the way that readers are able to tease out such relationships, they are dealt with subsequently. In addition, it is worth noting that exploration narratives designed to describe real journeys are rarely used for metaphorical reasons, unlike the situation in the field of fiction, although one should allow for this possibility when evaluating texts.

The first task that faces any author is the *organizational structure* to be employed. Compared to other prose works, any explorer seeking to write an account of the voyage or expedition has a huge advantage. The journey through time and space provides the basic structure in itself, since the sequence of events of the journey, as well as the sights seen, fall into a coherent narrative, without the need for any fictive invention. This means that the unexpected experiences, the shocks, fears, or even pleasures, as well as the days that pass like others, are automatically welded together by reason of the passing of time. Certainly the isolated fragments of new experiences, the series of anecdotes that are recorded, could be reorganized in different ways. But they usually retain their narrative position in exploration journals because they are integrated through the passage of time. Many of the earliest printed narratives of Renaissance explorers are little more than daily logs, but as the genre becomes more sophisticated, and authors respond to their reader's interests, there is less than a strict adherence to a daily accounting. The form may still dominate, but longer descriptions of the events or sights seen on particular days, are provided in the text. Days where little of consequence seemed to happen may be ignored. So even though the structure is still based on some temporal sequence, the relative balance of the text is based more on the features the author considers to be significant, than upon a strict adherence to the daily log.

One of the best examples of the use of a particular organization to stress the merits of a new land can be seen in William Vaughan's book, The Golden Fleece (1626), although this is a plea for colonisation, not strictly an account of exploration. Vaughan constructed his argument in the form of a play, rather than simply recounting the advantages of the island. Most of the action is based in a court presided over by a set of mythical Greek Gods. The court was addressed by a series of people with special knowledge of the potential of the new land and who argued the case for colonization. The approach has been heavily criticized by those reviewing Vaughan's work through contemporary standards, as seen in Cell's (1969; 1982) classic accounts of early English settlement schemes:

> The work is sound and practical, if not very original; however, such passages are so well concealed amongst pages of fantasy, classical, biblical and historical allusions … that as a propaganda document, the whole makes very little impact … its meaning is lost. (Cell 1982, 854)

Although Cell's conclusions seem apt in the context of our contemporary standards of argument, they are not appropriate if the precepts of the new historicism are followed. In view of the context of Vaughan's day, and the problem he wished to solve, the organization criticized by Cell makes perfect sense. It was the king and his courtiers who had to be persuaded about the value of colonisation. By presenting the discourse as an allegorical play, with arguments mediated by key figures from Greek mythology, Vaughan ensured that the work would appeal to an educated readership and, presumably, also give it the authority of classical scholarship. Although there is no evidence that the play was performed, Vaughan was well aware of the fact that the Stuart court revelled in masques based on classical themes. These were not just entertainments, but portrayals of some idealised world, in which the virtues of the wise and benevolent monarchy were exalted (Orgel 1965). So, the theatre was seen as the reflection of what the king hoped his kingdom would become. The structure of the discourse makes it probable that Vaughan adopted a typical organizational form of presenting an argument to the Stuart court, one which allowed a public airing of contested views about the benefits of colonisation. His organization may have looked like a frivolous entertainment; in practise it contained a serious message, whose value has been lost by being interpreted through modern views (Davies 2003).

The utility of exploration narratives is not only based on their organization. An important part of an author's personal style or gloss, relates to the *new insights and expressions* that are provided. These may be a result of some unique skill in perception that provided some evocative phrase, as much as the fact that the explorer was the first to record accounts of some new phenomena, whether area, animal, plant, or culture. But some explorers have been able to respond personally to the experience of the new environment. The raw sensations of the journey become translated into evocative words or phrases that frequently fix or shape the landscape for subsequent travellers. Jacques Cartier, the first European to sail down the St. Lawrence River in 1536, described the forbidding north shore of the estuary as 'the land God gave to Cain' – which we now know is part of the rocky, glacially scoured Canadian Shield in Labrador and eastern Quebec. This memorable phrase provided a strong image of a wilderness, one unsuitable for agriculture – a land that seemed only fit for those whom God had cast out. This ability to make a conscious connection to the land, to translate feelings about nature into words that ring down the ages is of course a creative act. Not all explorers were able to create such vivid expressions. In fact, it has already been argued that part of the limited attention paid to exploration texts as literary documents was a consequence of the fact that most explorers were rather limited in their writing skills. Many had little time, given the need to traverse unknown and often dangerous territory, to think beyond the practical and mundane in order to survive. It was the later generations of writers, now called the nature writers, from Wordsworth to Thoreau or John Muir who had the time, skill and leisure to spend time in the physical environment, creating their poems of praise to nature and articulating man's feelings about the land. In doing so, they taught others to see more clearly, to feel more profoundly, as well as showing how natural experiences can lead to a renewal of the spirit and create a closer identity with the living and inanimate world.

The third category to be considered in the construction of a narrative of exploration is the question of *specific writing strategies or tropes*. These are crucial to the readability of the exploration narrative. It is the writing strategy that creates or constitutes the image or representation of the place for the reader and helps convince them of the arguments put forward. After all, readers only 'experience' the newly discovered worlds through the rhetoric of the explorer. Part of the tropes involves the general organization of the text, which has already been dealt with. It also involves the choice of the language to write in. This is a key decision that may affect the narrative because of the constraints or advantages of expression, as well as the size of the audience that the work reaches. In the former context it has already been shown how the linguistic relativity thesis argues that different languages may 'construct' the world in various ways. In the latter, the switch from Latin, the language of educated people from the Roman Empire onwards, to vernacular languages in most post-sixteenth-century exploration narratives, did ensure a larger readership within a country. Many other features are also critical to the tropes adopted, which can be illustrated by a brief description of the style used, the choice of words to evoke particular images, the adoption of particular rhetorical forms, and the influence of gender.

In the seventeenth century it was typical for explorers to apologise in advance to their readers for what were considered the deficiencies of style. *Style* had long been regarded as the garment of an author's status, and a mark of learning, which had led to a grandiloquent, even florid prose form full of classical references and interpretations. Although this style continued into the early seventeenth century, many of the new explorers lacked the education to write in this way. Instead, an increasing number of the narratives of exploration were couched in the new plain style of the seaman, essentially a direct, vernacular and unadorned text. However many of the authors seemed self-conscious of their approach. Even James, an educated man, a lawyer, felt he had to apologise for what he called *this rude Abstract* (James 1633, 2). His rival, Foxe, may have had more excuse, since he was a seaman who does not seem to have had any formal professional education. Foxe, perhaps realising his prose did not compare with the already published book of James, used his preface to warn his readers not to expect any eloquence.

> *Gentle Reader, expect not heere any flourishing Phrases or Eloquent tearmes; for this Child of mine, begot in the North-west's cold Clime, (where they breed no Schollers), is not able to digest the sweet milke of rethorick.... (Foxe 1635, Preface, 7)*

The familiar environmental determinism of the seventeenth century may not be acceptable today – especially among academics that work in the Canadian Northwest! But these words establish a defensive tone – one that goes beyond the self-disparagement that was favoured by many explorers of the day. Indeed, is worth remembering that Foxe's book was published a year after James's work, suggesting that he was well aware of his literary deficiencies when compared to his rival.

The style of most explorer-authors in the early seventeenth century was quite unlike the verbose constructions found in many books of the period. These books were full of encoded meanings and classical or religious references that gave them authority, or a learned appearance. But we must be wary of interpreting most exploration texts as simplistic straightforward accounts; the choice of words or the features to record, as well as the organization used, frequently have more than a literal effect. For example, Luke Foxe seemed determined to ignore the hardships and dangers of his voyage to Hudson Bay, since such problems are rarely mentioned in his descriptions of the journey. Presumably these were seen as signs of weakness, which Foxe, a seaman proud of his practicality, did not wish to draw attention to. Foxe's narrative, therefore, is largely dispassionate and had little appeal to the emotions, unlike James's descriptions of dangers and near brushes with death, Not surprisingly, it was James's work which initially received popular accolade, But as we have seen, it was subsequently dismissed by those who were only interested in the 'hard facts' of exploration.

The choice of *themes or images* is always another critical task for any author. The choice of some themes may be a result of the need to justify exploration and its results. Greenblatt (1991, 73) suggested that Columbus deliberately used the rhetorical strategy of 'wonder' to describe the world he had discovered. By the third voyage Columbus was subject to many sceptics at court, because he had not found the immense sources of gold or trade goods that had been promised. So Columbus began to stress the 'wonders and marvels of the land' in his accounts, an approach that can be seen as a defensive strategy to disarm his critics.

> *Not to manifest and arouse wonder is to succumb to the attacks against him.*
> *The marvellous stands for the missing caravels laden with gold … it is a word*
> *pregnant with what is imagined, desired, promised. (Greenblatt 1991, 73)*

This example shows that even the choice of words and features described could be a deliberate rhetorical writing strategy to evoke some specific response. Of course, Columbus's constant use of words such as 'wonder' and 'marvel' could stem from an impoverished vocabulary, although Greenblatt dismissed this possibility.

Exploration narratives often favoured particular *rhetorical devices* to draw attention to the value of their discoveries. One of the new trends from the seventeenth century onwards was the way that many of the preferences of earlier authors, such as use of elaborate metaphors, or the use of classical analogies, were avoided in accounts of exploration. This was based on the belief that such devices obscured what was regarded as the new 'truth' about the new lands, or the sights that were seen. Many explorers from the seventeenth century really believed they were exercising what we have described as realism, of producing a mimetic account of what they saw – although it has already been shown that their representations were usually biased by their religious and social beliefs. Kittay (1987) has argued that the development of rationalism in the period known as the Enlightenment was a prime reason why many authors rejected, or at least reduced the use of metaphors in their prose. This view was buttressed by the adoption of the emerging scientific methodology, initially codified by Francis Bacon (Bowen 1981). It was left to the Romantics to reject the values of an increasingly rational and mechanized society and to stress the value of metaphorical writing, but this led to the separation of what was called literature from the rest of the written texts. However, the apparent objectivity of scientific procedures must be questioned; they are also a constructed methodology for creating information and controlling discourse, however much they seem natural and authentic. But since the scientific approach is one that has led to an enormous increase in a certain type of knowledge, the method is associated with a great deal of prestige, or even authority in the minds of many. The increasing use of scientific approaches in exploration narratives can be seen by the greater use of the latitude–longitude approach to represent location, and measurements of such environmental characteristics as tides, wind speed and climate characteristics. As such, the landscape descriptions become part of the emerging documentary record, producing more and more detail about the new environments that were discovered. Although explorer-authors may have been increasingly prone to use a sparse style and scientific approaches in their descriptions, their narratives still used other writing strategies. It is unclear whether these were conscious decisions, or strategies that reflect their values and ideologies. The study of the range of rhetorical devices used in exploration narratives is still in its infancy, Pratt (1992, 204) has shown how the texts of Victorian exploration writers used three approaches, in addition to the theme of survival, to create value for the discoveries, namely: aesthetics, density of meaning, and the element of mastery or dominance, which can be connected with acquisition (Brown 1993).

The first of these devices, *aesthetics*, is relatively well-known, since it was part of the late-eighteenth-century Romantic Movement in western Europe. British naval officers in northern Canada deliberately commented on, or even composed scenes that reflected their aesthetic preferences for the picturesque scenes of hills and dales from their homeland. MacLaren has summarized their favourite features:

> *Elevated prospect, animated foreground, meandering river, sunset, coulisses*
> *of tree-covered hills that govern the perspective and direct it to a single*
> *vanishing point ... (together with) the "ruins" motif by scattering driftwood.*
> *(MacLaren 1985b, 44)*

Such scenes of contentment parallel the pastoral images so favoured in early- and mid-eighteenth-century Britain, in which greatest value was placed on landscapes composed of well-watered grassy areas, interspersed with small woods. But this preference may not be a simple consequence of the Romantic Movement. Raleigh described the Orinocco Plains in similar terms at the end of the sixteenth century. Although he has been criticized for using this aesthetic to stress the area's suitability for settlement, Whitehead (1977, 5) maintained this is taking criticism too far; Raleigh's descriptions were reasonably accurate portrayals of the savanna, a mixed wood and grass countryside occupied by many native peoples. But readers must be careful of viewing such landscapes only in aesthetic terms. Trees provided essential fuel and building materials for natives and settlers alike and provide a useful marker of the fact that there is likely to be sufficient rain for arable cultivation. Also, the presence of grassy areas means that less land has to be painfully cleared of trees. So there are utilitarian reasons for the preference for such landscapes, at least for western and southern Europeans and their cultivation techniques.

Positive comments about scenes of pastoral harmony and mixed grass and woodland landscapes form a stark contrast to attitudes expressed about other locations that were newly discovered. For example, the rain-drenched, impenetrable, rocky and forested shores of the British Columbia coast north of Howe Sound were landscapes to be feared and were initially viewed with despair, or even horror, by European explorers. But the development of the aesthetic of the sublime led to a reversal of such views. This was based on new feelings about the cataclysmic environmental events, or apparently chaotic, unorganized natural landscape that initially overawed and terrified people. Burke (1757) noted that if the fear or terror of such environments did not lead to a severe injury, or even the death of an observer, it could often be transformed into a pleasure, creating a new appreciation of nature. This was the basic principle of the sublime as an aesthetic principle. It might even evoke a new spirituality in the observer, one linked to a more profound understanding of God's handiwork in creating such environments. In Canada, the concept of sublimity has often been applied to the unfamiliar and awe-inspiring sights seen in the Canadian Arctic, for most of the landscapes above the tree line provided real challenges to the first European explorers; they were unable to conceive of any way to live on, or exploit the land, unlike the indigenous Inuit. Moreover, the monotony, desolateness and vastness of the Arctic and subarctic landscapes – so frequently covered by a blanket of white snow – led Parry in the winter of 1824 to describe them with real horror. They produced

> *a picture calculated to impress upon the mind an idea of inanimate stillness,*
> *of that motionless torpor with which our feelings have nothing congenial....*
> *In the very silence is a deadness. (Parry 1828, vol. 5, 34)*

The underlying danger of these lands meant that they were normally viewed with fear and alarm; these were not landscapes that were valued in any way, at least through European eyes at this time. MacLaren (1985b, 54) has noted how Richardson's 1848 expedition in search of the missing Franklin viewed the tundra:

> *Even though possessed of a naturalist's intrepid curiosity. Richardson could only see the tundra as naked, a desolate reminder of wayward-ness, starvation, fatigue, and murder, in contrast to which the prospect of a landscape with trees was aesthetically most welcome.*

Only when the fear of death was removed could such lands be positively viewed through the concept of the sublime. In the case of Canadian exploration literature and early works of fiction chapter 1 has described how it has been traditional to suggest that the theme of survival was a recurrent motif, given the difficulty of surviving the Canadian winter. Recently, Glickman (1998) has criticised this view and suggested that nature was not always regarded as a hostile factor. Not only did the concept of sublimity mean that even extreme environments could be experienced with pleasure, but some nineteenth-century pioneers, such as Susanna Moodie who left descriptions of the harsh life of women in the Canadian wilderness, found their major solace in the natural environment that surrounded her (Thompson 1997). This example indicates the need to remember that few themes are exclusive; the multiplicity of experiences makes it likely that different authors with diverse values will express varied opinions about the land.

It must also be remembered that views of landscapes rarely remain static, at least if they are in accessible locations. Spectacular sites such as Niagara Falls were viewed with awe by white explorers after the end of the seventeenth century. But as travellers and tourists were attracted in increasing numbers during the next two hundred years, attitudes about the immense waterfalls changed drastically, in part because they became more familiar (Shields 1991; Dubinsky 1998). Initially, the falls were seen as the ultimate expression of the sublime; 'the prodigious, frightfull Fall' of Father Hennepin, the first white man to write about the site in 1697. Alexander Wilson's (1818) famous poem portrayed the same feelings as seen in these extracts:

> *With uproar hideous first the falls appear,*
> *The stunning tumult thundering on the ear...*
> *The islands, rapids, falls, in grandeur dread*
> *This great o-erwhelming work of awful Time*
> *In all its dread magnificence, sublime.*

But as the area became visited by more and more people, opinions altered:

> *Niagara Falls has changed from being a remote, exotic shrine, an icon of the*
> *sublime, through. ... processual rituals built around the rites de passage of*
> *first, pilgrimages, and later newly-weds; with the promotional discourses of*
> *commodities and tourism. (Shields 1991, 156)*

The result has been to displace the natural wonder of the site with new cultural formations, that were subsequently added to, by industrialization through water mills and power stations, and different types of mass tourism. Fortunately, some of the latter's most recent carnivalesque associations are now kept away from the falls by a narrow greenbelt of protected land established by government order, although this expression is based on another set of values.

Many of Canada's natural wonders, or at least those in accessible locations, have been humanized, or perhaps humiliated, in similar ways, despite the efforts of the National Parks Service to restrict development. Other parts of the Canadian wilderness were tamed by the hard work of pioneers and transformed into farming landscapes. But most of the country remained in a state of nature, only marginally affected by man; it was a wilderness that was viewed with fear by the majority of the white population. Today, much of the dread of the unknown has been removed by the new technologies of access, the prospect of contact and rescue, through plane, helicopter, radio and global positioning systems, increasing the ability of even humans inexperienced in survival techniques to operate in remote locations. Moreover, a widespread recognition of the ability of wilderness experience to provide renewal, a refreshment of the spirit from the congestion and artificial nature of modern urban life, has created new attitudes about such areas (Easley et al. 1990). To experienced back-country travellers, wilderness areas can now be traversed in safety and experienced with pleasure, rather than with the fear so characteristic of the past. Recognition of the need to protect some of these areas has led to their preservation through land-use regulations.

These examples show that aesthetic constructions have had a long history in exploration and travel writing. But two of Pratt's (1992, 204) other categories, *density of meaning* and *mastery*, are less familiar. Pratt proposed the phrase 'density of meaning' to describe the writing style in which a variety of modifiers are used to give additional meaning to a word. This provides the environment with a more nuanced interpretation; the river is never *green* but *emerald green*; the mist is *pearly*, rarely plain; mountains are *steel-coloured*, which implies strength. But the approach does not simply use adjectives to enhance description; the adoption of nouns to modify the word provides a similar effect. By introducing these additional objects into the description, the text becomes much denser, creating the impression that the new world being observed and described is rich and diverse – a parallel example of what Greenblatt (1991) showed, in the way that *wonder* was so frequently adopted in Columbus's narrative.

Pratt's third category of *mastery* in rhetoric becomes more and more apparent as the nineteenth century progresses, as explorers view the new lands from a position of superiority conveyed by their new technology and their own colonial and imperialistic hubris. A sense of mastery was projected upon many new lands by a new style of commentary, whilst exploration of wilderness was seen as a way of proving a man's courage (Schöene-Harwood 2000). Also, the areas described were frequently described from some prominent position, enabling the writer to stand above and dominate the scene. Frequently, the explorer also commented on how the scene would be *improved* through transport, vehicles, churches, gardens and mansions, the attributes of what was thought of as economic progress and civilization. But we must be careful. Many previous European explorers and promoters had viewed landscapes in terms of their potential for development; in the sixteenth century it was a familiar approach, one used to justify exploration as Whitehead (1997) showed in his interpretation of Raleigh's Guiana expedition. The nineteenth-century difference was that the landscape was increasingly being seen through the eyes of a master or potential possessor, one coming from a culture with the technological ability to transform the land. Yet Pratt (1992, 208) is careful to note that not all explorers adopt the approach. For example, in the case of the Lake Victoria area, Burton's normal rhetoric was one of mastery, whereas Speke viewed the region as an outsider in his descriptions of the ways of life of the peoples and lands. But again it is necessary to be careful of over-generalization, for there are other examples in which European explorers did not cast themselves in the role of master. Samuel Hearne is rightly remembered as the first white man to travel overland from the interior of what is now Canada to the Coppermine estuary on the Arctic coast in 1771. But Venema (2000) argued that Hearne's narrative clearly shows that it was the protection afforded by the Indian Chief Matonabbee, as well as his knowledge of the route, that made the journey a success. In this case Hearne was *taken* to the place he supposedly *discovered*. Venema has also argued that Hearne's narrative needs to be interpreted in terms of cultural and gender power dynamics. She shows that Hearne's cultural status as a white man meant little in the lands beyond the influence of the fur trade, since previous native guides had robbed him. Indeed, Hearne had to play the role of a subordinate to Matonabbee's leadership, for the journey took place on the native leader's terms. The account of the journey also revealed the role of women in the culture that he lived in. Although as subservient as in the western world, they still played a vital role in hunting and gathering societies, as pack carriers during the constant migrations. Moreover it was the women that taught many explorers to live off the land and comforted them during the severe winters. The ability of women to transport possessions left the males free to hunt if the opportunity arose, and in Hearne's case gave him time to carry out his astronomical observations. Unlike many contemporary writers, Hearne displayed an unusual sensitivity to the role of females in his descriptions, but Venema

(2000) argues his gendered observations were an expression of a survival strategy in an unfamiliar and harsh land.

This issue of *gender* as a variable in textual construction can be taken a stage further, for Pratt's (1992) three categories do not exhaust the possible range of rhetorical devices adopted by explorers. Her summary of Mary Kingsley's 1897 book on Africa displays the presence of a very different gaze, one linked to the observations of a different gender. Kingsley was certainly an advocate of British expansion, although she believed this interest was better served by traders, than by oppressive colonial administrators, missionaries or big companies. Hence, she advocated a third way, economic expansion without domination and exploitation. In addition, she was one of the first to view her travels in comic, ironic terms, by describing her mistakes and misunderstandings. But her descriptions also made it clear how much pleasure she took in the travels, although Pratt argued that such pleasures were often her imaginations projected upon the landscapes, usually in night travels down rivers, when her fellow-travellers were asleep. The result is a subjectivity linked to personal pleasure and feelings, not mastery and domination, itself, perhaps a product of a feminised approach (Blunt 1994; Blunt and Rose 1994). Pratt (1992, 168) starkly differentiates between the genders, with males undertaking

> *Quests for achievement fuelled by fantasies of transformation and dominance ... (whereas) ... the exploratresses employ quests for self-realisation and fantasies of social harmony.*

The journeys that led to a reinvention of self may be more characteristic of female travellers. Unfortunately it is difficult to confirm the distinction since there are relatively few female explorers until the nineteenth century, and most of these were probably better described as travellers rather than explorers, who were less prone to use the rhetoric of acquisition (Brown 1993). Indeed, Forster's (1990) review of the writings of female travellers in the period suggested they were caught in a paradoxical situation. To survive, they had to adopt the characteristics of a male voice, an assumption of superiority and pretension to objectivity. Nevertheless, most still managed to display more sensitivity and relational links to the land than the domination expressed by most male explorers. In a related context, gender and sexual conduct was also brought in to identify the character of peoples. Montrose (1993) has shown that Raleigh's account of Guiana used what could be described as a sexualised ethnology. For example, Raleigh described the Warao as "manlie" in speech and disposition; the English were represented as restrained and continent; whereas the Spanish were portrayed as lascivious and subject to their own lusts; not surprising views, given the power politics of the time and his bias.

These examples show that the landscape descriptions recorded by explorers have been *constructed* in a variety of ways, making it impossible to think of the narratives being expressed in neutral terms. The perceptions of explorers and later visitors may have been based on the elements that were present in the environment, but their landscape descriptions were also intimately associated with values, based on particular aesthetics, economic domination, or emotional feelings and varied by gender. But communication of the results of any journey is not only a matter of skill with words. An important skill of the author-explorer lies in *other forms of portrayal*, through the addition of maps, sketches or even pictures. Since the inclusion of an accurate and portable map makes it easier for others to repeat a journey, one of the important methods of the emerging scientific enquiry, namely replication, is fulfilled by their construction. However, it is important not to overstate the accuracy of the early Renaissance maps. All maps are flat, two-dimensional representations of the earth, from what is, in reality, a curved surface. So there are always distortions in any representation, which are resolved by various map projections. By the mid-sixteenth century the Mercator projection was in common use, since it had the advantage of providing accurate directions, but only at the expense of increasing the area of places towards the poles. With the increase in the knowledge of the world and technological advances, more sophisticated projections and maps were developed by mathematicians, surveyors and geographers, as historians of cartography have shown (Harley and Woodward 1987). But it is important to recognize that all European maps are indexical (Turnbull 1993). This means that the knowledge derived from them is not independent of their context, but depends on understanding the conventions and representations that are used to describe location and to portray a variety of other features. Through time, European maps became standardized in their representations, using latitude-longitude and conventional symbols, but these could only be understood by some explanation or period of training. However, their ability to precisely represent areas and locations implied that these aspects were objective, features untainted by social factors. Harley's (1992) classic essay *Deconstructing the Map* has shown the errors in such an interpretation. He has shown that maps may be vehicles for defining where places are, but the organization and the content of the map involve choices that reflect cultural values. Since maps define territory, they usually show ownership and control, thereby fulfilling the function of an external power. In an internal power context they condition readers to accept a particular view of the world, since only selected information can be shown and the data included are based on the map's function. So the map cannot be considered as some objective truth. A map may represent location reasonably precisely, but it also encodes cultural and power values, some of which may not be consciously understood by the map-maker, but are simply part of his cultural attitudes.

At the same time that European maps were being valorized as objective documents, the locational representations employed by indigenous peoples were ignored or denigrated by most Europeans. It is now recognized (Lewis 1979; Turnbull 1993) that indigenous peoples were also capable of representing routes and other locations in a very precise way, although these maps often took specific form in particular contexts, which confused Europeans who did not understand the forms of representation. This was particularly the case with the stylized way that Australian aboriginals constructed maps, using parts of animals to portray areas. Route maps were based on the ways that their ancestors had socialized the landscape, through past actions at particular places that gave these areas names and identities. So the environment is not portrayed by abstract qualities, such as length or width, but through the historic cultural events of the people. In other cases, travel time or difficulty, rather than actual distance, represented the differences between places, whilst linear portrayals rather than two-dimensional charts were used, although instructions were given at particular points to change direction, rather in the fashion of the maps used by coach drivers in eighteenth-century Britain. However, it must be noted that some authors have shown that aboriginal peoples did provide some accurate two-dimensional portrayals, both in size and distance (Harley and Woodward 1987; Turnbull 1993). In recent years, our openness to other cultures has given us a greater appreciation of the way that places may be represented by other cultures. But most would still agree with the utility of the latitude-longitude frame of reference in providing precise identifications that not only can be quickly obtained, especially with modern technology, but can also be easily understood once the basic principles are grasped.

It is not only cartographers who have become interested in the way that space is represented. A great deal of recent experimental work has been carried out by psychologists, as Deregowski's (1989) extensive review of the effect of cultural differences has shown. She showed the importance of understanding the difference between what are described as *2/3i* and *2/3d* portrayals in the representation of space, which has parallels to the portrayal of objects. In the former, there is no attempt to create an image with three-dimensional cues, unless the observer recognizes the object; representation is often made by the use of stick-like figures which provide ideographs that are not regarded as duplicates of reality. By contrast, the 2/3d approach attempts to portray the object by providing shadows or perspective to indicate the additional dimension, so as to imitate, not simply represent, the object. Obviously, lack of understanding of the conventions of the 2/3i approach can lead to serious misunderstandings of the objects being portrayed. Part of the problem of misunderstanding the maps of indigenous peoples by western explorers may stem from an inability to appreciate the type of representation being employed.

Maps are not the only forms by which the character of places can be communicated. Although the map remained the chief form of communicating locational knowledge about the world and the position of specific places, accounts of the new lands from the mid-eighteenth century contained more and more sketches and pictures to show the character of the land, its flora and fauna, and its peoples and their culture. The allocation of names and the use of illustrative material also communicated particular meanings, especially in the new continent of America. The assignment of the name Virginia to the Atlantic coast of America signified an untouched land; the word succinctly eradicated the previous use and claims of the existing inhabitants. In the same way, the terms New France, New England, or New Spain did not simply label the new lands, but fixed their possession in terms of the new power relationships. Pictures of unfamiliar objects, such as Ellis's (1578) sketch of an iceberg in his account of Frobisher's third expedition to what we now know as Baffin Island, along with his comment that it was a "great and monstrous peece of yce," helped communicate the ever present danger of sailing in the ice-infested seas. Pictures of strange animals and lands, naked or semi-naked people and what seemed to be their exotic practises, added to the popularity of many works, such as Raleigh's *Discoverie* (Whitehead 1997). Many of the earliest exploration narratives contained pictures of the Europeans encountering the new inhabitants, portrayals deliberately designed as allegorical representations. Researchers, such as de Certeau (1988), have shown how native peoples were deliberately shown as the opposite of Europeans: unclad (not clothed); adorned with paint or tattoos (not with fashionable clothes, or armoured to do battle); as defenceless females arousing desire (not masculine and ready for work or conquest), and devoted to leisure by reclining on a hammock (not ready for exploration or trade as seen by the addition of sextants and ships). Native peoples were viewed as being close to nature and therefore emotional (not controlled by reason), representing the *other* to Europeans who were increasingly influenced by the Enlightenment. Native peoples were interpreted either as simple people, noble savages living a Garden of Eden existence, or as a subhuman species; representations that had the effect of making it easier to justify conquest and control. Other continents were treated in different ways. For example, in the nineteenth century Africa was represented as the *dark continent* full of evils such as cannibalism, slavery, idolatry, and disease. It was a continent that needed to be saved from itself; again a representation that helped justify the nineteenth-century colonial scramble. This interventionist view had extra force when combined with the values of western economic rationality that argued that land should be improved and managed to increase its output – with goods destined for western markets, not local ones – rather than just being left in its original state for indigenous people to harvest the natural resources.

By the late eighteenth century such overly allegorical representations were less frequent, although never entirely lost, as the new rationalism took hold. Skilled artists and scientists were deliberately added to explorations of discovery to provide more realistic inventories of the character and resources of the new lands. Much more extensive portrayals of the plants, animals, and character of the land were made, part of the new inventory approach of the emerging field of natural science. So the new expeditions gradually took on a dual character, with the main narrative of exploration as well as voluminous supplementary material of a scientific nature, not all of which was published. By that time the ability to draw and to paint had also become one of the favourite accomplishments of British navy and army officers; many used these skills to illuminate their accounts. However, through the choice of content to include, and the vantage used, particular aesthetic values were being communicated, which can also be seen in the books of exploration from the mid-nineteenth century that used the new technology of photography.

The last category of issues that can be considered part of the author's gloss in the construction of exploration narratives involves the *extent of rewriting*. The most common type of rewriting simply involves changes made by the explorer-author at various stages of composition, from drafts of the text, to the proofs before final publication. Until quite recently, the primary concern of scholars of exploration lay in the completed text, the narrative or book that summarized the results of the exploration. But in recent years, students of exploration have shown a great deal of interest in the relationship between various written versions of the expeditions (Davis 1989), especially the completed text, usually referred to as the narrative, and the daily record, or journal (Davis 1995, 40), an issue that Greenfield (1992, 18–22) has also discussed in detail. Many editions of the daily records of explorers have been published in the last two decades, allowing more people to appreciate the first perceptions or at least the first written observations of explorers. They provide evidence of the daily progress and initial ideas of the explorer, before the inevitable rewriting that leads to the final text. In exploration literature, the so-called *formalistic* approach has traditionally priorized the final text or narrative. It was viewed as the sober, reflective, and final version, almost an authorized version of the journey.

Under the influence of modern literary theory it is increasingly recognized that the final narrative and the daily or other records should be considered as quite different *texts*. The final version frequently removed basic information found in the daily record, especially tables of calculations of distances and location, which had low readability for the general reader. Hindsight, particularly knowledge of the final result of the journey, was used to rewrite initial opinions; additional sources were often incorporated and different rhetorical structures adopted to appeal to the general public for which the narrative was often aimed. Davis's authoritative work on the first (1819–22) and second (1825–27) of Franklin's expeditions to the Arctic shores of Canada has shown the differences between the initial records, Franklin's daily logs and notes, and the final narrative (1991; 1995; 1998). The former was designed for the Admiralty who sponsored the expedition and his own use; the latter was written for a general public eager for information about the newly discovered parts of the world. The narrative written for such an audience created different images of the places explored, often using aesthetic ideas of the day, such as the picturesque. Davis also showed that the two texts displayed some subtle differences in attitudes to indigenous peoples. The reasons given for particular behaviours in the daily journal were often removed in the final narrative, so the reader is less able to understand the motives for particular decisions made by the aboriginal peoples. Together with the addition of pejorative adjectives, such as *gro-*

tesque to describe displays of dancing, native peoples are represented in quite different and often demeaning ways. This may well have been a deliberate strategy to emphasize the assumed *savage nature* of native peoples, the development of which Olive Dickason (1997) has described in detail. Indeed, Davis's (1991, 108) comparison suggested that:

> one might consider the narrative the most corrupt, in the sense that it panders to the perceived tastes of a popular audience, whereas the journal often seems to come closer to an expression of the author's own response to his experience.

However Davis concluded that the two texts should be regarded as "distinct but equivalent," and must be understood in relation of their contextual constraints. Indeed, he suggested that the ultimate irony was that although popular readers were seeking to learn about the lands Franklin describes, the final version or narrative had "their cultural views reaffirmed rather than expanded", for instead of a non fictional account "what they get is not *history*, but Franklin telling *his story*" (Davis 1991, 108). So the revisions in Franklin's texts seem to be appeals to the prejudices of the readers, another example of the way that narratives are "*shaped*" to win favour among his readers (Davis 1998, 75). However, explicit links between a description and the intended audience are more clearly seen in sensationalized newspaper accounts of exploration (Riffenburg 1993). They reflect the author's appreciation of the quite different expectations of different types of readers. In a related context, Sellick's (1973) study of the writings of explorers in Australia has shown the differences between the narratives written for government officials as opposed to those designed for the public at large. The examples show that explorers, like all authors, write for a particular audience and the final narrative is more likely to show a great deal of rewriting, modifying the initial written impressions.

The second type of rewriting goes beyond an author's reinterpretation or rephrasing of what had been recorded initially in the daily journal. It consists of the way that one or more new authors, or ghost writers, adds to, or modifies the original information. This can involve a complete or partial reconstruction of the original draft. Presumably, the changes are carried out to create what is considered a more readable and informative text. This trend becomes more and more important from the nineteenth century onwards, as the exploration narratives have more commercial prospects among an increasingly discerning readership. But one must not assume that all ghost writers or editors produce major changes. In the context of exploration literature, Lamb's (1970) careful editing of Alexander Mackenzie's journey to the Arctic in the summer of 1789 showed the difference between the original manuscript and William Combe's editorial additions, although Daniells (1969) concluded that relatively few substantive changes were made in this case. In addition, there is the question of intertextuality in the process of rewriting; other sources, ranging from information from subsequent explorations to speculative ideas, were often consulted, or incorporated by the explorer, *after* the journey was completed. This was an especially important factor in map construction, which often needed the involvement of specialist cartographers. It must also be remembered that the writing process is often a *construction* that may be created years or decades after the expedition, so the *timing of the writing* and the *site(s) of production* are other sources of variations. This means that the details of the journey, and the places and peoples seen, may not be accurately recalled, which could lead to textual inventions. Also, final narratives may reflect circumstances that could not have been known at the time of exploration. They frequently show the influence of hindsight, and influences such as the final result of the journey, which often modify the opinions held at previous stages which can be found in the daily log. In addition, they may show the effect of subsequent national or world events, as well as the incorporation of new ideas, self-justifications, or personal apologia. Sometimes the original draft of the narrative was rewritten; other times, only parts of it are rephrased from the descriptions made during the expedition. For example, the first published account of the Lewis and Clark expedition to the north central and western parts of the land that became the United States was extensively edited by Nicholas Biddle in 1809. Since it was published in two books, not the planned three, much of the projected *scientific* descriptions of the new lands, to be edited by Dr Barton, were left out (Ambrose 1996).

This rather lengthy review of the main categories that affect the organization, style, and content of an exploration text has demonstrated that the construction of an exploration narrative will be affected by a large number of influences. So far, it has been assumed that the author is concerned primarily with producing a literal, although embellished account of what was seen and experienced on the expedition. This means there is a vital distinction from a fictive text; in such works, the journey is designed to portray some underlying meaning, in which the objects or people seen are introduced for some symbolic value, or to reinforce some deeply held values. But, in practise, the division may not be as clear as initially envisaged. Although most post Renaissance exploration narratives may be written as literal accounts and lack metaphorical design, the mere fact of survival or success in completing a journey may reflect the author's belief in the guiding hand of some God or the superiority of his nation. These views may be deliberately encoded in the narrative. In addition, of course, the reader may be able to derive similar deeper meanings of which the author may be unaware – meanings that reflect the cultural conditions and processes in a society. These issues provide part of the discussion in a subsequent section, which deals with the way that readers interpret the text that has been constructed. Before this can be discussed the extent to which the author is subject to various constraints needs to be investigated.

D. CONSTRAINTS

Few explorers were able to write their books strictly on their own terms. All authors are subject to a number of problems that they have to resolve – difficulties that affect the construction of the narrative. Some of these are *personal constraints*, which may be considered as part of the author's intentions. The final texts may be deliberately designed to be promotional, rather than mimetic descriptions, creating propaganda for some desired end, such as inflating the prospects for agriculture in order to encourage settlement. The text may also be seen as a way of recouping some of the costs of a journey, or as an exercise of self-aggrandizement linked to the role of the explorer. The explorer may have been writing the book for a specific public and wished to sell as many copies as possible to achieve the fame and the wealth that his exertions seemed to justify. Moreover, few explorers are likely to record all the mistakes and misinterpretations that are almost certain to be made during the course of a journey through unknown lands. Almost without exception, explorer-authors all try to put themselves in the best light, or retroactively seek to justify their actions in their final text. This provides yet another source of embellishment, or exaggeration in the descriptions of the character of the places, peoples, and events that are part of the final written record. The result is to move the text even further from the initial record or memory of their observations. Moreover, there is little doubt that the characteristics of determination and single-mindedness that stood them so well on expeditions often became a stubbornness to admit that their opinions about lands or routes still in dispute could be wrong. Pratt

(1992, 206) has described how the domineering Burton quite viciously attacked the opinion of Speke in the 1860s, when the latter argued that the source of the Nile was in Lake Victoria. Although this opinion subsequently turned out to be true, Burton used every opportunity to denigrate his former subordinate who had become his rival, which may have helped lead to Speke's depression and probable suicide.

All books are also subject to a series of *external constraints and influences*. Given the amount of exploration literature that has been preserved and reprinted in the contemporary period, it is easy to lose sight of the fact that much of the original written records of exploration were not available for contemporaries to read. Many of the descriptions were written for private, not public use, and have only become available as private archives have been made accessible, or after the explorer's papers have been deposited in official historical collections. Since the costs of expeditions were so high, and often involved hard won permissions from state or royal authorities to undertake the journey, many patrons and commercial companies tried to preserve the results of the journeys for their own use. Explorer-authors subject to state or commercial control were perfectly aware of the power of their sponsors, adjusting their style, content, and textual construction accordingly. Explorers were usually deferential to the authority that financed or controlled their expeditions. The explorer-author had to make sure that the interests of their sponsors were at least partially fulfilled, such as by claiming possession in their name, pandering to their prestige by naming places after them, or by holding out the promise of finding additional riches in the new land. One frequent result was that explorers constantly praised their patrons. In addition, they justified their own actions in the hope of avoiding the blame for miscalculations, poor results, or to increase their chances of leading future expeditions. But constraints from other sources of authority also had to be taken into account from the Renaissance to the early nineteenth century, especially the influence of the major church or other spiritual authorities. Exploration authors had to ensure that these powerful influences were not upset by the descriptions and interpretations made in the text, otherwise they ran the risk of finding their work banned or unpublished. Nevertheless, an increasingly important influence on exploration narratives was the increasing appetite of the reading public for more information and stories about the new worlds being discovered. It led to more and more published books on the results of explorations, texts designed for general, not private consumption, inexorably moving narratives towards descriptions with entertainment value, rather than only incipient scientific, or commercial trade value.

Another important external constraint on an author comes from the process of publication itself. Few books are produced without a publisher setting limits on the book's size, or number of maps, sketches, or other material, as well as upon the content or organization. All the decisions set bounds on what the explorer can actually write down. It is the publisher who decides whether to aim for a cheap mass-market publication, or an expensive, well-illustrated and expensively-bound book for the rich. Additional editions can lead to reinterpretations of the original study and its principal conclusions, or the exclusion of parts of the original edition. Moreover, if the book is to be known and read by a wide audience, the text has to be promoted, as well as being published in sufficient quantities to satisfy the potential readers. It is often forgotten that most books are treated as *commodities* by the typical producer: the commercial publisher (Eagleton 1976, 59). As a result, it is the potential sales volumes that often influence the content, style, and appearance of the book, rather than the publication being dominated by the need to disseminate some scientific *truth*. In addition, it is worth noting that the publication of exploration descriptions may not take the form of a book. By the late nineteenth century, the growth of mass-circulation newspapers provided another source for publishing accounts of exploration, as Riffenburgh (1993) has recently shown. The late-nineteenth-century American newspapers, in particular, sensationalized the exploits of explorers as a means of selling more copies of their editions. New myths about explorers and exploration were created, myths that did not relate only to whether there were passages or routeways, new lands, or peoples of various character. The emphasis changed. The focus was upon the heroism of the explorers, or the national characteristics of the participants, that either contributed to the success of the expedition, or enabled the survivors to accept its tragic failure. In other words, new explorations created new iconographies, distortions, or stereotypes, perhaps not so much about the places explored, as about the individuals who traversed the previously unknown areas. This explains one of Riffenburgh's (1993, 198) surprising conclusions: *there was no relation between the success of expeditions in the nineteenth century and the coverage that they achieved in newspapers of the time*. The generation of controversy, as much as the exploratory achievement, was the real, yet latent objective of the journey. The sales of newspapers that contained such reports were increased by the creation of discussion and excitement, not the final success or failure. However, it is important not to overstate this factor; it only becomes a force from the mid-nineteenth century onwards.

So far, it has been assumed that the author-explorer was able to publish the result of the written labours. The biggest constraint on the writing process, or rather its dissemination, lies in those situations where the author was unable to get the work published. Even when there are no problems of national or commercial secrecy, potential commercial publishers may decide not to publish the work, usually because they do not see the work as a viable commercial proposition. This seems to be the reason why David Thompson's famous narrative of his major explorations in the Canadian interior in the nineteenth century was not published in his lifetime. But it has been the subject of two scholarly editions in this century (Tyrrell 1916; Glover 1962). In view of the current interest in Thompson's work, it is rather tragic that he was unable to find a publisher for his book and died almost penniless in 1857 after selling his surveying instruments to provide the basic necessities of life. Such a penurious fate was typical for many explorers; few seem to have experienced a comfortable old age, basking in the fame of their exploration.

This discussion of the four main categories of features that affect the writing of any exploration narrative, take one even further away from any core belief in the mimetic approach, what may be called the *personal experience-realist description* nexus. The land and its people are represented in ways that reflect the culture of the explorer, prior experience. and values and goals which may be additional to the simple discovery of new lands. This means the explorer-author is never able to write from some neutral position. The lengthy process of writing the narrative and the frequent delay in publication involves subsequent reflection and reconstruction of the initial descriptions and opinions in the daily log. Also, it has been shown that the final product may have as much to do with elevating the author's ego, the sales potential of a book, or improving the author's chances of leading future expeditions, and even illuminating the popular aesthetics of the day. Many features may be exaggerated, especially the suitability of a land for agriculture or mineral discovery. Doubts about the utility of a new land, or the prospects of a long-sought-after route, may be concealed in the interests of satisfying the expedition's sponsors. But the range of problems caused by rendering the explorer's perceptions into prose do not end the difficulties faced by analysts of exploration narratives. There is still another *construction* process that must be considered; one that further corrupts the concept of a simple connection between reality and description. This is the construction of meaning by the readers; again, a series of distinct influences can be identified.

✤ 4. THE READERSHIP CONSTRUCTION

Opinions about the value or utility of any exploration narrative are filtered through the attitudes and influences brought to bear by the readers. The way that a book is interpreted can affect the public views of the new environments experienced, and this is a function of four separate sets of factors: its publication and promotion; the way that discursive authority is assigned; the influence of authority; and the plural nature of reading.

The first issue is relatively straightforward and relates to *publication and promotional issues*. In the former case, it is important for the publisher to provide enough copies to satisfy a potential readership and to alert the public to the availability of the book through promotional activity. Obviously, multiple readership of any copy of a book can solve the first problem, word-of-mouth recommendations can help promote knowledge of a book, whilst in the last hundred years formal reviews in other media sources provide a major influence upon public attitudes and awareness. This feature overlaps with the second factor that affects the opinions of readers, namely the process of valuation that privilege some works of exploration over others and provide what is often called *discursive authority*. During the European Age of Discovery, the number of journeys of exploration, and the dissemination of many of their results through written texts, created a veritable mountain of words and other forms of representation, such as charts and sketches, as well as artefacts and products brought back from the new lands. An important question, therefore, is how or why a particular work achieves a high valuation? How is the authenticity of some narratives as valued representations of the new land and its peoples established over others?

In the general context of books, the superiority of some works over others is normally assumed to come from two sources. The first was provided through the wisdom of the author, as revealed by previous works, especially those of a philosophical nature. The erudition of an author was also revealed to readers through the adoption of a rich, diverse, and complex style, with interpretations linked to classical ideas or themes, all of which confirmed the education and hermeneutic skills of the author. A second source of authenticity came from the social or political status of an author. This was often the arbiter of success; only gentlemen of learning or family or power could be trusted to create what was regarded as the truth. The authority of such works was often reinforced by the approval, or even dictate, of royal or religious power; the latter either through the opinions of priests, or through what were regarded as divine messages. In the pre-Renaissance world, where few were literate and the number of texts was very limited, the circle of influential people was small, and they were often influenced, or biased by secular or spiritual traditions. This situation drastically changed with the voyages of discovery, the invention of the printing press, and the spread of literacy. The changes that took place from the late fifteenth century enormously multiplied the volume of information and the reading public. But the voyages created a new source of authenticity for knowledge about new lands. Far more of the leaders of the expeditions were literate and were able to write down their own versions of the journeys undertaken and the sights that were seen. These were not the second-hand opinions of intermediaries — individuals who passed on information about lands beyond the horizons that were not experienced at first hand — although such accounts are often included in the travellers' texts. Instead, much of the new information came from eyewitness accounts of explorers who had actually seen the new lands and sights. Their first-hand accounts authenticated the information provided. Some of this exploration literature was unique, in the sense that only one person may have travelled to an area. In these cases, the singularity of access to the new lands gave the explorer-author's words a great deal of authority — unless there was doubt about his veracity. They were the voices of the explorers who actually saw the new lands. Many were without a great deal of education, at least in classical languages. Their discoveries often ran counter to the speculations of their more learned predecessors, especially the classical scholars whose views on the world and the character and location of places had been reified to statements of undisputed authority. Now, the words of the sailor, or rather the educated explorer able to write and record his views — after all, most plain sailors of the day could not write — took precedence over what had passed as knowledge for centuries. Certainly there were still errors and inaccurate speculations; the history of attempts to find a Northwest Passage was based on quite inadequate knowledge of the geography of the Canadian Arctic islands and mainland and the extent of ice. But the repeated explorations gradually created more and more knowledge of the real situation in an almost scientific way. These explorations can be regarded as repeated experiments which, by trial and error, finally arrived at the truth. Replication is not simply a function of the laboratory. This new phase of writing valorized the experience of the new explorers. They fulfilled the important role of eyewitnesses, people who mediated between the environment of the new land that was explored, and the received knowledge of readers in the old.

Traditionally, the valuation of any book was not left in the hands of the reader. The third important issue to be considered as part of the readership filter of construction relates to the way that a book's reputation may well be enhanced, or even dismissed, by the *reception provided by various authorities*. Historically, the state or the church represented the principal gatekeepers between any narrative and the public. Their favour was important, since they often had the right to ban a book, or to dismiss its validity because of conflict over their own views. By the nineteenth century, such political or religious authority was rarely exercised, at least with narratives of exploration in the democratic world. But the decline of political and spiritual influences did not remove the constraints of authority. Attitudes are often guided by new guardians, or what may be called canonical authorities, namely the reviewers of texts who are chosen for their knowledge, insight, or learning. In the case of works of fiction, senior academics or other writers have provided reviews and interpretations of many books for much of this century; in doing so their opinions are often privileged, and they conditioned opinion. In the case of works of geographical discovery, old explorers were often asked to judge the new studies. The review process that created favoured interpretations may be less obvious when one deals with works such as exploration literature that profess to be based on facts and experiences, not upon fictive events. Yet, opinion can still be biased by unfavourable reviews that stem from the concealed motives of the reviewer, not the actual contribution of an explorer. Chapter 1 has shown that the work of Captain Thomas James suffered particularly badly in this way; Barrow's (1818) scathing critique of James in a book that reviewed arctic exploration must be interpreted by his own desire to stimulate new expeditions to find the Northwest Passage. So contrary opinions, like those expressed by James, had to be countered or dismissed. Barrow's influence and prestige meant that his views must to have affected public opinion about James. These examples show, once again, that there is no necessary and simple relationship between what the author wrote, and the subsequent public reception and opinions of the journeys described by the explorer-author.

The final issue questions the idea that a text is a closed entity, the belief that any reader is a simple consumer of what has been provided by the author, the words and meanings provided on the pages of the book, or from authority figures. It has already been shown in the previous chapter that readers bring their own perceptions, preferences, and biases to the written words, and are able to participate in the interpretation of the places described by the author. This approach is called the *reader's plural*, the concept that individual reader's are active participants in the production or construction of meaning. This view is based on two related features. One is the fact that each reader brings his or her own experiences, prejudices, beliefs, and even culture and context to their reading. In the pungent words of one literary critic:

> The reader does not come to the text as some kind of cultural virgin, immaculately free of previous social and literary entanglements, a supremely disinterested spirit or blank sheet on which the text will transfer its own inscriptions. ... all responses are deeply imbricated with the kind of social and historical individuals we are. (Eagleton 1983, 89)

This means that readers often derive what they want from a book, selecting some features to add to their corpus of beliefs, and ignoring or questioning others. Raleigh's work in particular was romantized by many of his subsequent readers. People critical of Stuart absolutism regarded him as a champion of freedom, an icon of the glorious Elizabethan age, a man who was the inspiration for the British attempt to promote overseas settlement – even though little came of his endeavours (Whitehead 1997). Moreover, it must be remembered that reading can involve quite different functions. Bonnycastle (1991, 140–2), extended the work of Barthes (1975) by identifying five different types of reading: the text taken as reality; the collection of fragments from the text or those which seem to encapsulate the work; the assembling of historical information about the author from the book; the pleasure derived from identifying complex structures, such as how the bits and pieces of the text fit together; and the search for themes or symbols which involve the reader in interpretative rituals. It can be argued that most of the reading of exploration narratives before the last twenty years was based on the first three of these functions. Only in recent years have the other functions of reading been applied to exploration texts, although it seems obvious that many exploration books have long been read for pleasure and for excitement – through the impression of *entering* the new world described by the writer, who often constructed the text to fulfill such functions.

Recognition of these issues means that it is very probable that there will be many interpretations of particular texts, so one must be careful of taking a singular interpretation. It has already been noted that many of the conclusions of what were privileged interpretations of texts have been not only questioned in the last twenty years, but mortally wounded by the rise of the post-structuralist school of literary criticism associated with authors such as Derrida and Barthes (Eagleton 1983; Bonnycastle 1991). They emphasized that readers were active participants in the production of the meanings that are derived from any text. Since meanings are only represented by words, in shifting and unstable ways, there cannot be any final or determinate truth or opinions. However, Eagleton is careful to note that Derrida's approach was not some anarchic plot designed to create a world in which all meaning and identity is dissolved. Instead, he argued:

> *Derrida is not seeking, absurdly, to deny the existence of relatively determinate truths, meanings, identities, intentions, historical continuities; he is seeking rather to see things as the effects of a wider and deeper history – of language, of the unconscious, of social institutions and practices. (Eagleton 1983, 148)*

In other words, the post-structuralist approach to reading emphasized that meanings are not created by what is seen from the outside, from literal interpretations of the text. They are frequently linked to the ideology of power that pervades the text – through interpretations that are made, such as by the way that the book is written, even upon decisions to finance the journey. Eagleton compared this with the realist tradition, as the following two extracts show:

> *Realist literature tends to conceal the socially relative or constructed nature of language: it helps to confirm the prejudice that there is a form of 'ordinary' language which is somehow natural. This natural language gives us reality 'as it is': it does not – like Romanticism or Symbolism – distort it into subjective shapes .... The sign is ... quite neutral and colourless in itself: its only job is to represent something else, and it must interfere with what mediates as little as possible. (Eagleton 1983, 136).*
>
> *Signs which pass themselves off as natural, which offer themselves as the only conceivable way of viewing the world are by that token authoritarian*

and ideological. It is one of the functions of ideology to naturalize social
reality, to make it seem as innocent and unchangeable as Nature itself.
(Eagleton 1983, 135)

These ideas can be illustrated by a derivative of one of the examples discussed previously, the eighteenth-century British passion for picturesque pastoral scenes. In settled landscapes, the preferred scene was of pleasant, peaceful views from country houses, showing grassy swards, tranquil pools and scattered copses – the harmonious composition of the picturesque. Farm buildings, animals, and the peasants who created the wealth, were strikingly absent, often literally so, in the sense that they were deliberately removed and placed out of sight of the houses by the new landscaping. Raymond Williams (1972) emphasized that the resultant landscapes and their pictorial representations were those of consumption, not of production. These were markedly different from the social reality of a countryside that was being enclosed, where new geometric fields absorbed the common fields and rough pastures of the past, and where tenants were dispossessed. These *created landscapes* were paid for by a class of people that elevated leisure to be a guiding principle. The landscapes they engineered, and landscapes immortalized in the paintings and poems they paid for, reflected this ideology. It was a landscape constructed for, and based on, the new rural power structure of the large capitalist landowners, not the social reality of the rural lower and middle classes. In a similar way, it has been noted above that Pratt (1992) and other researchers have shown the way that male western explorers wrote about the lands as potential masters and in the words of her title, viewed, or rather wrote about, the new worlds through what she called *imperial eyes*. Such interpretations may be obvious once they are pointed out. But few exploration texts were *read* in such ways until two decades ago. The texts were regarded as straightforward accounts of the new worlds, as realist observations useful for what they told about the discoveries, not the underlying values that infused the words and tropes used. Yet one must be careful of assuming that a narrative of exploration has only one interpretation. For example, Belyea (1990) criticized MacLaren's (1985b) discussion of the way that Franklin's narratives of his Canadian explorations adopted the aesthetics of the picturesque or the sublime in their descriptions. She noted that Franklin also selected and discussed other features that could not be attributed to these traditions, producing a double discourse.

The dominant discourse remains one of European superiority, but at the same time it is inconsistent, as though it were a fabric torn and repaired with foreign patches — indications of other knowledge, other values, other discourses.... (Belyea 1990, 22)

Belyea concluded that the New World experiences may have been translated into familiar European aesthetics, but is emphatic that *her reading* is different.

The illustrations and text of Franklin's published Narrative record the expedition's achievements despite all odds, even aesthetic ones: this is MacLaren's reading. But I prefer to think of the Narrative as patching together several discourses and exploring European conventions as well as the deserts of America. (Belyea 1990, 24)

These examples show that the interpretation of the published views about the lands that were discovered may be influenced by the voices of authority described above. But they are also dependent upon the previous knowledge, values, and character of readers. Moreover, readers may gain opinions or attitudes from what they get out of a book, such as the derivation of new information, pleasure, fear or other emotions, or from the way an exploration narrative may consciously or unconsciously represent a particular ideology, especially that of the 'right' of conquest. Whether these attributes are shared by others, or not, is always a moot point. What seems undeniable is the presence of what is described as the reader's plural; the possibility of many different views about the value of a book, and what it represents. Certainly, this may lead to the chaos of alternative opinions. But it has already been argued that these plural views are not necessarily a set of unique opinions; within certain groups there is often a more or less shared consensus, at least in one time and place. But opinions change. So, an exploration narrative can never be seen as a static representation. Just as the words on the page are never a simple mimetic representation of what was seen by the author, so opinions about the value or utility of a book will change through time. It is the presence of different attitudes, beliefs, and ideologies that provide a reader's construction of meaning about any text — a set of influences to set alongside the constructions linked to the initial cognition and subsequent writing. James's narrative of his exploration and wintering provides a particularly good case study of the changes in the way that his work was received, initially with enthusiasm, but with scepticism after the early nineteenth century. Obviously, the text remains the same. But opinions of James's worth or significance in exploration writing are themselves *constructed* by his critics, who may be reading the text from a particular point of view, or from opinions expressed by others, not from their own reading.

This lengthy review of the multitude of influences that affect the cognition of the new worlds discovered, and the writing and reading of any narrative of exploration, has been designed to show that all narratives of exploration only provide partial and constructed views of the new environments that were found. The discussion has attempted to identify the major components among the kaleidoscope of influences involved in the process of understanding, providing an antidote to the simple realist view. Yet it is important to stress that recognition of the many influences upon the production of any exploration narrative does not necessarily destroy its integrity or usefulness – after all, the narrative is the only surviving record we have of the first impressions made about the new lands. Instead, it simply reinforces the idea that these texts can only be representations, as much linked to the Old World of the explorer and its culture, as to the new world experienced. Traditionalists may be disappointed that there is unlikely to be any final truth about the nature of the landscapes and cultures that were observed by the first explorers, for new interpretations may provide additional insights within the texts. Yet there may well be partial consensus among many informed readers of the value or importance of particular texts. In addition, the criteria of valuation is likely to vary among people who view these works through different eyes – especially between those whose focus is upon fixing the location of a new land or new route, and those attempting to understand the forms of representation or emotional responses in the descriptions of the new worlds. At first sight, the alternative criteria for judging either a text's utility, or the variety of influences that affect its construction, seem to mitigate against the creation of any generalizations. If the study of exploration literature is viewed as a search for meaning, a process of signification, then the variety of forces that affect each narrative means that our knowledge is really the accumulation of multiple fragments of discourse. But there is no reason why at least some of these multiple fragments cannot be ordered in some way, to provide coherence to the study of any individual text and to help in its evaluation. This is the objective of the next section.

Most interpretations of exploration narratives have been based upon the literal results of the journeys, especially the locations of the lands discovered and the sights seen — what are sometimes called the first voice descriptions of the lands as seen by Europeans. But it has been shown that a large number of factors affect the way the initial sense experiences are translated into the form that is crystallized in the written text. Their scope and variety mean that the narratives are bound to be representations, with meanings profoundly affected by the historical circumstances and culture of the author. So far, most studies of exploration narratives based on these new hermeneutic approaches are individual, interpretative commentaries on particular explorers. The result is what Greenblatt (1991) described as the *fragmented discourse* of the field — not some interconnected body of literature. Exponents of this type of approach will always argue that this is inevitable. Since the events that took place on individual voyages, and the number of factors that affected the subsequent description are unique, they can only be treated as singular events. Moreover, the representations created, and the meanings derived, are so varied that there is unlikely to be a single interpretation, especially when one recognizes the importance of the reader's plural. Many analysts may prefer to keep these interpretations as singular examples, providing us with particular pieces of knowledge about the literature of specific explorations. But there does seem to be a great deal of value in trying to establish a framework for comparative work, creating a template by which individual exploration texts can be interpreted and judged. Germaine Warkentin (1993, xx) has begun this task in the context of Canadian exploration literature. Arguing from the perspective of the new interpretations, she maintained that exploration literature produced what she described as:

> *Four areas of deep concern to the emergence of discourse in English-speaking Canada....*
>
> i. *The insight we gain into the original inhabitants of this place;*
> ii. *The powerful access ... to variant ways of organizing its history;*
> iii. *The insight into power and its operation;*
> iv. *The evident pleasure many of these writers took in the new world.*
>
> *(Warkentin 1993, 20)*

It is to Warkentin's credit that she has tried to generalize beyond the specific texts of individual Canadian explorers, to identify new insights of relevance to the literature and history of Canada. Yet we must remember that these hermeneutic approaches rarely concern themselves with the representation and accuracy of the key objectives of exploration, such as: the location of the places discovered, the replication of the journey by the provision of accurate maps, the location of new resources. But this type of information is in danger of being ignored or downplayed by the new literary approaches. A more comprehensive approach to the valuation of exploration literature would be to find a way of integrating these older ideas with the type of themes identified by Warkentin. By identifying the principal themes that index the key content areas of exploration narratives, a general framework can be created, which will help readers being overwhelmed by the detail of individual studies.

Table 3.2 is a classification of the major themes that seem to be of most important in exploration narratives. They are summarized as: context, locational identification and cognition, interpretations and representations, and instrumental functions. Each of these themes summarize broad domains of understanding, all of which can be subdivided into a number of smaller and more focused categories. As in all attempts to subdivide a complex field, there are bound to be places where some overlap occurs, but this does not diminish the utility of the schema in providing a preliminary checklist of themes that can be used to review and evaluate the content and influence of any exploration text.

A. CONTEXT OF THE JOURNEY

The first issue to be investigated in any exploration narrative is the context of the journey. A vital part of this category relates to the *purpose or reasons* why the expedition was undertaken. It is worth emphasizing that the defined or specific reason for a journey may not be the only purpose of an expedition. Other motives may be deliberately concealed; they are hidden or latent, rather than apparent or manifest. Thus, explorations of discovery were often based not simply on the acquisition of new knowledge, but on the furtherance of objectives of particular organizations – such as a state or religious body wanting increased control or expansion, new or increased trade, more newspaper sales, or societies such as the Royal Geographical Society, in the nineteenth century, devoted to furthering British exploration and knowledge of the world. Yet explorers are rarely devoted only to discovery; they may be involved in their

TABLE 3.2 THEMES IN EXPLORATION LITERATURE

MAJOR DOMAINS   DETAILED DIMENSIONS

uyb *Interpreting*
Exploration

A
CONTEXT OF
JOURNEY &
NARRATIVE

1 Purposes of Exploration
2 Role of Imagination
3 Societal & Temporal Setting
4 Preparation & Financing
5 Characteristics of Explorers

B
LOCATIONAL
IDENTIFICATION
& COGNITION

1 Identifying, Measuring Locations
2 Portrayals in Maps etc.
3 Naming
4 Experiencing the Land
5 Choice of Other Features
        - Environment
        - Peoples

C
INTERPRETATION
&
REPRESENTATION

1 Purpose of Narrative
2 Internal Power Relationships
3 Organization
4 Style & Rhetoric
5 Representational Practices
        - Aesthetics etc.
6 Environmental Processes
7 Representation of Aboriginals

D
INSTRUMENTAL
FUNCTIONS

1 Utilization
2 Feelings Created
3 Stimulation of Other Artistic
   Endeavours
4 Self-Reflection
5 Metaphorical Meaning

own search for personal glory as can be classically seen in the fatal expeditions of Franklin and Scott, and the rivalry between Peary and Cook in the race to the North Pole (Riffenburgh 1993). But the purposes of the expedition are not the only factors that need to be considered as part of the context category. Other important factors are: *the role of imagination or speculation* in the expectations to be fulfilled; the *societal and temporal context* – the intellectual, socio-economic and political setting of the period – features often encoded in the narrative; the *preparation and financing* of the journey; and the *personal characteristics and previous experience of the leader and his crew*, which may influence the success or failure of the expedition.

B. LOCATIONAL IDENTIFICATION OR COGNITION

The second theme incorporates the more traditional approaches to the results of the journeys of discovery. In particular, it deals with the question of how locations are identified, portrayed, and shared with others through standardized representations. The act of identification is really an act of cognition and is never value-free, as has been described earlier. We identify objects and process information through the culture we live in – through the language and concepts we share. There is also a technological component involved. The age of exploration increasingly relied upon measuring devices that lie outside our bodies. The need for precision and standardization in our understanding of features such as distance and direction meant that measurement categories had to be invented; common scales were needed to represent the features in ways they could be understood by others. Such scales were often specific to individual nations at first, causing great problems in mutual understanding, until standardization became part of the application of scientific methods to such features in the eighteenth century. Distances, and then time, became standardized by the mid-nineteenth century. But not until 1888, after a conference in Washington D.C., was the Greenwich meridian adopted as the global prime meridian from which other lines of longitude were measured – an international decision that was linked to British political dominance and its comprehensive system of naval maps which used the system.

Four key areas seem to be of particular importance among the variety of features that comprise this category: the *identification and measurement of the location of places*; the *portrayal of the information in map and other forms*; the *naming or labelling* of locational features and associated acts of possession; and the *choice and communication of other features* that are described in the various locations, the so-called *facts*. It may also be worth separating out the way the environment is experienced, in terms of its effect on the explorers. However, parts of it, especially climate, land-sea distribution, or relief, are subsequently measured by the scientific and naval expeditions from the eighteenth century onwards. The peoples who are seen can also be identified, whether by verbal description or measurement, although the latter was rarely adopted until the anthropological expeditions of the past century. Much of the emphasis in this domain is usually placed on the application of the emerging scientific approach to the issues, but it has already been shown that western maps and standardized approaches to measurement are not simple objective devices. They are still cultural products based on utilitarian objectives to support or extend the power of western nations or companies. Humanistic insights into cartography have emphasized that many native peoples had alternative forms of finding and communicating locations, of identifying where places were, or how they may be reached – such as through signs, knotted ropes, or the ability to understand the nuances of environmental conditions (Turnbull 1993; Harley and Woodward 1987). However, these approaches are rarely as precise, or easily adaptable to different environments, which explains the popularity of the latitude-longitude system. The limitations of the system in trying to produce representations of a curved earth on a two-dimensional surface are well-known. But it may also be noted that the system is also an abstraction, one that takes humans away from experiencing and adapting to environmental cues in their travels, perhaps paralleling the way that the adoption of steam power meant that ships could virtually ignore wind conditions in their voyages.

C. INTERPRETATIONS AND REPRESENTATIONS

The third theme goes beyond identification. The various approaches in this category seek to *interpret* the way that places and peoples are represented in the book. They illuminate, and provide insight into, the representations and meanings of the journey and the discoveries of new lands and peoples. It must be emphasized that there is some overlap between this category and the previous one. The scientific practises discussed earlier – whether of location, typology, or physical process – are really particular types of interpretation. However, they seem to be best reviewed in conjunction with the same methodological practises that led to the measurements of location and to western mapping procedures. In this section, the emphasis is upon the cultural production of the exploration narrative. It has already been shown that no exploration narrative is simply *produced* from the experiences of the journey, since these experiences are processed through the perceptual apparatus of the explorer and the construction strategies employed, in which the cultural background plays a critical part. Moreover, readers can interrogate the text to uncover the meanings that may lie hidden within it, especially those that may not be consciously recorded. A number of specific features can be identified in this broad category: the *purpose of the narrative*, the *internal power relationships* within the crew and with the sponsors; the *organization, style, and rhetorical strategies* used in the narrative; the *nature of the representational practises* employed to describe and interpret the new lands and its peoples, not simply experiential issues but the application of particular aesthetic preferences or concepts to interpret the new landscapes, and the way that environmental processes and native peoples are portrayed.

D. INSTRUMENTAL FUNCTIONS

The fourth category is concerned with the subsequent consequences of the work – the *results that lie beyond* the actual journey. One of the most important of these issues is its *utilization*, not only of the text, but the way that the land, its peoples, or the route found, are subsequently used. In the first of these categories there is little doubt that the resources of many new lands were seriously misjudged initially.

The presence of lush forests often led Europeans to believe that the land, especially the soil, was fertile. The quick exhaustion of tropical soils after deforestation led to the failures of many settlements. The inability of Europeans to recognize edible plants in the new land also caused serious problems. The trial and error approach of their forefathers, that had identified or adopted useful various crops and fruits in their homeland, was of little use to them during short visits to strange lands, full of very different objects. This was especially true in the luxuriant tropical lands, where an abundance of edible plants was counterbalanced by many that were poisonous, or at least unpleasant. In their discovery of useful new food sources, explorers were dependent upon the guidance or the experience of the indigenous peoples, whose ancestors had domesticated many crops. Eventually, many of these new products from the New World added substantially to the European stock of foodstuffs, especially maize, tomatoes, and potatoes – with the latter providing a new basis for peasant agriculture and the growth of population. Elsewhere, the removal of crops from their areas of origin to new areas, led to vastly increased outputs in productive, yet often exploitive, production systems, such as the rubber and tea plantations of Malaysia, Ceylon, and India respectively. But in the early years of exploration, the European inability to assess and use the food resources of many unfamiliar landscapes often led to personal disaster. The absence of surface water in desert climes was often calamitous for Europeans used to watered lands, whereas aboriginal people such as the Bushmen of the Kalahari were able to catch the dew that falls every night and could find underground water sources, whether in plants or in seepages. In addition, Europeans were often unable to catch local animals that could be nutritious because they had inappropriate weapons or modes of transport; a feature especially important in arctic waters. More importantly, the food sources of the aboriginal peoples they encountered often consisted of creatures that the Europeans found repulsive or unclean – particularly snakes, lizards, rodents, and insects. Many explorers who died of starvation were surrounded by food sources that could not be touched – either because of ignorance of their value, or prejudice based on their cultural preferences. Even the members of the Lewis and Clark expedition were so acculturated to a diet of meat that they purchased dogs from local Indians when they reached the Columbia river, preferring dog meat to the abundant salmon of the river (Thwaites 1959). In addition, new and unfamiliar diseases also caused many deaths among explorers. But these numbers paled into insignificance before the calamitous effects of European infectious diseases on the native population of the Americas, which also contributed to the collapse of indigenous irrigation systems and agricultural organizations. Ronald Wright's (1992, 154) heart-wrenching survey of the effect of European conquest of the New World through Indian eyes, estimated that by 1568 the indigenous Aztec population of New Spain had fallen to 2.6 million, down to a tenth of its size fifty years earlier, with similar population declines in other areas. The instrumental consequences of journeys include more than the subsequent utility of the discoveries. Other major features of importance are: the *feelings created by literary accounts* of the journey, which may bring pleasure, or other emotional responses to readers; the *stimulation of new literary or artistic works* from the initial experiences described in the text; and the way that the interpretation of the new land and its peoples produced *self-reflection within the explorer's culture*. To this list could be added the concept of *metaphorical meanings*, but such an addition is more appropriate for fictive descriptions than the type of explorations considered here.

The four broad categories of table 3.2, and their subdivisions, are, of course, analytical abstractions; in practise, the features overlap and interact with one another. But when applied to any exploration narrative the schema identifies a number of key features that can be used to assess the value of the work. Nevertheless, the list of themes in table 3.2 is undoubtedly a provisional one. It must be seen as an initial classification, or a primitive conceptual model – a first stage in helping investigators to unravel the content, significance, and consequences of exploration and its associated narratives. As such, it may serve as an initial checklist of ideas or features that readers can look for in any book on exploration. Explorers vary in the degree to which their narratives deal with these various issues, so it must be accepted that not all these themes may be relevant in particular cases. This means that the schema is as useful in illuminating the silences – the features ignored or downplayed by the writer – as much as the features dealt with. In general, therefore, these themes can be seen as representing a guide to the multiple roles that exploration books play, as well as providing questions about the interpretations that can be derived. Of course, table 3.2 should not be construed as imposing some rigid straightjacket on either understanding, or approaches to the narratives of exploration. It must be remembered that explorers moved in an unordered world – or what seemed unordered to them – because they often did not have the conceptual apparatus to understand all that they saw or experienced. Their descriptions tried to order and interpret the chaos of individual and previously unknown events and experiences, for others. Obviously the isolated fragments of new experiences, the series of anecdotes that are recorded, could be expressed or reorganized in different ways. The meanings they represent may go beyond the literal, yet are not the metaphorical inventions of fictive journeys. The past that explorers described can never be a simple mimetic account of some objective reality – there are too many intervening features between the so-called reality, and the words and narratives that try to describe it. Nevertheless, one must not be too dismissive or pessimistic of the utility of exploration narratives. At least their representations provide us with partial access to the new worlds that have been lost, the worlds that the explorers so fleetingly glimpsed, and imperfectly understood, because of the filters of their own cultures and cognitive devices. So understanding the ways that individual narratives of exploration are constructed provides a framework of evaluation that can be applied to individual studies of exploration. This provides the methodological basis for a new assessment of the utility of Captain Thomas James's work in the chapters that comprise the next section of this book.

Interpreting
Exploration

Part B

EVALUATING THE WORK
OF CAPTAIN THOMAS JAMES

Chapter 4

The Lure
of the Northwest Passage:
Preparation and Journey

Having bin for many yeeres importuned, by my Honourable and wor-
shipfull friends; to undertake the discovery of that part of the world,
which is commonly called The North-west (sic) Passage into the South
Sea; and so to proceed to Japan, and to round the world to theWestward.
(James 1633, 1)

The quotation from the beginning of James's narrative makes his intentions clear; he had been asked by his commercial associates to try and find the Northwest Passage. So if he is to be believed, the venture seems to have been on the minds of James and Bristol merchants for years, which is contrary to Barrow's (1818) opinion that this was a ill-prepared venture, although as we shall see, it was hastily put together. Foxe seems to have a much longer interest in exploring the route, for he claimed on the first page of his narrative that he had sought the task since almost going on Knight's 1606 expedition (F 261). Significant markers of the expeditionary efforts to find the Northwest Passage to Asia range from: John Cabot's journey from Bristol in 1497 that led to the formal discovery of the eastern coast or islands of what is now Canada (Quinn 1974; 1990; Wilson, I., 1991; 1994); through Frobisher's (Symons 1999; McDermott 2001) three unsuccessful voyages in 1576–78; those of Henry Hudson and Thomas Button in the second decade of the seventeenth century, that preceded the journeys of James and Foxe; and the various expeditions of Parry (1828) and Franklin two centuries later (Morison 1978). Not until 1906 was the first successful voyage completed by Amundsen, although McClure had proved a passage did exist in 1850, even though he walked part of the way because of the presence of solid ice. But these are only the most prominent of scores of expeditions to find the almost mythical Northwest Passage for over four hundred years, which have been described in many books (Cooke and Holland 1978; Berton 1988; Savours 1999; Delgado 1999). James, in other words, was only one among very many explorers who sought the route.

The discovery of the previously unknown continent of America and its northern fringe of ice-locked islands was initially a disappointment to Europeans. The continent blocked a western passage to the rich spice, silk, and precious metals trade of Asia. More to the point was the fact that it was an unimagined continent to the Europeans (Greenblatt 1991). It was also the last continent, apart from Antarctica, to be inhabited by man – although it is still a matter of contention whether the first humans arrived either twenty or fifty thousand years ago by walking across a Bering Strait uncovered by ice during the lower seas of the last Ice Age. But it seems certain that there had been previous contacts between northern Europe and what was considered a new continent during the half millennium before the voyages of Columbus and Cabot in the last decade of the fifteenth century. Even if we believe in the reputed sixth-century voyages of the Irish monk, Brendan, or the Welsh prince Madoc in the twelfth century (Williams 1987), they left few marks and no real continuity of contact. But Fell (1982) as well as McGlone and Leonard (1986), have long argued that ogham-like carvings can be found in North America and betray evidence of a Celtic contact long before these travellers from the so-called Dark Ages and Medieval periods. Although it is a claim that most archaeologists dispute, one careful review of epigraphic evidence concluded more positively: "I have no personal doubts that some of the inscriptions which have been reported are genuine Celtic ogham." (Kelley 1990, 10). However, it is important to recognize that Kelley dismissed the authenticity of several of the examples identified by Fell. Whatever the truth of these early European contacts, it is accepted that the Vikings had previously established continuing links with at least the margins of the American continent (Fitzhugh and Ward 2000). They had sent out expeditions from their settlements in Iceland by the end of the ninth century, settled parts of western Greenland, and established L'Anse aux Meadows in Newfoundland around 1000 CE, a site rediscovered in 1961. It is difficult to believe that this was the only settlement that resulted from these Norse exploration parties, but this is the only one of which we have definite knowledge. The Norse settlements in western Greenland survived for between four and five hundred years, and had regular trading contact with ships from Bergen. Eventually they become victims of the climate recession of the medieval ice age as well as conflict with the forerunners of the Inuit peoples. It is one of the sad ironies of the North Atlantic history that the Greenland settlements died out only a mere half century or so before Europeans returned to the edge of North America.

Arthur Davies (1984) has shown that these Greenland settlements were served by a least a ship a year from Bergen, and ministered to by Christian bishops, so the Roman Catholic authorities in Rome must have had records of the history of the region. Knowledge of this distant and marginally inhabitable land did not seem to have led to any general understanding in Europe – certainly in the south – of the presence of a large and unknown continent west of the Atlantic. When the extent of the Americas was realized, it represented the shock of a real unknown land to Europeans. Combined with the presence of unimaginable wealth from the golden artefacts of the central and southern American cultures, the continent provided a real magnet to European adventurers. In the north, early explorers found no evidence of comparable mineral wealth, or the presence of complex, advanced societies that could either be enslaved or provide trading partners. Frobisher's excitement of finding 'gold' in the inlet named after him on Baffin Island in 1576 was short-lived; the metal proved to be the worthless fool's gold or pyrites (Symons 1999). Certainly, the immense fish resources of the Grand Banks attracted many fishermen from most western European countries. But there were only limited exploration and colonization schemes to Newfoundland, the St Lawrence, and Virginia before James's voyage; most were unsuccessful – a few barely survived (Quinn 1977; Cell 1982). Although vigorous efforts to promote settlement were made by advocates of plantations, most Europeans considered the settlement prospects of the northern part of the new continent to be very limited, especially when combined with the long, dangerous, and expensive journey across the Atlantic. A passage to Asia via the fabled Northwest route was still a more obvious and richer prize for any northern Atlantic venture, given the enormous profits possible from trade with the spice islands and the advanced cultures of the Orient. No wonder the search for a shorter Northwest Passage to the South Seas, which would replace the hazardous and long existing route around Africa, was so avidly dreamt of, and pursued (Savours 1999; Delgado 1999).

Cabot's successful voyage and landfall in 1497 had been preceded by an abortive attempt the previous year. Cabot, an Italian by birth, had deliberately moved to the city of Bristol and its famous port after many years in Spain. Not only had he been unable to raise sufficient money for an expedition to sail west to reach Asia, but he had seen his own hopes dashed with Columbus's apparent success, reaching islands off the coast of what was assumed to be the continent he sought. If Asia was located where Europeans believed it to be, then a northerly sailing across the Atlantic and down the eastern shore of Asia would still represent a quicker route to the trading areas, providing advantages to the emerging northern nations of Europe. So Cabot's decision to move to Bristol was probably made on strict navigational grounds. It could also have been influenced by the prospects of royal support in Britain, and financial assistance from the rich merchants of Bristol, the biggest port on the Atlantic coast of northwest Europe. In addition, it is very likely that Cabot knew that sailors in Bristol had experience of trans-Atlantic voyages. Yet it is difficult to be definite about this issue. The question of the first contacts between Bristol and a land across the Atlantic cannot be conclusively settled, given the limited historical records. Most authorities (Williamson 1962; Quinn 1974; Wilson, I. 1991; McGrath 1997) have shown that the first known expedition from Bristol was completed by John Jay in 1480 and was unsuccessful. After reviewing the available evidence, Quinn carefully concluded: "English discovery could reasonably have taken place between 1481 and 1491" (Quinn 1974. Also quoted in McGrath: 1997, 6). The main reason for this opinion comes from comments in various contemporary letters as well as the evidence of greatly increased catches by Bristol ships from the late 1480s. It was the latter that led Ian Wilson (1991) to argue strongly that some Bristol fishermen were experienced in transatlantic journeys, perhaps before Columbus's journey, and certainly before Cabot's voyage was authorized by the king. Exploitation of fish stocks from nearer sources, such as Iceland, would have led to recorded disputes with the Icelandic fishermen, leading to complaints at the English court, such as those that were made earlier in the fifteenth century. Moreover, since permission to trade was a royal monopoly, at least in theory, and new patents had *not* been granted to Bristol merchants, it would have been financially suicidal for merchants to admit that a new source of fish had been discovered. In any case, such an announcement would have been a foolish commercial decision, as merchants usually attempted to keep such information to themselves to ensure their exclusive profit. Even apart from this evidence of increased fish catches, it is very probable that there would have been knowledge – however shadowy – of lands across the Atlantic, given the long history of annual contacts with Greenland. In general, therefore, at least circumstantial evidence exists to suggest that Cabot's decision to base himself in Bristol was deliberate; it was a large port with sailors who had knowledge of, and experience in, Atlantic crossings, or at least to the edge of the continent in the Grand Banks. Unfortunately, Ptolemy's estimates of the circumference of the world, rather than the more accurate ones of Eratosthenes, were accepted at the time. This meant that the world was assumed to be over a third smaller than reality. So reports of the discovery of a new land and enormous, nearby fisheries would easily lead many to the conclusion that Asia had been reached, raising hopes that a short, northwestern journey to the Orient was feasible. But before dealing with the subsequent history of transatlantic contacts which forms a background to James's voyage, another association with James needs to be dealt with, namely, the evidence of some important Welsh linkages with these new discoveries.

The Lure of the
Northwest Passage

Many of these early expeditions in search of the Northwest Passage had a significant Welsh connection. The port of Bristol was as much a node for South Wales trade and seamen as for the rest of southwest England – indeed, one of the main harbours in its port was called the Welsh Back. Not surprisingly, therefore, Bristol became the home of many Welsh sailors and merchants, especially after the accession of the Tudor dynasty to the English throne in 1485. Family names of Welsh origin often dominated the lists of prominent officials in Bristol in the next decade. It is also possible that part of the Welsh connection with the exploration of North America and the mythical passage to the northwest came from the folk memory of some transatlantic sailing by the Welsh. Arthur Davies (1984) claimed that Madoc's reputed trans-atlantic twelfth-century voyage was well-known in Wales; a written review of this event was to achieve even wider fame by being reprinted in Hakluyt's famous compendium of voyages in 1600 and was used again in Harris's (1705, vol. 2, 12) survey of world exploration. But Davies went further. He claimed that a Welsh-born seaman John Lloyd, known as John the Skilful (or Jon Solvus, the latinized version of the German word *scholfuss* or skillful) led at least one voyage to Baffin Island in the 1470s. Although the presence of such a skilled navigator at this time seems to have been accepted by other authorities (Taylor, E.G.R., 1930, 266; Quinn 1961; Williamson 1962) the evidence for Solvus or Lloyd's journeys is still problematic. Cooke and Holland (1978) are far less definite about John Solvus's journey in 1476 and suggest he was Danish. But even if one discounts these shadowy ventures of Madoc and Lloyd, the Welsh association with attempts to find the Northwest Passage can be confirmed with John Cabot's pioneering voyage of 1497 – the first European discovery, or rather rediscovery, of North America. Reviews of the limited evidence available of Cabot's actual discovery have argued the case that the first landing was made on Cape Breton or other parts of Nova Scotia (Quinn 1977; Wilson, I. 1991; 1996, 38), whereas Morison (1978) and Williams (1997) among others, favour the Newfoundland connection. Cabot only spent part of one day ashore, so there is unlikely to be any archaeological evidence of his landing place. Yet Cabot's journey and discovery did not necessarily lead to the concept of a new continent. Henry VII's household books of 10 August 1497 (Morison 1978, 69 and 87) record a gift to "hym that founde the new Isle," which seems to support the belief that the discovery was of an *island*, that many regarded as being off the Asian coast. Only later were the same words used to create the compound word Newfoundland; even in 1521 it was still described as the Newefounde Iland by Henry VIII (Morison 1978).

Arthur Davies (1984) has shown that the sailing master on Cabot's vessel was a Welshman, Edmund Griffiths; the sailing master being the person who actually controlled the boat. More significantly, it has long been claimed (Hudd 1957; MacDonald 1997) that Cabot was financed by Bristol merchants, including Richard ap Merycke, who was one of the most successful men in the Bristol area: merchant, official, and landowner. Together with John Kemys, he performed the duties of customs officer in Bristol for the king. It was from these tax receipts that Cabot received an annuity of twenty pounds a year, authorized by the king as a reward for his success in exploration. Unfortunately, little is known of either ap Merycke or Kemys, although it is important to note that the spelling of the names varied considerably, with ap Merycke being also written as Ameryk in the Customs Rolls for 1497 and 1498, which list the expenditures of the customs officers, including the payment to Cabot (Scott 1897). Certainly the names suggest that these prominent individuals came from families of Welsh origin. Kemys is a name long associated with the famous manor of Cefn Mably in southwest Monmouthshire, the main house of which has recently been converted into high-priced apartments. Ap Merycke is a derivation of ap (son of) Merrick, an English corruption of the Welsh name, Meurig, and whose family seems to have originated on the Herefordshire-Radnorshire border. In gratitude to his main sponsor, Cabot was reputed to have named the new land after ap Merycke/Ameryk, whose merchant mark, 'Americ' was even shorter. Hudd (1957) and Ian Wilson (1991) maintained that contemporary letters of the period described how Cabot promised to name other parts of the newly discovered lands after his friends and sponsors, but since the original documents have been lost, the claim cannot be confirmed. Ameryck, who also served as mayor of the city, seems to have died in or around 1605, survived only by a daughter, Joan. The family name disappeared because she married a prominent official, John Brooke, later a sergeant-at-law for Henry VIII. Fortunately, links to Ameryck still exist in Bristol, in its famous church of St. Mary Redcliffe. A small, yet superb brass memorial to Ameryk's daughter and son-in-law can still be seen in the cross aisle before the main altar — unfortunately, it is usually covered by one of the carpets.

Cabot was not able to bask in his success for long. His next expedition in 1498 proved a disaster; the four ships that sailed out into the Atlantic were lost. No convincing evidence of their fate, or their leader Cabot, has ever been found. This tragedy led to a long hiatus in attempts to prove the Northwest Passage from Bristol; the seamen and merchants of the city became more interested in exploiting the rich fishing grounds of the Grand Banks.

In reopening this possibility of a Welsh and Bristol-based origin for the term America it must be acknowledged that most authorities still claim the term *America* was derived from Amerigo Vespucci (Quinn 1977). This Florentine worthy and self-publicist did participate in two Portuguese exploratory expeditions to the coast of America in 1499 and 1501 (Morison 1978; Wilson, I., 1991), but claimed to have been on two others, and to have been a principal navigator, which is almost certainly not true. The books publicizing his achievement in *discovering* a new world were written in Latin, and would have been regarded as having greater truth-value than other contemporary claims according to Quinn (1990). Vespucci certainly sailed along the middle Atlantic coast, a voyage that convinced him that a new *continent* had been discovered – whereas Columbus and Cabot seemed to think they had reached Asia, or islands off the coast. In 1507, a young German geographer, Martin Waldseemüller, published a new map of the world based on the recent discoveries. He added the portrait and name of Americi Vespucii along-side the outline of the new continent. Martin Waldseemüller argued it should be named Amerige – or Americus in the feminine form to correspond to Europa and Asia – after its discoverer, Americus (Wilson, I., 1994). The decision was a momentous one; others copied and used the term. Nevertheless, it is a decision that fails to acknowledge the rarity – except in the case of royal names – of the use of a Christian name to label a place, let alone a continent. Ian Wilson (1996, 61) suggested that it is possible that Vespucci had learned of Cabot's previous naming, linked to the Bristol merchant, Ameryk, from his participation on the Hojeda and La Cosa expeditions. He had seen the coincidence with his own name and recognized the opportunity to replace it, by deliberately promoting his own, similar name to influence Waldseemüller. The truth will never be known. The prior association of the name Ameryk with Cabot's pathfinding expedition – almost a decade before Vespucci's claims were formalized – does seem more than coincidental and is difficult to ignore. It is unfortunate that the documentary evidence of the continent being called America *before* Vespucci's work cannot be substantiated, for the letter using the word in a calendar describing the events of 1497 was destroyed in a fire in the last century (Hudd 1957). It can be suggested that it may be symbolic that the name America may well have been based on the name of an entrepreneurial promoter of Welsh origin, given the subsequent American emphasis upon free enterprise. Even if Richard Ameryk's name was forgotten, or manipulated in the naming of America, his association with Cabot's venture should have given him more credit, since it was probably his finance that made the pioneering voyage possible.

✢ 3. THE THREAT OF A LONDON VENTURE

In the century and a quarter after Cabot's discovery, Bristol's merchants were prominent in the Grand Banks fisheries, although Cell (1965) noted that they had started to lag behind the merchants in other smaller western ports by the end of the sixteenth century. In 1610, Bristol capital and manpower were involved in John Guy's attempt to settle Newfoundland (Cell 1969; 1982), the first to achieve any real success. Although Bristol men were the major settlers, only eleven of the forty-eight shares were held by Bristol subscribers – the majority of the finance and control came from London (Cell 1965; McGrath 1997). Guy's plantation was followed by a phase of sustained colonization activity, beginning with William Vaughan's venture of 1617 and which terminated with Calvert's (Lord Baltimore) departure in 1629 and the re-orientation of his interest to the more climatically favourable lands far to the south that became the state of Maryland. The failure of the settlement schemes, despite their promising beginning, meant that the seasonal fisheries were still the dominant interest of Bristol merchants. Indeed, settlement on the island was not something that many prominent Bristol merchants saw as desirable. Colonists would represent a threat to the commercial fishing interests of western Britain; the settlers would be able to fish earlier and get premium prices since they could send their catch back to Britain sooner than fishermen who had to cross the Atlantic from Bristol first. So colonization in Newfoundland was not regarded with favour by many merchants, and later on was actually prohibited by law for many decades. Despite the failures of expeditions in the Elizabethan period, interest in searching for the Northwest Passage revived in the seventeenth century, with the voyages of Button and Hudson being the most prominent. In 1629 the scene was set for another attempt, which if successful could have been a vital blow at Bristol's domination of the North Atlantic trade, and its future prospects, for it was one initiated by London merchants.

Bristol probably contained a population of between twelve and fifteen thousand people in the early seventeenth century and had long been the dominant port in the Atlantic trade because of its location and the wealth and acumen of its merchants. Its status was increasingly challenged by the other ports of southwest England, as well as the growing trading power of the dominant commercial centre of the country, London. The capital had a far bigger population, more financial resources, and easier access to the royal court – whose favour was so vital for permission to engage in exploration and trade, frequently via monopoly rights. In December 1629, a group of London merchants asked for royal approval to sponsor another search for the Northwest Passage. They proposed the bluff, yet experienced Yorkshireman, Luke Foxe, as captain of their endeavour. Belief in such a passage was widespread. In the public's mind it had been reinforced by the general world map contained in Purchas's mammoth study of the history of exploration published in 1626 (Purchas 1626, 44). Figure 4.1 is a reproduction of the part of this map that shows a clear passage around the North American continent. This roughly sketched map needs to be compared with part of a more detailed contemporary map of North America, which is shown in figure 4.2. This was produced by Henry Briggs, a mathematician and geographer at the University of Oxford, and was also published in one of Purchas's volumes (Purchas 1626, vol. 10). It was based on the discoveries of Hudson, Button, and other recent explorers who had searched for the Northwest Passage (Wallis 1997, 160). Briggs's map shows the broad outlines of Hudson Bay, with three major unknown areas which might be interpreted as potential passages to the Orient by observers: the first is beyond Davis Strait; a second is northwest of Hudson Strait, or Fretum Hudson; and another is to the southwest of Hudson Bay. Although the map places Hudson Bay further west than it should be, and much of the shoreline detail would be modified by later discoveries, there seems little doubt that Briggs believed that any passage to the west would be relatively confined by the main continental land mass. This means that the passage was revised from the broad, inviting sweep of water, providing a route around North America, that was shown in Purchas's world map.

FIGURE 4.1. PURCHAS'S MAP OF THE WORLD, 1626, PURCHAS
VOL.1, XLIV

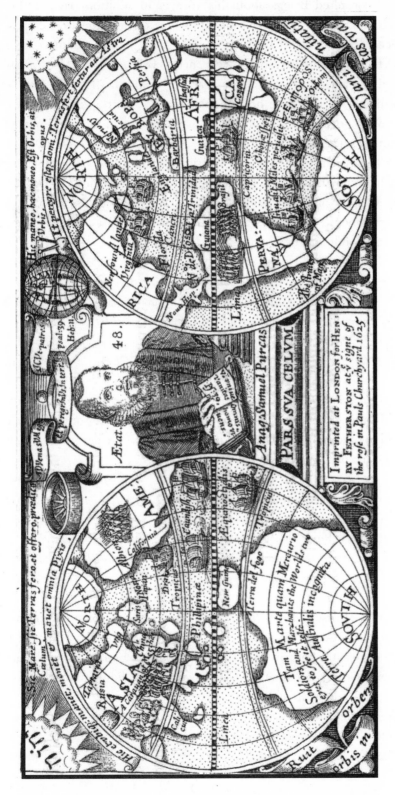

Foxe's book about his journey (Christy 1894, 262) described how he
had consulted Briggs about his voyage. In addition, Thomas Button,
the old South Walian hero of a previous exploration to the area, had
been asked by Lord Dorchester, the king's adviser, about the chances
of finding a Northwest Passage (Christy 1894, 68). Button was still on
active service for most of the year, patrolling the Irish Sea for pirates,
although by this time he was increasingly embittered about his debts
and the government's failure to repay money that he felt he was owed.
Button's letter to Dorchester of 16 February 1629–30 (DSP 1630,
189) was sent from his house outside Cardiff in the Vale of Glamorgan.
It began with the following comment – shown below in the original
spelling – which indicated that Button thought his exploratory work had
been ignored and shows his rather cynical view about the political and
social conditions in Britain at this time.

> *I outlooked my Journall and those notes and papers that long have
> lain by me, Wch I thought would never have bin made use on, consid-
> eringe that these later tymes amonge our nation rather studies howe
> to forgette althinges that may conduce to the good of prosperitye...
> (DSP 1630, 189. Also reprinted in Christy 1894, 65)*

Button restated his belief in a Northwest Passage, recommending that
only men of experience should tackle the task and regretting he was too
old for the task. He gave specific instructions of where to search in the
western part of Hudson Bay:

> *As soone as he comes to the the west parte or Cape of Notingham Iland where
> he is to anchor, and, according to the sett of that tyde which he shall finde
> there, to direct his course; w'ch must be and is the only way to fynde that
> passadge, w'ch I doe as confidently beleave to be a passadge... (DSP 1630,
> 189. Also reprinted in Christy 1894, 68)*

Button also stated that he would be prepared to bring his journal and
notes to discuss the issue with the king, but was not prepared to let
others use this information. This shows how explorers jealously guarded
their primary information – although Button did comment that he had
given the benefit of his experience to many other people, including
the mathematician Briggs. A long delay of over three months occurred
before King Charles gave permission for a voyage to find the Northwest
Passage on 8 June 1630 (Christy 1894, 71). The date meant it was too

FIGURE 4.2. PART OF BRIGGS'S MAP OF 1626 (NORTHERN PART)

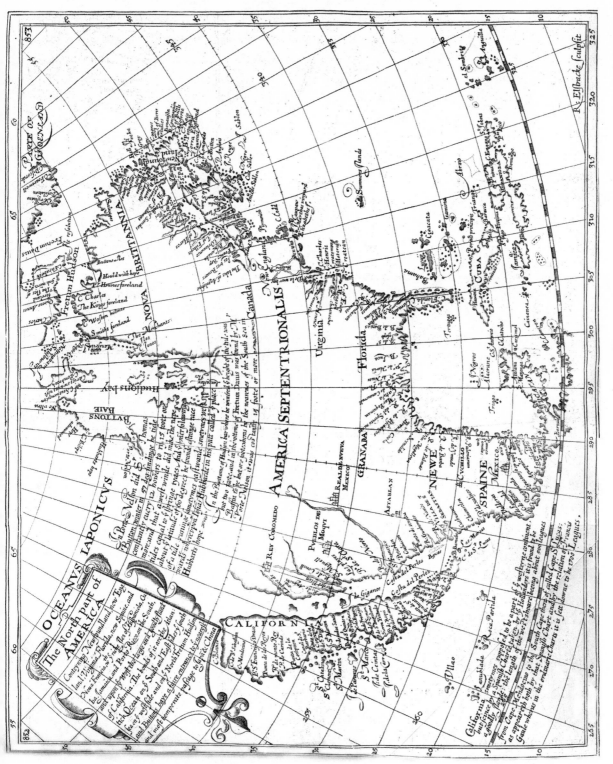

late to attempt the passage in that year, but there was a consolation, the loan of one of the king's ships, named the *Charles*. The court was subsequently asked whether Foxe should be allowed to bring back a cargo of spices from the Orient on his own account, if the voyage was successful. The request led to wrangling with the privileged monopolists who had run the East India Company since its charter in 1600. This shows that the Northwest Passage venture must have been regarded as a real threat to their interests.

✛ 4. BRISTOL PREPARES ITS OWN EXPEDITION

The trading ships that sailed from Bristol were usually sponsored by several merchants, in order to spread the costs and risks of the voyages. By the late sixteenth century the most powerful traders who had come to dominate the trade from the port had established a collective association with each other that had evolved into a formal organization – the Society of Merchant Venturers. McGrath (1952; 1968) has shown that the members of this society were mainly interested in trade; exploration and colonization received limited attention because the immediate material returns were so small. Hence the society's enthusiasm for the Northwest Passage venture in the late 1620s does seem unusual, and was almost certainly a reaction to the London venture. The Bristol merchants realized that a successful voyage to China and the Orient sponsored by London merchants could lead to the establishment of yet another monopoly that would cut across their own trade routes and exclude them from one of Europe's most profitable trading connections.

Thomas James was appointed as captain of the Bristol venture and was sent to London in late January 1631 to plead the Bristol case. This itself was a sign of the confidence that the merchants had in their captain, who had been trained as a lawyer. In early February, a formal letter from the society signed by the mayor and five associates was sent to Lord Weston, the lord treasurer, pleading their case. In it, their petitioner was described as:

> Captain Thomas James, a most deserving gentle born expert in the Arte of Navigation, Valiant and a good Commande. (BSMV 1631, 187)

Allowing for the hyperbole that was customary at the time, the words suggest that James had a reputation as a first class navigator. He must have proven himself in previous expeditions or raids on foreign ships, and was known to have good leadership qualities. Yet, before the formal petition was made to the king, the leaders of the Society of Merchant Venturers in Bristol followed the normal practise of sounding out their friends at court about the conditions their proposed venture would obtain. They were fortunate to be connected to Sir Thomas Roe, whose sister was married to John Tomlinson, the mayor of the city. Roe had enormous reputation as a traveller and diplomat; he had been ambassador at the court of the Great Mogul in India for fifteen years (Strachen 1987). Not surprisingly, he had been asked to oversee the organization of London's Northwest expedition. In addition, the Lord Treasurer, Lord Weston, had been made a steward of the city of Bristol some years previously, so there were expectations among the Merchant Venturers that Weston would also help their case. Also, they were encouraged by the fact that the king seemed to regard Bristol with favour, since the port had sent many ships to join the attacks on Spain in previous years.

On 25 January, Roe replied to the society that he had discussed the proposed expedition with James and recognized that the Bristol merchants would only proceed if they received equal privileges to the London venture. Despite Roe's commitment to the London scheme, he insisted he was working for the public interest in trying to help find the passage. Roe stressed that final approval could only be made by the king, but stressed that delay was inevitable since his majesty would not be back in London for a few weeks. Roe was encouraging in his opinion that the Bristol venture would be looked on with favour and had gone so far as to consult the lord treasurer on the matter. Roe's letter to the society quoted Weston as stating: "it is just that you have equal share with any who bear equal adventure" (BSMV 1631, 185). In the same letter Roe stated his own view: "it will be also convenient … that we may help one another and make the more expedition and the more exquisite [*sic*] discovery." Although comforted by this support, the Bristol merchants were alarmed that Roe seemed to believe that they already had a ship available to send on the venture. Speedily, they wrote to James, residing at the Three Cups, a famous London inn in Bread Street, reminding him of the need for caution (BSMV 1631, 186). This undated letter confirmed that they had procured the sum of 800 pounds from local adventurers to equip a ship. The venturers reaffirmed their interest in the expedition in this letter to ensure that James and others did not think their commitment was weakening. But they went on to warn him that the decision to proceed would not be made until the society had confirmation of the privileges to be received if a successful discovery was made. The society even suggested that they preferred all of the king's subjects to share in the trade equally – a surprising attitude for the group, given their previous preference for specific trading privileges linked to the port whose ship had proved the passage. However, the letter also emphasized that it would be difficult to procure "a fit ship suddenly" and drew James's attention to two potential ships – vessels that may have been the subject of previous speculation. It was observed that the White Angel, a vessel owned by the prominent trader, Gilles Elbridge, could not be obtained, whilst another prospect, called William and John, was not expected in Bristol for another month. They also suggested that James might find a suitable vessel in London. This demonstrates, once again, the trust they must have had in their captain's acumen, but also, perhaps, their increasing concern about being able to find a good enough ship in time to make the journey.

On 4 February, The Earl of Danby confirmed to Sir John Wolstenholme that the king was willing to see James and proposed an audience the following Sunday, at nine in the morning. James went to the meeting and presented the petition from Bristol – which asked for the same privileges as the London adventurers – a document that committed the society members to undertake a voyage the following May, even though they still had not found a suitable ship. Although the Bristol group seemed pleased at James's reception, subsequent letters show they were still worried about the need to obtain legal confirmation of their rights if the voyage was to take place. Nevertheless, their confidence seems to have been boosted by the royal audience. After congratulating James, they gave him a series of gratuitous instructions in their next letter: to see Thomas Button, the still famed explorer of Hudson Bay, and seek his opinions about the journey; to collect any books and charts about the passage; to obtain advice about the best time to sail, and how to provision the ship; and even to find two or three experienced men who had travelled in the area (BSMV 1631, 188). Royal approval for the Bristol venture was soon confirmed in a letter from Sidney Montague, written on behalf of the king at the Court in Whitehall, although it was dated 3 February, which must be a transcription error of around ten days. Permission was provided under the following terms: "grants to the petitioners such equal Liberties and privileges of trade as are already granted to the adventurers of the citty of London" (BSMV 1631, 190). The letter went on to state that both groups could trade with Asia via the Northwest passage, even if only one expedition was successful, with each having an advantage according to the proportion of their overall venture. James's accompanying message (BSMV 1631, 191) to the Bristol Society attempted to allay their legal concerns. He argued that since the London adventurers could not take a formal patent on trade until the voyage was completed, the Bristol group had the legal right to follow suit if their venture failed and Foxe's voyage was successful. Sir Thomas Roe also wrote to the society, asking them to trust the king's word.

By 26 February, the society seemed to have overcome their worries and wrote to both Roe and Danby thanking them for their help (BSMV 1631, 192). It must be noted that the Bristol merchants had set aside their wish for free trade, accepting the principle of sharing the potential spoils with London. Given their previous worries over their ability to find an appropriate ship, it is surprising to find the letter confirmed that they had found "a meet ship" for Captain James of "four score tons burden"; incidentally, this was far smaller than the 140-ton *White Angel* that had been of initial interest. In a judicious move to counter the potential favour that might accrue to Foxe's expedition in a ship named after the king, the society noted in the same letter that they decided to name their ship after the queen: "wee have destined the shipps name to bee the *Mary*." There is no evidence in the records to show where they obtained the ship from at such short notice, and, apparently, in James's absence. The society's fussy letter to James in early February had noted that Giles Elbridge, a prominent member of the group, had written to a friend in Barnstaple (Devon) asking about availability of ships. Was this port the source of the vessel, or could it have been one already known in Bristol? In the inventory of forty-eight ships at Bristol in March 1628 (DSP 16/38/14), the closest records to the date the vessel was purchased, there was a vessel called the *Marie*. This vessel was described as nine years old, with eight ordinances and eighty tons burden. There were also five other vessels with some version of Mary, or Maria, in their names. The tonnage is similar, but not identical to the ship that eventually carried James and his crew across the Atlantic, whilst the incessant leaks they had to cope with on their journey implies that such an elderly or poorly constructed ship could have been the one provided for the expedition. More to the point, two of the *Marie*'s five registered owners were none other than Humphrey Hooke and Andrew Charlton, who became principals in the Northwest Passage venture; Elbridge, however, was absent from the owner's list. Whether the Marie was the ship that was used by James and was slightly renamed must still be considered a matter of speculation. There is no real evidence of where James's ship came from; if the ship was renamed by the association of merchants, it may work against the argument that it was a local ship with a similar name. Within a few weeks, the ship described in the formal warrant of the society for the Northwest venture was called the *Henrietta Maria* – incidentally a more precise summary of the full name of the king's French-born consort. What may be more important than the ship's origin was its size, for James specifically noted in his journal that he wanted a small ship, one that could be pushed through the ice by the crew if necessary (J 2). Out of the forty-eight vessels registered in the port of Bristol in 1628 almost two thirds were in the largest size class of 100 to 250 tons, with most of the rest between fifty and 100 tons (calculated from DSP 16/38/4), indicating that the *Henrietta Maria* was among the smallest of the vessels in the area.

The speed with which the Society of Merchant Venturers could conduct its business, if it so desired, can be seen by the fact that the warrant for the journey was issued on 30 April 1631 (BSMV 1631, 194). This document noted that the objective of the voyage was to discover the Northwest Passage to China. It also outlined the liabilities of the venturers who were to manage and furnish the ship, as well as to pay the crew, etc. The sponsors are described as: Humphrey Hooke, master of the society; Andrew Charlton; Miles Jackson; and Thomas Cole. Thomas James is described in the document as an *assistant*, which implies he had a part share in the venture. Unfortunately, the list of the members of his crew that was supposed to be attached to the document has been lost. It is surprising to find that the names of the sponsors differed from those who signed the first letter to Sir Thomas Roe enquiring about the venture in London at the end of January. These were: John Tomlinson (mayor); Humphrey Hooke; John Barber; Richard Longe; John Tailor; Giles Elbridge (BSMV 1631, 187). It was, of course, normal for the various trading ventures at this time to be shared among a group of merchants, with different sets of memberships for each journey. How Hooke remained the only consistent member of the interested parties between late January and April, and why the membership changed, remains a mystery. It suggests that some of those originally interested had reverted to their habitual reluctance to finance explorations or settlement schemes, a not surprising caution in view of the previous poor results (McGrath 1952; 1968). The complete financial accounts of the venture are unknown, although a letter dated February 1631 showed that over 800 pounds had been subscribed by that date (BSMV 1631, 186). Another record shows that the wages of the crew had been guaranteed and amounted to 181 pounds, eighteen shillings, and one penny. (BSMVT 1631, 17). The events of the first few months of 1631 indicated that the Bristol venturers had scurried to create a rival venture in response to the proposed expedition from London. But there seems little doubt that the idea of a voyage to the Northwest Passage had been on many a Bristol merchant's mind for some time, as the quotation at the beginning of this chapter shows. Obviously, the venture was a major expedition. The *Henrietta Maria* was provisioned for eighteen months to enable it to reach the South Seas, China and Japan, and then was expected to sail back around the world. Such an expedition would need an outstanding leader; one trusted by the cost-conscious and experienced Bristol merchants. So, who was James? And what were his qualifications for this arduous task? It was, after all, a venture that had defeated many previous explorers and had led to so much loss of life.

✛   5. JAMES'S EARLY LIFE

The appointment of Thomas James to command Bristol's expedition does present investigators with a real problem. Very little is known of Thomas James's early life. The Latin phrase on the portrait in his book published in the spring of 1633 (fig. 1.1) described him as forty years old which means he was probably born in late 1592 or early 1593, rather than 1590–91 as suggested by MacInnes (1967, 4). He was a lawyer and a member of the Inner Temple, with a wide circle of well-connected friends, and interested in the arts, science, and exploration. One friend, Thomas Nash, a fellow Templar and a well-known jurist of his day, wrote a dedication of praise for James's book. Yet, standard references (DNB 1950; Cooke 1966; Kenyon 1975; Marsh 1985) are obscure on James's origin. MacInnes's profile of James's exploration (1967, 4) noted that there were several prominent men called Thomas James in Bristol at this period – including the Thomas James who was sheriff, mayor and M.P., for the city, but who died in 1619 – which led some sources to the erroneous conclusion the explorer was connected to these Bristol worthies (Cooke1966), even though Christy's authoritative survey (1894, 206) had previously discounted the connection. After reviewing the alternatives, MacInnes concluded that it was "probable" he was the younger son of James ap John Richard and Elizabeth Howel, from Wern-y-Cwm manor near Abergavenny – although he did not cite the source. A family tree for Thomas James the explorer is listed in the early-twentieth-century history of Monmouthshire under the entry for Llanvetherine parish (Bradney 1906, 267–69), which seems to confirm the link that MacInnes only described as a probability. A farm called Wern-y-Cym that derives from the Welsh Gwern y Cwm and would normally be translated as Alders in the Valley, still exists today, in a shallow valley below the eastern flanks of the spectacular Skirrid Fawr mountain. Yet given its location in this depression, it is also possible that the word *gwern* may have been derived from an older Welsh meaning of the word, namely swamp or meadow. Close to Offa's Dyke, the farm and former manor were part of the parish of Llanvetherine, whose early medieval church lies hidden in a hollow along the B4521 road, a few miles east of Abergavenny, in the ancient border county of Monmouthshire. Figure 4.3 shows that this Thomas James was part of a family of five who survived infancy: three sisters, Catherine, Margaret, and Alice, and an elder brother John, who inherited the farm and manor. Incidentally, the use of the Welsh *ap* (son of) seems to have lapsed with Thomas James's father, showing the recent anglicization of names and the adoption of a surname. James's great, great grandfather was Phillip Vaughan of Grosmont, base son of William Fychan (Herbert) of Llanhyddol, and therefore linked to one of the premier families of the county. The will of James's mother was proved in February 1596, so he obviously lost his mother at an early age. No records have been discovered which throw any light on his early life. However, it has been shown that the registrar of admissions to the Inner Temple admitted James to study law in 1612 in the following words, which surely confirms his Monmouthshire background and the probable original spelling of the word *gwern* of his farm: "Thomas James de Gwerne y combe in com. Monmouth..." (Bradney 1906, 268). The spelling of 'Gwerne' and 'combe' seem to be corruptions of the original Welsh.

Although James qualified as a lawyer, it is not known whether he ever practised law. At some stage, he turned to the sea to seek his fortune, for as a second son he would not have any claim on the manor in which he was born. There seems little doubt that he must have acquired a considerable knowledge of the sea, for by 1628 he is listed as a captain in the Bristol shipping inventory (DSP 1628: 16/38/4). This was the year in which letters of marque were issued to many ships because of

Pedigree of the Family of James (Herbert) of Wern-y-cwm
ARMS – HERBERT with a difference for illegitimacy.

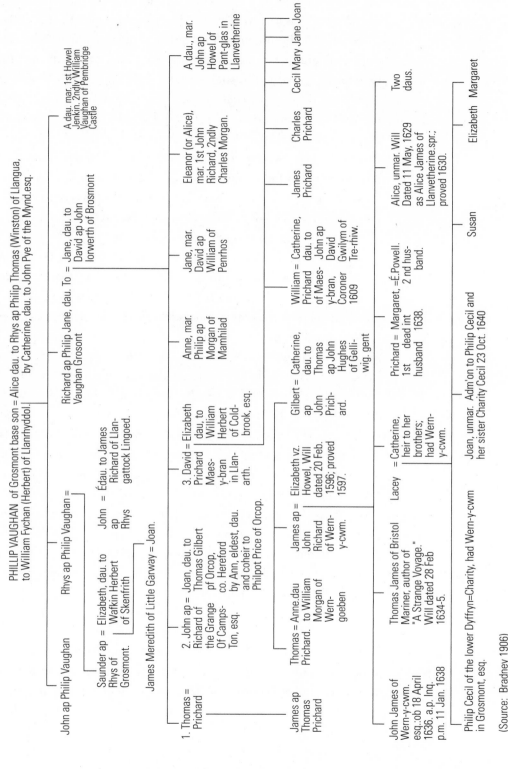

FIGURE 4.3. JAMES'S FAMILY TREE

(Source: Bradney 1906)

the war with France, one, incidentally, in which Kirke captured Quebec in 1629, but was forced to return it in the subsequent peace settlement. Some idea of the potential profit that could be obtained by capturing ships from another nation in this way can be seen from the fact that over twenty ships engaged in such ventures had sailed from Bristol in 1626 alone, and the famous *Eagle* of Humphrey Hooke brought back a prize worth 40,000 pounds sterling. In July 1628, Captain Thomas James was provided with the legal right to act as a privateer, as captain of the Dragon, a 140-ton ship, six years old, and with ten guns, according to the inventory of forty-eight vessels registered in Bristol in March 1628 (DSP 1628: 16/38/4). At first sight, the name of his command seems to emphasize James's Welsh links. However, the inventory does not list him as one of the four co-owners, as previously suggested by Powell (1930, 75). There is no evidence that James was successful in his privateering ventures. The fact that prominent Bristol merchants, such as Colston, were among the co-owners of the Dragon, demonstrates James's close connections with the commercial elite of the city. James next appears in the historical record as the captain chosen by the Society of Merchant Venturers to undertake their sponsored voyage to the Northwest Passage and is recorded in their records as resident at 25 Guinea Street, Redcliffe. This street is near the spectacular medieval church of St. Mary Redcliffe. Located outside the old walls of Bristol it acted as the parish church for many of the sailors and merchants of the city who lived in the surrounding area. Figure 4.4 shows one of the most detailed seventeenth-century maps of Bristol. Although the map is somewhat later than the period of James's voyage, most of the streets and buildings shown must have been present in James's day. Unfortunately, the detail is largely restricted to the city itself. The areas outside the boundaries are only barely noted, including James's home. However, Guinea Street still exists, a narrow thoroughfare that dips steeply down from near St. Mary Redcliffe Close. The street runs past the existing Golden Guinea public house to the still surviving old Ostrich hostelry that is partially built into the famous red cliffs on the docks that gave the church its name. The old quays on the meandering river Avon, and its tributary the Frome, are now gentrified — new bijou residences have replaced the busy commercial port buildings of James's day. The mid-nineteenth-century changes that heralded the age of steam and the advent of bigger and bigger ships made Bristol's old river port largely redundant, and in the last twenty years most of the old docks have been redeveloped, piecemeal, changing into a series of leisure, residence, and office complexes. None

FIGURE 4.4. MAP OF BRISTOL IN 1671

Ⓖ Guinea Street   (this has been added to the original map)

of the wooden houses of James's time survive. The specific site of James's former residence and its immediate neighbours are now part of the area occupied by the Bristol Infirmary Hospital, a large Victorian construction that led to the destruction of the houses in Guinea Street near the docks, and now dominating its lower portion. Most of the surviving buildings in the street are the narrow, yet originally rather elegant townhouses of the eighteenth century – which, although rather dilapidated today, still reflect the profits made by Bristol merchants in the city's heyday as a centre for Atlantic trade.

Unfortunately, no historical evidence from which one can gauge James's previous experience as a seaman has ever been found. It is improbable that the financially acute merchants of Bristol would venture their money on a maritime neophyte. James may have made previous journeys to the Straits of Magellan or even to Hudson Bay, for he claimed in his journal to have previously experienced ice conditions (J 2). This might explain why he was given command of such an important venture and was held in such high regard. James's narrative subsequently describes how he had spent time and money collecting all the information available about the area that he was to traverse. Although it is clear that James had become a *Bristol man* by residence and profession, his Welsh origin seems to have been important to his identity, as can be seen in two facts from his voyage. First, he named the new land that his ship discovered along the southern shore of Hudson Bay after his homeland of South Wales (James 1633, 24). In this decision he followed the lead of his countryman Thomas Button, who had been the first to explore and winter on the west coast of Hudson Bay in 1612–13 and called the area New Wales, which after James's dedication often became New North Wales. Additional cartographic decisions also suggest his Welsh heritage. For example, one of the principal rivers on the south coast of Hudson Bay became the Severn on James's map, the northwest part of the coast was relabelled New North Wales on his chart, whilst a cape in James Bay was called Monmouth. Curiously, these decisions are not described in his journal. A second clue to his Welsh origins comes from the entry that described a traditional Welsh festival in March:

> *The first of this moneth being Saint Davids Day, we kept Holyday, and solemnized it in the manner of the Ancient Britaines: praying for his Highnesse happinesse Charles Prince of Wales. (J 65. All extracts from James use the spelling in the original text)*

FIGURE 4.5. JAMES'S JOURNEY 1631–32 ON MODERN MAP

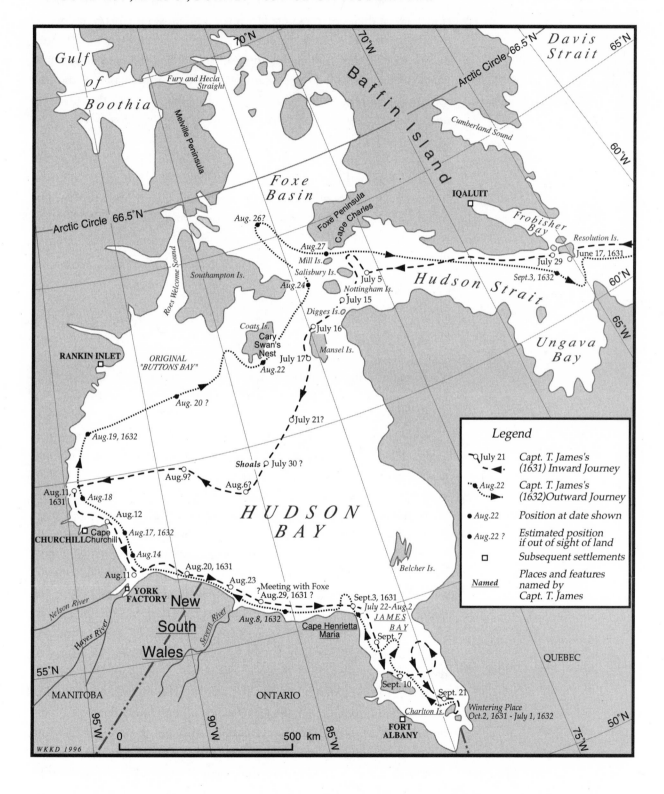

Legend

⊶July 21   Capt. T. James's (1631) Inward Journey

•••Aug.22   Capt. T. James's (1632) Outward Journey

• Aug.22   Position at date shown

• Aug.22 ?   Estimated position if out of sight of land

□   Subsequent settlements

<u>Named</u>   Places and features named by Capt. T. James

WKKD 1996

Who else but an individual of Welsh origin would celebrate the traditional day of their patron saint? However, one must note his reference to the *ancient Britons* as a descriptor of his origins – although many educated people from Wales were calling themselves Cambro-Britains at this time (Vaughan 1626). Like many acculturated fellow countrymen of the day, especially from the border counties, his allegiance lay with the relatively new polity of England. Less than a century previously, Henry VII, a king of Welsh origin, had ended decades of civil war and his son formally absorbed Wales into the English state (John Davies 1994, 232). With the death of Elizabeth I, the throne passed to the Scottish Stuart dynasty, which meant that Scotland was effectively added to the new union. The monarch, Charles, was glorified in Thomas James's journal (J 112) as the King of England, Scotland, and Ireland, as well as France – an ancient claim – without mention, it must be noted, of Wales.

✛ 6. JAMES'S VOYAGE

The broad outline of James's voyage is shown in map form in figure 4.5. James's book summarized the journey in four parts: Preparation (J 1–5); A Voyage for Discovering (J 5–53); Wintering (J 54–89); Discovery and Coming Home (J 90–111). Much of the section describing the voyage is a daily description of events and locations, but the last two sections contain far more discursive and speculative information, interspersed with accounts of the events of individual days. James hosted a reception on board his vessel before he left, which included prayers for a safe voyage read by Thomas Palmer. The records of the church of St. Mary Redcliffe, the building that so dominated the wharves on the river Avon, show that Palmer was the vicar of the church between 1623 and 1639. James and his crew sailed out of the Kingsrode anchorage on 3 May 1631. The dependence of his vessel upon favourable winds can be seen by the fact that it took the ship nineteen days, that is until the 22 May, to weather the southwest coast of Ireland. But the crew sighted Greenland thirteen days later, on 4 June. Despite fog and icebergs, they reached Resolution Island, outside Hudson Strait, on 18 June. Contrary winds, a strong tidal outflow and heavy ice conditions meant that James was unable to complete his estimated 120 leagues (circa 360 miles) of the strait until 5 July, reaching Nottingham Island on 15 July. The next day they reached latitude 62° N, but solid ice conditions made it impossible to pursue their plan to go further north. Turning west and south their journey was made difficult by continuous pack ice – on frequent occasions they were forced to break a passage with crowbars and push the ship with their shoulders (J 20). Eventually they found open water and despite the hazards caused by patches of ice, fog, and storms, reached the western shore of the bay at 59°40′ N near Hubbert's Hope on 11 August. They then turned south along the shore, taking the route that his fellow countryman, Thomas Button, made twenty years previously.

James and his crew followed the general trend of Hudson Bay shore south and then east, making considerable progress until the end of the month when they were checked by adverse winds. On 29 August, they had the extreme fortune to meet the rival expedition of Luke Foxe from London, who had probably sailed past them when they were investigating Resolution Island, and was probably at anchor out of sight up the Nelson River when James's ship crossed its estuary. The two ships spent a few days together, which led to quite conflicting accounts in the two rival captain's journals, before Foxe sailed north and returned to Britain at the end of the summer. After parting from Foxe, James sailed further east and on 3 September (J 28) named the prominent cape, Henrietta Maria, after the queen of England. He then turned south into the bay that continues to immortalize his name, in the hope that it might lead to what he called (J 33) the *River of Canada* – the present St. Lawrence. The weather degenerated; the shallow water, rocks, and tidal flats on the coasts, and deteriorating weather, made sailing treacherous and dangerous. His journal entry for the last six days of September described how they failed to get further east:

> The winde shifted so in our teeths, that it put us within a quarter of a mile of the very shoare: where we chopt to an Anker and rid it out for life and death. Such miseries as these, we indured amongst these shoalds and broken grounds: or rather more desperate then I have related;(very unpleasant perchance to be read) with snow, haile, and stormy weather, and colder than ever I felt it in England in my life. … we were driven amongst rocks, shoalds, over-falls, and breaches round about us; that which way to turne, we knew not.…All these perils, made a most hideous and terrible noyse, in the night season. (J 38)

By October, snow had become a regular event; ice was freezing on the ship on the masts and rigging "as bigge as a mans middle" (J 42) and was difficult to chop away. Their condition was becoming desperate. On 7

October they found a small island, approximately eighteen miles long, where they eventually found a reasonable mooring and began to establish a winter camp. Three separate huts were eventually built, separated to avoid the danger from fire. The largest was twenty feet square with wooden walls, a canvas roof made out of their sails and with double bunks on three of its sides. The settlement was subsequently named Charles Town to honour their prince – but was subsequently abbreviated to Charleton or Charlton.

During November the increasing ice and storm conditions led to the ship being battered in its anchorage. After failing to beach it and recognising that it would soon be destroyed, through the constant grounding, by the tides and the grinding by ice, James and his crew resorted to the extreme decision to sink their ship at sea, after removing all their stores, hoping to raise it the following spring. The survivors were not convinced they would ever refloat the ship, for when it was sunk James noted in his narrative: "we were leapt out of the Frying pan into the fire" (J 52). So in subsequent months the crew took the precaution of building a pinnace, some 27 feet long, 10 foot wide, 5 foot deep and 12 to 14 tunnes in weight (J 76), in case they were unsuccessful in refloating their ship and needed an alternative escape vessel.

During the long and bitter winter and spring that followed, most of the crew were prostrate with scurvy and devastated by the bone-chilling cold. Many had lost their shoes and were forced to wrap their feet in cloth; the majority of their tools had broken and they were reduced to the use of one or two axes, limiting their labours. There is little doubt they had many periods of despair, especially in late April when practically all the men were suffering from painful sores on their legs and bodies that needed daily attention. In all, four men died during the winter period, although two were involved in accidents. In early April, they made the decision to rescue the ship, and despite their weak condition began the arduous task of chopping out the ice that had accumulated in it. They managed to refloat the ship in mid-June 1632, leaving the island in early July – sailing back along the southern Hudson Bay shore to the west because ice prevented them from sailing north or east. Before leaving the island, they erected a wooden cross, leaving behind not only portraits of the king and queen and the coat of arms of Bristol to establish possession, but a summary account of their journey in case they perished. This letter was also reproduced in James's book as an appendix. Another cross was erected at Cape Henrietta Maria to fulfill the same function. Their journey to the northwest was again filled with potential danger after danger. James and his crew were forced to sail for weeks in a narrow and shallow band of open water, often only a few miles wide, between the treacherous shore and the pack ice. Danger from rocks, storms, and thick fog was ever present; at one stage James described how the ship was battered by ice five hundred times a day (J 94). This new attempt to find the Northwest Passage that had eluded them the previous summer — in full recognition of the appalling conditions they had already experienced — surely demonstrates the heroic nature of James and his crew. Yet, in some ways their ordeal was unnecessary. They could have sailed back to Britain the previous fall and been back in time to try to explore to the northwest in the following summer — although it is dubious whether such a journey would have taken place, given the negative results that had achieved previously.

Much of the 1632 journey duplicated the passage of the previous summer, but they eventually found open ice and were able to sail northeastwards to Coats and Nottingham Islands and then northwest into what is now known as Foxe Channel, searching for the passage to the Orient. On 26 July 1632, at a latitude estimated at 65°30′ N, the *Henrietta Maria* encountered unbroken ice. Disillusioned with the prospect of ever finding a clear passage to the west, James and his crew turned east and set sail for home. James's journal tells the reader little about the journey back to Bristol. They left Hudson Straits on 2 September and managed to avoid being sunk the next day when they encountered ice that was described as the highest they had seen (J 106). Not until 22 October were they finally able to bring their battered and leaking vessel to Bristol Roads. James's description of the condition of the ship when it finally reached harbour leaves little room for doubting the severity of their voyage.

> *All her Cut-water and Sterne were torne and beaten away, together with fourteene foote of her Keele; much of her sheathing cut away: her bowes broken and bruised, and many timbers crackt within boord: and under the Star-boord bulge, a sharpe Rocke had cut thorow the sheathing, the planke, and an inch and a halfe into a timber that it met withall. Many other defects there were were besides, so that it was miraculous how this vessel could bring us home againe. (J 110)*

The fact that the ship survived such a battering testifies to the robust nature of the ships that plied the Avon and the Severn Estuary, whose rapid tidal fall meant that ships were stranded on the mud every day.

James ends his description of the voyage with the comment that his crew all went to church – although it was not named – to give thanks for their deliverance.

Although James was not successful in his voyage it is worth remembering that for over two hundred years all the subsequent expeditions failed. Indeed, it is a mark of the difficulty of James's task to remember that it was not until William Parry wintered on Melville Island with his naval expedition in 1819–20 that anybody had come at all close to completing the passage (Parry 1828). Despite the short distance to the open Beaufort Sea, solid ice blocked the last part of his route. Incidentally, it may be noted, given James's background, that Parry's grandfather, Joshua, was born in the small Welsh village of Llangam (Pembrokeshire), although this heritage had little to do with his success as an explorer. Parry's father became a doctor in Bath and had a whole series of social connections with the British elite, which certainly helped Parry's career. Final proof of the existence of a passage through the Arctic islands had to wait another thirty years with many failures in the meantime, especially the disappearance of Franklin which caused so much anguish in Britain, but rekindled interest in the Northwest Passage. Partial success came with the naval expedition of McClure and Collinson who had been sent by the Admiralty to try to prove the passage from the west, beginning in the Beaufort Sea. It was probably McClure's intense ambition to be successful that led to the separation of the two ships and the fact that he became the first to traverse the passage. McClure had been unable to penetrate the strait that bears his name because it was blocked by ice. He sailed around most of Banks Island before being forced to abandon his vessel on the northeastern shore and sledged across to Melville Island in 1850 (Berton 1988). He and part of his crew then had to walk back eastwards through the ice-bound passage before being picked up by a rescue ship and taken back to London. Although attempts to make the passage by sea continued, it was not achieved until Roald Amundsen and his crew in the Gjoa, who had left Oslo in June 1903, passed through the Bering Strait on 30 August 1906. Initially he attempted to sail through the Lancaster Sound-Barrow Strait route but was unable to penetrate the known direct passage via Viscount Melville Sound and McClure Strait because of severe ice conditions, which meant he was forced to winter in the area. Amundsen's final route went south through Queen Maud Sound and then northwestwards to the Beaufort Sea, sailing with extreme difficulty in the shallow, rock-infested passage between the mainland and the Arctic islands, before being forced to winter yet again off the Mackenzie

Delta in the winter of 1905–06. Now confident of success, because the Beaufort Sea was known and frequented by whalers, Amundsen actually spent five months on a trek to Eagle City in Alaska to send a telegram confirming that he had achieved the long-sort-after passage, illustrating his intense desire to make sure his achievement would be the first to be recognized. This ended the longest search in exploration history, spanning the time from the early Renaissance to the modern period. The intense difficulties experienced by McClure and Amundsen, and the number of years they took to achieve their journeys, even with the technology of an industrial society, shows that the Northwest Passage was never achieved easily. Their experiences demonstrate the impossibility of James's task in the early seventeenth century, even if he had chosen, or been allowed by his instructions, to take a more northerly route.

Chapter 5

Locational Identification
and Cognition

I had all the men to acknowledge immediate dependence upon my selfe alone; both for direction and disposing of all, as well of the Navigation, as all other things whatsoever.... In the meantime, the better to strengthen my former studies in this businessse, I seeke after Journals, Plots, Discourses; or whatever else might helpe my understanding. (James 1633, 4)

It is usual to judge exploratory ventures by their success in finding new lands or new routes – whether serendipitous or calculated. But equally important in the growth of knowledge about the world is the extent to which the explorer is able to produce accurate and replicable portrayals of where places are – in terms of some reference system that is understandable to others. The explicit comments from James's narrative that are quoted above demonstrate that he was the undoubted leader and pilot of this venture. Moreover, he deliberately adopted an intellectual approach to the journey by finding and reviewing all the available evidence of previous discoveries and opinions about the area that he was exploring. In addition, it will be shown that James was meticulous in the calculations of his location and paid careful attention to the accuracy of the instruments he carried. Any review of other exploration journals will show that explorers varied in the degree to which they were able to calculate accurate locations and distances. This competence can be related to the innate ability of the explorers and their attitudes to written sources over practical experience. But it also depended upon the quality of the instruments they carried and the ability to measure location accurately in frequently severe climatic conditions, a particular problem in arctic and subarctic climates. From the sixteenth century onwards, and especially from the late eighteenth century with the presence of reliable clocks (Sobel 1996), the European system of representing location by the latitude-longitude system became more and more accurate, producing replicable results that enabled locations to be fixed with a high degree of precision. But this system is only one of a range of alternatives. It has already been noted in chapter 2 that recent humanistic insights into map-making practises have rediscovered the fact that indigenous peoples around the world knew how to reach quite distant places and had alternative forms of locational representation (Harley and Woodward 1987; Turnbull 2000). Many European explorers of the Americas used native peoples to guide them in the interior of continents, which proved essential in way-finding, as well as in ensuring peaceful passage through areas occupied by potentially hostile peoples. But once the exploration had been made, the navigational skills of the indigenous peoples were often dismissed, and the forms of representation they used were virtually obliterated, as Turnbull (2000) has shown in the case of the superb seafaring abilities of Polynesian navigators. Yet one must be careful of accepting some relativist position that all alternative location-fixing practises are equally useful. By the nineteenth century, the longitude-latitude system was able to be applied with a high degree of accuracy through the use of instrumentation – and could be carried out by people with some minimum level of training – providing an alternative to skills achieved by those with innate ability and years of personal practise.

Once the location of places was established, it was necessary to find ways of communicating this information to others. The practise of compiling lists of latitude and longitude of places had been created by Greek geographer-mathematicians such as Ptolemy in the famous library at Alexandria, but had fallen out of use. Not until the late eighteenth century onwards was the idea revived by the British navy, which was determined to precisely identify the location of major ports and topographic features (Owen 1827). However, such compendia are clumsy and difficult to use. By contrast, a map based on the latitude-longitude system is simultaneously able to record the position of these places, and provide an image of these locations in a single form. Certainly, maps and charts were found in Europe before the age of exploration in the Renaissance. Portolean charts had been widely used by seafarers in the medieval period, but they were based primarily on dead reckoning, and were limited to areas that were known, or to journeys that did not take travellers far from land. Also, the medieval maps produced to support the claims of the Christian church, often with Jerusalem at the centre of the world, were as much symbolic representations of the world as seen through Christian mythology as accurate portrayals of location. The new intellectual ideas of the Renaissance, followed by the beginnings of a scientific revolution, led to the development of new skills of map-making and to the calculation of more accurate locations, aided by new and better navigation instruments. It enabled the construction and dissemination of far more accurate portrayals of the newly discovered land and the routes to them, and through the printing presses made them widely available. It is obvious that the production of an accurate map makes it possible to repeat a journey. This means that the principle of replication is fulfilled – one of the important methods of the emerging scientific enquiry. Yet it is important not to overstate the accuracy of the early Renaissance maps. All maps are flat, two-dimensional representations of the earth, which in reality is a curved surface. So there are always distortions in a map representation, which are only resolved, in part, by various map projections. By the mid-sixteenth century, the Mercator projection was in common use, since it had the advantage of providing accurate directions, but only at the expense of increasing the area of regions towards the poles. With the increase in the knowledge of the world, more and more sophisticated maps were produced, as cartographic historians have shown (Harley and Woodward 1987). Although the map remained the chief form of communicating locational knowledge about the world, accounts of the new lands increasingly used sketches and pictures to show the character of the land, its flora, fauna, and its peoples and their culture. However, the use of such supplementary material only become commonplace from the mid-eighteenth century onwards, when skilled artists and scientists were deliberately added to the crews engaged in explorations of discovery. By that time, the ability to draw and to paint became one of the favourite accomplishments of British naval and army officers; many used these skills to illuminate their accounts of the areas they visited or explored.

⊹ 2. ESTABLISHING LOCATION

James, as an educated man, took a great deal of care in reviewing all the known information on the areas to which he was going to explore. In addition, he was specific about the navigational aids and other materials he consulted and took on the voyage, describing them in detail in the first appendix to his book (table 5.1) – a list which includes specific mention of the fact he included the books of Hakluyt and Purchas. It is inexplicable that Barrow (1818, 244) accused him of "being in total ignorance of all that had been done before him." Unfortunately, James's care in planning was not always understood by subsequent readers, for many subsequent editions of his narrative did not contain all these technical sections. Presumably the omission was made to emphasize the results and experiences of James's journey, forgetting the need to show how the locations that were identified were measured by the instruments he carried and used – an essential part of what we would call scientific proof today. Moreover, James's careful preparation is also seen in the fact that he described how he employed "skilfull workmen" to make his instruments, not trusting to what he called "Mechannicke hands," and had them calibrated by "an ingenious practitioner in the Mathematicks" (J A4).

This intellectual approach to the problem of establishing location on his voyage contrasts with his rival. Foxe's practical approach to ocean

TABLE 5.1. LIST OF INSTRUMENTS TAKEN ON THE VOYAGE

THE NAMES OF THE
seuerall Instruments I prouided
and bought for this *Voyage*.

A *Quadrant* of old seasoned Peare-tree-wood, artificially made, and, with all care possible, diuided with *Diagonals*, euen to minutes. It was of foure foote (at leaste) *Semi-diameter*.

An *Equilateral Triangle* of like wood, whose *Radius* was fiue foote at least, and diuided out of *Petiscus Table* of *Tangents*.

A *Quadrant* of two foote *Semi-d.*, of like wood, and with like care *proiected*.

The *Sights*, *Centers*, and euery other part of them lookt to, and tryed with conuenient *Compasses*, to see if they had been wrongd or altred; and this continually before they were made vse of.

Staues for taking *Altitudes* and *Distances* in the heauens.

A *Staffe* of seuen foote long, whose *Transome* was foure foote, diuided into equall parts by way of *Diagonals*, that all the *figures* in a *Radius* of tenne thousand might be taken out actually.

Another of sixe foote, neere as conuenient, and in that manner to be vsed.

Masters *Gunters Crosse-Staffe*.

Three *Iacobs Staues*, *proiected* after a new manner, and truly diuided out of the Table of *Tangents*.

Two of Master *Davis Backe-staues*, with like care made and deuided.

Of *Horizontall Instruments*.

Two *Semicircles*, two foote *Semi-diameter*, of seasoned Peare-tree wood, and diuided with *Diagonals* to all possible exactnesse.

Sixe *Meridian Compasses*, ingeniously made, besides some doozens of others more common.

Foure *Needles* in square boxes of sixe inches *Diameter*, and other sixe of three inches *Diameter*.

Moreouer, foure speciall *Needles* (which my good friends Master *Allen* and Master *Marre* gaue me) of sixe inches *diameter*, and toucht curiously with the best *Loade-stone* in *England*.

A *Loade-stone* to refresh any of these, if occasion were; whose *Poles* were marked, for feare of mistaking.

A *Watch-clocke* of sixe inches *Diameter*, and another lesser *Watch*.

A *Table*, euery day *Calculated*, correspondent to the *Latitude*, according to Master *Gunters* directions in his booke; the better to keepe our *Time* and our *Compasse*, to iudge of our *Course*.

A *Chest* full of the best and choicest *Mathematicall bookes* that could be got for money in *England*; as likewise Master *Hackluite* and Master *Purchas*, and other books of *Iournals* and *Histories*.

Study Instruments of all sorts.

I caused many small *Glasses* to be made, whose part of time I knew to a most insensible thing, and so diuided and appropriated the *Logg-line* to them, making vse of *Wilbrordus Snellius* his numbers of feete answering to a *Degree*, and approoued of by Master *Gunter*.

I made a *Meridian-line* of 120 yards long, with sixe *Plumb-lines* hanging in it, some of them being aboue 30 foot high, and the weights hung in a hole in the ground to avoyde winde; and this to take the *Sunnes* or *Moones* comming to the *Meridian*. This line wee verified by setting it by the *Pole* it selfe, and by many other wayes.

Two paire of curious *Globes*, made purposely, the workeman being earnestly affected to this Voyage.

(Source: Appendix 1 James in 1633. Original spellings and italics used except for ſ being changed to s as in normal convention to improve modern comprehension.)

navigation led him to boast that he had no need for books. His experience had convinced him that it was necessary to act in an emergency, for there would not be time to consult a "waggoner booke" (F 265) – a derogatory reference to the contemporary word for a guide or aid to travel. Yet Foxe may have overstated his practical orientation. He did admit that he had used a number of globes and other navigational aids and had previously scrutinized the journals of other explorers who had been to the area (F 262). In addition, Foxe had consulted the famous mathematician and geographer, Henry Briggs, in Oxford. Indeed Briggs seems to have been influential in helping to persuade the king and the London merchants to make the attempt to find the northwestern route to Cathay. Hence this contact means that Foxe must have been aware of Briggs's map of North America published in Purchas in 1626 (Wallis 1997), which shows the broad outlines of Hudson Bay (see figure 2.4.) But Foxe's mean spirit is seen by the fact he took delight in describing in his journal that James was not able to avail himself of Briggs's expertise, since the theoretical geographer and mathematician had died in the winter before their voyages took place (F 263).

What was significant about James's voyage was that he established definitive evidence of the positions of the new lands around Hudson Bay. In a strictly exploratory sense, there is little point in denying that James's achievements were limited. The prior achievements of Hudson, Button, and Munk have already been noted. But James was the first to explore and map the southern shore of Hudson Bay and the western part of James Bay. Although Briggs's map of 1626 (Wallis 1997) shows the presence of this western shore in what became James Bay, it is likely that Hudson only sailed along the eastern coast, but probably wintered in the south of the bay. James's voyage added another several hundred miles to the known extent of the southern shores of Hudson Bay, confirmed its broad outlines, and provided the most accurate map of the area to date. Despite James's two brave attempts to sail through the ice to the northwest, it seems likely he did not penetrate further than 65°30′ N in his second attempt in the summer of 1632. His rival, Foxe, claimed to have reached 66°47′ N in 1631: The area of this achievement was subsequently named Foxe Channel in his honour. Also, Foxe explored more of the area in the northwest of Hudson Bay, in the region known as Roe's Welcome Sound. However, it must be emphasized that the achievements of previous explorers in the area, such as Hudson and Button, were not fully recognized in print in James's day. Button's journal was never published – only the fragments published in Foxe (1635) survive today

— whilst the mutiny in Hudson's ship ensured that the detailed record of this voyage was largely lost, although its broad outlines were known from the information brought back by the survivors (Asher 1890). This meant that it was James's more detailed account of the Hudson Bay area that created the biggest impression upon the public, especially since it was published almost two years before Foxe's work (1635). Moreover, the journal was written with the imaginative flair that his rival lacked. Although the normally critical Barrow admitted that Foxe was a talented sailor, he was also described as "conceited," with a style "so uncouth and the jargon so obscure and comical as in many places to be scarcely intelligible" (Barrow 1818, 236). In addition, Foxe was greatly criticized in court circles for returning after six months and for not wintering in the area to enable him to try again to prove the passage during the following summer — an issue he was at pains to try and counter in his journal.

James's narrative frequently described the great care he took when measuring his location. The care and persistence taken over his calculations demonstrate, once again, how unfair many of James's critics have been. Clearly these tasks were treated as crucial intellectual exercises; James's approach to measuring location can be considered exemplary. Foxe, by contrast, always critical of James, did not display the same care — or at least did not bother to record the fact. The difference between them may be the fact that Foxe was a practical seaman, whereas James, a more educated and scientifically orientated individual, placed more dependence upon instruments. Yet we must be careful. James was not the maritime neophyte that his critics have portrayed him. He must have spent a lot of time at sea before the voyage to Hudson Bay was made, given his obvious knowledge of ice conditions, his work as a privateer captain, and his decision not to include any other crew member with extensive knowledge of arctic navigation and conditions. In addition, he made the brave decision to winter in Hudson Bay and, more to the point, again tried to search for the passage to Asia in the following summer of 1632. This ignored his previous hardships and disappointments — whereas Foxe returned home in the late summer of 1631, despite also being provisioned for an eighteen month journey.

James's approach to calculating his location went further than simply describing how he had taken care in making the measurements. He also provided appendices to support his methods and calculations, so that others could judge the utility of his results. One appendix (figure 5.1) listed the large number of navigation instruments that he carried — a compilation that shows the seriousness with which he approached the problem. James, like all sailors of his day, had little trouble in estimating his latitude by the height of the sun, except when the sky was overcast, although the problems caused by reflections from ice surfaces were noted and were shown to create difficulties in northern voyages. What is clear from his book is the care he took to record his positions by frequent recalculation of his observations before arriving at a definitive answer, whether of magnetic variation or latitude. The need to take several confirmations of the noontime positions, rather than depending on a single measurement, may have been standard. But James seems to have always aimed for the greatest accuracy possible. For example, he commented (J 81) that he had practised his observations for two weeks in June 1632, before concluding that Charlton Island was located at latitude 52°3′ N, a surprisingly accurate value given the instruments that were available to him. Unfortunately, some of the tables made were lost "by negligence of my Boy" (J 123) – one of the few occasions he provides any criticism of his crew. But in general, like all of his contemporaries, James was not able to identify his longitude during his journey with any accuracy. The precise clocks suitable for sea voyages that were needed to achieve the task were not invented until the late eighteenth century (Sobel 1996). But James did have timepieces with him, and specifically described the fact that the cold was so severe in winter that his clocks froze (J 64) – surely indicating that he was aware of the importance of accurate mechanical devices to recording time, if not distance from Britain. In the second appendix to his book, written by Master Gellibrand, an astronomer-mathematician of Gresham College, the general problem of establishing longitude was described. Gellibrand noted there were several ways of identifying latitude, whereas "the longitude of a meridian is that which hath and still wearieth, the greatest Masters of Geography." (J A2, 1) The appendix describes a series of calculations used to identify the position of James's wintering place. Basically, they are based on two principles. The first came from estimating the altitudes of fixed stars at the time of maximum elevation of the moon. James always made a series of calculations of what he described as azimuths and summarized the range of values by a mean. Most of these were at indeterminate locations at sea, often taken on ice floes, so they cannot be evaluated properly. Yet it is worth noting that James always provided a series of estimates, subsequently calculating a mean value as a final conclusion, demonstrating his command of the emerging scientific approach to measurement and the need to report these variations. The second estimates were based on the observations of the solar time of a major eclipse of the moon on 29

October (J 45). These were subsequently compared with the time of the same eclipse in Britain and adjusted by a series of additional calculations to produce estimates of longitude. Gellibrand's methods produced values between 79°30′ W and 78°30′ W for the longitude of Charlton Island. Gellibrand maintained his calculations only varied by four minutes of time, or one degree of difference. He considered the result to be very accurate, given that his review of the calculations made by various leading European mathematical and geographical authorities of the estimated positions of the cities of Rome and Nuremburg had revealed major differences. This led Gellibrand to his concluding comment that the minor difference in the calculated values of longitude for Charlton Island should

> ... *be a means to incourage our English Sea-men and others, to make such or the like observations in forraine parts, as the heavans shall be offered unto them. (J A2, 6)*

Since contemporary maps show Charlton Island to be at 79°15′ W, it seems clear that James's calculations, and the subsequent use of his information by a renowned mathematician-astronomer, provided much better estimates of his longitude than previous work by his contemporaries. But it is not simply the results that must be praised; it is the careful methodology he used to provide proof for the calculations. By comparison, it is worth noting that Foxe did not provide any reasonable mathematical estimates, or evidence of how he solved this crucial problem of longitude – other than by dead reckoning on his maps. Of course, the limitation was that James was unable to derive longitudes with accuracy during the voyage; Gellibrand's calculations were estimated after the voyage was completed.

James was not content with simple assertions of the need for empirical accuracy in establishing geographical position. An important addition to his journal was the third appendix written by another Cambridge academic, only identified by the initials WW, probably the cleric William Watts (Christy 1894, 628); in some editions XY was used as the pseudonym. Although rather long-winded and often obscure in meaning, the essay was designed to demonstrate that the voyages of James and his fellow explorers produced information that was at variance with the work of theoretical geographers or classical philosophers. James had shown his awareness of the problem facing the navigator, as can be seen from one of his first observations off the coast of Greenland, near Cape Farewell:

I know very well these Latitudes, courses and distance, doe not exactly agree with Mathematicall conclusions; but thus we found it by practice. (J 7)

This shows James's awareness of the differences that can occur between theoretical and observed locations. It demonstrated his preference for observations, rather than using either values from theoretical speculations, or calculations that might be based on false premises, both of which could produce inaccurate results. This issue is more widely addressed in the third appendix, where the author, WW, argued that the theoretical interpretations of classical philosophers, such as Aristotle, should be modified or replaced by the knowledge brought back by the new breed of explorers. This means that James's work should be seen as providing philosophical significance, in producing precise statements for locations and other facts that were derived from experience. Moreover, it was the type of evidence that could be replicated, or confirmed, by subsequent expeditions. Hence James's work should be seen as having a philosophical purpose, one that in our contemporary world may be described as linked to the *logic of justification*. As Livingstone (1992) has argued, it means that the conclusions based on the authority of theoreticians, or classical authors, were challenged and overthrown by the seamen of the day; their empirical observations showed that previous ideas were incorrect. Unfortunately, this philosophical commentary was dropped from the 1740 and 1973 editions of James's book, along with the two previous appendices, seriously reducing the value of the book as an example of the need to provide scientific justification for statements about location. This means that the scientific significance of James's calculations, and the justifications of location, cannot be appreciated by those who have only read later and shorter editions of his work. Perhaps these omissions led subsequent critics to underestimate his work.

Although one can commend James for the care he took in his locational observations, not all of the calculations in James's book were accurate. Given the problem of establishing longitude during the voyage with accuracy, and the constant changes in direction he was forced to make at sea, it is hardly surprising that James's estimates of distances which were based on dead reckoning are not entirely accurate, especially those across Hudson Bay. Distances at sea were notoriously difficult to make and to communicate since the common term *league* or sea mile varied.

FIGURE 5.1. JAMES'S MAP OF HUDSON'S BAY AND VOYAGE

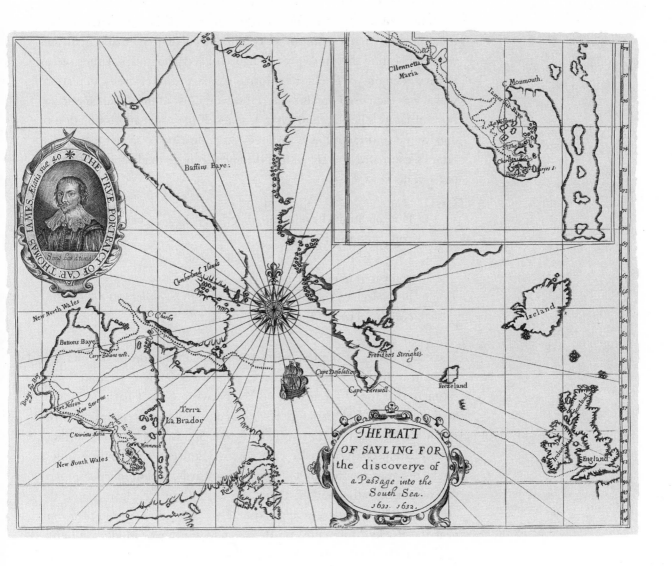

Eva Taylor (1934) showed that the Portuguese navigators had long used 17.5 leagues or four Roman miles each to a degree, which produced an equivalent of 64.4 statute miles to the degree. Although British sailors usually adopted the value of sixty miles to a degree, mathematicians were advocating the more precise figure of sixty-six miles. James seems to have been one of the first explorers to accept this revised calculation, which was then used on his maps. However, most of the distance calculations in James's book are given in leagues. If the usual approximation of one league to three miles is adopted, the following equivalents between James's estimates and the actual distances can be made for several key parts of his voyage:

i.   Hudson Strait (Resolution–Digges Is.): 120 leagues (360 miles) compared to 415 miles;
ii. Digges Is. to site of western landfall: 160 leagues (480 miles) compared to circa 575 miles;
iii. Pt. Nelson to Cape Henrietta Maria: 130 leagues (390 miles) compared to 395 miles.

The congruency of the last estimate may be a function of the fact that James travelled this distance twice. James was far less accurate in his estimate that the difference, at 66° N, between Cape Charles and what he described as "Califurnia" (J 109) – a contemporary description of the whole Pacific coast north of Mexico – was 500 leagues. At this latitude, the panhandle coast of Alaska – unknown to Europeans at the time, unless Drake did traverse the coast – trends westwards, so a modern comparison would be rather unfair. Using the latitude of Charlton Island, the estimate of 500 leagues, or approximately 1,500 miles, would place one near the Rocky Mountains, on the western border of modern Alberta. So, James's estimated distance to the Pacific is a third less than the actual value – another example of the way that the early transatlantic explorers significantly underestimated the distance to the Pacific.

✢ 3. MAPPING AND THE QUESTION OF THE NORTHWEST PASSAGE

The rapid publication of James's book meant that his map and descriptions were published before Foxe's (1635). James's chart provided firm evidence for subsequent explorers to duplicate his journeys, whilst his descriptions of the areas visited left useful information about the conditions to be found on the frightening and inhospitable shores of Hudson Bay. But only one map was included in his book – which is shown in figure 5.1. James did not provide any other illustrations about the lands he visited. However, the map does contain a small sketch of a two-masted ship travelling along the route he identified, which does provide useful evidence of the type of vessel he used. Figure 5.1 can be compared with the modern representation of James's journey that was shown in figure 4.5, which was constructed by locating the key positions identified in his book from the latitudes, landfalls, and dead reckoning of distance that were described in the narrative. In the cases where his estimated positions can be related to some landfall, James's locations are virtually within sight of the real position – a real achievement since James had to make measurements in difficult conditions, on an often pitching and freezing ship. James's map of Hudson Bay represented the first comprehensive portrayal of the area, but it is far from accurate, as a comparison of figures 4.5 and 5.1 will show. James exaggerated the large southern extension of Ungava Bay, extending it too far to the west. Similarly, the bays that James shows on the west coast of Hudson Bay are too large. Coats Island (Cary Swan's Nest to James) is shown inaccurately as an extension of the mainland – as is Southampton Island. It is worth noting that the location known as Roes Welcome is identified, but as a bay, not a channel separating Southampton Island from the mainland. It is rather curious how James identified this feature, since he did not sail into it. Foxe certainly explored there, and may have passed this information on to James during their meeting. The area north of modern Churchill is also incorrectly shown as a larger bay than exists in reality. Incidentally, James labels it Briggs's Bay on his map, honouring the Oxford mathematician-geographer, although there is no comment about this designation in the narrative itself.

The biggest inaccuracy lies in James Bay itself, where James's map portrays the area divided into two by means of a major peninsular whose tip was labelled Cape Monmouth, which honoured his home county. Again, there is no written comment in the journal to justify this strange decision – strange because James did not really explore much of the east coast of Hudson Bay itself. He knew that Hudson had wintered in the area and was probably aware that Hudson's map, or rather one drawn by Hessel Gerritz in 1612 (Armstrong 1982, plate 9) based on reports of Hudson's journey, contained this hypothesized major bifurcation of the bay. The example shows how the process of intertextuality probably affected James's opinions. In the absence of other evidence we must assume that James simply modified this map from his own explorations in the west, but kept Gerritz's view that there was a separate eastern part. Incidentally, this was a conclusion shared by Foxe (1635), although his rival never sailed anywhere near this area. In practise the bay does separate into two parts at its end, but with nothing like the extent shown by James and his contemporaries.

What is tantalizing about James's map is the identification of a relatively wide channel to the northwest of Hudson Bay, in what was subsequently called Foxe Basin to mark his rival's pioneering journey. The presence of what became Foxe's Basin and Channel provided continued hope for those who believed in the Northwest Passage. Yet the evidence of the map contradicts the conclusions of James's written narrative, which produced the first definitive statement from any knowledgeable British explorer that questioned the long accepted belief in a Northwest Passage. James was dismissive of reports that the Portuguese and Spaniards had sailed through such a passage from the Pacific. He listed four principal reasons (J 108) why he discounted its presence in the Hudson Bay area: the fact that the flood tide in the bay comes from the east; the limited presence of fish, whales, or driftwood in the bay, all of which would indicate a western passage, rather than an enclosed sea; recognition that ice filled the northern part of the bay to 65°30′ N, even in summer, making any journey difficult and probably precluding a passage; and finally, that the ice drifted out to the east. In his subsequent discussion, James also observed there were large compass variations in the west, which suggested a large land mass in this direction – not the presence of open water. Moreover, the prevailing westerlies were also seen as making a westward journey difficult, whilst the presence of so much ice in the bay during summer would always make a journey extremely hazardous – especially for the bigger vessels needed for commerce. James's comparative knowledge led him to note that although a Northwest Passage to Asia would be shorter at the higher elevations, it contained few commercial prospects, whilst the Cape route was better known and easier to travel. The wealth of evidence that James presents against the presence of the long anticipated passage is really overwhelming. Even a casual reader must be impressed with James's acumen. It must have convinced his financially astute Bristol backers that a commercial passage was impossible. Of course, contrary opinions were expressed by James's contemporaries – such as Button and Foxe, who both continued to believe that a passage existed, either via Roes Welcome Sound or Foxe Basin. Subsequent compilers of Arctic voyages (Harris 1705; Barrow 1818) also accepted the idea of a passage. James is specific about the disappointment of the voyage, as these telling, and perhaps even poignant words show.

> *And although wee have not discovered populous kingdomes, and taken speciall notice of their Magnificence, power, and policies, brought samples home of their riches and commodities: pryed into the mysteries of their trades, and traffique: nor made any great fight against the enemies of God and our Nation: yet I wish our willingnesse in these desart parts may be acceptable to our Readers. (J 105)*

Despite these sentiments, James was reluctant to completely close the door on the question of a Northwest Passage. His map (fig. 5.1) leaves a gap in the north, which *implies* that a passage could be found. James's conclusion also shows signs of equivocation.

> *I very well know, that what I have here hastily written, will never discourage any noble spirit, that is minded to bring this so long tryed Action to absolute effect. And it is likely withall, that there be some, who have a better understanding, and a surer way of prosecuting of it, then my selfe have. To whose designes I wish a happy successe. And if they doe but make a review of what hath beene done, and give more certaine Celestiall observations, Hydographicall descriptions or exacter practice in Navigation: it will be a most commendable labour. (J 110)*

James's final prevarication does seem surprising, given the evidence he had accumulated and the litany of hazards that would have to be faced by future travellers – of storms, shallow seas, icebergs, pack ice, impenetrable fog, impossibly freezing winters followed by fly-ridden summers. Indeed, despite James's hard-won knowledge, expeditions to find a Northwest Passage continued for centuries, although most of the attempts at a passage in the late eighteenth and nineteenth centuries were publicly sponsored ventures of the Admiralty, and contrast with the desire for commercial gain which motivated James's backers. The last part of the quotation is also worth noting. It demonstrates, once again, another aspect of the scientific side of James's quest; his recognition of the need of what is called replication today – of repeated observation and experimentation under constant conditions. In retrospect, one cannot fail to be impressed by the accuracy of his observations, given the conditions of the time. In addition, he was assiduous in providing information about the conditions that he found within the book: the run of the tide, directions of winds, magnetic variations, and depth of the sea. However, reviewers of James's text will always be unable to pinpoint all his locations, because of the problem of measuring accurate longitudes, making it difficult to use many of these observations. In any case, it would be unfair to judge his work by the standards of the nineteenth-century naval surveyors. It must be remembered that James's task was *not* to provide detailed maps of the coast, but to *find* a passage to the west.

⁜ 4. LABELLING THE LAND

Another important feature of the cognitive approach relates to the labels that are allocated to a new land. The names usually signify the act of discovery or possession – labels that index their incorporation into the consciousness of the European world. Perhaps the most obvious of these designations were the labels that signified national possession, such as New England, New France, and New Spain. But areas within these kingdoms were also used to designate new lands: Button called the west coast of Hudson Bay, New Wales; whilst Sir William Alexander used the term Nova Scotia for the area he tried to colonize. Hence, it is not surprising that James followed this approach, labelling the south shore of Hudson Bay after the area where he was raised:

> The 20 (August) at 6. in the morning, we saw the land; it being very low flat land.... At noone wee were in lat. 57.00. We named it, The new Principality of South Wales; and drank a Health in the best liquor we had to Prince Charles, His Highnesse, whom God preserve.... (James 1633, 24)

However, the precision of the label allocated by James can be questioned. At other points in James's journal the area is described as "The South Principality of Wales" (J 27) and "The New South-west Principalitie of Wales" (J 115).

Table 5.2 lists all the other names allocated by James. It shows that James did not label many places, at least when compared to nineteenth-century explorers who often charted and named every bay and headland as part of their detailed mapping. Still, the designations show that

TABLE 5.2. PLACE NAMES DESIGNATED BY JAMES

1631

RESOLUTION ISLAND

23 June   Harbour of God's Province (Saved by Divine Intervention) Price's Cove (Master of Ship)

HUDSON BAY: SOUTH COAST

20 Aug.   57° N. The New Principality of South Wales
2 Sept.   Cape Henrietta Maria (Queen of England, 1609 - 69, Daughter of Henry IV of France)

IN JAMES BAY

10 Sept.   My Lord Westons Island (Richard Weston, Lord Portland; Baron W. of Neyland, Lord High Treasurer 1628 - 33)
19 Sept.   Earl of Bristol's Island (John Digby: Diplomat, Statesman, 1580 - 1653)
23 Sept.   Sir Thomas Roe's Island (Diplomat and Ambassador, 1581? - 1644)
2 Oct.   Earl of Danby's Island (Henry Danvers: Privy Counsellor, Statesman, 1573 - 1644)
25 Dec.   Winter's Forest (Sir John Winter: Queen's Secretary, 1600? - 1673). Caryes Island (Sir Henry Cary, Viscount Falkland, Lord Deputy of Ireland d.1633)

1632

6 May   Brandon Hill (near Bristol)
29 May   Charles Town (abb. to Charlton) and Island (Charles I, 1600 - 49, Prince of Wales, 1616, King 1625)

His charts also show five other names: James His Bay, New Severn River, Cape Monmouth, New South Wales, Briggs's Bay.

SUMMARY OF INFLUENCES ON NAMES

Named After:

Royalty	2	Crew	2	Wales and Borders	4
Nobles or Sponsors	6	Mathematician	1	Bristol Area	1
God	1				
Sub-totals	9		3		5	17 in Total

James either named places after areas he was familiar with – in this case to areas around the Bristol Channel – or for influential people, such as royalty, his sponsors, and influential courtiers. But the names are simply the empirical signifiers of these connections. In semiotic terms they reflect the presence of important principles: the power relationships behind James's journey; emotional connections with his homeland; as well as the resolution of rival claims, since the naming identified the first Europeans on the land, which was an accepted claim to possession. Most of James's labels were accepted by most subsequent mapmakers, and remain to mark the first European designation of the land, although the use of *New South Wales* died out in the mid-nineteenth century.

It must be recognized that the survival of the terms New Wales and New South Wales may have been fortuitous. Foxe also named this land. His narrative (1635, 217) described how he had found and re-erected the cross that Thomas Button had raised to claim the land for the British sovereign in 1612, about a mile up river from the mouth of the Nelson River. Foxe accepted the designation that had been given to the area, namely New Wales, rejecting – if he knew it – the name, New Denmark, that the Danish explorer Munk later gave to the same area in 1619. Subsequently, Foxe sailed along the south shore of Hudson Bay and recorded his negative opinion of the area. But the comments also describe the fact that he had named the area after his home county in England and had told James about this decision when they met on 29 August.

> *I had beene ... on the land, also, before they came; and had named it new Yorkshiere; but, being a barren waste Wilderness of Birds, and wild beasts of prey (and chiefely for that it is out of the roade of trading, and the passage) ... where none hereafter will desire to come), I conceive that I can have no great honour thereby (although I have given it a name), and therefore doe leave it to those that are disposed to intitle themselves therein. (F 358)*

This rather dismissive account implies that Foxe did not seem to care whether his label was accepted by others – although it could have been a recognition, two years after James's publication, that James's book had already popularized his own name: *New South Wales*. The British domination of subsequent explorations and trade connections explains the persistence of James's labels, ensuring that English language names would be maintained. Unfortunately for the name's longevity, the forbidding climate and limited agricultural potential of the region meant the area was never settled by Europeans – except for the small fur factories and forts controlling the subsequent fur trade of the interior – so the name South Wales was rarely used. The label *Wales* does not appear on maps of the area today. It was displaced when the new Dominion of Canada took over the Hudson's Bay Company lands in 1870 and decided to return to more indigenous naming traditions in its late-nineteenth-century maps. Had the area proved to be fertile and attracted many settlers, it is very likely that this *Canadian* New Wales, both North and South, would have become part of the common parlance. Then Captain Cook would have been unlikely to have used the term in Australia on 23 August 1770, when he proclaimed English possession over the area around Botany Bay – the area that grew to become the state of New South Wales. Other names given by James to major features in the area still survive: Severn River, Cape Henrietta Maria, Charlton Island, and James Bay. All remain as major memorials to the Anglo-Welsh explorer's discoveries.

✛ 5. EXPERIENCING THE LAND

In an experiential context, James's voyage and the descriptions of his wintering clearly show he was exploring a land at the margins of human existence for Europeans – given the level of contemporary technology and resources. The problem was compounded by the absence of native peoples to share their environmental expertise by showing how travellers or settlers could live off the land. James is often quite specific about the capability of the land, as a comment about Resolution Island shows: it is "utterly barren of all goodness" (J 18). The winter proved to be a real challenge in survival, despite the precautions James and his crew took in the construction of their houses and in their diet. James did not simply describe the cold; he reinforced impressions of its effect by vivid imagery and telling examples. For instance, when the men were rescuing their possessions from their sunken ship, eloquently described the scene in the following words.

> The men therefore must wade thorow the thicke congealed water.... Every time they waded in the Ice, it so gathered about thé, that they did seeme like a walking piece of Ice, most lamentable to behold. (J 57)

If the frozen men moved too quickly to the fire in their cabins during the winter, "the cold raised blisters as bigge as wall-nuts" (J 58). In another passage, the cold of winter was so severe that James noted it would "so freeze the haire on our eyelids that we could not see" (J 64). During most of the winter, the majority of the crew had their feet wrapped in rags; their leather boots had been burned by too close contact with the fires in their huts. Even the inside of their main house was only marginally habitable. James's descriptions drew attention to several of the problems that were experienced: permanent icicles inside their house; the fact that all their wines and medicines were frozen; and the daily presence of hoarfrost on their bedding in the mornings (J 65).

These examples must have convinced readers that James and his crew lived at the very edge of survival – saved by their ability to get enough fuel for their permanent fires. Yet, warmth was not enough. The excess of salt in their diet and the presence of too few juices or vegetables meant that most of the crew suffered from scurvy. The explorers only recovered because they discovered vetches growing in late May – a fortuitous discovery that soon improved their health. An adequate water supply was also a problem – they not only found that the ponds contained foul smelling water but discovered that melted snow was unwholesome to drink. Fortunately, they found a good spring that flowed all the winter (J 59). In summer, another set of hazards was found – just when the melting ice gave them hope that they could soon leave the place where they had wintered. From mid-June onwards, the crew members were plagued by clouds of biting flies and insects of many different varieties. James describes how they were was especially perturbed by one type:

> *Such an infinit abundance of bloud-thirsty Muskitoes, that we were more tormented with them, than ever we were with the cold weather. (J 81)*

James and his crew even wore bags on their heads in a vain attempt to keep the insects away (J 87). Despite such efforts, the flies and mosquitoes raised pimples on the faces of sailors and they could not stop scratching. The problem of this new hazard can be seen by the fact that James repeats the point made earlier in his laconic conclusion to the section on June 1632: "these flyes, indeed, were more tormenting to us than all the cold that we had heretofore indured" (J 87).

When all these experiences of life on this new land are added together, it is difficult to accuse the author of exaggerating their difficulties and discomforts. In any case, it must be remembered that their life had not been much better on board ship because of the constant soaking and the need to constantly chip the ice off the rigging. At other times they were exhausted from the effort of pushing the surrounding ice away with poles, of physically hauling the ship through the ice when it was jammed, and the constant need to constantly pump out the water that seeped through its seals. Perhaps the only positive feature of their stay, in a medical sense, was that James was able to report (J 79) that nobody suffered from any chest or lung infections!

✦ 6. IDENTIFYING AND MEASURING ENVIRONMENTAL CONDITIONS

James's care in calculating his positions provides strong evidence for the view that he can be regarded as a scientist in relation to this particular task. But these achievements were ignored by such a prominent critic as Barrow (1818); instead he chose to focus upon the constant crises faced by his crew during the eighteen months of his journey, suggesting these problems reveal James's lack of preparation and knowledge of the conditions to be experienced. This is clearly a reading or interpretation that ignored the fact that James chose to emphasize these events as part of the perils of his journey. It has already been shown that such criticisms are unfair, given James's description of his careful preparation for his journey, and his thoroughness, such as revealed in his measurements of location. In addition, Barrow's comments conceal the value of James's book in providing the first informative descriptions about the part of Canada he explored. For example, it has already been shown how some of James's empirical observations can be regarded as the first experiential comments about life in the area. It can also be argued that James provided what can be regarded as the first scientific evidence of the character of the environment and the physical processes at work.

Given the limited scientific knowledge of the day, it may be expecting too much to find James's journal providing major advances in the field, given the absence of any trained scientist on board – unlike the voyages of Cook and later Darwin, from a century and a half to two centuries later. Nevertheless, despite Barrow's critical comments to the contrary, James's descriptions do provide some of the first real insights into the character of the Hudson Bay environment. Apart from the locational references, the journal is replete with references to the flow of tides, direction of winds, and depth of the sea; one important conclusion was the description of the shallowing of Hudson Bay halfway between Nottingham Island and its southwest coast. James, like Baffin before him, was also one of the first to appreciate the extent of the refraction of the sun in arctic and subarctic environment, which meant the sun seemed to rise earlier, causing problems in estimating latitude and the ability to see distant places (J 69). But in contrast to these measurements and observations, it must be admitted that James's descriptions of the environment are not very informative. Some of these deficiencies can be attributed to the fact that much of the area consists of uninspiring, low, sandy shores bounded by islands, where land and sea are difficult to distinguish – hardly the raw material for inspired comment. Occasionally, there are flashes of insight that draw attention to some key environmental changes, such as the sandy red and muddy water which marked the flow of the Nelson River into the bay (J 24). But such insights are few and far between. They are far less important than the climatic observations that resulted from James's decision to winter in Hudson Bay. These comments provided the first informative summaries of the climate of the area that were available in print. They confirmed the environmental hazards that made the region so difficult for Europeans to survive.

James's search for a favourable place in which to winter, was complicated by the development of ice in the bay from October 1632 onwards. His subsequent descriptions of the onset of the freeze-up provides the first real summary of the sequence of ice formation in late fall and early winter. James's entries for mid- and late November describe how the growth of ice led to the water becoming congealed, which made it difficult to row boats through the icy sea. A telling point is made in the 1 December journal entry, when he describes how they were able to walk over the ice to their ship. Yet on the previous day they had rowed out – a clear indication of the speed with which solid ice could form (J 56). James also noted that the surface of the sea around Charlton Island was not completely frozen until the new year, although his observations of the rise and fall of ice in the bay in winter led him to doubt that it was completely frozen to the bottom of the sea. By contrast, he noted that the land around his winter quarters was frozen to a depth of ten feet by the end of January (J 63). James did not seem able to understand that some parts of the area were permanently frozen, for modern observations confirm that this is part of the discontinuous permafrost zone. February was described as the coldest month, but it was April that brought the greatest snow – a snow which was noted as being moist, unlike the dry, small flakes of winter. The size of the winter snowfall can also be gauged from his comments, since he described how it covered two thirds of the height of their huts (J 64). James also indexed the onset of spring, noting that some of the snow melted on the land by 3 May. But his records show that it was not until 24 May that some of the ice in the sea started to melt, although clear patches of water were not seen until 19 June. Even the attempt to sail away from Charlton Island on 1 July was hindered because the bay was still blocked with ice to the north and east. So James and his crew had to sail west through the shore-lead, the narrow band of open and shallow water between the shore and the ice. This was a dangerous task at any time. Their journey to the northwest, into the area now called Foxe's Channel, was halted by the presence of continuous pack ice in late July. Combined with Foxe's experience in the area during the previous year, this observation established the southerly limits of the pack ice, although subsequent explorers continued to believe there was a way through to the sought-after Northwest Passage.

All this information clearly provided important markers of the key climatic events of the winter. This must have helped subsequent expeditions to appreciate and prepare for the conditions – despite the absence of more precise measures subsequently derived from the use of thermometers. Despite the unequivocal evidence of the severity of the climate in winter, James maintained that he found the combination of hot days and freezing nights from mid-May to mid-June as being especially difficult to bear – "this unnaturalness of the season, did torment our men, that they now grew worse and worse daily" (J 77). This clearly illustrates the fact that James's representations of the climate conditions were based on the standard of his previous experience; a western European spring. The return of daily warmth in June did not solve all their problems, for the water was still very cold. When working to refloat the ship, James noted that even the fittest and youngest of his crew could only manage less than ten minutes in the water in June (J 79), but this was a result of the contrast between air and water temperature, not of the water temperature itself. Later, as has already been described, the pestilence of flies added to their discomfort.

James's observations on the flora and fauna are not as informative as those on the climate. Perhaps his most useful passage on this topic is found in the summary of the conditions in Charlton Island, although the brevity of the passage illustrates the limitations of his biogeographical observations.

This Iland and all the rest, (as likewise the maine) is a light white sand;
covered over with a white mosse, and full of shrubs and low bushes: excepting
some bare hills, and other patches. In these bare places, the sand will drive
with the wind like dust. It is very full of trees, as Spruce and Juniper: but the
biggest tree I saw, was but a foote and a half over. (J 89)

This passage goes on to note that few animals and birds were seen, or fish in the sea, or any sign of their bones on the shore. A reader is left with a clear impression of a marginal land in terms of available resources. In combination with the severe climate, this poor soil and vegetation was hardly likely to attract much further interest. James was a little more forthcoming in his comments on the fauna, recording some aspects of the seasonal migrations in the area, although one must remember he was on a small island. He noted the appearance of geese and cranes on 3 May, maintained that all the foxes had migrated elsewhere by May (J 89), and recorded that all the birds and animals had left by 17 June (J 81). But his comments on the fauna are often tinged with irritation, for his crew were rarely able to catch any birds or animals to supplement their meat supply. Despite several determined hunting expeditions and the assistance of two hounds, they were able to capture only a dozen foxes throughout their sojourn, which shows the technical limitations of his seamen in an unfamiliar environment. Although the dogs were kept all winter, they were released at Cape Henrietta Maria on the return journey, because the crew thought the dogs had not justified their care. The inability of James's crew to carry out successful hunts contrasted with the experience recorded by Button's expedition. Members of his crew killed hundreds of birds on the Nelson River – perhaps a function of this expedition's greater numbers and more guns, and of greatest significance, a mainland, not an island location – that was on a major seasonal migration route. James's only positive comment about the animals in the area comes from the one brief observation to his crew that the pelts of the foxes would be valuable (J 46), which is very different to Newman's (1986, 30) conclusions that James identified the area as a source of major fur-bearing animals! Contrary to Newman's view, James seemed to have had little idea of the potential of the area's fur trade – although again it must be remembered that it was the native peoples that really provided the trapping skill that enabled the Europeans to accumulate wealth from the fur trade in later years. In general, therefore, James's journal must have reinforced the attitudes of later explorers that there was no guarantee of being able to live off the resources of the land in this northern environment. James and his crew rarely found many fish, whilst they found it difficult to trap birds and animals; as is shown by the summary descriptions about animal life made in July 1632, as they were about to leave Charlton Island.

> *At our first comming hither we saw some Deare and kild one; but never any*
> *since. Foxes, all the winter we saw many, and kild some dozen of them; but*
> *they all went away in May. Beares we saw but few, but kild none: we saw*
> *some other little beasts. In May there came some fowle, as Duckes and Geese:*
> *of which we kild very few. White Partridges we saw; but in small quantities:*
> *nor had we any shot, to shoot at them. Fish we could never see any in the Sea*
> *... excepting a few Cockle-shels: and yet nothing in them neither. (J 89)*

The book leaves the clear impression that their survival depended upon the large supply of fish and meat they had brought with them. Although the land and sea had few resources, the problem was exacerbated by their location on an island, which must have reduced the available fauna. Even when the sailors discovered the ponds were full of frogs in June they were wary of trying to eating them – because of their speck-led appearance – although their cultural prejudices would probably have made frogs an unlikely food supply! The conclusion must be that James's journal left the impression of a land of little value. If it was to be conquered, it could only be achieved by the use of outside resources; Europeans would be unable to live off the land.

Viewed from the perspective of late-twentieth-century knowledge in locating and mapping places or in describing environmental conditions, James's work seems primitive. But related to the technology of his time his work has to be commended. The care he took in establishing his position, and more to the point, his concern in trying to prove the accuracy of his calculations, represented a scientific practise far ahead of his time. James's work is unique in the detail of his description when compared to his contemporaries. In addition, his identification of the seasonal migrations in the southern part of Hudson Bay was another important breakthrough in description. James has often been criticized for not making major new exploratory achievements. But his work was in an area where such achievements were impossible given the enclosed nature of Hudson Bay and the ice conditions. But what must not be forgotten was his *methodological achievements* in locational and environmental description, which made him a pioneer in these contexts. Subsequent techniques made it possible to provide greater and greater precision in measurement, but it must be emphasized that James achieved all that was possible given the technology of the day. In addition, his vivid descriptions of the actual experience of winter must have captured attention and convinced his readers of the vicious nature of the climate of the area. But it is the way that he interpreted the conditions, as much as the journey undertaken, that makes James's work so important. James took his experiences and constructed a literary account that provided new interpretations of both the journey and the hazards that had to be overcome. These interpretative issues form the basis of the next chapter.

Chapter 6

Interpretation
and Representation

Many a Storme, and Rocke, and Mist, and Wind, and Tyde, and Sea, and Mount of Ice, have I in this Discovery encountered withall; Many a despaire and death had, almost, overwhelmed mee; but still the remembrance of the Accompt that I was to give of it to so gracious a Maiesty, put me in heart againe; made mee not to give way to mine owne feares, or the infirmities of humanitie. ... since your Maiestie was pleased to signifie your desires, of having a Briefe of my Voyage presented unto you: that word became a Command unto mee. (James 1633, Preface)

James's preface shows that the perils of his journey were still very much on his mind when he wrote the account of his journey at the command of his king. Given his failure to find the Northwest Passage, it may not be surprising to find that it was these encounters that dominated much of his text. Certainly the narrative was bound to deal with the discovery and locational indexing of new lands – through the latitude-longitude co-ordinate system and mapping – as well as their character. Yet the written text also contains a great deal of other information that can provide additional understandings about the journey, the area explored, and the interrelationships among the crew. But any interpretation of the textual evidence of the narrative must also consider the way that it was organized and phrased, for these provide evidence of the goals of the writer and the way that he seeks to communicate with his readers. This means that the discourse of the text is not simply about the results of the exploration and the nature of the land; it can relate as much to the objectives, abilities, and character of the author – especially his fears and values – which influence how the text is constructed. This chapter uses six key categories to review these interpretive issues: the purpose of the journey and the narrative; the internal power relationships, especially leadership and spiritual values; the organization and style used in the narrative; the aesthetic representations; the interpretation of environmental processes; and finally, attitudes to the inhabitants of the land explored, both in terms of the culture of the aboriginal peoples and his own.

✛ 2. PURPOSE OF THE NARRATIVE

There seems little point in doubting that the manifest purpose of James's *voyage* was to find the much anticipated northern passage around the recently discovered continent of America to the rich trading lands of Asia and to sail back around the world. The boat was provisioned for eighteen months, so there was a clear objective, a specific quest. The experienced merchants of Bristol were not interested in some speculative voyage to discover unknown lands, some kind of odyssey or adventure cruise through unknown waters – which may, or may not have produced knowledge of new resources and new lands. Their rapid assembly of the resources to finance the venture was motivated from fear of trade competition, since the possible success of Foxe's expedition sponsored by London merchants would inevitably lead to a new trade route close to the Grand Banks, which would intrude on their dominance of the North Atlantic fisheries and exclude Bristol from any prospect of entering the lucrative Asian trade. When James was constructing his book, its final conclusion – the failure to find a commercial route to the Orient and his arguments that such a passage did not exist – must have weighed heavily on his mind. Who would be interested in a voyage that failed in its objective and showed that Hudson Bay was a dead end? This might have explained why James chose to deliberately emphasize the problems of coping with the unknown lands and environment he experienced, and the multitude of difficulties that he faced. Figure 5.1 shows that even the title – *The Strange and Dangerous Journey of Captain Thomas James* – reflected such a purpose. The relative size of the letters used in the title, and the subsequent description "the miseries indured," (James 1633) seem to have been deliberately chosen – either by James or his publisher – to focus attention on the difficulties. Surely this title makes as much an appeal to the senses, to the prospect of an account of adventure, as to any geographical discoveries? The title page draws attention to the way that the author coped with the unknown and its manifest dangers. It described a book that sought to astonish, entertain, as well as instruct, readers about the new lands. It was James, as a writer, who orchestrated the emphasis, not the commercial traders who sponsored him, for he must have been aware of the interest in exploration writing. This new genre contained descriptions of what seemed to be strange and exotic lands and brought examples of the sufferings that explorers endured into the drawing rooms of the readers. Given his failure to find the much sought after geographical passage it is surprising that James was granted a long audience with King Charles. But the king was so fascinated with James's tribulations that he encouraged him to write the book. Indeed, James's preface is dedicated to the king and clearly indicates that royal support was crucial to his decision to write the book – despite his initial forebodings that were shown in the extract which began this chapter.

No records exist to inform us whether James deliberately set out to write a book that would sell, or whether the book produced is the inevitable consequence of the fact that James was a natural storyteller – one with the gift of description possessed by so many of his countrymen from Wales. James chose to focus on the difficulties he experienced on the journey, which meant that he decided not to sweep aside his mis-

FIGURE 6.1 THE TITLE PAGE OF JAMES'S BOOK

THE
STRANGE
AND DANGE-
ROVS VOYAGE OF

Captaine THOMAS IAMES, in
his intended Discouery of the Northwest
Passage into the South Sea

VVHEREIN

THE MISERIES INDVRED, BOTH
Going, Wintering, Returning; & the Rarities
observed, both *Philosophicall* and *Mathematicall*,
are related in this Iournall of it.

Published by His MAIESTIES
command.

To which are added, A Plat or Card for the
Sayling in those Seas.

Divers little Tables of the Author's, of the Variation of the Compasse, &c.

VVITH

An Appendix concerning *Longitude*, by Master
Henry Gellibrand, Astronomy Reader,
of *Gresham* Colledge in *London*.

AND

An Aduise concerning the Philosophy of these late
Discoueryes, By W. W.

LONDON :
Printed by *Iohn Legatt*, for *Iohn Partridge*.
1633.

takes, avoid his constant apprehension, or his actual fear of being over-whelmed by the elements. Since his voyage always seemed on the edge of destruction, some readers took this as evidence of James's lack of skill. Foxe, his rival, was contemptuous of James's sailing ability, boasting that experience, not book knowledge, was the key to success. Barrow (1818) used the constant emotional outbursts found throughout the book as evidence of James's limited ability as a sailor and navigator, although he was undoubtedly prejudiced against James because of the latter's insist-ence that there was no commercial Northwest Passage. Barrow failed to recognize that such descriptions were *precisely* the passages that would entertain a popular readership. So it seems very likely that James's deci-sion to describe the problems and potential disasters was a deliberate rhetorical strategy – one designed to make the book popular. So when one evaluates the purpose of what can be called James's *work or contribu-tion to knowledge*, a dual approach is needed. The *voyage* was motivated by the fear of the powerful Bristol merchants of being outmanoeuvred by their rivals in London. But in the *book*, James deliberately used the fear of a hazardous environment to create the tensions that sustained the explo-ration narrative. In doing so, James transformed a *failure* of exploration into a literary *success*.

It may have been the need to emphasize the practical value of James's work as a journal of exploration that probably accounted for the word "strange" being dropped in the title of Payne's 1740 revision and in the reprinting by Coles in 1973 (James 1740; 1973), together with a series of other omissions, such as the exclusion of some appendices. This makes it also possible to argue that the initial editions of James's book should be regarded separately from the description of the voyage. Adams (1983) has argued quite convincingly that the development of exploration lit-erature helped stimulate the appearance of the novel, a very different genre since it was fiction. James's book may well be one of those works that helped this process, for it transcends its descriptive basis as an unemotional account of what happened. Of course, James's book does not complete the passage to the fictional base of the novel. His locations and descriptions were not invented; its daily log is a journal of actual exploration, whose text is enlivened with accounts of the ship's close calls with destruction. The result is a work that provides its readers with vicarious exposure to experiences in an extreme climate, in addition to the charting and describing a new land. But in focusing upon such issues, the book can be thought of as anticipating the sensationalist approach that characterized the accounts of exploration in the competitive nineteenth-century newspapers (Riffenburgh 1993). In these accounts, the *perils of the journey*, rather than the *result*, stimulated the interest of readers. Hence, it can be argued that two traditions – the imaginative experiences of the novel, and the facts of exploration – are combined in James's work. In this context it may not be without significance that there is another Welsh and Bristol literary association with North America in the development of one of the first American novels, but like James's work has been underestimated. Although there is a great deal of debate over the question of what constitutes the first novel in North America, Adams (1983) suggested that a strong case could be made for the work of William Williams (Dickason, D. H., 1970). Although Williams grew up in Bristol, his family was Welsh. He ran away to sea, and later settled down as a portrait painter in the New World, but returned to Britain during the American Revolutionary period and died, impoverished, in his hometown in 1791. But Williams seems to have completed his fictional account of the adventures of a Welsh castaway in 1789 – one that he called Lewellin [*sic*] Penrose, from the small, historic castle town of Caerphilly, in South Wales. But this was not published until 1815, and then only in heavily revised form (Dickason, D. H., 1970). This is another example of a Bristol–Welsh literary connection whose significance has been largely forgotten.

✢ 3. POWER RELATIONSHIPS

Exploration journals can also provide important insights into the power relationships that surround voyages of exploration, not only those external to the journey, but those that are internal to the group – such as the leadership qualities displayed and the interactions between the various members of the crew. Since a previous description of the context of the journey has described the external power relationships, it remains to show how the journal provides insights into the relationships within the crew – the internal associations. Since James provides the only voice providing information about such issues, there is always the possibility that the text could be self-serving. But, even allowing for this fact, the evidence shows that James displayed considerable prowess as a leader, which confirmed the character reference made by his sponsors in their letter of introduction to the court that was quoted in chapter 4. James's journal describes the care with which he organized and equipped the expedition in such a short time. Also, throughout the journey he makes a series of key decisions which display the mark of a true leader – issues that were all ignored by Barrow (1818) in his assessment of James's worth. For example, it has already been noted that he had prepared his navigational instruments with great care and visited a "practitioner in the Mathematicks" (J 4) to calibrate them. When he was on shore James took precautions against the possibility of attack by mounting guards in the camps – although he never saw any indigenous peoples. In the winter, he emphasized the need – both for psychological and nourishment reasons – for a hot meal every day and made many attempts to avoid the ravages of scurvy. In this context, he was quick to plant seeds in the spring in the hope of having fresh vegetables. However, it was the discovery of native vetches a few days later that probably saved the sickest members of the party. Even when he found these plants he told his readers that he gave instructions that they should be washed and boiled before they were eaten (J 80). Also, James deliberately chose a wooded area, protected by a bank to the north, for the construction of the three dwellings in which the crew survived the winter. Unfortunately, the discovery of the water table at two feet meant he was unable to set the main house into the ground as originally planned. It is curious how Barrow (1818, 244) came to the conclusion that it "was the sick men who wished for a hovel on shore." Although this was technically true he fails to give any credit to James's careful planning (J 59) of the three huts that were eventually constructed for the winter, using the derogatory term *hovel* to describe the winter camp.

James described how he deliberately set out to conserve fuel during the voyage. He also kept reserves of food and drink for emergencies – noting that he felt sure that the party would be at their weakest in the spring, keeping back a "tun of Alegant Wine" for this period (J 73). James ensured that the paths between the huts that constituted the winter quarters were kept clear and available for physical exercise and, given the constant fear of fire, made sure that the cooking building was separated from the others; another indication of Barrow's (1818) inaccurate views of James's preparation. Moreover, James was aware – the phrase employed in the journal is rather opaque – of the need to sink his ship in shallow water to keep it safe in the winter; otherwise it would be lost by being crushed by the ice or pounded in the shallows during the thaw. He also recommended that the ship used in the expedition had to be a small one, noting "a great Ship (as by former experience I had found) was unfit to be forc'd thorow the ice" (J 2) – an aside that surely confirms that he had been on a previous expedition to the Arctic.

After their ship was sunk to protect it from the ice, James gave instructions to build a pinnace during the winter, as an alternative, if limited, escape vessel. Another mark of his caution was the decision to build a large number of casks during the winter to help the flotation process to raise his ship when the ice melted. During the actual voyage James frequently made use of the practise of grappling his vessel to ice floes, not only to provide buffers from other icebergs, but to get advance warning of a shallow shore. This indicated either a man of experience, or one who could quickly adapt himself to the local conditions – although the first attempt to make the boat fast to an iceberg, in the Hudson Strait almost crushed them (J 9); later a large and unexpected drop in the tide almost pulled the ship over when they had tied up to a large rock (J 11). J. Barrow (1818, 244) used this latter example to illustrate James's incompetence since he had not chosen crew with Arctic experience, individuals who may have been able to anticipate this mistake, although the size of the tide may well have taken even experienced sailors by surprise. But it was the decision to use only one small vessel that may have been James's master-stroke. Not only did this avoid the need to make rendezvous with accompanying ships, but it also meant that the boat could be worked by half of the complement of his crew. This made allowance for the loss of crew members through accidents and ensured that the sailors would have longer rest periods between their watches. The use of a small vessel also meant that the vessel could be moved by brute human force if they got stuck in ice.

Good organization and sensible responses to crises were not James's only strong points. He also had a compassionate side. When it was clear that his gunner was dying after an accident, James allowed him to drink sherry at any time – the most valuable drink they possessed (J 46). Throughout the journal, he provides examples of the ways he sought to encourage the crew, to divert them when spirits were down, or to inspire them at moments of crisis. For example, he held a funeral service before they left their winter camp on 1 July – a service held in memory of the crew who had died – and deliberately made it an occasion to remember. He marched his men, with "Arms, Drumme and Colours, Cooke and Kettle," to the burial site on Brandon Hill where those who had died were buried under their tomb of stones. He followed this with a eulogy to inspire his crew (J 88–9), demonstrating James's obvious compassion and need to boost morale. When such qualities are added to all his other attributes, it seems clear that James displayed leadership skills that were rarely matched by other explorers.

These glimpses into his own character were not augmented by many insights into his relationships with his crew, or to their individual personalities. James was probably much older than most of the crew – for he describes them at one point as my "young and tenderhearted companions" (J 88) – although he was only in his early middle age at the time. In addition to James, the ship had a complement of nineteen men and two boys, but only the following officers and some other key men are named at various parts in the journal.

Lieutenant: William Clements.
Master: Arthur Price.
First Mate: John Warden.
Second Mate: John Whittered.
Boatswain: John Palmer.
Surgeon: Nathanial Bilson.
Gunner's mate: John Barton.
Gunner: Richard Edwards.
Carpenter: William Cole.

Only two of the twelve sailors were named: George Ugganes and David Hammon.

Many of the names seem typical of the Bristol area and the West Country, but the presence of names such as Price and Edwards suggest the possibility of some additional Welsh influences. Unfortunately, little is known about his crew, other than James's decision to only hire men if they were recommended, and were "unmarried, approved, able and healthy Sea-men" (J 3). His journal tells us that he recruited enough individuals for the crew in a few days. But he refused to hire anybody who had been on a similar arctic voyage, "for private reasons unnecessary here" (J 3). This represents a contrary decision to the advice received from his sponsors when he was in London seeking the royal favour. Foxe, by comparison, specifically stated he wanted crew with experience of ice conditions (Christy 1894, vol. 2, 264). James also stated in his book that he ensured the crew was dependent on the captain alone for "both for Direction and Disposing of all, as well of the Navigation" (J 4). At first sight, the absence of experience might appear foolhardy, as Barrow (1818) seemed to believe. But it was less than two decades since Hudson's crew had mutinied in the bay that bears his name, abandoning their captain and his companions to their death in an open boat. James's hiring practises were almost certainly taken to reduce the possibility of a similar result.

James only provides meagre comments about his crew. Practically all are positive, although they are rather shallow and repetitive, as the following extracts show. James described the gunner as "an honest and a strong-hearted man," (J 47) and the steward as "an honest man" (J 64). The surgeon merited a few extra phrases – "as diligent and sweet tempered a man, as I ever saw," (J 72) – whilst the carpenter had an even higher rating – "a man … of innate goodness … and quality" (J 75). By contrast, the boatswain was criticized as a "painfull man," although there is a possibility that this might have been a reference to his illness (J 30). James's prose contained few incisive statements to flesh out the character of the men with whom he shared the voyage. The impression is created that he was surrounded by what a late-nineteenth-century adventure novelist would have described as *jolly good blokes*! Perhaps James was merely describing his good luck in having such good and capable companions. Indeed, he may have been fortunate to find such individuals – given the haste in which they were chosen, and the apparent lack of previous contact among the crew which meant they had to learn to work together – although this may have had an advantage, in leading to an absence of previous resentments or cliques. Only in a handful of places in his journal did he criticize his men. On three of these occasions James described how he had overheard the men grumbling that the icy conditions were overwhelming, but he managed to divert them before the concerns escalated to a confrontation. In another passage, James showed irritation when reporting that some of the observations of the compass variation were lost "by negligence of my Boy" (J A2). But the only serious criticism of the crew came at a time when the ship ran aground; he wrote that the lookouts had failed in their task because they were "blinded with self-conceit" (J 32). James subsequently admitted he had to control a "little passion" in himself to check the bad counsel that had been given – before he was able "to revenge myself upon those that had committed this error" (J 32). This is the only time in the journal that he shows any sign of a vindictive attitude – although the *revenge* only took the form of making the miscreants work harder to save the ship.

The descriptions of such a passive crew may seem improbable in view of the hardships the crew suffered, the aggravation produced from close confinement, their illness, and inevitable worries about the prospects of survival. It seems very unlikely that these tribulations would be borne in stoic silence. It is far more probable that James chose to understate the real situation – but one can go too far in hinting that the silences about interrelationships in the journal covered up a hive of discontent. There is little evidence to suggest he was other than an able, compassionate, and fair captain. Unlike many of the captains of his day who strode the upper deck – the martinets, or the haughty and ineffective gentry – he seems to have believed in consultation. James's book described how he consulted his crew on eight critical times in the journey. The most significant of these occasions was on 26 August 1632, when the ship was virtually surrounded by solid ice as they still tried to force a passage to the northwest in the Foxe Channel area (J 104). Upon his request, James's five senior associates provided a written statement of their collective opinion; seven reasons were given for abandoning the search and sailing home. Today, one would take such an unusual action as the mark of an early democrat. More likely, it was evidence of his training as a lawyer. By reprinting the arguments in the book, the judgment of his senior crew is clearly shown. Obviously, he could not sail the boat alone. So this demonstration of a common attitude from his colleagues became a safeguard against criticism from his sponsors or court gossips – who may have claimed, since they knew little of the conditions – that James had not tried hard enough to find the Northwest Passage. James proved judicious in expressing regret at not being able to contradict the arguments that could be made about his lack of success. However, he hoped "his Majesty would graciously censure of my endeavours and pardon my returne" (J 105). He realized that his failure to fulfill the voyage's objective needed to be justified in his book – in the clearest possible way.

The evidence of the narrative surely displays James as a resourceful leader, one who often listened to his crew, on occasion asking them to speak freely (J 54). One must remember he provided the only evidence; as in all autobiographies, the descriptions may be self-serving, coloured by hindsight and subject to the pitfalls of memory loss. Yet it does seem unfair to take the absence of informative comment on the crew, or other silences in the journal, as evidence – or rather potential evidence – of a crew riven with discontent. Indeed, there are few grounds for even qualifying the conclusions that have been reached by using the evidence of other sources. Only one contemporary example could be found that provides an outsider's insight into James and the crew – the journal of his rival Luke Foxe (1635). This is a work that seems tinged with envy and bitterness. James met Foxe's ship, the *Charles*, accompanied by two smaller boats, the *Mary* and the *Bonnet*, shortly after seven in the evening of the 29 August and parted early in the morning of the 31 August. James provided only the barest description of the meeting in 26 lines of text, almost half of which describes how the ships had to be managed to ensure they did not lose contact, the rest commenting on the fact that they exchanged information on their discoveries. By contrast, Foxe (F356-362) allocated 153 lines and revealed his mean spirit by the following comment:

> *This 17 houres was the worst spent of any time of my discovery. My men told me his men gave them some Tobacco, a thing good for nothing. (F 361)*

This was James's reward for entertaining his fellow explorer! Foxe's antipathy to tobacco extended to drink – the mark of a true contemporary Puritan. But he was hardly a man of Christian charity, as can be seen from other passages. Foxe described how he obtained a lot of useful information about where James had explored, and the conditions experienced, concluding: "and what else I desired to have, I had" (F 357). The way that he and his men questioned James's crew extensively about their discoveries in the morning *after* the first meeting surely provides a clear insight into his guile. This second approach had a clear objective:

> *To reiterate the last evenings discourse ... to the end I might understand the difference of severall reports (for every man will report the best of his owne Actions). (F 358)*

Foxe admits that nothing new was learned from James – making the previous comment an astonishing statement – yet reveals his cunning and desire to take advantage of the findings of fellow explorers. Such naked honesty in a journal – in literary terms, a *considered* piece of work, not an instant commentary like a daily log – may also be seen as a mark of Foxe's insensitivity to others. Foxe's comments may be compared with the summary of the journey that James left on Charlton Island in case the expedition perished: "I entertained him ... and made him relation of all our endeavours" (J 115). Foxe also ventured the opinion that James was "no Sea-man" (F 359) and criticized the seaworthiness of James's ship – which few can disagree with, since James and his crew were always pumping water out of the *Henrietta Maria*. This comment is made in the context of blaming those who had provided James with such a poor ship to undertake a journey of such length. However, from what we know of the sudden decision to purchase the ship, as previously noted in the commentary of the letters from the Society of Merchant Venturers in the spring of 1631, it was probable that James had little say in the matter. Foxe, of course, was fortunate enough to obtain a ship from the king's service. Grudgingly, however, Foxe does commend James in one area.

The Gentleman could discourse of Arte (as observations, calculations, and the like) and shewed me many Instruments, so that I did perceive him to bee a practitioner in the Mathematicks. (F 359)

Coming from such a critic as Foxe, this surely adds to the sum of James's qualities, confirming that James really was an educated man – one skilled in pursuits other than those of law. When the ships parted at six in the morning of 31 August, Foxe reported that he was told that James was "in his cabbin" (F 362). Was this the consequence of the dinner James hosted? It was one that went on until the early hours – and Foxe admitted the liquor had flowed and that they had argued. Or was James's action a deliberate snub from a man of a very different social stratum? Unless James really was incapacitated, the snub seems very likely. After all, it is almost inconceivable for anybody on board either ship to miss the last opportunity to see fellow Europeans, given the fact they were on a remote and inhospitable coast from which they might not return. James's book provides no clue to the puzzle.

Any discussion of the power relationships present in the journey cannot rely on societal or internal group dynamics alone, after all, James lived at a time when spiritual forces were often given primacy in explanations. Yet his voyage was part of that series of grand explorations that helped to demonstrate the errors of many of the teachings of the church. The explorations demonstrated the value of observation, experiment, and rationality – some of the key approaches of the subsequent scientific revolution. James obviously adopted these emerging scientific values in the journey, but it seems clear that he was also an advocate of the religious beliefs so typical of pre-industrial western society: the need to depend upon faith, upon God's providence, to keep them safe. Again, it is impossible to know whether James was a man of deep religious belief, or simply that he subscribed to the mores of the day – especially since his venture had royal approval. But it is probable that he was religious, since there are many references to regular church services on Sunday. Also, James takes the trouble to note in his narrative that the voyage began and ended with services of dedication and deliverance respectively.

James's book has significance in being the first publication that provides descriptions of Hudson Bay and its environs. But the content that James chose to include in his journal, and the organization he used to present this information, must also be subject to scrutiny. The approach points the way to the development of a new style of description, emphasizing the dangers that were present and how they were overcome, rather than primarily being concerned with the results of the expedition. The approach is quite unlike that adopted by Foxe and what little we know of Button's journal describing his journey to Hudson Bay, as seen in the extracts quoted in Foxe (1635). The most distinctive feature of James's book was its avoidance of two traditional forms of the travel literature of his day: one represented by the repetitive daily listing of estimated location and weather, little different from the daily log; the other, adopting a florid, grandiloquent style, full of classical allusions and Latin asides, the type of approach adopted by individuals such as Walter Raleigh (1596) – people with social status who were using the accepted forms of court language. Although accounts using these styles in the period in which James lived provided important insights into the new lands, and described the dangers experienced, they are often full of myth and speculation dressed up as proven fact, for many writers were concerned with personal aggrandizement, or with promoting their next voyage.

James's journal, however, does not fall into either of these extremes. He apologized in the dedication to the king, for what he calls "this rude Abstract," and even asks pardon for "a Seaman's Stile" (J P 2). This comment showed that he recognized his literary style was sparse and direct – quite unlike the weighty prose familiar in court and educated circles. But by using the vernacular, and adopting such a direct description of events, James produced a journal that could be easily read and understood by a readership beyond the elite. Indeed, although allowance has to be made for the length of sentences, the early modern spelling, and the older style of transcribing certain letters, even a contemporary reader has little difficulty in following and enjoying the narrative. It has already been noted in chapter 1 that the style and clarity of expression made a good impression on readers for the simplicity and effectiveness of its prose. But in some ways it can also be viewed as an example of the emerging scientific style (Bowen 1981); the approach is an empirical reporting, a straight forward description of the conditions and events that are seen, with little metaphorical or classical embellishment. Unlike many travel narratives of his period, there are only about half a dozen references to themes from classical or biblical literature; one is a reference to Jonah and the whale (J 30); another is the comment about fishing with "a golden hooke," (J 44) an expression normally attributed to Augustus Caesar. This described the unnecessary death of the gunner's mate during a hunting expedition — he took a short cut across a frozen lake and was drowned when the ice gave way. In this case, the loss of the man (a golden hook) was more valuable than any return (a fish or animal) from the journey. Despite the criticisms from Barrow (1818) that he exaggerated the environmental problems, most readers will find that James's sparse, often laconic style actually underplayed the dangers of sailing and living in such a hostile and hazardous milieu. Allowing for the seventeenth-century words and sentence construction, James's action-packed narrative provides a gripping story of unparalleled heroics. The narrative describes an almost unbelievable sequence of physical dangers that were faced in Hudson Bay and on its shores, one of the harshest environments in which man is able to survive. It included: battering by severe storms; of being pounded by surf on shoaling or rocky lee shores; being in frequent peril from looming icebergs that towered over the masts; the fear of being crushed by pack ice, in which the din of grinding ice floes provided a never ending assault on the senses — one that was probably worse in the dark when nothing could be seen. On other days, dripping fog enveloped the crew, marooning them in a grey, invisible world from which there seemed no escape. Such fogs provided additional hazards when they ran into ice, or were in danger of running aground in the uncharted and often vicious coasts, where harbours were few, and rocks and shoals were constant dangers. As if such conditions were not enough, the unspeakable and numbing cold of winter frequently brought the sailors to the edge of despair — especially after they were forced to sink their vessel to prevent it being crushed by the ice. This is an area in which there are very few months without ice. Even after the granting of the royal charter that created the Hudson's Bay Company in 1670, the area was only marginally connected to Britain for the next two hundred years. The regular contact was a single vessel, normally sailing once a year from London to the trading post at York Factory on the Nelson estuary. It rarely arrived before mid-August and left by the end of the month to ensure a safe passage home. Even today, with the ice-breaking technology of the contemporary period, the modern grain port of Churchill in Manitoba is only open for a few months each year, which indicates the severity of the climate.

James's choice of events or objects to describe means his book is more than mimetic – a literal description of what he saw on various days. After a passage detailing the problems they faced just before the decision to return to Bristol, James noted:

> At breake of day, we wayed; and fought all wayes to cleere our selves of Ice: but it was impossible. I conceive it impertinent to relate every particular dayes passages; which was much alike to us. (J 94)

This demonstrates an acute awareness of the need for an explorer to *select* from his daily log – with its descriptions and initial impressions – in order to make his book readable. However, his skill in this selection, and the prose style he used, all seem designed to make his book an adventure – with the passages deliberately constructed to build up tension in the reader. Using MacLulich's (1979) typology, James's *quest* for the Northwest Passage became an *ordeal* in a dangerous environment, with its ever-present spectre of tragedy. This is not to suggest that James resorted to fiction. It is difficult to deny that for weeks on end he and his crew faced extreme danger from sailing through such ice-infested and stormy waters. Rather, it is the fact that James lays so much stress upon the various hazards that were experienced; by contrast, other explorers mentioned these problems once or twice, if at all, then ignored them once they became commonplace.

The argument presented above can be illustrated by a brief comparison between Foxe and James. Foxe, the rugged sea captain from Yorkshire apparently took the environment in his stride. Was it because he was a more experienced sailor, more used to the hazards of the sea or weather, and was more accepting of the problems he encountered, perhaps as everyday events that were not worth describing? By contrast, James's journal is a description that contains one crisis after another. The descriptions of the events of July and August 1631 provide a good point of comparison between Foxe and James since they sailed within days, if not hours of one another through the same area, meaning that they experienced similar conditions. But the impressions of the environment provided by the author-explorers are very different. In one important character of the area there is little variation, namely in the number of times that the ice hazard is mentioned. James mentioned the word *ice* forty-nine times in the nine pages that describe his journey between

TABLE 6.2. DESCRIPTIONS OF INCREASING ICE HAZARD

229

Location	Date	Extract from Narrative

GREENLAND

Location	Date	Extract from Narrative
East Coast	June 4	Completely surrounded by ice.... **serious and fearful buffeting.**
	June 6	**Unusually large** pieces of ice.... **great** floe.
	Evening	Surrounded by **great** pieces as **high as our poop.**
Cape Farewell	June 7/8	Still pestered by **much** ice
Cape Desolation	June 10	Pieces as **high as our mast head.** Tormented, pestered, and beaten by the ice; **many pieces as high as our mast-top head.**

HUDSON STRAIT:

Location	Date	Extract from Narrative
Resolution Island	June 17	**Terribly pestered** by ice, blinded by a **thick** fog.
	June 20	Swept so close to **towering icebergs** that we were afraid they would fall and crush us.
	June 23	**Great** pieces of ice.... **twice the height of our mast head.**
Left Resolution Island	June 29	Into the Strait Sea was **infinitely** pestered with ice.
Salisbury Island	July 5	Sails northwest
Approx. 63° N	July 18	**Solid wall** of pack ice.... sailed south-southwest
	July 19	Slabs of ice as thick **as any we had yet seen.** Jammed in the ice.
60° 33' N	July 21	Again trapped by ice.
	July 27	Trapped in ice
	July 28/29	Trapped solidly in the ice.... ice in **large flat cakes** 1000 paces long - **the most difficult to deal with that we had so far encountered.** This was the first day that the men started to grumble.
	July 30	Moved the ship forward by heaving it with our shoulders, breaking up the ice with crowbars...

(Source: Comments from James's narrative at the dates shown with emphases shown in bold print)

Resolution Island, at the east side of Hudson Strait, on 17 June 1631 and Salisbury Island on 5 July. Foxe completed the same passage between 22 June and 7 July and used the word *ice* fifty-five times in the twelve pages of narrative, a slightly smaller average of 4.6 mentions per page compared to James's 5.4. But although the frequency of use is approximately the same, it must be noted that James emphasized the size of the ice and the dangers it caused, creating a 'density of meaning' that heightened the dangers. By contrast, Foxe gives the impression he almost sailed serenely through these difficult conditions; even if he describes the environmental problems, he is careful to downplay them.

Table 6.2 is derived from the phrases used in James's narrative. It illustrates how he described the ice as bigger and more menacing as his voyage into Hudson Strait and Bay progressed. Of course, it is possible that James's descriptions may be literally true. One cannot go back in time and check. But it is much more likely that the icebergs calved off the Greenland glaciers were bigger and more dangerous than those he encountered in Hudson Bay. Some icebergs do drift across the Baffin Strait and into Hudson Bay, but rarely the biggest — given the narrow channel and frequently strong eastward tidal flow. Perhaps it could be argued that the smaller icebergs were more of a hazard for such a small ship in a narrow channel, with little sea room to manoeuvre. But table 6.2 shows that James's descriptions are quite specific: the icebergs increased in size, with the danger getting worse. Foxe, by comparison, barely acknowledged the size factor and even reduced the scale of the danger by the comment that the ice is "seldom ... bigger than a great Church" above water, although he noted that it was bigger under the sea (F289). Later on, Foxe does describe how his crew became fearful as they were surrounded by ice, but downplayed the situation: "we feare more danger than wee are in. God, for his mercies' sake set us at libertie" (F 292). In other words, the same type of danger that is almost *dismissed* by Foxe becomes a big *menace* for James, or at least is described as such in his journal. In the next page of his book Foxe described how an "easie gale breathed in from the East by South" (F 294) — even the choice of the word *breathed* has the effect of reducing the potential danger in the mind of readers. Foxe went on to describe how his crew became worried at the storm, but commented that "the matter was not great" (F 189), illustrating, once again, that he felt that their fears were exaggerated.

James, by contrast, seemed to take every opportunity to emphasize the hazards posed by the environment. Table 6.3 shows that when the peril of the ice faded, other difficulties appeared: gales, shoaling shores,

TABLE 6.3. ADDITIONAL HAZARDS FACED, JUNE 29 TO JULY 19, 1631

Date	Ice Hazard	Other Hazards	Attitudes / People
June - 5 July (Sailing through Hudson Strait)	Sea infinitely pestered with sea ice to N.N.W.	Variable winds and fog Driven back by winds	*Thought ship would be smashed 1,000 times Realizes no route to N.West 'this year'*
15 July (Between Digges-Nottingham Island)			*Some open water for a few hours Unable to go North*
16 July (Mansfield Island)		Fearful blows from ice Foul Weather Fog	*Sick men Cut rations Fired guns to guide men back from land Evidence of savages*
17 July (Vista Island)	ice very thick, unpassable	No driftwood, animals, or fish Few ponds; utterly barren of goodness	*Signs of savages*
18 July	Ice all about us. Wall of pack ice to West Sailed S.S.W. Open water at first... Large flat cakes of ice— "the most difficult to deal with we had so far encountered"	Rut of ice ⟶ Thick black fog	*High Spirits did not last Hideous noise of ice*
19 July	No way through ice Jammed in ice	Blinded by fog	*Ship pounded by ice*

rocks, fog, adverse winds, etc. In total, the book describes over thirty major crises. Given their range and number, it is surprising that James and the *Henrietta Maria* continued to find ways of escaping from what seemed to be impossible situations. But these were not just continuous environmental threats, but extreme and previously inexperienced dangers. On 17 August 1632, a few days before they finally turned for England, at latitude 50°20′N, James concluded:

> For we were hourely, for the space of six weekes, as it were in the Jawes of death: yea never any (that I have heard of) have beene so long, in such long nights, upon a foule shoald shoare, tormented with Ice, as we have now beene. (J 101)

The result of James's narrative is to overwhelm readers with the constant hazards, perhaps even to strain their credibility – which might have been the reason for criticisms from those promoting later expeditions to the Arctic (Barrow 1818). It is hard not to resist the conclusion that James and his crew seemed to possess what three centuries later would be described as a *Buchanesque* ability to surmount the perils – although it must be remembered that John Buchan, the future Lord Tweedsmuir and Governor General of Canada, invented his adventure stories. James's descriptions were supposed to be a real life portrayal. Yet it is fascinating to note that the survival of James's ship was never accidental. James wrote his journal as a testimony to the helpful intervention of a spiritual guiding hand. There are over fifty references to God and to divine intervention. Scarcely a page in the discussion of the voyage itself is free from references to God. It is worth detailing these features. There are fifteen instances when James described how he conducted general prayers among his crew to thank God for delivery from the perils experienced. On nine occasions, divine intervention was thought to cause the wind to change and move them out of danger. In addition, God preserved the *Henrietta Maria* from either shoals or rocks eight times, and from various ice hazards another six times. Problems getting the small boats back to the ship were solved by divine guidance on three occasions, whilst God resolved a potentially disastrous nighttime crisis by suddenly illuminating the scene with moonlight. James also made God responsible for preserving their beer and cider! However, such libations must not be seen as simply being important for convivial events, but for helping to maintain a vitamin balance for the crew. Since James was carrying a letter from King Charles to the emperor of Japan – itself a mark of hope that there was a Northwest Passage – it may be appropriate to view his descriptions in the context of the famous late-twentieth-century Japanese production systems. The voyage exhibited a *just-in-time* salvation: one that emphasized the role of God in life. Yet there was no fatalism in James's beliefs. The emerging contemporary Protestant ethic of self-help can also be seen in his prose. For example, there are passages in which James maintains that it was "work" which brought salvation, such as when he observes: "it pleased God to favour our labour so" (J 98).

Given the passage of centuries, it is difficult to know whether these references identify a man of deep religious belief, or one who simply accepted the beliefs and convention of the day. After all, many of his contemporaries believed that divine intervention occurred when forces beyond human knowledge or control were involved. It seems more likely that the former view is the more appropriate, given the fact he often refers to religious services that he organized. At first sight, these religious overtones seem to contradict the adoption of what we have described as a Baconian scientific style. But it must be remembered that Francis Bacon advocated a dual approach: one was the realm of nature and reason, using empirical description and invoking induction to arrive at generalizations; the other was the realm of God and the unknowable, linked to theological truths and the word or oracles of God (Bowen 1981). Today, we may revere Bacon for developing or popularizing the former approach, but we should not forget his alternative method based on belief. James's narrative should be seen as representative of the Baconian dual approach to explanations. As such, it does not emphasize our contemporary preferences in interpretation; a good example of the need to avoid what some recent historians of geography describe as a presentist approach to the work of past authors (Livingstone 1992; Mayhew 2000).

So far, it has been argued that James's style is rather basic, with few adjectival descriptors. Yet there are occasional attempts to create more evocative images. Some are phrases that are almost identical to some of the classic clichés of contemporary writing. James may have been one of the first to use such words: "It proved a faire Moone-Shine night," (J 93) or "we endured a most dangerous, darke night" (J 95). Elsewhere, he used other prose forms to enliven his text. The addition of references to sound, with adjectival emphasis, is particularly effective in increasing the drama of his descriptions, such as when icebergs or ice floes: made "a most fearefull noyse" (J 93); "did grate us with violence" (J 15); were "breaking with a terrible thundering noyse" (J 12); or "made a most hideous noise" (J 31). The threat that a fire posed when it was accidentally created so close to their winter camp was made more stark by James's reference to its "terrible, rattling noyse," (J 85) and to its speed. The privations faced by the scurvy-ridden crew in the spring of 1632 are dramatized by James's comment that the three men who requested to sleep aboard the ship from mid-April 1632 "avoyded the hearing of the miserable groanings: and lamentings of the sicke men all night long." (J 69, 70).

Despite these ever-present dangers, James is not averse to providing some wry humour, which can only have been included to relieve the tension and to entertain the reader. Part of the disappointment of finding land at the position that Button had labelled Hubbert's Hope is relieved by noting the place should be called "Hopeless" since it marked the end of a hope for a passage to the Pacific (J 39). On another occasion, James described the problems in the winter quarters caused by the smoke from burning dry wood, which was so full of turpentine that it produced a sooty residue blanketing the hut and its contents. James remarked that it made his companions look like members of the company of Chimney Sweepers" (J 67) – surely an aside that would appeal to many of his readers, the moneyed residents of big cities or large houses. Readers are also likely to chuckle at the chivalry described in the eve of a May Day party – organized to cheer up the spirits of the crew after the long and extreme winter – in which each person wore the name of a woman in his hat (J 71). It is possible that James's demeanour may have imposed some gentile standards upon his rough crew. Knowledge of subsequent life on the fur frontier in Canada as described by Newman (1986), would suggest that the occasion was far more likely to have been a party characterized by squalid innuendo from a group of sexually-deprived males, marooned in a wilderness, and with limited hopes of returning to their homeland.

It is also worth noting that James did not shrink from adding what is known today as gothic horror in his descriptions of the effect of physical conditions upon the human body. Such passages must also have titillated his drawing room readership – long before the gothic became a nineteenth-century fad in literature. When one of the winches spun out of control on the evening of 21 August, eight men were hurt and the leg of Richard Edwards, the ship's gunner, was crushed. The summary account (J 25) may have described a commonplace accident in a society where agricultural injuries accidents were frequent. Moreover, it was a society brutalized by the ever present physical abuse to those who transgressed against contemporary mores. In the case of Edwards, the surgeon had to remove his leg. Unfortunately, Edwards died on 22 November. Later, James observed: "we had committed him to the Sea at a good distance from the Ship and in deep water" (J 76). Later, James provided a morbid and laconic description of how the gunner's body floated back to the ship, and was rediscovered on 18 May – months after its original burial at sea. The body was clearly visible, frozen in a block of ice, but was upside down and with his one leg sticking up. It had also drifted under the ports of the very gun room, which James had described as the place where the gunner had made himself comfortable in the past. Surely this introduced an element of the macabre into his book: it reads like a page from a book called: '*The return of the dead gunner!*' But after chipping the body out of the ice, James observed that it proved to be perfectly preserved, except for one gruesome and remarkable fact:

> *... He was as free from any noysomenesse, as when we first committed him to the Sea. This alteration had the Ice and water, and time onely wrought on him: that his flesh would flip up and down upon his bones, like a glove on a mans hand. (J 76)*

James then returned to standard mores in his description, that of respect for the dead, by observing that in the evening they buried the gunner with the others who had died.

Similar incidents may have occurred in other contemporary voyages of exploration; if so, they are rarely mentioned in the narratives. James may have sensationalized a harrowing event – but in doing so added *reader appeal* to his book. Similarly, when so many of his men were prostrate with scurvy in the late winter of 1632, he praised the work of his diligent doctor:

> *Our Surgeon ... would be up betimes in the mornings; and whilst he did picke their Teeth, and cut away the dead flesh from their Gummes, they would bathe their owne thighes, knees, and legges. (J 72)*

Since practically all the crew suffered from scurvy at various stages this must have been a ghastly daily task. The condition of their mouths meant that many had to "boyle Pease to a soft paste, and feed as well as they could, upon that" (J 72) – surely a diet of what amounted to mushy peas! Compared to such personal afflictions, the perils of coping with freezing drizzle, of soaking clothes, rigging so ice-encrusted that the ice that could only be removed by hard labour with axes, as well as the discomfort of large blisters raised by the cold, began to seem commonplace as the narrative progresses. All these descriptions must have provided additional shivers of horror for readers in their comfortable English homes. Certainly few could read such descriptions and derive a positive view of this part of the future Dominion of Canada!

Although there seems some evidence that James overdramatized the perils of the journey, the privations were certainly real enough and cannot be easily dismissed. Obviously these were real experiences and provided the basis for his description – but his textual construction used them to sustain interest for the reader. Yet there is one element whose repetition does point to exaggeration for effect. Time and time again James emphasized that "I have never seen" or "never did I see" such a dangerous thing, place, condition, bird, or event. This constant expression of wonder at the new sights may, of course, reflect the Celtic propensity to exaggerate when telling stories, and may be a survival of the personalized, old storytelling approaches that emphasized the very different experiences found in the environment. It may not be too fanciful to suggest that this 'Did you ever see' style of reporting may be one of the first printed examples of the famous humorous folk verses of early-twentieth-century South Wales that begin with this phrase.

It is also possible to regard James as some kind of ingénue, struggling in the subarctic environment – certainly Foxe and Barrow seemed to regard him as such. It is fascinating to note that Adams (1983) has described how the ingénue, usually a companion of the hero, is a frequent character in fictionalized travels, a person whose naiveté can be mocked or used to illustrate the pomposity of various customs. James could have adopted the style of an environmental neophyte by emphasizing the dangers he faced on his journey. But it is difficult to sustain the argument. The fact that he survived on so many occasions was not a matter of luck or of God's hand; rather it testifies to the fact that he was a skilled seaman who successfully managed to deal with the many and varied dangers faced by the *Henrietta Maria* and its crew.

James did not restrict himself to prose in his journal. On 30 September, his journal turns to verse, when he recalled that the conditions were "rather more desperate than I have related" (J 38). The threat of winter was upon them – "with snow, haile, and stormy weather, and colder than ever I felt in England in my life" (J 38). It was at a time when they could not discover a safe harbour amongst "the shoalds and broken ground" (J 38) and did not know which way to turn. James observed that he was stimulated to express his thoughts in a different form. The result was a twenty-six-line poem, which may be one of the first examples in which the hazards of the Canadian environment were explicitly evoked to produce an emotional response in verse. This is worth quoting for its historical significance, as well as providing a glimpse of his thoughts and his expectation of divine salvation.

> Oh, my poore soule, why doest thou grieve to see
> So many Deaths muster to murther mee?
> Looke to thy selfe, regard not mee; for I
> Must doe (for what I came) performe, or die.
> So thou mayst free thy selfe from being in
> A dung-hill dungeon; A meere sinke of sinne,
> And happily be free'd, if thou beleeve,
> Truly in God through Christ, and ever live.
> Be therefore glad yet: ere thou go from hence,
> For our joynt sinnes, let's do some penitence,
> Unfainedly together. When we part,
> Lie with the Angels Joy, with all my heart.
> We have with confidence relyde upon
> A rustie wyre, toucht with a little Stone,
> Incompast round with paper, and alasse
> To house it harmelesse, nothing but a glasse,
> And thought to shun a thousand dangers, by
> The blind direction of this senselsse skye.
> When the fierce winds shatter'd blacke nights asunder,
> Whose pitchie clouds, spitting forth fire and thunder,
> Hath shooke the earth, and made the Oceane roar;
> And runne to hide it, in the broken shore:
> Now thou must steer *by faith*; a better guide,
> 'Twill bring theee safe to heaven against the tyde
> Of Satans malice. Now let quiet gales
> Of saving grace, inspire thy zealous sayles. (J 39)

The style, especially in the first half, may be crude. Indeed, James prefaced the poem with the hope that it would not be considered "ridiculous," describing it as "ragged and teared rimes" (J 38). In any case its structure consisted of sets of couplets, whose rhymes are often forced, which hardly attains the heights of immortal poetry. But as the poem develops, its lines display a primitive poignancy that is appealing — especially during the last eight lines that deal with the storms that provoked him to express himself in verse. Its portrayal of violent weather and perilous shores must have reinforced the message of his prose that the Hudson Bay area was an environment to be feared. The comment about dependence upon the fragile rusty wire and stone"– clearly the compass – is significant. This rather dismissive reference means that the technology of the day was not considered good enough to save them. Instead, the end of James's poem reflects the religiosity of his times. The problems posed by the storms can only resolved by faith in a loving God. This was the eternal Christian message.

The second poem is associated with virtually the last action they carried out at their camp on 1 July 1632. Before embarking on the ship to continue their search for a Northwest Passage, the crew, led by James, visited the tomb of their dead companions. James composed a eulogy of thirty-six lines to mark the occasion.

> I were unkind, unless that I did shead,
> Before I part, some teares upon our dead;
> And, when my eyes be dry, I will not cease
> In heart to pray their bones may rest in peace.
> Their better parts, (good soules) I know were given,
> With an intent they should returne to heaven.
> Their lives they spent, to the last drop of blood,
> Seeking Gods glory, and their Countries good,
> And as a valient Souldier rather dyes,
> Then yields his courage to his Enemies:
> And stops their way, with his hew'd flesh, when death
> Hath quite depriv'd him of his strength and breadth:
> So have they spent themselves; and here they lye.
> A famous marke of our *Discovery*.
> We that survive, perchance may end our dayes
> In some imployment meriting no praise;
> And in a dung-hill rot: where no man names
> The memory of us, but to our shames.
> They have out-liv'd this feare, and their brave ends,
> Will ever be an honour to their friends.
> Why drop ye so, mine eyes? Nay rather powre
> My sad departure in a solemne showre.
> The Winters cold, that lately freze our blood,
> Now were it so extreme, might doe this good,

As make these teares, bright pearles: which I would lay,
Tomb'd safely with you, till Doomes fatall day.
That in this Solitary place, where none
Will ever come to breathe a sigh or grone,
Some remnant might be extant, of the true
And Faithful love, I ever tenderd you.
Oh, rest in peace, deare friends, and let it be
No pride to say the sometime part of me.
What paine and anguish doth afflict the head,
The heart and stomache, when the limbes are dead:
So griev'd, I kisse your graves; and vow to dye,
A Foster father to your memory.
Farewell. (J 87)

Although James is once again apologetic for the verse, acknowledging the lines might procure "laughter in the wiser sort," he observed that they "moved my young and tendered hearted companions" (J 88). If true – and there is no reason to doubt his words – the response provided the true worth of the poem, authenticating the spirit in which it was composed. The verse was designed for a *particular occasion*, not for posterity, when later readers might judge its worth in the context of different values, or without the same sense of personal loss. Moreover, James's decision to remember their fallen shipmates in a formal ceremony again demonstrates his compassion for his crew. When such a quality is added to all his other attributes, James does display leadership skills that were rarely matched by other explorers. The content of the poem shows that James was at pains to emphasize that his fallen companions had played an important part in the expedition, laying down their lives for their country, as well as for God – just like soldiers. Their death provided a symbol and testament to their discoveries. James's words may be a mark of his awareness of the fate of so many explorers who had died forgotten in their old age. It was an attempt to argue that they would be better immortalized if they had died *in action*. But he is not above being sentimental in hoping for some alchemy, based on the frozen days in which they had barely survived, that would transmute his tears into pearls – to provide a lasting gift to the men that had lost their lives because of the expedition.

Whatever opinions are held about the literary merits of these poems, they deserve a place in history for being some of the first English-language poems – perhaps even the first – composed in northern Canada.

It is unfortunate that subsequent editions of James's book (Payne 1740; Coles 1973) excluded these verses. The exclusions certainly reduced the literary value of James's book, relative to its utility as a journal of discovery. It probably contributed to the lack of recognition of James's verse, for they do not appear in Davies and Gerson's (1994) comprehensive survey of early Canadian poetry. Some critics may argue that the poems were afterthoughts, written when he was back in England. However, there is no evidence for such a view. After all, the crew was witness to James's verse, so there is no reason to assume that James made up these poems at some later date. The verses may be added to William Vaughan's (1626) literary efforts describing Newfoundland, providing more evidence of the contribution of Welsh explorers and promoters to the emergence of a literature in Canada – one based on knowledge and experience of a barren and harsh land.

✢ 5. AESTHETICS AND ENVIRONMENTAL REPRESENTATION

James's descriptions of the environment he explored provide insights and connections with the land that go beyond the experiential and scientific. Certainly they were developed long before such Romantic concepts as beauty or the picturesque were used to view landscapes in Britain (Burke 1756) and which were later applied by many writers in Canada (Glickman 1998). James may have thought that some of the lands in which he travelled were beautiful – but there is no real evidence for such a feeling for natural beauty in his text. Rather one can point to the fact that James's prose seems more in tune with the aesthetics of sublimity, in which heightened sensations and feelings of awe and inspiration were derived from the raw and savage aspects of nature, once the fear of being killed was removed. Although feelings of what we call sublimity today may have been experienced and implied by his descriptions, the concept was not invented until a century after his writings, so we would be unwise to apply such a conceptual abstraction to his writings. But it can be argued that part of the attraction of James's narrative to subsequent readers, especially to the Romantic poet Coleridge, was the way that he described and stressed the often terrifying environments and situations that were experienced. After all, the Hudson Bay region produced conditions that were unknown in the relatively gentle and much subdued climates and landscapes of Britain. Hence, readers interested in what amounted to the sublime could find evidence of such an aesthetic in James's writing, albeit second-hand and without the concept. But one must be careful of interpreting James's book as containing passages that deliberately contributed to the creation of higher emotions or feelings; it has already been suggested that it may be more appropriate to see James's book as one of the first examples of the type of sensationalism in travel writing. Evidence for such an interpretation comes from the fact that a significant part of James's journal describes a series of potential calamities and the hazards of living in such an extreme environment. Hence the emphasis is not upon any abstract aesthetic feelings; instead, the voyage and the wintering are always seen as being on the brink of calamity – surely the heart of a sensationalist approach. Riffenburgh (1993) made a persuasive case for the replacement of *sublimity* by *sensationalism* in the way that exploration was treated in the new, or rather mass-market newspapers of the late nineteenth century. Yet it may be a mistake to regard the sensational as a new approach at the time. After all, most historic descriptions of discovery and exploration were full of exaggeration and often mythic in tone. Hence, the sensational style could be considered to have been the most typical approach *before* the empiricism of the post-Renaissance explorers. In other words, it preceded the classic aesthetic principles of beauty or sublimity as a focus for environmental description. But even here, there was room for an emphasis upon the sensational. James's laconic style may not have contained the adjectival excess of future, or even previous, years, but it was still marked by descriptions on the events that would excite, and therefore, interest, his readers. So it is difficult to place James's book within a single genre with respect to its representation or interpretation of the environment; in any case, previous sections have shown the narrative had scientific, as well as literary value.

✢ 6. INTERPRETING THE ENVIRONMENTAL PROCESSES

The early seventeenth century was not a period in which there was a great deal of knowledge about the nature of environmental processes. It is to James's credit that his observations helped the development of knowledge in several areas and was recognized by one of the principal

English scientists of the seventeenth century, Robert Boyle (1620–91), whose works were collected and published by Birch in 1744 and have been reproduced with a new introduction by McKie in 1965. Boyle's lengthy set of observations and experiments on cold and its various effects made extensive use of James's observations, which were judged to be excellent because of "his breeding in university and by his acquaintance with mathematics" (Boyle in McKie 1965, 478). Indeed, Boyle went so far as to state that James was

> *A person from whose journals I have borrowed more observations than from those of any other seaman … this gentleman was commended to me both by some friends of mine, who were well acquainted with him, and by the esteem that competent judges appear to have made of him.… (Boyle in McKie 1965, 478)*

Boyle (McKie 1965, 462–718) quoted James in several points within his treatise of over 250 pages, such as sections dealing with: the effect of cold in stopping corruption of bodies (532); recognising that the earth and sea in winter was only frozen to a limited depth (567); describing the unusual presence of freezing nights and very hot days in the change of the seasons in Hudson Bay (610); noting how cold's power restricted the spread of a fire's heat (614); commenting on how his crew found the water in June more difficult to bear than in the much colder time in December (661); and describing how more stars could be seen in the very cold nights at the end of January, which demonstrated the effect of cold on visibility (604). Boyle compared these observations with data from other areas and sources to produce a survey of the effects of cold, and completed experiments to demonstrate many of the effects that were identified. Certainly, Boyle was the superior scientist because he completed experiments and tried to integrate observations, but there seems little doubt that James's careful observations were of great value to the development of science in this area.

In addition, James did try to speculate on the origin of some of the features he saw – although with very limited success. One of his most important comments described how he thought that snow disappeared from the land: it is "exhaled up by the Sunne, and suckt full of holes, like honey-combs" (J 77). This process was sufficiently unusual to be worthy of comment, since it seemed so different to the familiar processes seen in Britain, where snow was more likely to melt first into water and, if a very heavy snowfall is involved, usually led to floods. James's description provided a vivid illustration of the importance in these climates of what we know as the process of sublimation today, where snow or ice can pass directly into vapour, missing out the phase of water. It also shows the dryness of the air in the subarctic, which meant that the snow seemed to vanish. Supplementing this observation was his comment (J 106) that he never found any dew – even after the hottest day – obviously a matter of some surprise. But despite recognizing these indicators of the low humidity, James did not have the concepts in his language to describe, let alone the technology to measure the condition. So he was unable to derive implications from this environmental feature. One result was that James underestimated the dryness of the vegetation in late June. Just before their departure from their winter quarters, a tree was deliberately set alight to see if local native peoples could be attracted. The fire spread to the area around and quickly got out of control, eventually burning a large part of the island, including their huts. They were very fortunate to have already transferred everything of value to their ship (J 84), so their losses were minimal.

James was also the first to try and explain the formation of sea ice and the way it melted in the area – albeit it with limited accuracy. He postulated that the snow forming on the tidal zones was a primary cause (J 63). Since the snow was being constantly swept out to sea, James suggested that the snow cooled the sea and thickened the water; then, through compaction and wind action, it created continuous ice. Such an explanation has long been dismissed. Contemporary texts (Smith 1990, 78) describe a five-fold process of ice formation: the development of thin elongated crystals or frazils; their concentration into a slush or a greasy soup; the formation of thin pancakes of ice, whose edges collide and ride over each other due to tide and wind action; the coalescence of the ice into floes; and their final building up of thickness by accretion from below. Yet James did help future understanding in a part of this sequence. His descriptions of the difficulty of getting to the ship and back to shore in November noted the "thicke, congealed water" (J 56) that made their progress extremely difficult. This vividly identifies the character of the second stage of ice formation. He also observed the importance of the action of wind and tides in compressing small pieces of ice together, causing them to push over one another. The result was that the sea ice became two or three inches thick in a single night, cooling the sea and leading to greater ice thickness. James also speculated on the way that the sea ice broke up in the spring. He noted that the ice in the bay was rarely more than six feet deep, except by what he calls accident (J 86), where tides or wind pushed floes over one another. James also observed how the ice first melted along the shores, a product of the way the sun's heat was more effective in these shallow waters. In addition, he described how the motion of the tides cracked the ice, grinding the pieces together, which assisted the process of summer thaw. In late August, when James was further north than his winter camp, he was astonished at the length of time ice took to melt. Indeed, he used experiments to show that a two foot square piece of ice took eight days to melt – despite being exposed to the sun and being close to the warmth of the ship (J 101). On other occasions, when the ship remained in the same place, he marked the surrounding ice to try and estimate the rate of melting, but never produced any conclusive results.

Obviously, many of James's ideas have been superseded by later research. But they demonstrate that he was one of the first visitors to northern Canada to speculate about, and occasionally to experiment on, how the unusual conditions he observed were created by physical processes. Again, this provides an example of the emerging scientific tradition, in which conclusions could be derived or refuted by new observations, rather than being based on belief or prior speculation. Yet one must not exaggerate James's scientific endeavours. His journal shows gaps in his perceptiveness. James's descriptions made it obvious there was a difference between what we now call sea ice and icebergs, but it was Foxe (F 289 and 292) who postulated that the latter were composed of fresh water and formed in mountainous areas. Foxe argued that their weight made them fall into the sea – not quite the link to their origin in glaciers or shoreline ice, but close. Also, James either seems to have been deficient in his observations of certain physical features, or simply decided not to include them, for reasons that are unknown. For example, it is very curious that he makes no mention of the northern lights, although most expeditions to the north often comment on this spectacular phenomenon; for example, Foxe described what he calls the "pettie-dancers" several times (e.g., F 313–17). Although the Hudson Bay area does not abound with wildlife, it is also odd – given the fact that that they were travelling within a few days of one another in the same area, for two months in the summer of 1632 – how Foxe chose to describe far more animals than James. This may be a function of the fact that Foxe's crew was more successful in supplementing their food by killing fish and sea mammals. Despite these omissions, and his protestations that the "secrets of nature are past my apprehension," (J 101) James's work can be regarded as the beginning of the growth of published scientific knowledge of the Hudson Bay environment. His pioneering interpretations, especially about the winter conditions, were made even more valuable when one considers that many of his predecessors did not publish journals, so their experiences were lost to posterity.

✤ 7. REPRESENTATION OF ABORIGINAL PEOPLES

Any evaluation of an exploration narrative should consider two important cultural issues: one is the way the aboriginal peoples are represented; the second is whether the contact led the Europeans to introspective reflections upon their own societal mores and values. The early seventeenth century was a time of endless fascination for Europeans about what were described as the barbarous peoples from other worlds – some of whom were brought to London and other capitals and displayed at court. Even though the native peoples were often ridiculed, they helped Europeans to survive in many of the first colonies in America (Dickason, O. P., 1997; 1998). In Canada, the adoption of the canoe, snowshoes, and the use of native guides who showed the fur traders the routes to new environments, provided the difference between success and failure for many an explorer and traveller. Many individual explorers acknowledged the help they obtained from particular aboriginal guides and often had good relationships with them, as described in David Thompson's journal (Tyrrell 1916). In addition, explorers, and particularly traders, entered into liaisons with aboriginal women, who provided a source of comfort, support, and more intimate familial contact with the rest of the native peoples. Inevitably, the associations produced children, but these mixed-blood offspring did have the ability to work in both cultures – at least before the Canadian frontier became settled and such people were looked down upon and became marginalized by the more rigid social mores of the mid-nineteenth century. But there is always the impression that these contacts between native peoples and the explorers and traders were personal ones. The social superiority of the Europeans meant that aboriginals, as a group, were rarely treated as equals, and were represented as savages (Dickason, O. P., 1997). Native cultures were often dismissed as being too alien for most Europeans to respect – unless the white commentators had lived in the land for many years. Not until the last thirty years have Caucasians started to question the driving expansionism and exploitation of resources that underlay their society and to look at the culture of the peoples they conquered in other than Eurocentric ways. It has led to greater understanding of the very different attitudes that native peoples have had to their environment – especially to the sharing of resources and the need to ensure sustainability.

James was unable to contribute to the growth of knowledge of other peoples in America – perhaps one of the most important limitations of his work. Again, it was not his fault that he was one of the few explorers who failed to meet any aboriginals on his journey. This was almost certainly to his regret, for a discussion of their appearance and customs would have added to the interest of the book. Foxe had a similar lack of success, although he found many native remains, especially in the location described as Sepulchre Island, which contained hundreds of human funeral sites. Merbs (1971) suggested that this was probably the island now known as Silumiut island in Roe's Welcome Sound, an area which James did not explore because he turned south, rather than north, after his landfall on the west coast of Hudson Bay in 1631. Certainly Sepulchre Island was a macabre sight to any European – but only because their culture interred the dead, moving bodies out of sight, unlike the Hudson Bay native practise of placing them on platforms exposed to the elements.

The absence of actual contact with aboriginal peoples did not mean that James's book is without reference to the inhabitants of the area around Hudson Bay. On three occasions James reported that he found signs of native camps; in one of these he drew attention to the presence of sharpened poles, probably indicating a group that had iron tools, implying earlier European contact (J 90), or perhaps evidence that Hudson's expedition had been there before him. In another four places in his book, James specifically noted the absence of native peoples, even though he described how he searched for them, took precautions against the possibility of an attack, and even as he was about to leave the area, burned a large tree as a signal to try to attract local peoples. In many ways it is puzzling why James made so many references to what amounted to *non-events*. One explanation is that the brief references would remind any reader of the ever-present fear of native attack. After all, Frobisher's expedition in 1577 had experienced a short skirmish with natives; four of Hudson's crew, including one John Williams, lost their lives in another attack (Christy 1894, 154). Moreover, the educated classes in London were familiar with the threat posed by the native population in some other parts of America. So, it is possible that James's references are more of a literary device, adding to the drama of his journey. By mentioning the *absence* of natives he raises the possibility of their *presence* in the minds of his readers. Moreover, it is curious that many of the references to natives come after a series of physical hazards had been resolved. It suggests the reader is given tantalising clues to the possibility of additional threats in the environment, other than those of a physical nature. It seems that James used this device to add to the overall suspense of his descriptions, sustaining interest by maintaining the threat of disaster – even when there was little else to report. This means that the non-events may well have been a deliberate rhetorical device to increase the book's readability. Perhaps anticipation of another threat or fear – one different to the constant physical dangers – may have been more thrilling to readers than the actual appearance of aboriginal peoples. Indeed, the potential threat posed by native peoples was enhanced by their description as *savages* (J 91). The meaning of this racially biased representation would have been clear to James's readers, although Olive Dickason's (1997) review of early white-native contacts in Canada has shown that most contacts were peaceful and that the term *savage* was unjustly applied.

All these examples demonstrate, once again, how James's narrative has been misrepresented in the past and needs to be considered separately from the journey of exploration itself. Of course, the two were intimately connected; but the book has achievements that go beyond the facts of discovery. The narrative seems to have been carefully designed, not simply to identify the exploratory achievements, but to appeal to the imagination of the readers by emphasizing the dangers that were overcome. In focusing upon this task, James produced a cleverly constructed narrative, which went far beyond the typically arid, daily logs of many of his contemporaries. In addition, the book provides important clues about the interpersonal relationships and insights into James's character and leadership skills, which can be set alongside the merchant and state power relationships that created the expedition. There is little point in doubting that the experiences of James and his crew were actual ones, not fictive events. But James's ability to make them readable, represented an appeal to the readers' emotions, as much as to any of their rational senses – especially the passages that deal with their survival in winter. Surely it was these literary skills that account for the initial popularity of the book – not the results of the geographical discoveries. Yet James's enquiring spirit also led him to speculate about the new environment he found and how some physical processes operated. Certainly his ideas were not always accurate, but they were part of that process of scientific reflection that led to the explosive development of scientific knowledge in subsequent centuries. James needs to be remembered as an author of quality, and a budding scientist – not simply as an explorer and leader who had compassion for his men. Of course, we are largely dependent upon James's voice for this opinion, but the fact that his work was so well-known and reprinted in subsequent centuries testifies to its utility in literary terms. But utility depends on more than the ability to complete a journey, or to construct readable descriptions of the new lands; significant pieces of exploration influence future actions or fields of enquiry. It is to these instrumental functions that we must now turn.

Chapter 9

Instrumental Functions

It did snow and freeze most extremely. At which time, we looking from the shoare towards the Ship, she did looke like a piece of Ice, in the Fashion of a Ship; or a Ship resembling a piece of Ice. The snow was all frozen about her, and all her fore-part firme Ice, and so was she on all both sides also. (J 46)

Some narratives of exploration also have important consequences beyond the specific results of the expeditions. In other words, particular texts can be reviewed or interpreted in the context of the ways they fulfilled other functions – those beyond the immediate effects of the journey of discovery. Some of these instrumental functions may stem from the imagery that was used to describe events on the journey; for example, the quotation used to begin this chapter indicates James's ability to create a unique and certainly memorable picture of his ship when viewed from the shore. But James's text produced a large number of additional instrumental functions. These can be summarized within five broad categories. The first instrumental function consists of the way that the expedition's results had subsequent utility, such as in stimulating future exploitation – or even avoidance – of the lands and seas that were discovered. The second category relates to the goals of the narrative, as compared to the journey of exploration; many narratives are written with rather different objectives in mind. A third major category consists of the extent to which the book stimulated other artistic or literary endeavours. Geographical explorations had a romantic aura in the circumscribed world of most people before the age of steam made travel easier. They were hazardous journeys into the real unknown, glimpses of unimaginable sights, products, and peoples, and where the prospects of immense riches were often dangled before the reader. A fourth major instrumental category is produced by the clash of cultures between the explorers and the native peoples – which sometimes led to self-reflection about the customs and practises of the Europeans. Finally, there is an individual instrumental effect upon the participants. The active life of an explorer, and, perhaps, his crew, rarely ended after the expedition's return; the leaders of successful expeditions and their crew were often sent on other journeys, or rewarded with other posts because of their experience or success. Each of these issues will be dealt with in subsequent sections.

Many of the most famous fictive journeys described in literature, from Pilgrim's Progress to Gulliver's Travels, were designed as allegories, to draw attention to some conditions or issues other than those described literally in the text. In the case of James's work, it seems unlikely that the book was an extended metaphor for something else; it was, after all, a description of an actual journey, with a deliberate aim or purpose. However, it is important to remember that the manifest reason of many journeys may be outweighed by purposes that remain hidden from sight or only subsequently appear after the journey has been completed — what are now called latent functions. Some of these may be quite unexpected. These are additional to the consequences that stem directly from the issues discussed in previous chapters, the new cognitions, or the new meanings that are uncovered. Two different features of this category can be illustrated from James's journey: the consequence of his failure to fulfill the primary function of the voyage; and the effect upon the explorer.

The first issue to be addressed is the primary or manifest function of the voyage. James never discovered the passage to the South Seas. The only feasible route was far to the north of where he explored, north and west of Baffin Island, winding its way through the Canadian Arctic islands. It was a passage that was blocked in ice for all but a few weeks of the year and probably impossible to traverse in a ship of James's size and vintage — unless there was an unusually warm summer that melted the ice. However, James's journey was not a complete failure in the context of exploration. Although it has been shown that James did leave the door open to the prospect of a Northwest Passage, any dispassionate contemporary reader of his journal must have been convinced that such a passage did not exist — at least in the sense of an easy passage to Asia for commercial vessels. Yet, despite his hard-won knowledge and the wide publication of his book, a succession of explorers continued to search for the passage for centuries afterwards (Berton 1988). This provides a valuable illustration of John Allen's point (1975b) about the power of myths or preconceived ideas in influencing actions, even when the emerging facts show that the image was incorrect. Although James's evidence may have been ignored in subsequent years, in local terms it seems to have had an extremely powerful effect. The voyage virtually ended the interest of Bristol merchants in financing ventures of this kind. Part of this may have been due to the greater caution of investors at a time of increasing domestic political turmoil that led to the Civil War, but the far richer prospects of trade with the Caribbean began to interest Bristol merchants. Yet it is tantalizing to realize that James's journey could have produced a positive benefit – that of helping to prove an alternate route to the continental interior in order to exploit its fur resources. But the route that James helped to pioneer and map was not used for almost another forty years, when Gillam sailed to James Bay in 1668 – probably the first European ship to do so since James, on a voyage to find furs. This journey to obtain furs had been suggested by Pierre Radisson and Sieur de Groseilliers, two French Canadians who had trading experience in the area north of the Great Lakes and realized that the Hudson Bay passage was a quicker route to the fur-rich areas. The successful voyage led a group of London merchants and the Crown to create the Hudson's Bay Company in 1670 (Williams, G., 1970; Newman 1986). This was an enterprise that initially monopolized access to the heart of the continent. The company's reluctance to penetrate into their hinterland enabled the Montreal fur traders to extend westwards and outflank it north of the Prairies in the late eighteenth century, before the Hudson's Bay Company also moved into the interior and eventually absorbed their St. Lawrence-based rivals. This means that a positive economic return was eventually obtained from the hinterland of the area explored by James. Perhaps it was ironic that those who obtained such great profits from the area were based in London; it was the nation's capital, not Bristol, which eventually reaped the benefits of the exploration. One consequence was that the western hinterland of Hudson Bay is often described as Rupert's Land, after the prince who was the first royal sponsor of the Hudson's Bay Company. This does mark the first European exploitation of the area, rather than its discovery, for which the terms New Wales, Button's Land, or James's Land would have been more appropriate acknowledgments of the work of the initial explorers.

A second important consequence of many journeys of exploration is the immediate effect upon the explorer. Explorers were far from being simply instruments of what can be called the manifest purpose; many plunged into the voyages and endured extreme hardships in their search for personal glory and financial gain. Some were successful, lionized by their contemporaries and turned into heroes – or martyrs if they died – by the subsequent public adulation. The public perceptions of explorers, either as intrepid travellers or tragic figures, were created by the image-makers. Such writers frequently sensationalized the actual events and character of the explorer for their own ends. Of course, this process was not new. Our knowledge of Greek myths, and the practise of the ancient Celtic bards, show how actual and imagined discoveries were immortalized – perhaps the Madoc myth about Welsh-speaking Indians was created and kept alive in such circumstances (Williams 1987). It has previously been shown how nineteenth-century newspapers created their own heroes by sponsoring expeditions to Africa and the Arctic to boost their circulations. The seventeenth-century explorers had far fewer opportunities to enhance their own images, or their fortunes, without recourse to piracy. The experience of Button was remembered and the court consulted him when the journeys of James and Foxe to Hudson Bay were contemplated. But it has already been shown that his responses to the royal enquiries provided some useful observations. However, they also reveal that he had become an embittered and debt-ridden old man, one who had only a few years left to live. Judging by James's failure to find the passage to the riches of the Orient, it is curious how he seems to have been held in very high esteem by the court and the public. This may be evidence, once again, of the mismatch between achievements – at least in the manifest function – and subsequent fame. It could be a function of the second instrumental function to be discussed; James's decision to write a book on his experiences, which had very different purposes to the journey.

✣ 3. CHANGING PURPOSE: FROM JOURNEY TO NARRATIVE

James's popular esteem in the 1630s does not seem to have been simply a consequence of the exploration itself. James's reputation may also have been enhanced by the fact there was considerable anticipation that he had made a successful journey because of the events in the year before he returned. It is easy, with hindsight, to exaggerate the significance of voyages of exploration and colonization schemes to contemporary observers at court. To the self-centred courtiers, focused on their daily joust for power and influence, such issues about a far-flung land or voyage were usually of little import. But the coincidence of the two parallel voyages of James and Foxe, linked to the rivalry between Bristol and London, and regarded with apprehension by the powerful monopolists in the East India Company, must have provided more interest than usual.

Foxe returned with news of his failure after only six months – when he was provisioned for eighteen – to immediate criticism. But since the fate of James remained in the balance, there was a lot of speculation of his whereabouts, almost certainly adding to interest in James's voyage. Sir Thomas Roe's letter to the Bristol Society dated November 1631 (BSMV 1631, 197–98), informing them of the Yorkshire captain's return, displays considerable irritation at the failure of the London venture, in part because the Yorkshire captain had not appeared at court to explain what had happened. Roe was quite blunt in his assessment that Foxe had disobeyed his orders in proceeding to the southern shore of Hudson Bay, rather than staying and searching for the Northwest Passage near Button's Bay. Roe admitted that the explorer had tried to redeem his error by subsequently going north and heading past Nottingham Island into the Arctic Circle. But the fact that Foxe had sight of land to the east, led Roe to the contemptuous comment that he had been searching for a northwest passage on a northeast shore! Of course, much of this criticism is unfair, since the initial decisions to proceed south into Hudson Bay were both taken by Foxe and James because of the presence of solid ice to the northwest in early July. It demonstrates the savage nature of comments at court by people who had not experienced – and probably could not imagine – the solid ice that blocked the way, perhaps demonstrated by the fact that Roe does not mention the word *ice* in his critique of Foxe. By contrast, there is special praise for James, even though it was obvious that he was also on the southern shore when last seen. Roe's favour is seen by the following comment:

> All our hopes now reste upon captain James who will attempt it next yeare and resolved to lose his life or returne with more honour and though you cannot find it (if it bee there) yet hee shall hath gained infinite reputation to have taken this resolution and not to come home like a sluggard. (BSMV 1631, 197)

Comments about hazarding a life for honour and glory may have been Roe's interpretation, rather than reflecting the opinions of James – unless James sent letters back with Foxe, in which such opinions were expressed. However, there is no evidence of such communication. Obviously, such heroic attitudes were prized at the time. They were not simply the preserve of nineteenth-century exploration, linked to the travails and tragedies of the likes of Franklin and Scott. Their reputation was enhanced by jingoism, almost turning them into martyrs for their country; indeed, contemporary reports tended to ignore the way the journeys of these individuals were flawed by so many errors of judgement (Riffenburgh 1993; Davis 1995). Also it must be remembered that James was seen as a scholar and gentleman – unlike Foxe, who is usually represented as an uncouth, sea dog – although his own words did much to create such an image. Since the appearance of style was as important as substance, especially where duty and honour was involved, James's continued absence during the winter of 1631–32 may well have built-up expectations in the English court. These helped mitigate the disappointment of his actual findings, especially when he was able to describe a tale of heroic survival against so many perils. Indeed, the groundwork for such a change in the way that James's journey would be judged, may have been laid well before James's book appeared.

Less than two weeks after James brought his battered ship into Bristol, the exhausted captain was travelling to London bearing letters of introduction from his sponsors to both the lord treasurer and to Sir Thomas Roe – a list of names that now included one of Bristol's leading merchants, Thomas Colston. The letter asked for a royal audience for James as "abundant compensation of his labour and our charge" (BSMV 2 November 1632, 200). It is fascinating to observe that the brief letters do not even mention James's failure to find a Northwest Passage. Instead, stress is laid upon quite different goals, as the following extracts from the letter show.

> Having escaped manifold dangers and extremities in the voyage through good merit he doth now address himself to your Majesty the first account of his industrie and endeavours. ... that his faithfull, and indefatigable service. ... in the voyage tending principallie to the honour of his Majesty, and common benefit of our native countrie. (BSMV 2 November 1632, 200)

Such a rapid shift in opinion, transforming the objectives of the venture, at least from its initial goals, was not unknown in courtly circles! Few would wish to bring bad news to the king. But since James was acting on behalf of Bristol merchants, few among the royal court had financial links with the venture and negative views of James. However, the hints of adventure and discussion of perils that are contained in the letter surely sets the scene for the emphasis upon James's exploits – his *ordeals* rather than his *quest* – long before James's own presentation at court and the publication of his book. This may be a good historical example of *putting a new spin on the news,* illustrating that the approach is hardly an invention of the contemporary media.

Some idea of the anticipation raised by James's journey can also be gauged from the fact that he was able to have his audience with the king in mid-November. On 19 November, James wrote to the society describing his presentation to the king. He also commented on how he was being entertained to dinner by many important people in London. When compared with the odium that had been heaped on Foxe the previous year, it indicated that James had already become a celebrity. Yet James's letter shows how he was at pains to acknowledge that he was really the instrument of the Bristol Society of Merchant Venturers:

> *By experience I have found that they respect the worstest of your servants the more amplie to make it appear how much they favour you in general, and any of the noble minded of the Citty in particular. (BSMV 1632, 204)*

The audience with the king lasted an unprecedented two hours; James presented his plot or chart, described the journey, and answered questions. In the same letter, James observed that the king "was pleased to say it satisfied his expectation" and that he had been asked to return with Foxe and Bruton – the latter was presumably Foxe's second in command, who may have been incorrectly described as captain. They were supposed to discuss the journeys at some later date, although such an audience never took place. What is extremely important was James's comment that he was commanded to visit the king in the future and was asked to bring "an abstract of my Journall and perfect my observations." It was obviously a task that James took seriously. He must have set to work immediately and obtained the co-operation of his publisher to produce his book early in 1633, even though he was busy in his new post by April, as captain of a king's ship, patrolling the Irish Sea in search of pirates. The speed with which James's work was produced, especially given the fact that the appendices involved considerable work by others, seems to testify to the value of the royal favour which had been bestowed on James.

This discussion of the events that took place between the end of the journey and the publication of the book may also illustrate additional positive effects upon the organizations involved. The sponsors, the Society of Merchant Venturers from the City of Bristol, seem to have gained prestige from their involvement in the expedition – even allowing for the typical courtly flourishes of the day and the standard self-abasement of James's comments about his own worth that were quoted above (BSMV, November 1632), But, transcending these commercial and personal considerations are the effects upon state policy, especially the claims to the new lands. At both Cape Henrietta Maria and Charlton Island, James raised flags and took possession of the land in the name of his king. The ritual of possession was adhered to and, in European minds at least, established unequivocal British claim to sovereignty over this part of the future Dominion of Canada. This was a necessary prelude to the future development of the fur trade in the lands that drained into Hudson Bay. So James's sponsors, recognizing the failure of the attempt to reach the expected goal of the Northwest Passage, may have quickly and deliberately emphasized the royal and national benefit of the journeys. They seem to have conveniently forgotten their pre-venture concern with reaping the benefits of trade with Asia, on an equal footing with their London rivals. But for James, the production of a book about his adventures represented an opportunity to establish *his* reputation as a survivor – one who had battled extreme environmental conditions and had lived to tell the tale. Certainly, James's narrative did perform the function of describing his discoveries. But it did so in a way that appealed to the imagination of his readers – thereby fulfilling a different purpose to the original intent of the journey: to discover a passage to the Orient.

✣   4. STIMULATION OF OTHERS

It has already been shown that James's short book provided significant achievements in a number of different areas. Those associated with discovery and with scientific method have been dealt with in previous sections and need not be repeated. In an environmental context, it can be argued that James's journal provided one of the most effective descriptions to date of living in, and coping with, an extremely cold environment. It had the effect of stimulating subsequent work, especially alerting others to the effects of the extreme cold – a cold well beyond the experience of the British Isles. It has already been shown that the eminent scientist, Robert Boyle, used, with gratitude, many of James's observations on cold; even the normally critical Barrow (1818, 250) acknowledged this relationship – quite an admission from an otherwise critical source. However, the work had another value in the context of the environment. Germaine Warkentin (1993) suggested that exploration journals may sometimes be seen to demonstrate the *pleasure* of the author in experiencing the new lands. It is dubious whether James's journey could have been viewed in this way by the author. Arctic explorers may be a separate *breed*, relishing the challenge of overcoming extreme weather conditions. Yet one would have to be a masochist to derive enjoyment from the bone-chilling winter, or the frequent exhaustion from the physical effort needed to keep a ship afloat during weeks of severe icing – even apart from the deleterious effects of their monotonous diet, attacks of scurvy, or the frequent fear of being sunk by gales, ice or rocks. Yet, from a reader's perspective, not an author's viewpoint, James's narrative may have produced a vicarious pleasure – or at least respect for his fortitude – among his readers. After all, the dangers and potential disasters exposed his readers to the sensations of the journey, albeit at second-hand. These sensations may have stimulated the imagination of many a reader who was able to relive James's journey in the comfort of their own home, as well as authors who produced their own literary work. MacLaren (1984; 1985b, 41) suggested that James's description of the dreadful conditions experienced in the winter at James Bay may have been echoed in Milton's images of hell in *Paradise Lost*. However a much clearer and extensive connection to subsequent literary works can be seen in the work of the Romantic poet, Samuel Taylor Coleridge. It is very possible that one of Coleridge's most famous poems, *The Rime of the Ancient Mariner*, bears the mark of experiences first described by James.

Questions such as how any author arrived at the chosen theme of a book or poem, or came to describe the conditions that either form part of the text or create meanings within it, are standard investigative issues among literary scholars. Without explicit evidence from the author, the truth is always elusive; there is always the possibility that they may have been derived by some unconscious or purely random process. In any case, it is not unknown for authors to conceal their sources. The situation is made even more complex because modern literary theorists emphasize the need to accept multiple interpretations of a work. The canonical traditions of the past, involving a single privileged interpretation from major scholars, are rarely accepted today. What the author intended, and what was achieved, may be very different. The concept of the reader's plural adds another layer of difficulty because it authenticates the derivation of varied interpretations and feelings from any text. But there seems little doubt that one of the most famous genres in literature, the

Romantic Movement that began in the mid-eighteenth century, turned to nature and to previously unknown or disregarded lands to obtain their inspiration. This proved to be a real reversal from the classical, religious, or personal themes that dominated most previous prose or poetry. Romantic poets in particular derived new and inspired insights into feelings from the environment, finding pleasure in the landscape: first of beauty and then sublimity. Most of the landscapes immortalized in the works of the Romantic poets were those that were local and accessible to these writers – especially the famous English Lake District or the more dramatic mountainous parts of Wales – which were given quite new interpretations (Zaring 1977). But the Romantic poets also described situations that could not have been grounded in their personal experience. It is accepted that the extensive exploration and travel literature of their day provided a large and readily available source material for such themes. Coleridge's biographers have shown that he was a voracious reader of such books (Lowes 1927; Gallant 1989). The poet seemed to have a phenomenal memory for things that he had read, but also frequently jotted down ideas and phrases from a variety of sources. Coleridge was always fascinated by the twilight stage between the conscious and unconscious state, in which new ideas and sequences were created. Indeed, the poet maintained that he composed his famous poem, *Kubla Khan*, after waking from a sleep that followed reading about this Asian potentate in Purchas's (1626) famous compendium of explorations (Lowes 1927, 324). Naturally, it took Coleridge's imagination and poetic ability to weave a tale of mystery and delight from the raw material at hand that had led to the dream, from which he awoke and quickly composed the basic structure of his poem. But the stimulation provided by these accounts of exploration should be noted. Similarly, there seems strong circumstantial evidence that James's *Strange and Dangerous Journey* provided the inspiration for at least part of an even more famous poem – although without the intervention of a dream.

Coleridge's poem *The Rime of the Ancient Mariner* was written between mid-November 1797, when he was in the Quantock Hills of Somerset, and the following March (Lowes 1927, 128). Published late in 1798, it was reprinted and revised on at least six occasions, as an authoritative account of the various editions by Wallen (1993) has shown. We can never know all the circumstances that led to the creation of the poem, although it is often suggested that some of the key ideas came from books or ideas provided by Wordsworth, especially the albatross sequence (James, I., 1890). However, it seems very likely that James's epic adventures in Hudson Bay provided the source of many of the winter sequences described in the poem. Over a century ago, the link between James's book and Coleridge's poem was first suggested in a small booklet written by Ivor James, registrar of the University of Wales (James, I., 1890). A score of relationships between the poem and the explorer's narrative were identified, but some of these linkages were criticized in a review of this comparison by an anonymous critic in a contemporary journal (Atheneum: March 1890, 355–56). Although many of the associations were repeated in Lowes's (1927) authoritative study of Coleridge's use of imagination, the relationships between poet and explorer seem to have been largely forgotten over the last half century, although Delgado's (1999) recent study of the exploration of the Northwest Passage does re-emphasize the linkages.

Five main points seem relevant to the debate that there are close connections between the poem and James's narrative. First, there seems little doubt that Coleridge knew of James's book. It was available in the library at Cambridge where the poet studied, and was known to even more people because of the 1740 reprint (Payne 1740). Coleridge spent a lot of time from the autumn of 1794 to 1798 in the Bristol area when he visited his close friend and collaborator, Richard Southey. He was known to be a voracious reader who borrowed books from the public library in Bristol. Although Ivor James (1890) claimed that James's book was part of the Bristol library, the unidentified Atheneum critic (1890) and Lowes (1927, 452) cast doubt upon the evidence, although the latter maintained that Harris's (1744) book on voyages, which included a major extract from James's work, was available. More convincing proof of Coleridge's awareness of James's voyage can be seen in the book entitled Omniana (Southey and Coleridge 1812). This is a collection of what can only be described as *fragments*, containing pieces of verse, prose, commentaries, essays, and poems collected over many years. The volume included the two poems printed in James's journal, together with some favourable comments: the poems are described as having a "fine and manly feeling breathed into them." (Southey and Coleridge 1812, 230). Incidentally, this is another example of the way that masculinity has been portrayed (Schöene-Haywood 2000). Southey seems to have played a leading role in the compilation of this work and was probably responsible for the comments. Together with the other evidence, there seems little doubt that Coleridge knew of James's work and could well have adapted some of the descriptions in his own poems.

The second, and perhaps most important set of associations, stem from the accounts of particular events in the poem that seem to come from James's journey. Lowes (1927) observed that the verses contain features he could not have experienced personally. Coleridge's first boat journey took place six months *after* the poem was finished, whilst the descriptions of the dangers and characteristics of sea ice go far beyond the experiences that could be derived from a British winter. Even the poet's choice of words parallel many of those found in James's descriptions of the Canadian North. It may be too commonplace to pay much attention to the fact that James described his own verses as "rimes" (J 38), a word that appears in this spelling in the title of the poem. What is more important is that few northern explorers before the nineteenth century provided much detail about the dangers of ice and the noise it produced – in part because there was little interest, expertise, or tradition in describing nature, or landscapes in general. James's work was unusual in this respect and provided several descriptions that are paralleled in Coleridge's verses. The most obvious is the way that James was almost obsessive about ice; it has already been noted how he mentioned the word several times a page when he was sailing in ice-infested waters. In total, the term *ice* is mentioned over four hundred times by James. It has already been shown that Foxe (1635) also used the word frequently, but with far less emphasis, and rarely associated it with emotions, such as fear. These repetitions are very different to the descriptions provided by previous subarctic explorers. For example, the word *ice* is only used on some fifty occasions in all of Frobisher's descriptions of his three expeditions in 1576–78 (Stefansson1938). More to the point, is James's frequent description of the way that he was '*enclosed* or *surrounded*' in ice. The enclosure even extended to a third dimension, as the following passage shows.

> In the evening, wee were inclosed amongst great pieces, as high as our Poope, and some of the sharpe blue corners of them did reach quite under us. All of these great pieces (by reason it was the out-side of the Ice) did heave and set, and so beat us that it was wonderful how the Ship could endure indure one blow of it. (J 6)

There seems little point in disputing James's literal observations. But this constant repetition of enclosure by ice is a unique feature of James's book and may well have been a stimulus for many of Coleridge's famous lines.

The ice was here, the ice was there,
The ice was all around:
It cracked and growled and roared and howled,
Like noises in a swound!

Later on, the poem refers to the way the pack ice disintegrated:

The Ice did split with a thunder-fit;
The helmsman steer'd us through!

It is worth noting that the precise wording, as well as the punctuation of the poem, were constantly altered by Coleridge over the next twenty years, as Wallen's (1993) detailed study has shown. All quotations used here are from the last major revision by the poet in 1817.

It is not only the fact of enclosure that is so significant. Many of the words found in the extracts describing the noise of the ice first appear in James's book. He described how the sea ice broke in late June 1632: it "crackt over the Bay, with a fearful noyse" (J 77). There is even a passage which describes "steering betwixt great pieces of Ice … twice as high as our top–mast head" (J 14). The previous discussion about James's use of sound in his narrative has described how the ice made a "most terrible thundering noyse" (J 12), or a "most fearfull noyse" (J 93) and "did grate us with violence" (J 15). Yet, it is worth observing that it was the wind, not the ice, that was violent and roared. This created the image of "a great rowling sea" in James's account (J 49). Indeed, James did not use the word *growled* in this context, although it must be remembered that the associated word, *growler*, is a common surrogate for an iceberg in the Maritimes of Canada. It may have been a term known to Coleridge through the West Country fishermen of his day who fished off Newfoundland. It is curious that Kenyon's translation of James's work into modern phrasing used the term "growler" (Kenyon 1975, 121) when James actually referred to the *rut* of the ice on the seashore. The archaic word "swound" in these circumstances may have been used to simply fit the metre. James did use the word in his book, but in the sense of a swoon, as shown in the italics added to the quotation below. James described how his youngest men went into the water to rake away the sand from around the ship so that they could replace the rudder:

But they were not able to indure the cold of it halfe a quarter of an houre,
it was so mortifying; yea, use what comforts we could, it would make them
swound and dye away. (J 79)

Parallels in phrasing between poem and voyage can be seen in many other places, although James's journal may not be the only source. For example, Coleridge's lines described the initial onset of the ice as follows:

> And now there came both mist and snow,
> And it grew wondrous cold:
> And ice, mast-high, came floating by,
> As green as emerald.

However, the immediacy of the cold and the ice is not found amongst the phrasing used by James. It is also worth noting that although James does use the word "wondrous" to describe the climate, it was with reference to the heat of the day (J 81). James also frequently described the height of the ice by reference to the ship and its masts, not — as was common practise at the time — by reference to some standardized, yet abstract measure of distance, such as fathoms or paces.

All these examples provide a great deal of circumstantial evidence for proposing James's book as a primary source for the winter sequences of the poem. But one cannot attribute all these sequences to James alone. Lowes shows that other arctic explorers may also have provided sources used by Coleridge — especially for the last extract. He noted that the voyage of Martens to Spitzbergen in 1694 used the juxtaposition of "mist and snow" and of "ice floating down," whilst ice was described as "green as emeralds" (Lowes 1927, chapter 9). By contrast, James only used colour once in all of his references to ice — it was a singular example, in which the ice was described as "blue" (J 6).

A third major association comes from the fact that some of James's descriptions may have been transposed to fit a different theme — a typical approach in poetry. Perhaps the most suggestive lines in Coleridge are those describing the Mariner's ship marooned in the Doldrums.

> Day after day, day after day,
> We stuck, nor breath nor motion,
> As idle as a painted ship
> Upon a painted ocean.

The effect of being becalmed in the tropics would have been well-known to any eighteenth-century reader of travel literature. But it is worth quoting the words used by James to describe how his ship was held fast in the northern ice. These certainly provide a possible source of imagery used by Coleridge.

> The 28 and 29 (July 1632) we were fast inclosed in the Ice, that notwithstanding, we put aboard all the saylethat was at yards, and that it blew a very hard Gale of Winde; the Ship stirred no more than if shee had beene in a dry docke. ... we went all boldly out upon the Ice, to sport and recreate ourselves, letting her stand still, under all her Sails. It was flat, extraordinary large Ice: the worst to deal withal, that we had yet found. I measured some pieces, which I found to be 1000 of my paces long ... wee dranke a health to his Majestie on the Ice; not one man in the Ship, and shee still under all her sails. (J 19)

Later, on the 17 November (J 46), after describing how the crew were in misery on theshore because of their frozen condition, James wrote the words that were used to begin to this chapter. James's images of an empty ship, marooned in ice – sails billowing but not moving, despite the gale – are certainly moving and memorable. Did Coleridge take the idea and relocate it in the tropics, adding colour where James would only see shades of white in the ice and snow of the subarctic? Or, could this have been the passage that led the poet to conceive a spectral ship, a phantom vessel in the poem – one with all its sails set, yet moving without a wind? Again, it is impossible to be sure. What can be said is that James certainly provided a vivid, and more to the point, unusual word-picture of the conditions he experienced. It is one that seems unique in early exploration journals and, as such, could well have stimulated Coleridge's imagination. After all, his biographers frequently observe that he was always searching, however unconsciously, for raw material for his poems.

But one can go further in the analogies. Ivor James (1890) suggested several other possible transpositions, although these are not so clear. For example, he proposed that the lines that every school child used to know in Coleridge's poem, "water, water everywhere and not a drop to drink," may also have been inspired by James. During his winter camp, James and his crew were surrounded by snow and ice and all their drinks were frozen. But he complained that they were unable to use these possible resources: melted snow made them breathless; their frozen beer and spirits had to be split with an axe before they could be thawed to drink. In addition, it can be argued that the poem's description of dead men on the spectral ship, its charnel house atmosphere, and the *Life in Death* woman, may have been suggested by the condition of James and crew by April 1632. Most were exhausted and ill from the prolonged effects of the severe cold and scurvy, with festering gums, and sores on their legs. They were still alive, but some were visibly rotting; clearly, death was approaching. However much James and his crew suffered from their privations, the majority survived. This was very different to Munk's disastrous expedition from Denmark to Hudson Bay in the winter of 1619–20, when most of the crew died during the winter (Hansen 1970). The captain's own survival may have been due to the fact that he managed to drag himself out of the ship – undoubtedly a charnel house that was full of dead, dying, and disintegrating humans – to the habitation that had been built on shore. Munk's experience, therefore, would have provided a more vivid source for Coleridge's imagery. But it is not clear whether the poet was aware of the Danish explorer's journal that described the gruesome scenes of lingering deaths.

A fourth argument can be based on some of the key themes in the poem – especially the journey home which was described as being powered by spiritual, not earthly, winds. Initially, this seems to have no relationship to James's voyage. Yet Coleridge's concept of a *dream voyage*, of a ship being powered by spiritual power, does have a basis in James's book, as the Atheneum critic (1890) correctly observed. It can be illustrated by the phrasing of the quotation provided below. James's diatribe against the veracity of Spanish and Portuguese explorers who were reputed to have sailed in these seas through a Northwest Passage, includes the following suggestive words "fables" and "meere shaddowes":

> *What hath beene long agoe fabled by some Portugales, that should have comne this way out of the South Sea, the meere shaddowes of whose mistaken Relations have come to us, I leave to be confuted by their owne Vanitie. (J 107.)*

After emphasizing that he paid little attention to those whom had proposed and supported the idea of a Northwest Passage, James observed that the Iberian explorers did not mention any of the extreme environmental difficulties that are found in the area. This made it improbable that they found such a route. It led James to explicitly suggest that the Iberians had been on a *dream* voyage.

> *I give no credit to them at all, and as little to the vicious, and abusive wits of later Portugals and Spaniards: who never speake of any difficulties: as shoald water, Ice, nor sight of land: but (write) as if they had beene brought home in a dreame or engine. And, indeed, their discourses are found absurd: and the plots ... mere falsities. (J 107.)*

More specifically, the idea of a dream voyage in Coleridge's poems may have been inspired by another passage. One of James's own poems concludes with the opinion that survival, even salvation, is more likely to be achieved if the sails were powered by *grace*, rather than by *nature*. The relevant lines are worth repeating.

> *Now thou must Steere by faith; a better guide,*
> *'Twill bring thee safe to heaven, against the tyde*
> *Of Satan's malice. Now let quiet gales*
> *Of saving grace, inspire thy zealous sayles. (J 39.)*

Coleridge's own spirituality may well have been especially moved by this passage, since James described how it was composed and then delivered to encourage his crew after a series of disasters. But there is another relationship that can be linked with these ideas. The poem described how the Mariner went to the limit of the southern hemisphere – to a zone of continuous ice. On leaving it the poem states:

> We were first that ever burst
> Into that silent sea.

Subsequently, the Ancient Mariner's ship turned north and home. Geographically and temporally, this sequence does not make sense. There was no unknown sea to *burst into* in the area after which they turned north; after Antarctica it is possible to use Magellan's Straits to enter the Pacific, but this part of the southern Pacific was reasonably well-known by the early seventeenth century. If the Mariner did continue north to the north Pacific then he would have to have taken a route through the Bering Strait and the Canadian arctic before returning home. This is the route that some early-sixteenth-century Iberian explorers were supposed to have taken – the journeys so heavily criticized by James in the quotation above as a *dream*. There is no convincing evidence that such journeys did take place. If there was an exceptionally warm summer or two, the passage may have been open – a possibility that might have occurred in the late fifteenth or early sixteenth century when there was a slight warming trend. In the early seventeenth century, when Hudson, Button, James, and Foxe were searching for the elusive passage, the pattern was of a colder period, so ice locked the potential passage through the arctic islands.

A fifth and more conjectural set of relationships between the poem and James' journey can be seen in some of their common settings. The Ancient Mariner poem begins and ends with an encounter between a wedding guest and the seaman, who accosts the guest with his horrific story. At first sight, this link to a celebration has little relationship with James's journey, although any wedding at this time would have had a religious basis. Yet it must be noted that James's exploration narrative is unusual in describing how he and his crew began and ended the journey with religious services. This means that both the book and the poem have a spiritual framework, initial settings for the subsequent descriptions of both extraordinary, yet real, other-worldly experiences, as well as similar ones that are fictive. Coleridge's gloss, or short marginal comments, may also be regarded as a parallel to exploration journals. Added to the editions of the poem that appeared in and after 1817 (Wallen 1993), the gloss provided what amounted to a *rational* summary of the poem, contrasting with what has been described as "the naked power of the pantheistic, elemental forces that the verse exemplifies" (Gallant 1989, 89). Gallant may have a point in seeing the gloss as a moralizing agency, to alert readers to their habitual way of thinking – thereby providing a vivid contrast to the spiritual themes of the poem. But one can go further and suggest the gloss may be another link to James's narrative or rather to exploration journals in general; after all, marginal comments and summaries are typical in exploration journals and logs of this time. In James's book, only the daily dates are provided as marginal entries. These mean that the most extraordinary events of the voyage are constantly anchored by the mundane, the daily sequence of the log, a time-keeping familiar to the readers since it was part of their everyday life. It is possible that Coleridge intended to provide the same type of link to experience and rationality when he added the gloss to his fictional, yet spiritual poem.

Despite the number and closeness of these associations, one must not take the parallels too far. Not all of 'The Rime of the Ancient Mariner' can be attributed to inspiration from James's epic journey. There are many events in the poem that have little to do with James's journey. This does not destroy the argument. It is enough to have shown that *some* of the passages of the poem parallel James's journal in events, and in word use. This provides a strong possibility that Coleridge's poem could have been partly inspired by James's voyage – in other words it can be seen as an instrumental consequence of the narrative. Certainly there are other sequences that seem to be based on quite different sources, as shown by Lowes's (1927) still authoritative book on the poet. One of the most obvious examples concerns the killing of the albatross and the subsequent advent of bad luck in the poem. There is no parallel for this in James's journal. Indeed, he frequently bemoaned the inability of his crew to capture many birds and animals. However, it was an event that had prominence in the work of another explorer – in George Shelvocke's (1726) voyage to the South Atlantic, which may have been brought to Coleridge's attention by Wordsworth, who had been reading the book in November 1797 (DNB 1950, vol. 18, 47). The actual incident reported was the shooting of the albatross, which was thought to have brought the ship contrary winds in the southern hemisphere. Coleridge transposed the idea, linking it to a becalming in the Tropics. This adaptation of one of Shelvocke's descriptions may be used to demonstrate another Welsh borderland link between a real exploration and the fictive. Little is known of Shelvocke's origins, but his name is a very unusual one and may derive from the family that lived in the large farm of that name between Oswestry and Shrewsbury, a farm that was one of the Ruyton XI Towns established after the Norman Conquest.

This discussion of the way that James's journal may have stimulated or affected other artistic endeavours does not stop here. Gustav Doré, the master engraver, was so entranced by 'The Rime of the Ancient Mariner' that he created a series of illustrations to illuminate the scenes described by Coleridge in another publication of the poem edited by Millicent Rose in 1878 (Rose 1970 reprint). James's descriptions of a ship encrusted and surrounded by ice, almost indistinct in the mist, are given life in another artistic medium. Yet one must be critical of the some of the features illustrated. Doré's fanciful portrayals of seals in some of his illustrations look more like the hounds that James carried on board; they show that artistic licence has been carried too far. In any case, one of the major features of James's journal is the fact that during his months at sea he saw relatively few signs of life – whether fish, mammals, or fowl.

269

A fourth major instrumental function of exploration texts is the extent to which they contain observations that demonstrate how the explorer's experience leads to reflection about his own culture – especially about values, ways of doing things, of moral attitudes, etc. In other words, contact with previously unknown peoples may result in introspection about the accepted mores and philosophies of the explorer's culture. It is difficult to find any evidence for such cultural self-reflection in James's narrative. It has already been noted that James did not meet any native people. His preparations against the possibility of attack merely confirmed the general view that explorers ought to be concerned about ambush, and indicated that he was aware of the need for defence against what were usually thought of as aggressive aboriginal peoples. So there is little room for any critical reflection in a comparative cultural context. But the same conclusion can be applied to many of the early European explorers, who can be regarded as simply visiting other lands, using the mind sets and attitudes of their home country. This had particular relevance to seaborne explorers. They were largely insulated against the day-to-day activities of other cultures by reason of their life on board ship – unless, as in the case of later South Seas explorers, they spent a lot of time on islands, or in trading posts. For land explorers, daily contact with aboriginal guides and the necessity of frequently moving camp, as well as meeting other native groups in their travels, ensured closer connections. This led to more intimate associations with different native peoples, allowing comparisons and introspection. Even in these circumstances, the self-centred Europeans were usually convinced of their own moral superiority. In this they were buttressed by an increasingly sophisticated technology – especially after the Industrial Revolution – as well as a belief in a single God who was assumed to support their ventures. Hence most explorers disparaged local cultures – the differences they saw rarely dented their own views. One example from the area originally called New Wales may illustrate the point. In 1832 the aboriginal peoples were described by the Reverend Thomas Jones, the Welsh-speaking missionary in the Red River settlement area (Manitoba), as: "the untutored heathen tribe, a dark bewildered race" (quoted in Davies, W.K.D., 1991, 226). The effect of intercultural contact also led him to make the following derogatory comment about the fur traders, many of whom were white: "I have often been astonished at the amazing degeneration which they have shown, in falling by degrees into the habits of the Indian" (quoted in Davies, W.K.D., 1991, 230). There is no prevarication here. Despite Jones's sympathy with his native flock that is shown in many other letters, the comments indicated his clear sense of cultural superiority and the problems that could come from too close a contact with such peoples. Missionaries, such as Jones, or explorers like James, may be best seen as part of that group of visitors to North America who were still European in every respect. They might have produced discoveries of new lands or ministered to its people, but were never really part of the land; they remained outsiders.

Although James's experiences produced little in the way of cultural self-reflection, there is one area in which his book did show new insights into what may be described as New World views and new reflections. This is the primacy of the explorer's *gaze* over the once authoritative views of classical philosophers. It has already been shown how the findings of the eyewitness, many of whom had little education, were priorized over ideas described in the classical texts. Yet James did not write the words that confirmed this important new approach to what we might call *evidence* about the location and character of the new lands. James took it upon himself to persuade a respected Cambridge cleric-scholar to make the case in an appendix. The fact that James included it in his book may again be the mark of a trained lawyer. He recognized that an expert may be better able to make the case. His own advocacy could be construed as biased in favour of the eyewitness approach; after all, he was one of the explorers whose findings were replacing the previous *truths* of the classical philosophers. In the last resort, however, James's narrative is not only important for providing vivid descriptions of what he had seen. It was also significant for its convincing case against the possibility of a Northwest Passage. James's work did not discourage future attempts to search for the passage. But it seems to have convinced his sponsors to turn their interests elsewhere. However, in doing so, it has already been noted that Bristol missed sharing in the huge profits subsequently realized from the Hudson Bay fur company. Yet to achieve these profits the company needed a monopoly, which was dependent upon royal favour – perhaps an unlikely reward for a city such as Bristol, so distant from the seat of political power. So perhaps the biggest instrumental impact of James's journey was to keep the Bristol merchants' sights on the fisheries of the Grand Banks off Newfoundland, and later to the Caribbean, the southern American states, and to West Africa – the trade that subsequently generated so many fortunes for Bristol's leading merchants.

It has proved possible to trace some of James's subsequent life, although little is known of the history of James's battered ship and nothing seems to have been recorded about the crew that shared his gruelling expedition to the northwest. A state survey in April 1635 (DSP 1635) listed the English ships that were ready for sea. Among these, is a vessel called the *Henrietta Maria*, which sailed from Chatham in August taking Lord Aston, the English ambassador, to Spain. This is not the same Henrietta Maria; along with the *Charles*, it was one of two new royal warships that took their names from the royal couple. But in James's case, some personal instrumental utility resulted from his exploits. James received preferential treatment from the crown – the typical reward of an office in the king's service. On 6 April 1633, James was appointed captain of the *Ninth Lion's Whelp*, one of the two king's ships in the Bristol Channel – Irish Sea area, under the overall command of Captain Plumleigh. His orders were to suppress pirates – some of whom came from as far away as the North African coast – a continuing menace to maritime trade in the area (DSP 1633). The fact that James took such an appointment implies that he had limited financial resources and was unable to retire to some landed estate, or gain access to trading opportunities with his previous masters. It is worth noting that his Welsh predecessor to Hudson Bay, Admiral Button, had been captain of the same ship until July 1631, but had been relieved because of growing sickness, and died in the spring of 1634. Although James's career as a king's officer was a short one, it started well. With his usual efficiency, James reported to the authorities that it would take six weeks to get the ship fit for duty. He managed to fulfill his promise by setting sail for Ireland on 20 May 1633, a few days later than his historic transatlantic journey two years previously. By 6 July, he had captured a small pirate ship and had brought the vessel to Milford (DSP 1633). The following October, James's diligence and honesty was rewarded with a recommendation for promotion, although it was not followed up by the royal officials. It is clear from James's requests to the admiralty for more guns, pistols, and pikes in January 1634 – requests that were rejected – that he thought his ship was not fully prepared for the tasks that he had been set. In addition, James's naval service was not without controversy. The previous captain of the *Ninth Lion's Whelp*, Captain Cooper, had obtained an admiralty warrant for the arrest of three members of its crew, who had been accused of dishonesty with the stores: William Brooke, master; John Greene, boatswain; and John Dudley, gunner. After checking with the mayor and merchants of Bristol as to the honesty of those accused, James argued that the loss of these key men would deprive his ship of its ability to perform its duties. He then took matters into his own hands and sailed as planned, thwarting the attempt of Cooper's agent to arrest the men. By the following January, James was formally accused, not only of slighting the admiralty's warrant, but of making the derisory comment that he would do the same, for five shillings a head, for others who had been similarly charged (DSP 1634, 421). The warrant and the charge of disrespect were never pursued. James, the mayor, and aldermen of Bristol all wrote supporting letters for those accused, and the charges seem to have been dropped within a few months.

On 19 February 1634, James was again appointed as captain. By 15 March, he sailed down the Bristol Channel and the Irish Sea searching for pirates. During the next month, James reported that he heard that Button had died and that the master of his ship intended to sue the admiral's widow to recover the money that the master was owed. But by the winter of 1634–35 it was clear from the letters in the State Papers that James was very ill himself. On 29 January 1635, James reported that sickness "utterly disabled him from employment this year" (DSP 1634, 480). But this did not prevent him from writing a strong letter of recommendation for William Purser, the master's mate, whom he described as being the most qualified person he knew in the art and practise of navigation. By the next month, James's brief naval service had ended. His illness meant he could not complete his duties and Sir Beverly Newcombe replaced James as captain of the *Ninth Lion's Whelp*.

James was only in his early forties when he died, hardly the *old seaman* of subsequent description (Southey and Coleridge 1812). But he was still relatively old when compared to the typical seaman of the day. An inventory of the sailors in the Bristol area in 1628 (DSP 16/138/4) listed their ages as well as names and parish of residence. From this information, it was calculated that 63 per cent of the seamen in the Temple and Redcliffe parishes, the areas around the docks, were under thirty years of age. The exact date of Thomas James's death is unknown, but he probably died in the spring of 1635. In his will, dated 28 February 1635, he commended his soul into God's hands and itemized his bequests (Christy 1894, 204). He forgave his elder brother, John, a debt of over 250 pounds. The document went on to note that he had paid his debts, had already disposed of his lands by deed, and left the rest of his possessions to his sister, the widow Katherine Lacie, who was appointed as his executor. The fact that he was able to lend his brother such a considerable sum indicates that James must have been successful in privateering or trade before he went to Hudson Bay. However, his elder brother did not have much time to reflect on Thomas James's generosity. John died in April 1636 and Katherine inherited the Wern-yr-Cwm manor (Bradney 1906, 268). Since her sisters, Alice and Margaret, died in 1629 and 1638 respectively, it is clear that the family were not characterized by longevity. James's will was witnessed by William and Francis Yeamans, George Bowcher, Richard Pownall, and Richard Henry, most of whom were members of the Society of Merchant Venturers. Perhaps James's political sympathies can be seen by the choice of friends, for Bowcher was executed in the Civil War as a Royalist ringleader. Captain Thomas James was probably buried in St. Mark's Church, the Lord Mayor's Chapel in Bristol, despite his previous association with St. Mary Redcliffe. Located opposite the cathedral, the chapel was the religious sanctuary favoured by the city council and the major merchants. Given the variety of less worthy people whose time on earth is marked by memorials in Bristol's churches, it is unfortunate that there is no memorial tablet to mark the resting place of James, or his life and achievements in the service of Bristol. This omission seems typical of the limited attention paid to James's work in so many ways. Perhaps James had a premonition of this subsequent fate. It is worth quoting again an extract from the poem he composed in memory of his dead crew.

> We that survive, perchance may end our dayes
> In some imployment meriting no praise;
> And in a dung-hill rot; where no man names
> The memory of us, but to our shames.
> They have out-liv'd this feare, and their brave ends,
> Will ever be an honour to their friends. (J 89)

James's published eulogy was designed to praise and immortalize his dead companions. Perhaps the fact that his own grave is unknown, makes his verse prescient. Nevertheless, he did create his own memorial: a vivid narrative of an adventure-filled journey to the Canadian Northwest.

Chapter 8

A Passage Not Found, Passages Created

But thou (great James) hath by thy actions fram'd
A trophie that, hereafter, thou being name'd,
Men shall rise up with reverence, and keepe
Thy fame from freezing, when thy Ashes sleepe.
(Thomas Beedome 1641)

296 *A Passage Not Found, Passages Created*

The poet Thomas Beedome (1641) was stimulated enough by James's exploits to compose two epigrams to "the Heroicall Captaine Thomas James"– of which an extract is shown above – that were published after the writer's death and reprinted in Christy (1894, 187). Beedome was certainly not a major poet, but making James the subject of his verse indicates the high regard in which James was held after he returned from his harrowing voyage. But as we have seen in the first chapter, most students of exploration from the early nineteenth century had a quite a different view of James – as an incompetent seaman. This means that Beedome's poetic hope for James's immortal renown was not achieved. Certainly there is some residual knowledge of James's exploration because it has been indexed by the name of James Bay, but few seem to know of his connection with, or even of the existence of, the use of the name New South Wales in Canada. Captain Thomas James's *New South Wales* did survive for over three hundred years on the maps of British North America. But after the mid-nineteenth century, the mapmakers of Britain and the new Dominion of Canada, which took over the vast interior possessions of the Hudson's Bay Company in 1870, dropped the term, and began the process of applying names to the area that were derived from the indigenous cultures. Perhaps this Canadian New South Wales would have survived had it been a fertile land that attracted settlers. But its remoteness, limited resources, and harsh climate repelled Europeans, apart from those manning the handful of scattered fur trading posts – only marginal outposts on the rim of the European commercial world. The New South Wales of the land that became Canada, did not come to even mark – let alone symbolize – some valued location. Its existence as a label has gradually been forgotten; a disappearance that provides another example of the way that the Welsh rarely even merit a footnote in the history of Canada – a land created by the efforts of immigrants from so many lands – although some efforts have been made to rectify this matter (Bennett 1985; Davies, W.K.D., 1986). The disappearance of this Welsh label parallels the fate of the Anglo-Welsh explorer who named the area; James's achievements have been either downplayed or misunderstood in the past. Even some of the people who live close to his birthplace had a curious opinion of his work a few years ago. The official town guide to Abergavenny, the market town closest to James's home, made the following boast several years ago:

Captain Thomas James, the famous 17th-century navigator, was born in Llanvetherine in 1593. When he reached Australia, he named the place where he landed, New South Wales. (Waller, Town Guide of Abergavenny: 1986, 64)

Of course, this is a stunning travesty of the truth – in time and space. It was the Dutch, not navigators from the British Isles, who were the first Europeans to have sighted what turned out to be the landmass of Australia in 1605. They explored a large part of its shores in 1611 and continued exploration in the area for decades, culminating with Tasman's famous voyage in 1642. The laconic sense of humour James displayed in parts of his book might have led him to appreciate the symbolic association of such a remarkable mistake. Although his local market-town boosters had him exploring in the wrong direction – and almost a century and a half after his death – the incorrect attribution could be seen as realizing part of James's dream – that of reaching the Pacific and Asia by sailing northwest. So the hometown misunderstanding about the significance of James's journey may have unconsciously – and certainly inaccurately – tried to realize James's ambition of finding a Northwest Passage.

Despite the false information on which this example is based, it can be used to remind us that the knowledge that we have of many explorations, and the apparent facts they recorded, is not direct or mimetic. It is conditioned as much by the prior beliefs of explorers and sponsors and the cognitive filters by which the explorers see the world, and by the way the writer constructs, represents, or distorts what is seen, as well as by the subsequent interpretations placed by readers on the words recorded and the transmission of their opinions in secondary accounts. Recognition of the importance of these influences means that exploration narratives should no longer seen in empirical terms, only valuable in what they tell the reader about the results of expeditions, or providing the first descriptions of the new lands and peoples seen by European explorers. Instead, chapter 3 has shown that the descriptions the explorer-authors provided in their narratives are influenced by a large number of factors, other than the experiences of the expedition – factors which have been categorised as the filters of cognition, writing, and reading. These sets of factors condition the sense experiences of the explorer-author *before* the journey is undertaken, affect what is seen, influence how the narrative is constructed, and to some extent, how it is interpreted by readers. Exploration narratives are not simple copies of some assumed reality – of *what was there* – but are constructed representations of the sense experiences of the journey of discovery that have been intimately conditioned by the cultural and contextual influences of society. But as chapter 2 has argued, once one accepts the principle of the reader's plural, the creation of meaning to the reader depends upon the context of the reading, its consumption, and especially the reader's purpose. Now that the evidence provided by James's narrative has been evaluated in detail in the last four chapters, it is worth returning to the question of why James seems to have been regarded in such contradictory ways.

✢ 2. JAMES AND HIS CRITICS

The third section of chapter 1 described how James's work seems to have been praised, at least in general, until the early nineteenth century, but with the exception of his prose style he was criticized by most authorities after this period. But this does not explain *why* such contradictory opinions emerged. This issue can only be understood by providing an analysis of the way that reviewers represented James in their accounts. This means the focus is not upon how James described his experiences and the lands he saw, but the way *other readers represented* James's narratives. Chapter 3 has discussed how the creation of any exploration text is influenced by a large number of factors. The same motives and constraints apply to how the various written comments on James were derived. It has already been shown that intertextuality is a powerful influence on the way that representations are made. In other words, knowledge of James's work, character, and skills, has been communicated to the present by writers who often depend as much upon previously written reviews of this explorer as the original source material. These initial commentators may have had their own reasons for wishing to praise, ignore, or denigrate any explorer's achievements.

It has already been observed that until the new edition of Harris's (1705) survey of voyages was published in 1744–48, most commentators praised the value of James's work. But this edition did not simply publish extracts from James's voyage and wintering, as in the original version of 1705, it also added a series of comments upon James's achievements and opinions. Indeed, the editor argued that James's book was so good there was little point in using the narratives of James's predecessors to describe the conditions to be experienced in the vicinity of Hudson Bay, for James's work was the exemplar. Moreover, Harris lauded James at various junctures as the following extracts show:

> The Author is a knowing, careful and experienced seaman (Harris 1705, 407); never any Enterprize of this kind was better concerted or more Deliberately used to providing for its success (Harris 1705, 407); the wisest precautions were taken to prevent Factions and Mutinies (Harris 1705, 407); James is a very honest man, a very experienced Seaman. (Harris 1705, 434)

Despite this praise, the author argued that James was absolutely wrong in his conclusion that a Northwest Passage did not exist, but was gracious enough to admit that it was the progress made in the century since James sailed that had mainly altered the answer to the question of whether a route did exist. It was noted that later expeditions had leaned how to sail safely through ice-infested waters, and Hudson Bay Company personnel had lived comfortably throughout the winter at far higher latitudes than James suffered in. Moreover, the fur traders had extracted considerable wealth from the area, whereas it was noted that James had viewed the area negatively:

> It is plain he thought a more barren, more inhospitable and more worthless, Part of the World, was not to be found. (Harris 1705, 433)

The editor concluded his evaluation with the following strong opinion about how James had come to his conclusion and why new attempts to find a passage should be prosecuted.

> All the Difficulties and Discouragements which, from too strong a Sense of his Own Disappointment, Captain James has conjured up, sink to nothing, when duly considered and compared with the Circumstances that later Discoveries brought to light; so that there seems to be no reason his (James) conjectures should have any weight to determine us from prosecuting Attempts on this side, even though they still continue to prove, in several instances, as they have hitherto done, abortive. (Harris 1705, 433)

It is noteworthy that the criticisms are restricted to James's conclusions about the existence of the passage, not on the voyage itself, or James's seamanship, character, and leadership. But the conclusion that James was wrong, printed in such a well-known source, seems to have initiated the largely negative views of James's achievements in future years. The critical views were continued by the scathing comments made about James by Second Secretary of the Admiralty John Barrow (1818), in his extensive review of all previous Arctic expeditions. Barrow's book, which has been referred to previously, was designed to set the scene for a new thrust by Britain to fill in the maps of the unknown parts of the globe. It was published as Ross's expedition was sent out under admiralty aegis to explore the Arctic.

Barrow spent ten pages in his 379-page book describing James's expedition, a little larger section than that devoted to Foxe. Although most of the description faithfully records the voyage and the wintering, the passages contain a series of pointed criticisms. He began by comparing the two captains, suggesting that although Foxe may have been conceited in his knowledge of previous expeditions, James was a neophyte in exploration for he was

> *even more culpably conceited in his total ignorance of all that had been done before him … he appears to have been totally unacquainted with the narratives of preceding voyages. (Barrow 1818, 244)*

This was followed by accusations of James's mismanagement in exposing his crew to danger. The point was repeated at the end of his account, by suggesting that James contributed nothing to what former navigators had found, whilst his arguments against the existence of a passage "could well have been assigned prior to the voyage and saved his people the suffering" (Barrow 1818, 251). Throughout the review Barrow uses disparaging words to describe James's exploration, such as: James's *slowness*; the building of a *hovel* to winter in; and in the following remarkable passage uses the word *contrived*, which implies that James deliberately put himself in danger.

> *Captain James, indeed, contrived in the whole of his northern voyage, to be hampered with ice daily and almost hourly. (Barrow 1818, 250)*

In this vein, Barrow ended the review by quoting, with approval, part of the critical statement previously quoted from the 1748 revision of Harris's (1705) monumental survey of world travels:

There seems to be no reason his (James) conjectures should have any weight to deter us from prosecuting attempts on this side. (Quoted in Barrow 1818, 252)

What is important to emphasize here, is that Barrow was no ordinary author and critic. He was born in humble circumstances on a farm in the parish of Ulverston in northern Lancashire, but became the influential second secretary of the admiralty in 1804 and was subsequently knighted (Fleming 1998). He had come to the attention of several powerful individuals because of his organizational skills and the unusual ability to speak some Chinese, which he had learned during an earlier position as tutor to a young linguist. This accomplishment meant he held the post of translator in Lord Macartney's abortive attempt to visit the Chinese Emperor's court and establish an embassy in 1792–94. Later, Barrow was involved in expeditions to the Orange River and organized Cape Colony's first census. His bureaucratic ability and experience in several parts of the world – which led to well-received books on China and Africa – as well as political patronage, helped him obtain a key position in the admiralty, a post which he held for most of the period until 1845. Barrow's role was essentially that of chief administrator of the admiralty, carrying out the orders of his political superiors. But this position, and friendships with respected scientists such as Joseph Banks, especially after his election to the Royal Society in 1806, meant that Barrow was in a unique position to affect policy. It was Banks who had the influence and the opportunity to put into practise the idea of using some of the surplus British ships that had been laid up at the end of the Napoleonic Wars to explore and map the unknown world. He argued the work should be carried out for its own sake, to help future trade prospects and for national pride, which would be hurt if other countries carried out the task before Britain. In addition, there were a number of keen young captains whose hopes of fame had been dashed by the reduction in the size of the navy and their subsequent beaching on half pay. Barrow's advocacy of exploration was successful. A series of naval expeditions were fitted out in the next thirty years to explore various parts of the world, from the Antarctic to Africa and the Pacific. Barrow was the key administrator of these expeditions. The ventures attracted enormous public interest and did map many miles of previously unexplored areas. Yet the author of a recent book on Barrow argued that they were all worthless, in either failing to meet their goals, or in finding new commercial prospects (Fleming 1998).

Barrow's position, experience, and his administration of so many expeditions meant that his critical views of James were bound to carry a great deal of weight. Barrow was the spider at the centre of the expanding web of new naval explorations, and his book on the Arctic (Barrow 1818) became a primary source material for accounts of the explorations prior to the nineteenth century. In addition, Barrow was also influential in the organization of the Royal Geographical Society. The lecture series and journals of the society became increasingly full of accounts of exploration as the century wore on. So it is not surprising that many subsequent reviewers accepted Barrow's critical opinions of James, which seemed to be justified by the subsequent arctic voyages, from Ross and Parry onwards, that discovered more and more passages through the Canadian arctic islands as the geography of the area was revealed. However, it is worth repeating that James did hedge his opinion by suggesting that even if a passage were found, it would be useless in commercial terms. James's caution in presenting this opinion was ignored by Barrow. The results of the new explorations, combined with Barrow's authority, provided a powerful twin force in influencing opinion against a long dead explorer who seemed to have only provided original knowledge about a remote, dead-end bay in the Canadian northwest. For many subsequent readers, therefore, it is hardly surprising that Barrow's opinion became the authoritative view, with the result that James's work was regarded negatively.

But the uncritical acceptance of Barrow's opinion missed a telling point. Barrow was not writing his criticism of James as an unbiased observer of the past. It was a time of peace, and one of increasing popular and scientific interest in the unexplored parts of the world as demonstrated by the creation of Geographical Societies in many western countries (Livingstone 1992). Barrow's career and personal interests could be advanced by new Arctic expeditions in search of the much sought-after passage. It was, after all, one of the big geographical puzzles still to be resolved. Hence Barrow had a powerful motive in dismissing explorers, such as James, who had concluded that a viable Northwest Passage through the Arctic, or at least through the area he explored, did not exist. What does seem clear after the discussion in chapter 2 of the concept of the reader's plural and the need to relate *interpretation to context*, is that that a critic such as Barrow seems to have written about James in the light of his own interests in stimulating Arctic expeditions. His critique of James was *constructed* to fulfill this purpose. This was not achieved by arguing that James's conclusions were wrong, but by denigrating James's other skills, repeating the critical material from the influential 1748 edition of Harris's Travels, and ignoring the positive parts. Barrow went much further in his censure. He belittled James's seamanship, ability, and leadership, which he assumed to be bad, for how else could one explain how the expedition seemed to lurch from one crisis to another? Yet it can be concluded that the literary device used by James to create excitement for the reader, and to draw attention to the problems of sailing and living in the area, is literalized in Barrow's critique and used as evidence of poor technical skills. The virulence of Barrow's attack on James does seem unfair, now that the work of James has been reviewed in more detail in previous chapters. The injustice can be illustrated by rebutting Barrow's opinions in five critical examples: James carefully built three winter huts not one *hovel*; he could hardly have *contrived* to sail in icy seas: they were an environmental fact; James was clearly *aware* of previous explorations, because he had so many books and instruments on board; and could hardly have been *slow* since he and Foxe met on the southern coast of Hudson Bay after leaving Britain within a few days of one another; and finally, has been shown to have taken extraordinary *care* over his men, as previously acknowledged in the 1748 review of James's work (Harris 1748). These rebuttals of Barrow's criticisms demonstrate that Barrow's comments on James had moved from disagreement with his conclusions about the presence of a Northwest Passage, to what does appear to have been an unjustified, fully-fledged attack on all aspects of James's work, except the readability of his prose. Barrow's scorn for James became the accepted opinion. The accusations by such an influential authority figure have influenced most of the subsequent commentaries about James. They have reverberated over two centuries, disguising James's actual achievements. Since the criticisms are difficult to sustain if James's original book is read, the received opinions must indicate the influence of intertextuality, in which secondary sources, such as Barrow, provide the evidence for the critical opinions. Of course, this attempt to rehabilitate James does not deny his failure to find a geographical passage to the Orient, or the limits of his original geographical discoveries. What it does question is the unfair condemnation of many other qualities displayed by James, and the need to recognize his creation of what can be described as *passages to new interpretations*, most significantly in locational representation, early scientific description, and in literary practises – both as a pathway to the fictive form of the novel and to the development of early Anglo-Welsh and Canadian literature.

James's inability to successfully complete the task he was set, to find the Northwest Passage via the Hudson Bay route, will always mean that he can never be considered as a member of the first-ranking group of explorers. How could he be? He had the misfortune to be sent to explore for something that did not exist in the area he explored. The only outlet to the west in the area he sailed in proved to be the tiny Fury and Hecla Strait to the northwest of Foxe's Basin, between the Melville Peninsula of the mainland and Baffin Island, a route found by Parry in 1821–23 and one difficult to traverse by sailing ship. James's map of the area (fig. 5.1) seems to have consciously closed off the northwest corner of the Hudson Bay. This may be considered to be a rather dogmatic conclusion on James's part, since he did not sail into Thomas Roe's Welcome Sound, part of the area initially thought to be a large bay, labelled Button's Bay. The presence of such a bay was gradually disproved and James's chart does not show it. However, the persistence of older ideas can be seen in Sansome's map of New France and the Hudson Bay area in 1665, which still showed a large embayment in the west of the main bay, although further south than its original location, one that led into the Nelson River and was still labelled with Button's name in 1665 (Armstrong 1982). It is possible that James's experience of the icy conditions found when he sailed through the east of this area led to this conclusion. Also, it is possible that he obtained information from Foxe, during their famous meeting off the southern coast of Hudson Bay, which might have also convinced him that there was no route through the lands discovered on the western coast of the bay. Moreover, one must remember the tentative evidence of historical climatologists (Harington 1983), that a colder phase of climate had set in after the first few decades of the early seventeenth century, which would not have helped explorers at this time.

Foxe, as has been shown previously, seemed to have held a different opinion about the existence of the Northwest Passage, judging from the opinions expressed in his book. But we should be cautious here. Roe's letter to the Bristol Society of Merchant Venturers of 28 November 1631 (quoted in Christy 1894, 106) alerted them to the news that James had met Foxe and was trying to continue his journey. It has already been noted that Roe, who had been very critical of Foxe's decision to return to Britain at the end of the summer, reporting that the mariner believed the Northwest Passage did not exist in the area that they had searched.

However, Christy (1894, 106) argued that this opinion was probably derived from Foxe's sailing master and mate. Foxe makes it clear in his journal that he thought there *was* a passage; of course, he could have changed his mind from the time of the letter written by Roe, to the publication of his book, four years later. By contrast, James's evidence clearly contradicted the popular image of a commercial route to the Orient via the Northwest Passage. It has been shown that Campbell (1748, 434) in the revision of Harris's compendium of world travel, praised James's expedition in most aspects, even though he concluded that James's final opinion was incorrect. Indeed, Campbell suggested that James's book did a lot of mischief in helping to discourage new expeditions to the northwest until the successful 1667 voyage of the *Nonsuch* stimulated the creation of the Hudson Bay Company. Again we must be cautious about accepting such an opinion; it must be remembered that Britain was involved in a Civil War and an unsettled political situation for much of the time between the voyages of the *Henrietta Maria* and the *Nonsuch* was not conducive to new explorations.

Even if James did not discover major new lands, he did make important additions to the seventeenth-century knowledge of Hudson Bay and made reasonably accurate identifications of the location of many places given the instruments at his disposal, and published the first informative map of the area, which must have been a boon for subsequent explorers. It has often been argued, by reviewers from Barrow (1818) onwards, that Foxe was the better seaman and navigator. For example, the short entry on James in the latest Canadian Encyclopaedia made the same old accusations: "James's voyage was less productive than Foxe's, who was the superior navigator" (Marsh 1985, 912). The fact that James is still regarded with suspicion by most contemporary commentators has been shown to be a product of selective reading of James's journal by individuals such as Barrow who had an interest in denigrating James's conclusions, and whose opinions were passed on in subsequent reviews – a classic example of intertextual negative influence. But it must be noted that since James's narrative can be read on so many planes, it was still possible for Marsh (1985) to provide some praise, noting that James produced an effective harrowing tale and was the *first* to deliberately winter in the area – which does ignore three previous major expeditions to Hudson Bay, unless the reference is simply to James Bay.

The review of the available evidence from the journals of both explorers makes it clear that it is difficult to sustain the received negative opinions about James. Foxe may have penetrated further to the northwest, but James discovered more of the Hudson Bay coast. In any case, it has been shown that James seems to have taken far more care in the calculation of his positions using the latest and carefully calibrated instruments, and, more to the point, explicitly provided *evidence* for many of these calculations. The difference between them may be the fact that Foxe was a practical seaman, whereas James, a more educated and scientifically orientated individual, placed more dependence upon his instruments, the sign of a more rational, scientific approach. Yet we must be careful. James was not the maritime neophyte that has often been portrayed; he must have spent a lot of time at sea before his voyage to Hudson Bay, as was previously noted. In addition it must be remembered that he deliberately selected a crew whose members did not have previous experience of the area, so he was the only one with the skills to take the vessel to the area he explored and back! Moreover, the carping comments of James's many critics ignore the fact he was one of the few early explorers not to lose many of his crew during such a long voyage — especially one into arctic regions that involved the long and arduous task of surviving the frigid winter. Perhaps one can agree with James's critics that there would still have been considerable knowledge of Hudson Bay and its environs, even if he had not voyaged to the area. Yet this does downplay the fact that he was the first to explore hundreds of miles of coastline around Hudson Bay, even though he was quite wrong in thinking that there were two parts to the southern extension of Hudson Bay. Yet whatever opinion is held about James's seamanship, in the last resort it seems impossible to deny that he created a very readable description of the region. It was one that not only brought pleasure, through the thrill of horror, to his readers, but also provided useful data about conditions in the Hudson Bay region, which must have added to the knowledge of subsequent explorers. Hence, it can be concluded that James's ability to survive his ocean travels, as well as to endure the harsh conditions of winter, in the face of so many potential disasters, and with only the technology of the early seventeenth century, was exceptional. James surely deserves the accolade of *master mariner*. In addition, it must not be forgotten that James displayed considerable leadership skills during his expedition; skills that related as much to the encouragement of his men, as to making crucial decisions that kept them alive. Of course, this conclusion comes from only James's voice in the narrative. It is possible that James created his own character in the narrative, to make himself look heroic. But such an interpretation does seem dubious; James must have realized that the descriptions of so many brushes with disaster would not show him in the best light. Unfortunately, no other confirmation about James's ability have been found in other written contemporary sources, although Beedome's second poem about James (1641; quoted in Christy 1894) does suggest the intrepid explorer survived the various environmental challenges because of his courage and leadership.

Far less attention has been paid to what can be summarized as James's scientific work by his critics. The phrase must be used with caution since the new methods of science were only gradually making their appearance and were still intimately linked with older ideas of alchemy and theology (Livingston 1992). James's narrative shows that he deserves credit for being the first explorer to begin the collection of scientific knowledge about the area. Apart from providing hard evidence for the calculation of his locations, he provided useful descriptions of the effect of cold, the climate in the area, ice conditions and the experiences of winter, and the onset of the changing seasons. Even as eminent a scientist as Robert Boyle acknowledged the utility of James's work. Also, it is also possible that knowledge of the way he survived on Charlton Island was the reason why the Hudson's Bay Company established a collection and trading post on the island in the 1680s. This survived for several centuries before being abandoned (Kenyon 1975), with the result that there is no permanent habitation on the island today. In general, James's narrative does provide evidence of measurement and observational skills that merit the additional accolade of *scientific observer*, in addition to the others that have been given. Hence James's work provides another important passage to the development of a different kind of writing – to the provision of informed commentary on the area explored, and to a more rigorous process of perception and organization – that helped the gradual evolution of scientific methods among explorers.

✠ 4. LITERARY SIGNIFICANCE

Master mariner and scientific observer are not the only descriptive attributes that can be allocated to James. His literary skill must also be praised. Although several critics of James's work noted that the narrative was well written and easy to read, few have dealt with the construction and emotional appeal of the work. To be fair, Christy did quote Ivor James's (1890) opinion that Captain Thomas James's narrative was an exciting account – "once taken up, the book is not to be laid aside.…

The narrative is one long thrilling description" (Christy 1894, 171). But the general criticism of James's work stems from the content that he chose to emphasize. His descriptions of the problems experienced, and potential disasters surmounted, were not viewed kindly by those who reviewed exploration narratives in search of the *results* of journeys of discovery. Barrow (1818), in particular, may have seen James's style and emphasis as inappropriate for an explorer; by the early nineteenth century, explorers were expected to display the appropriate stoic behaviour and use the favoured dispassionate scientific style. After all, most explorers — at least in James's time — did not bother to describe many of the physical conditions they faced in any detail. In any case, in the *considered* writing that is represented by the final narrative, as opposed to the daily journals, the explorer-author usually took care either to avoid describing those occasions when they made navigation or other mistakes, or tried to justify these errors. Yet we must be careful of over-generalizing this point. Barrow, in his role as second secretary of the admiralty, was not unaware of the popular interest in tales of endurance and potential disaster. He was an author himself and made sure that all the expeditions associated with the admiralty were published (Fleming 1998). Davis's (1995) introductory comments on Franklin's 1819–22 overland expedition to the Canadian Arctic, has described Barrow's influence on the expedition and shows that he was well aware of the public interest in the journey — especially with its many brushes with disaster. Indeed, Barrow encouraged the early publication of Franklin's narratives, which was followed by three more printings within eighteen months of first publication, with two others by 1830 — in addition to several foreign editions. Perhaps Barrow had changed his mind about the value of such descriptions since his 1818 book! But as we have seen, Barrow seems to have *read* James in the light of his own interests in stimulating Arctic expeditions. His resultant critique of James seems to have been *constructed* to fulfill the purpose of downplaying the utility of James's conclusions.

Barrow's principal criticism of James's work, that it was full of *lamentations* and descriptions of crises, missed the main point of the narrative in literary terms. It was precisely these exciting passages of potential disaster, and fortuitous survival through God's intervention, that gave James's work such a wide appeal, whose purpose was not simply the results of the exploration. Crone and Skelton (1946) noted that by the eighteenth century, narratives of travel and works of theology were the two most popular types of books; James had probably appealed to both sets of readers a century earlier. Chapter 1 has shown that James does receive a brief positive mention in most accounts of the development of literature in Canada, but his achievements always seem to be downplayed. It is less easy to understand why James has been virtually ignored by influential Canadian authors such as Atwood (1995) in her description of survival as a theme in Canadian literature. After all, it was James who first brought detailed written descriptions of the frigid experiences of a winter in Hudson Bay to the general public in Britain through his writing. Button and others may have been on the lands of Hudson Bay before him and Foxe probably went further north. Yet it was James who was the first to create the written images by which his readers could imagine they had experienced the cold and endless ice at first-hand. In addition, he wrote the first two poems that were produced in the Canadian subarctic, poems that have their own poignant value, providing a memorial to their dead companions and to deliverance from the severity of the storms. Indeed, they may be two of the first poems in Canada to display an environmental theme based on Canadian experiences. James's descriptions could leave few readers in any doubt of the severity of the physical conditions and the limited prospects for settlement in the areas he visited. As one of the first books that described the environs of Hudson Bay for the popular reader in English, it left an enduring impression of an inhospitable and often brutal land, one that seemed to be beyond the margin for settlement by Europeans. James attributed his successful survival to God. This is the deep faith that shines through his narrative. But anybody who reads James's journal cannot help but conclude that the mere act of his survival, in the face of so many hazards, was a major triumph over great adversity. In fulfilling this task, he provided the raw material that helped stimulate Coleridge to write one of the immortal poems of the English language: *The Rime of the Ancient Mariner*. It has been shown that many of its passages bear witness to the original images that James created. Yet one must accept that beyond the imagery that attracted Coleridge lay a tale of endurance – the general tone of James's narrative was that of surviving a journey that turned out to be full of adventure.

James's work can be seen as an important contribution to the development of literature in Canada through its early use of environmentalist themes, but his narrative may be of more significance in the development of the genre called Anglo-Welsh. The global spread of the English language has led to the identification of many different hyphenated Anglo traditions in literature, using national or geographic areas as the suffix.

Of course, the process by which a distinctive genre emerges in a literary language is not a product of the past few centuries. Peter Ellis's (1990, 68–71) incisive review of the Celts in history described how the Roman conquest of Cis-Alpine Gaul in the second century B.C. – the area we would call the Po Valley and its environs today – led to the imposition of Latin upon a Celtic-speaking population. Several of the famous Latin writers of the next generation, such as Catullus Cinna and Pomponius – authors possessing a new style and fresh insights – were of Celtic stock from this area. The racial or cultural mixture helped create a new literary style. Ellis argued that their distinctive writings might have been based on their ethnic heritage and its language. But the expanded opportunities available in the growing and literate Roman Empire gave these writers a larger audience, resulting, of course, in a bigger reputation. This would not have been possible had they remained in the small and localized tribal societies of their forefathers, in which the oral tradition, rather than a permanent literary form, was dominant. By writing in Latin, a language that became the standard in Europe, their achievements survived even the fall of the Roman Empire. Two thousand years later, the same sort of process can be seen in the development of Anglo-Irish and Anglo-Indian writing, although active nationalistic forces – whether culture, or politics of both – added an additional developmental force to the creation of such distinctive schools of writing and provided an appreciative audience. Similarly, the concept of Anglo-American, or simply American writing, implies a distinctive school of work. But as Mathias (1986) emphasized, the type of literature that is now described as Anglo-Welsh predated the form by many centuries. It has already been shown that the authoritative sources on the development of this genre have only paid cursory attention to the work of James in this milieu; indeed the attention in Wales is even less than that received by James in the context of Canadian studies.

Some may consider Anglo-Welsh literature as a regional school of writing within the context of Britain, since the language of use is English. Most would argue that it is more – given its *national* flavour. In a historical context, most of the writers considered as Anglo-Welsh have been influenced either by the language, culture, and traditions of Wales, or by the new economies and the radical non-conformity of the eighteenth and nineteenth centuries that was so much a part of the English-speaking parts of Wales. The decline of the Welsh language and in chapel attendance since World War II has meant that the first of these factors may be of marginal importance for many new contemporary authors from Wales who write in English, although since the language decline has been arrested in recent years, its influence may survive and increase. But even the diminution in the numbers of people who daily use the native language does not necessarily mean that the unique expression of a different people is lost. It may appear in distinctive types of insights or in singular organizational forms – especially in poetry that is based on, or mimics traditions in another language, as was noted above in the case of the Celts in Italy. Yet those who have reviewed Anglo-Welsh writing have been unable to find a single style, content, or set of associations that are common to all people who have been classed as Anglo-Welsh writers (Garlick 1970; Mathias 1986), which does cast doubt upon the usefulness of the genre in an interpretive sense.

James's childhood in Wales and family heritage clearly qualifies him as an Anglo-Welsh writer in the terms of Mathias's review (1986, 16). Yet it is difficult to find any evidence that James's work displayed much in the way of a cultural or technical link to the organizational forms of Welsh language, or to any Welsh theme. James's narrative dealt with the events on a voyage to a new and forbidding terrain – one far from the Welsh experience. But it can be suggested that within the broad field of Anglo-Welsh writing there is an important distinctive niche to which James belongs – to the Welsh-born writers who described other lands. Mathias (1986) has described a series of categories in which Anglo-Welsh writing developed in the sixteenth and seventeenth centuries – such as poetry, religion, medicine, science, and technical subjects, such as map-making, although it was the historians and antiquarians that represented the largest group, producing what can be called topographic accounts of parts of Wales. One of the curious omissions in Mathias's survey is that small, yet significant group of Welsh-born writers who have written in English about foreign lands, using their personal experiences; for example: Button (Foxe 1635; Christy 1894); the promotional works of William Vaughan (1626); through the scientific and ethnographical comments of the naval surgeon, Dafydd Samwell, who sailed to the Pacific with Cook (Bowen 1974); to the nineteenth-century sensationalist accounts of Stanley in the African savannas and jungles; and finally, to the entertaining and incisive portraits of cities in other lands crafted by Jan Morris in the contemporary period. Vaughan and Samwell are mentioned by Mathias – but in rather different contexts. James, however, is not referenced. Yet he is probably the *first* Anglo-Welsh writer to produce a major piece of literature describing a voyage to a foreign land. Button never published his journal but from the fragments that were incorporated in Foxe's journal (1635; Christy 1894) it is apparent it was little more than a daily record of events. The omission is understandable. Welsh literature, whether in Welsh or in English, focused on the land of Wales, its problems, or the people – but it seems clear that some Anglo-Welsh writers have described the larger world beyond such parochial or national concerns. James was one of the first to do so. Surely he deserves credit for undertaking a task beyond what can sometimes be *little Wales* – adding to the influential effect that Anglo-Welsh writers and artists have had on the wider western culture in general, even though they come from such a small area.

At first sight, it is difficult to claim that James's writings displayed much in the way of a separate identity from his English counterparts, one that could help the case for regarding him as a pioneer Anglo-Welsh writer. Indeed, the term would not be one that he would have been familiar with; James certainly did not use the description. This means that if we situate his work within the terms and culture of his times, as demanded by the new school of historicism (Hamilton 1996), one might conclude it would be a distortion of James's *reality* to use the term *Anglo-Welsh*. Even though the label may not be one that was appropriate in the seventeenth century, there seems little doubt that James still made some literary decisions that can be linked to his Welsh origins, so the term applies to more than the simple fact of his Welsh birth. James named the area he explored *New South Wales*, and used other common borderland terms for particular topographic features he discovered. Surely this implies that he had at least some residual feeling for the land of his fathers? Yet James's writings never betray a feeling that his heritage produced any new or different identity, unlike another important contemporary of his who was prominent in the promotion and settlement of Newfoundland. Sir William Vaughan (1626) tried to create a Cambriola on that island – which would have been the first overseas colony for the Welsh had it been successful. In any case Vaughan frequently used the term Cambro-Britains for his fellow countrymen, a hyphenation that cleverly identifies the Welsh part of the larger political entity of Britain that is emerging, by adopting words that described the ancient peoples of the land.

These glimpses of some basic Welsh identity need to be balanced by some other facts that counteract the argument. James never used the word *Wales* to describe the land in which he was born, or *Welsh* to describe its people. In the historical context of the time it must be remembered that it was not a word that was much in contemporary use, as John Davies's authoritative history of Wales shows (1993). Those seeking latent nationalistic feelings or a subdued Welsh identity in James's work, will be disappointed that the summary map of the voyage (fig. 5.1) even had the word *England* scrawled across the land of his birth and the rest of southern Britain, indicating the political fact of the new English-dominated state. In another passage it has already been noted that he refers to the customs of his fellow countrymen as "Ancient Britaines" (J 65). Both points illustrate the way that James and so many of the gentry and the emerging professional or commercial middle classes from Wales had been acculturated in the mores of a new anglicized identity following the accession of Henry VII in 1485, a new king of England with Welsh ancestry. The new Tudor dynasty reduced the social and economic isolation of many people in Wales: many gentry were able to build upon their links to the new king, but the growth in prosperity of the kingdom led many to migrate to London and improve their economic prospects (Jones, Emrys, 1986). The Act of Union in 1536 consolidated and formalized the incorporation of Wales into the English state. One important cultural consequence was that English had to be used in courts in Wales and became essential in professional circles. This was more than a legal change: Mathias (1986, 14) noted that the use of English by the gentry became a mark of their rank and title. These social and political changes certainly led many Welsh-born people – at least those with land, or with a trade or profession – to increase their economic wealth. But it helped accelerate the process of shattering the cultural cohesion between landowners and their tenants in Wales. James's family was undoubtedly affected by these changes. It is not known whether James was Welsh-speaking. Many landholders in Monmouthshire had adopted English as their language for centuries. The fact that James's family tree (fig. 4.3) shows Welsh forms of family description, with the explorer's father described as James ap John (son of John, in English), means that the subsequent family name, James, was really the Christian name of his father. Hence this does suggest a Welsh-speaking connection within the memory of his generation.

So far, the evidence means that one cannot be conclusive about the impact of James's Welsh background and upbringing on his literary style. There do not seem to be any direct relationships between James's work and Welsh cultural traditions or forms of writing. But there is one literary form that may provide an exception. In a literary context, James's strengths lay in his ability to tell a tale and the skill to maintain the tension of a story. His narrative is not about fictional events, but his real tribulations. In this context, it is not hard to make the association with the oral style of storytellers – which are so well represented in Welsh and Celtic cultures – where the flow of words and the excitement of the action kept the attention of the audience. James's prose managed to achieve this task. He transmuted what could have been the sterile recitation of the events of the daily log into a narrative that sustained the interest of his readers. This was a harder task than appeared at first sight. James saw no exotic peoples, and few unusual plants or animals. Nor was he able to hold out the promise of rich agricultural lands. James never hints at valuable minerals to be mined, or treasures to be found – the usual components of dreams of wealth and adventure. Much of the world that he described was dominated by ice – an ice that took many forms. Its ubiquitous presence added to the dangers of a barren, frequently stormy sea and the hazardous, rocky or shoal-infested coasts. These are hardly the rich and varied features from which to weave a spellbinding tale. Unlike Raleigh's expedition to the Orinocco, he did not encounter a land teeming with many unusual and startling forms of vegetation, animal life, and human cultures. James's journey to James Bay revealed a much more sterile land, even at best, it was a stunted environment, for he did not experience the bird and animal migrations that sometimes gave it abundance. These were not landscapes of wonder in which to dream of a softer life, surrounded by the rich fruits of the mythic Eden – the lands that many explorers and armchair travellers fantasized. James lived in landscapes of horror and danger, at least to a man of his time. Concepts such as sublimity were developed much later; perhaps they could only be generally adopted when the technology of transport allowed people to visit and survive in the arctic environment, to look upon the icy scenes, and know that they had the competence and ability to survive, and leave the area.

It is to James's credit that he managed to achieve so much in such a short book, given his limited resources and a very tight timeline, producing the book and the appendices within six months. It has been noted that James's narrative was written in a very sparse literary style – one that contrasts with the circumlocution so typical of much of the literature of his day. In a literary context, it is this laconic, yet action-packed narrative that represents James's achievement in 1633. Adams (1983) has convincingly argued that such books point the way to the fictional inventions of the typical novel. As such, James's world and the events he describes, can be *read* as a type of escapist literature – even though he was describing some real events. It was a style that was far ahead of his time, and without parallels for centuries among those who are normally considered pioneers of the Anglo-Welsh tradition in literature. Yet these literary achievements must not obscure the fact that he still managed to provide an informative account of his explorations, with important, if primitive, scientific comments, plus precise locations and informative descriptions of the places he visited. It is the literary importance of his narrative, not only his discoveries, that make him significant.

✛ 5. CONCLUSIONS

This discussion has provided a new assessment of the work of Thomas James situated within the problems of representation and textual construction in exploration writing. The principal theme of the contextual analysis has been to demonstrate, rather than to assert, that exploration narratives and travel writing in general cannot be viewed as realist accounts. Exploration narratives, like any book, are constructed and influenced by innumerable factors, other than the experiences of the new lands explored; also, the meanings derived from these texts are a product of the intentions of the author as well as the reader. The discussion on these issues has been organized around a framework by which the normally fragmented discourse of geographical discovery and exploration writing can be interrelated and ordered. Although all narratives represent unique insights in the last resort, this template, although provisional, may be of help in assessing the work of other explorers. The framework might ensure that parallels or differences between different books of exploration can be more easily understood, and missing features swiftly identified.

It has been shown that James was not the incompetent neophyte that his critics have argued, a construction that comes from focusing on one type of reading of his book. James managed to survive in a dangerous and numbing environment. His skills in navigation and leadership saved the lives of most of his companions. Barrow's critical comments on James's 'lamentations,' as illustrating the incompetence of a poor seaman, missed the point of James's creative purpose in his book. The narrative's constant reference to the tribulations of the voyage was *not* designed to appeal only to those whose interests lay in issues that were strictly *scientific* or navigational; James's prose was aimed at the *emotions* of his readers. Yet we must not exaggerate James's appeal to sentiment and imagination – it was not *only* about escapism and novel experiences.

James's search for the Northwest Passage revealed, and more to the point *publicized*, important scientific evidence that was used by subsequent explorers. It added to the slowly constructed corpus of geographical knowledge about where places were, and the conditions that were found at various locations. Moreover, James's ability to provide accurate locations, despite the limitations of the instruments he had to use, must be praised, as should the evidence he provided for the observations and the methods he applied. James was an important contributor to that intellectual progress that helped improve the technical basis of seventeenth-century European explorations, through cumulative improvements in the measurement of locations. The Renaissance voyages of discovery were stimulated by the revival of classical knowledge. But much of the older geographical information was shown to be false by the experimental work of the new explorations and the valorization of empirical individual experiences – as James showed in an appendix, although he persuaded someone with a more scholarly reputation to undertake the task. Unfortunately, the realist assumptions of so many readers created the belief that the written narratives of explorers were largely mimetic descriptions of what was seen on the expeditions of discovery.

James certainly failed in his primary task of discovering the Northwest passage. But his conclusion that a passage to the Orient did not exist – or at least was not a commercial one – was a significant achievement, since it contradicted the general opinion of his time. James's evidence must have convinced his sponsors, the Society of Merchant Venturers, of the futility of more expeditions pursuing this quest, undoubtedly saving money for future Bristol merchants and perhaps the lives of its seamen. However, he did fail to recognize the possibilities of a trade in furs from the area, which led to the subsequent fortunes for the partners of London's Hudson's Bay Company – a crucial limitation of his work. But if James's search for a *geographical passage* proved a disappointment, his ability to create *passages in scientific and literary terms* do need to be stressed – especially to the development of the novel, to adventure writing, to emerging scientific approaches, as well as by providing imagery that was used by one of England's foremost poets. This means we should reassess James's rather dismissive comment underneath the portrait (fig. 1.1) that adorned the map of his voyage. "Some have a time" may have been accurate in identifying his *temporary* renown as an explorer. Fame *is* usually short-lived; in later years the achievements fade, and others will travel further and achieve more worldly success. Yet as an author, who was a pioneer in so many ways, James's *time* marked significant achievements that set him above most of the contemporaries. James was a true Renaissance product – a man of many talents. Practical, as well as imaginative, he contributed to the development of an emerging science, as well as to literature. Captain Thomas James should be seen as a *master mariner*, not the incompetent sailor he has often been portrayed. He was also a true *leader*, exhibiting personal bravery and displaying skills in leadership. This evaluation has shown that he also deserves the designation of *master author* in addition to the other accolades. James created, or helped create, passages to the development of new genres, in literature and science, for his work was subsequently recognized by two of the most notable individuals in the history of these fields: Samuel Coleridge and Robert Boyle. So Captain Thomas James, who came from the little parish of Llanvetherine in Monmouthshire, achieved renown in the wider world beyond Wales. Certainly his exploration was only made possible by the commercial ambitions of the merchants of Bristol and the emerging British State, and was not particularly successful. Yet in this latter context it was observed by the editor of the revised volumes of Harris's Travels that an explorer has to have *luck* to succeed, and may chose another way to achieve celebrity:

> *If he cannot be transmitted to Posterity as a fortune man, he may, at least, transmit the memory of his prudence, by which an Error long received was detected. (Harris 1748, 432)*

This was the approach James followed. He used the raw material of his experiences in Hudson Bay to create something new – in prose. James's fame should really result from his *writing* about exploration – upon what Beedome called his "trophie" in the poem that began this chapter – not on his unfulfilled geographical quest. Hence, it was Captain Thomas James's *narrative, not his voyage and wintering*, that should be seen as his true memorial – one that led to so many other passages of enquiry and representation.

A) MANUSCRIPT AND ARCHIVAL

BSMV. Manuscript records: The Bristol Society of Merchant Venturers' Book of Trade: 1631–32; Merchants' Hall, The Promenade, Clifton, Bristol.
BSMVT. Manuscript records: The Bristol Society of Merchant Venturers' Treasurer's Book: 1631–32; Merchants' Hall, The Promenade, Clifton, Bristol.
DSP. Domestic Calendar of State Papers. James 1, 1628–9 (1864; reprint Liechtenstein: Kraus Reprints, 1967). Charles I: 1631 to 1635. (1864; reprint Liechtenstein: Kraus Reprints, 1967). This contains a summary of the letters; the originals are held in the Public Record Office, Kew, London.

All page references to Thomas James (1633) relate to the original edition and are summarized as "J" followed by the page number, for example: (J 10). Appendices are listed as "J A," followed by page number, for example: (J A 2).

All page references to Luke Foxe (1635) are shown as "F," followed by the page number, based on Christy's 1894 edition (reprinted 1963), vol. 2: 261–445.

B) BOOKS AND ARTICLES

A.C.M.L. *John Mason's Map of Newfoundland, 1626*. Ottawa: Reproductions of Historic Maps of Canada, The Association of Canadian Map Librarians, 1982.
Adams, Percy G. *Travel Literature and the Evolution of the Novel*. Lexington: University Press of Kentucky, 1983.
Allen, J. L. *Passage Through the Garden: Lewis and Clark and Images of the American West*. Urbana: University of Illinois, 1975a.
Allen, J. L. "Lands of Myth, Waters of Wonder: The Place of the Imagination in the History of Geographical Imagination." In *Geographies of the Mind: Essays in Historical Geography*, edited by D. Lowenthal and M. J. Bowden, 41–61. Oxford: Oxford University Press, 1975b.
Allen, R., ed. *Regions of the Mind*. Regina: Canadian Great Plains Centre, 1973.
Ambrose, Stephen. *Undaunted Courage*. New York: Simon and Schuster. 1996.
Arensburg, C. M., and S. T. Kimbal. *Culture and Community*. New York: Harcourt and Brace, 1965.
Armstrong, J. *From Sea to Sea: Early Maps of Canada*. Plate 11. Scarborough, Ontario: Fleet Books, 1982.
Asher, C. M. *Hudson*. London: Hakluyt Society First Series No. 27, 1890.
Atheneum. "Review of the Source of the Ancient Mariner." *Atheneum* 3255 (March 1890): 335–36.
Atwood, Margaret. *Survival: A Thematic Guide to Canadian Literature*. Toronto: Anansi Press, 1972.
——. *Strange Things: The Malevolent North in Canadian Literature*. Oxford: Clarendon Press, 1995.
Baker, J. N. L. *History of geographical discovery and exploration*. London: Harrap, 1931.

Barnes, T. J., and J. S. Duncan. "Introduction: Writing Worlds". In *Writing Worlds: Discourse, Text, and Metaphors in the Representation of Landscape*. London: Routledge, 1992, 1–17.

Barr, W., and G. Williams. *Voyages to Hudson Bay in Search of a Northwest Passage: 1741–1747*. Vol. 1. London: The Hakluyt Society, Christopher Middleton, 1994.

——. *Voyages to Hudson Bay in Search of a Northwest Passage: 1741–1747*. Vol. 2. London: The Hakluyt Society, William Moor and Francis Smith, 1995.

Barrell. J. *The Idea of Literature and the Sense of Place: 1730–1840*. Cambridge: Cambridge University Press, 1972.

Barrow, John. *A Chronological History of Voyages Into The Arctic Regions*. London: John Murray, 1818. Reprinted C. Lloyd, ed. New York: Barnes and Noble, 1971.

Barthes, R. *The Pleasure of the Text*. Trans. R. Miller, New York: Hill and Wang, 1975.

Bawlf, R. S. *The secret voyage of Sir Francis Drake: 1577-80*. Vancouver: Douglas and McIntyre, 2003.

Beedome, Thomas. *Poems, Divine and Humane*. London: 1641. (Quoted in Christy, op. cit., 1894: clxxxvii.)

Belsey, Catherine. *Critical Practice*. London: Methuen, 1980. Reprinted 1999.

Belyea, B. "Captain Franklin in Search of the Picturesque." *Essays in Canadian Writing* 40 (1990): 1–24.

——. *Columbia Journals of David Thompson*. Montreal: McGill-Queen's Press, 1994.

Bennett, Carol. *In Search of the Red Dragon: The Welsh in Canada*. Renfrew, Ontario: Juniper Books, 1985.

Berry, J.W.B., and P. R. Dasen. *Cognition and Culture*. London: Methuen, 1974.

Berry, J.W.B., and S. Irvine. *Human Abilities in a Cultural Context*. Cambridge: Cambridge University Press, 1988.

Berton. P. *The Arctic Grail: The Quest for the Northwest Passage and North Pole, 1818–1909*. Toronto: McClelland and Stewart, 1988.

Blanco, W., and J. Roberts, eds. *Herodotus: The Histories*. New York: Norton, 1992.

Blunt, A. *Travel, Gender and Imperialism*. New York: Guildford 1994.

Blunt, A., and G. Rose, eds. *Writing Women and Space*. New York: Guildford Press, 1994.

Bodilly, Ralph. *The Voyage of Captain Thomas James*. Toronto: Dent, 1928.

Bonnycastle, S. *In Search of Authority: An Introductory Guide to Literary Theory*. Peterborough, ON: Broadview Press, 1991.

Bowen, E. G. *David Samwell (Dafydd Ddu Feddyg): 1751–98*. Cardiff: University of Wales Press, 1974.

Bowen, M. *Empiricism and Geographical Thought*. Cambridge: Cambridge Geographical Series, 1981.

Boyle, Robert. "New Experiments and Observations Touching Cold." In *The Works of the Honorable Robert Boyle,* edited by W. Birch. London: 1774. 3rd ed. edited by D. McKie, Vol. 2, 462–718. Hildesheim: G. Olms, 1965.

Bradney, J. A. *A History of Monmouthshire: Part II*. London: Mitchell, Hughes and Clark, 1906. Reprinted, London: Academy Books, 1991.

Brannigan, J. *New Historicism and Cultural Materialism*. New York: St. Martin's Press, 1996.

Brown, Laura. *Ends of Empire: Women and Ideology at the End of the Eighteenth Century*. Ithaca: Cornell University Press, 1993.

Burke, Edmund. *A Philosophical Enquiry into the Origin of Our Ideas of the Sublime and Beautiful*. London: Dodsley, 1756.

Buttimer, Anne. *Society and Milieu in the French Geographical Tradition*. Chicago: Rand McNally, 1971.

Buttimer, Anne, and D. Seamon, eds. *The Human Experience of Space and Place*. New York: St Martin's Press, 1980.

Campbell, Mary. B. *The Witness and the Other Word: Exotic European Travel Writing: 400–1600*. Ithaca, New York: Cornell University Press, 1988.

Carter, Sarah. *Lost Harvests: Prairie Indian Reserve Farms and Government Policy*. Montreal: McGill-Queen's Press, 1990.

Catlin, G. *Illustrations of the Manners, Customs and Condition of the North American Indian.* London: H. Bohn, 1845.

Cell, Gillian T. "The Newfoundland Company: A Study of Subscribers to a Colonizing Venture." *William and Mary Quarterly*, Third Series, 22 (1965): 610–14.

——. *English Enterprise in Newfoundland, 1577–1660.* Toronto: University of Toronto Press, 1969.

——. *Newfoundland Discovered: English Attempts at Colonization, 1610–30.* London: Hakluyt Society, 1982.

——. "Sir William Vaughan," In *Dictionary of Canadian Biography.* Toronto: University of Toronto Press, Vol. 1 (1966): 654–56.

Certeau, de M. *The Writing of History.* Trans. T. Conley. New York: Columbia University Press, 1988.

Chomsky, Noam. *Language and the Problems of Knowledge.* Cambridge, MA: MIT Press, 1988

Christy, Miller, ed. *The Voyages of Captain Luke Foxe of Hull and Captain Thomas James of Bristol in Search of a North-West Passage.* London: Hakluyt Society, First Series No. 88: Vols. 1 and 2, 1894. New York: Ben Franklin, 1963.

Clifford, James. "Introduction." In *Writing Culture: The Poetics and Politics of Ethnography*, edited by J. Clifford and G. Marcus, 1–26. Berkeley: University of California, 1986.

Cohen, E. "Authenticity in Commercial Tourism." *Annals of Tourism Research* 15, no. 3 (1988): 371–86.

Cooke, Alan. "Thomas James." *Dictionary of Canadian Biography*, Vol. 1. Toronto: University of Toronto Press, 1966: 384–85.

Cooke, A., and C. Holland. *The Exploration of Northern Canada.* Toronto: Arctic History Press, 1978.

Cresswell, T. "Writing, Reading and the Problem of Resistance." *Transactions of the Institute of British Geographers*, 21 (1996): 420–24.

Critchley, J. *Marco Polo's Book.* Aldershot: Variorum, 1992.

Cromer, R. F. "The Cognition Hypothesis Revisited." In *The Development of Language and Language Researchers*, edited by Frank S. Keissel, 223–46. Hillsdale, N.J.: Erlbaum, 1988.

Crone, G. R., and R. A. Skelton. In *R. Hakluyt and his Successors,* edited by E. Lynn. London: 1946. Quoted in Davis, 1998 op. cit.

Daniells, Roy. *Alexander Mackenzie and the Northwest.* London: Faber and Faber, 1969.

Davidoff, J., I. Davies, and D. Roberson. "Colour Categories in a Stone Age Tribe." *Nature* 398 (1999): 204–5.

Davies, Arthur. "Prince Madoc and the Discovery of America in 1477." *Geographical Journal* 150 (1984): 363–72.

Davies, Gwendolyn, and Carole Gerson. *Canadian Poetry from the Beginning to the First World War.* Toronto: McClelland and Stewart, 1994.

Davies, John. *A History of Wales.* London: Allen Lane, Penguin Edition, 1994.

Davies, W. K. D. "The Welsh in Canada: A Geographical Overview." In *The Welsh in Canada*, edited by M. Chamberlain. Swansea: Canadian Studies in Wales Group, University of Wales, Swansea, 1986: 1–47. Reprinted 2001.

——. "A Welsh Missionary at Red River, Manitoba 1822–35: The Work of the Rev. David T. Jones." *National Library of Wales Journal* 27 (1991): 217–44.

——. "Capt. William Owen and the Settlement of Campobello, New Brunswick, Part 1: Owen's Life and Character". *National Library of Wales Journal* 31, no. 2 (1999): 189–213.

——. "Capt. William Owen and the Settlement of Campobello, New Brunswick, Part II, The Settlement Scheme and Aftermath." *National Library of Wales Journal* 31, no. 3 (2000): 217–42.

——. "Globalisation: A Spatial Perspective." In *Common Heritage*, edited by D. Herbert and J. Matthews. London: Routledge. Forthcoming.

——,ed. *Human Geography from Wales: Proceedings of the E.G. Bowen Memorial Conference.* Llandysul: Gomer Press, 1986.

——. *Vaughan and the Cambriol Dream.* Unpublished manuscript, Geography Department, University of Calgary, 2003.

Davies, W.K.D., and M. Gilmartin. "Geography as a Cultural Field." In *Geography, Culture and Education,* edited by R. Gerber and M. Williams. Netherlands: Kluwer, 2002: 13–30.

Davies, W.K.D., and D.T. Herbert. *Communities Within Cities.* New York: Halstead, Wiley, 1994

Davies, W.K.D., and I. Townshend. "Identifying the Elements of Community Character." *Research in Community Sociology* 9 (1999): 219–51.

Davies, W.K.D., and I. Townshend, eds. *Monitoring Cities: International Perspectives.* Calgary and Berlin: International Geographical Union Urban Commission, 2002.

Davis, R. C. "Thrice-Told Tales: The Exploration Writing of John Franklin." In *The Canadian North*, edited by J. Carlson and B. Steigffort. Lund: University of Lund Press, 1989.

——. "History or His/Story? The Explorer cum Author." *Studies in Canadian Literature* 16 (1991): 93–111.

——. *Sir John Franklin: The First Arctic Expedition.* Toronto: Champlain Society, 1995.

——. *"Sir John Franklin's Journals and Correspondence: The Second Arctic Land Expedition, 1825–27."* Toronto: The Champlain Society, Toronto, 1998.

Delgado, James P. *Across the Top of the World: The Quest for the Northwest Passage.* Vancouver: Douglas and McIntyre, 1999.

Deregowski, K. "Real Space and Represented Space: Cross Cultural Perspectives." *Behavioural and Brain Sciences* 12 (1989): 51–119.

Devitt, Michael and Kim Sterelny. *Language and Reality.* Oxford: Blackwell, 1987

Dickason, David H. *William Williams: Novelist and Painter of Colonial America, 1727–1791.* Bloomington, Indiana: Indiana University Press, 1970.

Dickason, Olive P. *The Myth of the Savage.* Edmonton: University of Alberta Press, 1997.

——. *Canada's First Nations.* Oxford: Oxford University Press. 2nd ed., 1998.

DNB (Dictionary of National Biography) "Thomas James." Oxford: Oxford University Press, 1921. Reprinted 1950: Vol. 10, 660–61.

——. Vol. 18. "George Shelvocke." Oxford: Oxford University Press, 1921. Reprinted 1950: Vol. 18, 47–48.

Draper, Diane. *Our Environment. A Canadian Perspective.* Toronto: Nelson,1998.

Dretske, F. I. *Naturalizing the Mind.* Cambridge, MA: MIT Press, 1995.

Dubinsky, Karen. "The Pleasure is Exquisite but Violent: The Imaginary Geography of Niagara Falls in the Nineteenth Century." *Journal of Canadian Studies* 33 (1998): 64–65.

Eagleton, T. *Marxism and Literary Criticism.* London: Methuen, London, 1976.

——. *Literary Theory: An Introduction.* Minneapolis: University of Minnesota Press, 1983.

Eames, Aled. "Thomas Button." *Dictionary of Canadian Biography*, Vol. 1. University of Toronto Press, Toronto, 1966: 144–45.

Easley, A. T., J. F. Passineau, and B. L. Driver, eds. *The Use of Wilderness for Personal Growth Therapy and Education.* USDA Forest Service, General Report RM-193, 1990.

Ellis, P. B. *The Celtic Empire.* Durham, NC: Carolina Academic Press, 1990.

Ellis, Thomas. "A True Report of the Third and Last Voyage into Meta Incognita, 1578." Woodcut (Plate 25) reproduced in W. Franklin, *Discoverers, Explorers and Settlers.* Chicago: University of Chicago Press, 1979.

Fell, Barry. *Takhelne: A North American Celtic Language.* Epigraphic Society Occasional Publications, 7, no. 140 (1979): 21–42.

——. *Bronze Age America*. Boston: Little Brown and Co., 1982.

Feltes, N. N. "Yoy(ag)euse: Gender and Gaze in Frances Anne Hopkins's Canoe Paintings." *Ariel* 24, no. 4 (1993): 7–20.

Fitzhugh, W. W., and E. J. Ward. *The Vikings: The North Atlantic Saga*. Washington: Smithsonian Institution Press, 2000.

Fleming, F. *Barrow's Boys*. New York: Atlantic Monthly Press, 1998.

Forster, Shirley. *Across New Worlds: Nineteenth Century Women Travelers and Writers*. New York: Harvester, 1990.

Fowler, A. *Seventeenth Century Verse*. Oxford: Oxford University Press, 1991.

Foxe, Luke. *Northwest Foxe*. London: Alsop and Favvcet, 1635. Reprinted New York: S.R. Publishers, Johnson Reprint Corp., 1965.

Fraser, A. *Cromwell: Our Chief of Men*. London: Weidenfeld and Nicolson, 1973.

Frye, N. "Conclusion." In *Literary History of Canada*, edited by C. A. Klinck. 1st ed., Toronto: University of Toronto Press, 1965: 821–59. 2d ed., 3, 1976: 318–33.

Gage, John. *Colour and Meaning: Art, Science and Symbolism*. Berkeley: University of California Press, 1999.

Gallant, C., ed. *Coleridge's Theory of Imagination Today*. New York: A.M.S. Press, 1989.

Galloway, D. "The Voyagers." In *Literary History of Canada*, edited by C. A. Klink. Toronto: University of Toronto Press, 1965. 2d ed., 1983: 1–13.

Garlick, R. *Introduction to Anglo-Welsh Literature*. Cardiff: University of Wales Press, 1970.

Garvie, A. *Odyssey*. Cambridge: Cambridge University Press, 1994.

Gerritz, H. "Plate 9." In Armstrong, J., ed. *From Sea to Sea: Early Maps of Canada*. Scarborough, Ontario: Fleet Books, 1982.

Gilovitch, T. "How We Know That Isn't So." New York: Free Press, 1993.

Gilpin, W. *Three Essays: On Picturesque Beauty, On Picturesque Travel and On Sketching Landscape*. London: Blamire, 1792. Reprinted Westmead: Gregg International, 1974.

Gladwin , T. "Culture and Logical Processes." In *Culture and Cognition*, edited by J. W. Berry and P. R. Dasen, 28–37. London: Methuen, 1974.

Glickman, Susan. *The Picturesque and the Sublime: A Poetics of the Canadian Landscape*. Montreal and Kingston: McGill-Queen's Press, 1998.

Glover, T. *David Thompson's Narrative: 1784–1812*. Toronto: The Champlain Society, 1962.

Godlewska, A. "Map, Text and Image." *Transactions of Institute of British Geographers*, New Series, 20 (1995): 5–28.

Gould J. *Herodotus*. London: Weidenfeld and Nicholson, 1989.

Graff, G. and Robbins, B. "Cultural criticism." In *Redrawing the Boundaries,* edited by S. J. Greenblat and G. Gunn. New York: Modern Language Association of America, 1992: 419–37.

Greenblatt, S. J. *Marvellous Possessions*. Chicago: University of Chicago Press, 1991.

Greenblat, S. J., and G. Gunn, eds. *Redrawing the Boundaries*. New York: Modern Language Association of America, 1992.

Greenfield, B. *Narrating Discovery: The Romantic Explorer in American Literature*. New York: Columbia University Press, 1992.

Gregory, D., and J. S. Duncan. *Writes of Passage: Reading Travel Writing*. London: Routledge, 1999.

Griffin, D.R. *Unsnarling the World-Knot: Consciousness, Freedom and the Mind-Body Problem*. Berkeley: University of California Press, 1998.

Hakluyt, R. *The Principall Navigations, Voyages, Traffiques, and Discoveries of the English Nations*. Three volumes. London: 1600. Reprinted in 12 volumes, Glasgow: Under the title: *The Principal Navigations, Voyages, Traffiques, and Discoveries of the English Nation Made by Sea or Over-land to the Remote and Farthest Distant Quarters of the Earth at any Time within the Compass of these 1600 Yeeres....* J. MacLehose 1903–5.

Hamilton, P. *Historicism*. London: Routledge, 1996.

Hansen, T. *The Way to Hudson Bay: The Life and Times of Jens Munk*. New York: Harcourt and Brace, 1970.

Harley, J. B. " Deconstructing the Map." In Barnes and Duncan, op. cit., 1992.

Harley, J. B., and D. Woodward, eds. *The History of Cartography*. Chicago: University of Chicago Press, 1987.

Harington, C. R. *Climatic Change in Canada*. Syllogeus, 49. Ottawa: National Museum of Natural Sciences, 1983.

Harris, John. *Navigantium atque itinerantium bibliotecha: A Compleat Collection of Voyages and Travels*. 2 vols. London: T. Bennett, 1705. Revised and enlarged by J. Campbell, ed. Reprint, London: T. Woodward et al. 1744–48. New edition, 1764.

Heawood, J. *A History of Geographical Discovery of Seventeenth and Eighteenth Centuries*. Cambridge: Cambridge University Press, 1912. Reprinted, New York: Octagon Press, 1965.

Helfrich, H. W. "Captain James: Fool or Hero." *Beaver* (1972): 42–45.

Hopwood, Victor. "Explorers by Land: to 1860." *Literary History of Canada*. ed C.F. Klinck. Toronto: University of Toronto Press, 1965: 14–40.

Hudd, A. E. "Richard Ameryk and the Name America." In *Gloucestershire Studies,* edited by H. P. R. Finberg. Leicester: University of Leicester Press, 1957: 123–29.

Innes, H. *The Fur Trade in Canada*. New Haven: Yale University Press, 1930.

Ironside, E. *The Art of Deception*. London: Hodder and Stoughton, 1998

James, Thomas. *The Strange and Dangerous Voyage of Captain Thomas James*. London: John Legatt for John Partridge, 1633.

——. *The Strange and Dangerous Voyage*. Republished Amsterdam: Theatrus Orbis Terrarum, 1968.

——. *The Dangerous Voyage of Captain Thomas James*. London: Revised and reprinted by O. Payne, 1740. Reprinted Toronto: Coles, 1973.

James, Ivor. *The Source of The Ancient Mariner*. Cardiff: University of Wales, 1890.

Jones, Emrys. "The Welsh in London in the Nineteenth Century." In *Human Geography From Wales,* edited by W. K. D. Davies. Special issue of *Cambria: A Welsh Geographical Review* 12 , no. 1, (1986): 149–69.

Jones, Emyr W. "Captaine Thomas Iames A'I Fordaith." *Transactions of the Honorary Society of Cymmrodorion*, New Series, 2 (1996): 59–78.

Jones, Glyn. *The Dragon has Two Tongues*. London: Dent, 1968.

Keating, Berne. *The Northwest Passage*. New York: Rand McNally, 1970.

Kelley, David H. "Proto-Tifinagh and Proto-Ogham in the Americas." *The Review of Archaeology* 11, no. 1 (1990): 1–10.

Kenyon, W. A. "Charlton Island." *The Beaver* (Summer 1974): 24–31.

——, ed. *The Strange and Dangerous Voyage of Capt. Thomas James*. Toronto: Royal Ontario Museum, 1975.

——. *The Journal of Jens Munck*. Toronto: Royal Ontario Museum, 1980.

Keynes, R. D., ed. *Charles Darwin's Diary and the Voyage of H.M.S. Beagle*. Cambridge: Cambridge University Press, 1987.

Kittay, E. F. *Metaphor*. London, Clarendon, 1987.

Kreisel, H. "The Prairie: A State of Mind." *Transactions of The Royal Society of Canada* 6, no. 4 (1968): 169–73.

Lai, C.S.L., S. E. Fisher, J. A. Hurst, F. Vargha-Khadem, A. P. Monaco. "A Forkhead-Domain Gene is Mutuated in a Severe Speech and Language Disorder." *Nature* 413 (October 4, 2001): 518–22.

Lamb, W. Kaye, ed. *Journals and Letters of Sir Alexander Mackenzie*. Cambridge: Cambridge University Press, 1970.

Lateiner, D. *The Historical Method of Herodotus*. Toronto: University of Toronto Press, 1989.

Lave, J. *Cognition in Practice*. Cambridge: Cambridge University Press, 1988.

Lewis, M. "The Indigenous Maps and Mapping of North American Indian's." *Map Collector* 9, 25–32. 1979.

——. "The Origins of Cartography." In *The History of Cartography,* edited by J. B. Harley, and D. Woodward, Vol. 1. Chicago: University of Chicago Press, 1987.

Livingstone, D. M. *The Geographical Tradition*. Oxford: Blackwell, 1992.

Lowenthal, D. "Geography, Experience and Imagination." *Annals of Association of American Geographers* 51, no. 3 (1961): 241–60.

——. *Environmental Perception and Behaviour*. Chicago: University of Chicago Press, 1967.

Lowenthal, D., and M. J. Bowden, eds. *Geographies of the Mind: Essays in Historical Geography*. Oxford: Oxford University Press, 1975.

Lowes, J. L. *The Road to Xanadu*. Boston: Houghton Mifflin, 1927.

Macdonald, P. *Cabot and the Naming of America*. Bristol: Petmac Publications, 1997.

Marsh, J. "Thomas James." *Canadian Encyclopaedia*. Edmonton: Hurtig, 1985: 912.

Martens, F. M. *The Voyage into Spitzbergen and Greenland*. London: 1694.

Mathias, Roland. *Anglo-Welsh Literature: An Illustrated History*. Cardiff: Poetry Wales Press, 1986.

Matsuzawa, T. *Primate Origins of Human Cognition and Behaviour*. New York: Springer, 2001

Mayhew, Robert J. *Enlightenment Geography: The Political Languages of British Geography: 1650–1850*. New York: St Martin's Press, 2000.

McDermott, J. Martin. *Sir Martin Frobisher: Elizabethan Privateer*. New Haven, CT: Yale University Press, 2001.

McGlone, W. R., and P. M. Leonard. *Ancient Celtic America*. Fresno, California: Panorama West Books, 1986.

McGrath, P. *Records Relating to the Merchant Venturers of the City of Bristol*. Bristol: Bristol Record Society, 1952.

——. *Merchants and Merchandise in Seventeenth Century Bristol*. Bristol: Bristol Record Society, 1968.

——. *Bristol and America: 1480–1631*. Bristol: Local History Pamphlets, Bristol Branch of the Historical Association, 1997.

MacInnes, C. M. *Captain Thomas James and the North West Passage*. Bristol: Historical Association Local History Pamphlets, Bristol, 1967.

MacLaren. I.S. "Samuel Hearne and the Landscapes of Discovery." *Canadian Literature* 103 (Winter 1984): 27–40.

——. "Arctic Exploration and Milton's 'Frozen Continent.'" *Notes and Queries*, New Series 31 (1984): 325–26.

——. "Aesthetic Mapping of Nature of the West by the Palliser and Hind Survey Expedition." *Studies in Canadian Literature* 18 (1985): 24–52.

——. "The Aesthetic Mapping of Nature in the Second Franklin Expedition." *Journal of Canadian Studies* 20, no. 1 (Spring 1985): 39–57.

MacLulich, T. D. "Canadian Exploration as Literature." *Canadian Literature* 81 (1979): 72–85.

Menzies, Gavin. *1421: The Year China Discovered the World*. London: Bantum, 2002.

Merbs, C. "Sir Thomas Rowe's Welcome: An Island of the Dead." *The Beaver* (Spring 1971): 16–24.

Miles, Sarah, *Discourse*. London: Routledge, 1997.

Miller, G. *Arctic Journeys: History of Exploration for the Northwest Passage*. London: Lang, 1992.

Milton, G. *Nathaniel's Nutmeg*. London: Hodder and Stoughton, 1999.

Montesquieu, C. de S. *Persian Letters*. Original edition, 1743. Translated by J. Ozell. New York: Garland Press, 1972.

Montrose, L. "The Work of Gender in the Discourse of Discovery." In *New World Encounters*, edited by S. Greenblatt. Berkeley: University of California Press, 1993: 177–217.

Moodie, Susanna. *Roughing it in the Bush or Life in Canada*. 1st ed., New York: Putnam, 1852. New ed. edited by Elizabeth Thompson. Ottawa: Tecumseh Press, 1997.

Moore, Alexander. "Rosanzerusu in Los Angeles: An Anthropological Study of Japanese Tourists." *Annals of Tourism Research* 12, no. 4 (1985): 619–43.

Morison, S. E. *The Great Explorers*. Oxford: Oxford University Press, 1978.

Morris, Jan. *Travels*. London: Faber and Faber, 1976.

——. Personal communication. Calgary Winter Olympics Writers' Festival, 1988.

Morton, William L. *The Kingdom of Canada*. Toronto: McClelland and Stewart, 1963.

Neatby, L. *In Quest of the North West Passage*. London: Longman Green, 1958.

Newman, Peter. *Company of Adventurers*. Toronto: Viking Books of Canada, 1985.

Orgel, S. *The Jonsonian Masque*. Cambridge, MA: Harvard University Press, 1965.

Osherson, D., S. Kosslyn, and J. Hollerbach, eds. *An Invitation to Cognitive Science*, Vols. 1–4. Cambridge, MA: MIT Press, 1990.

Owen, W. FitzWilliam. *Tables of Latitudes and Longitude by Chronometer of Places in the Atlantic and Indian Oceans*. London: 1827.

Parry, J. H. *The Age of Reconaissance*. New York: New American Library, 1964.

Parry, W. E. *Journals of the First, Second and Third Voyages for the Discovery of a North-West Passage from the Atlantic to the Pacific in 1819–25, in His Majesty's Ships Hecla, Griper, and Fury*. Vols. 1–5. London: John Murray, 1828.

Payne, D. G., and M. J. Wenger. *Cognitive Psychology*. Boston: Houghton Mifflin, 1998

Pennington, L., ed., *The Purchas Handbook: Vol. 1 and 2*. London: The Hakluyt Society, New Series No. 186–7, 1997.

Pharand, D. *International Straits of the World: The Arctic North West*. Dordrecht, Netherlands: Kluwer, 1984.

Philbrick, N. *In the Heart of the Sea: The Tragedy of the Whaleship Essex*. New York: Viking, 2000.

Phillips, J.R.S. *The Medieval Expansion of Europe*. Oxford: Oxford University Press, 1988.

Piaget, J. *The Construction of Reality in the Child*. New York: Basic Books, 1954.

Posner, Michael I., ed., *Foundations of Cognitive Science*. Cambridge, MA: MIT Press, 1989.

Posner, Michael I., and M. E. Raichle. *Images of the Mind*. New York: Scientific American Library, 1994.

Powell, J. W. Damer. *Bristol Privateers and Ships of War*. Bristol: Arrowsmith, 1930.

Pratt, Mary Louise. *Imperial Eyes: Travel Writing and Transculturation*. London: Routledge, 1992.

Pressman, N. *North Cityscape: Linking Design to Culture*. Yellowknife, NWT: Winter Cities Association, 1995.

Purchas, S. *Haluytus Posthumus or Purchas, His Pilgrims*. London: Fetherstone, 1626. Reprinted Glasgow: J. MacLehoe, 1905–06. Reprinted New York: A.M.S., 1965.

Quinn, D. B. "The Argument for the English Discovery of America between 1480 and 1494." *Geographical Journal* 127 (1961): 277–85.

——. *England and The Discovery of America, 1481–1620*. London: 1974.

——. *North America from Earliest Discovery*. New York: Harper and Row, 1977.

——. *Explorers and Colonies: America 1500–1625*. Hambleton, Hants: Hambledon Press, 1990.

——. *Sebastian Cabot and Bristol Exploration*. Bristol: Local History Association, Bristol Branch, Rev. ed., 1992.

Quinn, D. B., and R. Skelton, eds. *R. Hakluyt: The Principall Navigations, Voyages and Discoveries of the English Nation*. 1st ed., 1589. Reprinted with editorial introduction Cambridge: Cambridge University Press, 1965.

Raleigh, Walter. *The Discoverie of the Large, Rich and Beautiful Empire of Guiana*. London: 1596. Reprinted London: P. Robinson, 1966.

Review of *The Source of the Ancient Mariner*. *Atheneum* 3255 (March 1890): 335–36.

Rich, E. E. *The History of the Hudson's Bay Company, 1670–1870*. Montreal: McGill University Press, 1966.

Ricou, L. *Vertical Man in a Historical World*. Vancouver: University of British Columbia Press, 1973.

Riffenburgh, B. *The Myth of the Explorer*. Oxford: Oxford University Press, 1993.

Roberts, Lewis. *The Merchants Map of Commerce*. London: R. Mab, 1638.

Rogoff, B., and J. Lave. *Everyday Cognition: Its Development in Social Context*. Cambridge, MA: Harvard University Press.

Rose, Millicent, ed. *The Rime of the Ancient Mariner: Illustrations by G.Doré*. Original edition, 1878. Reprint, New York: Dover Press, 1970.

Rundall, Thomas. *Narratives of Voyages Towards the North-West in Search of a Passage to Cathay and India: 1496–1631*. London: Hakluyt Series, No. 5, 1849. Republished New York: Ben Franklin, 1964.

Russell, Peter. *Prince Henry "The Navigator."* New Haven: Yale University Press, 2000.

Saunders, B. "Disinterring Basic Colour Terms: A Study in the Mystique of Cognitivism," *History of Human Sciences* 8 (1995): 19–38.

Savours, Anne. *The Search for a North West Passage*. London: Chatham, 1999.

Schacter, Daniel. *Seven Sins of Memory*. New York: Houghton-Mifflin, 2001.

Schöene-Harwood, Berthold. *Writing Men*. Edinburgh: University of Edinburgh Press, 2000.

Scott, E. *The Customs Roll of the Port of Bristol A.D. 1496–99*. Bristol: Georges and Son, 1897.

Searle, J. R. *The Construction of Social Reality*. New York: Free Press, 1995.

Selburne, David. *City of Light*. London: Little Brown and Company, Abacus edition, 1998.

Selden, R. *Cambridge History of Literary Criticism*, Vol.8: *Formalism to Post Structuralism*. Cambridge: Cambridge University Press, 1995.

Sellick, R. *The Epic Confrontation: Australian Exploration and the Centre: 1813–1900*. Unpublished PhD thesis, University of Adelaide, 1973. Quoted in Davis, op. cit., 1995, 40.

Seymour, M. C. *The Bodley Version of Mandeville's Travels*. Oxford: Oxford University Press, 1963.

Shelvocke, George. *Voyage Around the World by the Way of the Great South Sea*. London: 1726.

Shields, R. "Niagara Falls: Honeymoon Capital of the World." In *Places on the Margin*. London: Routledge, 1991.

Simpson-Housley, P., and W. Mallory. 1986. *Geography and Literature: A Meeting of Disciplines*. Syracuse, New York: Syracuse University Press, 1986.

Smith, W. O. *Polar Oceanography: Part A, Physical Science*. New York: Academic Press, 1990.

Sobel, D. *Longitude*. London: Penguin, 1996.

Solomon, S. *The Coldest March: Scott's Antarctic Expedition*. New Haven: Yale University Press, 2001.

Southey, R., and S. Coleridge. 1812. *Omniana or Horae Otiosiores*. London: Longman, Hurst, Rees, Orme, and Brown, 1812. Reprinted London: R. Gittings, 1969.

Stefansson, V. *The Three Voyages of Martin Frobisher*: Amsterdam: N Israel, 1938. Reprinted 1971.

Steiner, G. *Homer in English*. London: Penguin, 1996.

Stephens, M. *Oxford Companion to the Literature of Wales*. Oxford: Oxford University Press, 1986.

——. *Cydymaith i Lenyddiaeth Cymru*. Cardiff: University of Wales Press, 1997.

Stoddart, D. *On Geography and its History*. Oxford: Blackwell, 1986.

Strachen, M. *Sir Thomas Roe (1541–1644): A Life*. London: M. Russell, 1987.

Swift, Jonathan [L. Gulliver]. *Travels into Several Remote Nations of the World*. London: B. Motto, 1726. New ed. edited by J. Barzan. Oxford: Oxford University Press, 1977.

Symons, T.H.B., ed. *Meta Incognita: A Discourse of Discovery*. Ottawa: Museum of Civilization, 1999.

Taylor, Eva G. R. *Tudor Geography: 1485–1583*. London: Methuen, 1930.

——. *Late Tudor and Stuart Geography: 1583–1650*. London: Methuen, 1934.

Taylor, T. Griffith, ed. *Twentieth Century Geography*. New York: Philosophical Library, 1951. 3rd ed. London: Methuen, 1957.

Thomas, Colin. *Semenov, P. P.: Travels in Tien Shan, 1856–57*. London: Hakluyt Society, No. 198, 1998.

Thomson, George. *The North-West Passage*. London: Secker and Warburg, London, 1975.

Thwaites. R. G. *The Original Journals of the Lewis and Clark Expedition*. New York: Antiquarian Press, 1959.

Tower, T. "The Grand Tour: A Key Phase in the History of Tourism." *Annals of Tourism Research* 12 (1985): 297–333.

The Travels of Marco Polo. Trans. R. E. Latham. London: 1958.

Trudel, M. "Jacques Cartier." *Canadian National Bibliography*, Vol. 1. Toronto: University of Toronto Press, 1966.

Tuan, I. F. *Space and Time*. Minneapolis: University of Minnesota Press, 1973.

——. *Topophilia: Environmental Perception, Attitudes and Values*. New York: Prentice Hall, 1974.

Turnbull, David. *Maps are Territories*. Chicago: University of Chicago Press, 1993.

——. *Masons, Tricksters and Cartographers*. Amsterdam: Harwood, 2000.

Turner, V., and E. Turner. *Image and Pilgrimage in Christian Culture*. New York: Columbia University Press, 1978.

Tyrrell, J. B. *David Thompson's Narrative of his Explorations*. Toronto: The Champlain Society, 1916. Republished New York: Greenwood Press, 1960.

Vaughan, William (Orpheus Junior). *The Golden Fleece*. London: Williams, 1626.

Veeser, H. A., ed. *The New Historicism*. London: Routledge, 1989.

Venema, K. "Under the Protection of a Principal Man." *Canadian Writing* 70 (spring 2000): 162–90.

Venuti, L. *Rethinking Translation: Discourse, Subject and Ideology*. London: Routledge, 1992.

Wallen, M. *Coleridge's Ancient Mariner*. Barrytown, New York: Clinamen Studies, Station Hill, 1993.

Waller, A., ed. *Abergavenny and District Official Guide*. Bristol: Regional Publications, 1986.

Wallis, H. "Purchas's Maps." In *The Purchas Handbook*: Vols. 1 and 2, edited by L. Pennington, 145–66. London: Hakluyt Society, New Series No. 186–7, 1997.

Warkentin, Germaine, ed. *Canadian Exploration Literature: An Anthology*. Toronto and Oxford: Oxford University Press, 1993.

Warkentin, John, ed. *The Western Interior of Canada*. Toronto: McClelland and Stewart, 1964.

Warkentin, John, and R. Ruggles. *Historical Atlas of Manitoba*. Winnipeg: Manitoba Historical Society, 1970.

Waters, D. W. *The Art of Navigation in Elizabethan and Early Stuart England*. London: Hollis and Carter, 1958.

Watson, James Wreford "The Role of Illusion in North American Geography," *Canadian Geographer* 13, no. 1 (1969): 10–27.

——. "The Soul of Geography." *Transactions of the Institute of British Geographers*, New Series 8 (1983): 385–99.

Whitehead, Neil L., ed. *The Discoverie of the Large, Rich and Bewtiful Empyre of Guiana by Sir Walter Raleigh*. Manchester: Manchester University Press, 1997.

Whorf, Benjamin. *Language, Thought and Reality*. Cambridge, MA: MIT Press, 1956.

Williams, Alan F. *John Cabot and Newfoundland*. St John's, Newfoundland: Newfoundland Historical Society, 1996.

Williams, Glyndwyr, ed. "Highlights of the Hudson's Bay Society: 1670–1970." *The Beaver* (Autumn 1970).

——. *The British Search for the Northwest Passage in the Eighteenth Century*. London: Longmans, 1962.

Williams, Gwyn. A. *Madoc: The Legend of the Welsh Discovery of America*. Oxford: Oxford University Press, 1987.

Williams, Raymond. *The Country and the City*. Oxford: Oxford University Press, 1972.

Williams, William. *The Journal of Llewellin Penrose, A Seaman*. 4 vols. London: John Murray, 1815. Revised edition edited by D. H. Dickason. *Mr Penrose: The Journal of Penrose, Seaman*. Bloomington: Indiana University Press, 1969.

Williamson, J. A. *The Cabot Voyages and the Bristol Discovery under Henry VII*. London: Halkluyt Society, Second Series, No. 120, 1962.

Wilson, A. 1818. "The Foresters." in *Port Folio* New Series II (June 1909–March 1910), 2059–62. Reprinted in *The Poems and Literary Prose of Alexander Wilson*, edited by A. B. Grosart. New York: Gardner, Paisley, 1976.

Wilson, Ian. *The Columbus Myth: Did Men of Bristol Reach America before Columbus?* London: Simon and Schuster, 1991.

——. *John Cabot and the Matthew*. Bristol: Redcliffe, 1996.

Wilson, Scott. *Cultural Materialism: Theory and Practice*. Oxford: Blackwell, 1995.

Wood, Frances. *Did Marco Polo Go to China?* London: Secker and Warburg, 1995.

Wood, H. T. *Exploration and Discovery*. London: Hutchinson, 1951.

Wright, John K. "Terrae Incognitae: The Place of the Imagination in Geography." *Annals of American Geographers* 37 (1947): 1–15.

Wright, Louis B. *Gold, Glory and Gospel*. New York: Atheneum, 1970.

Wright, Ronald. *Stolen Continents*. New York: Viking, 1992.

Wyer, R., and T. Srull. *Handbook of Social Cognition*, Vol. 3. Hillsdale, NJ: Erlbaum, 1984.

Zaring, J. "The Romantic Face of Wales." *Annals of Association of American Geographers*, 67, no. 3 (1977): 397–418.

INDEX